Electronic Drama: Television Plays of the Sixties

The National Academy of Television Arts and Sciences series on *Television and American Culture*

Richard Averson and David Manning White, General Editors

Electronic Drama: Television Plays of the Sixties, selected by Richard Averson and David Manning White

Electronic

DRAMA

Television Plays
of the Sixties

Selected by Richard Averson
and David Manning White

With an Introduction by
Hubbell Robinson

Beacon Press   *Boston*

Copyright © 1971 by Richard Averson and David Manning White
Library of Congress catalog card number: 75–136220
International Standard Book Number: 0–8070–6178–6
Beacon Press books are published under the auspices
of the Unitarian Universalist Association
Published simultaneously in Canada by Saunders of Toronto, Ltd.
All rights reserved
Printed in the United States of America

Contents

v

INTRODUCTION

By Hubbell Robinson

Among the memorabilia of a long career in television are certain documents one preserves solely for the light they cast on the odd folkways of the medium. They may never be usable, but, who knows, the time may come. I have two whose time has come. They shed light on some of the problems commercial network television faces in attempting serious drama.

In February 1959 I was serving as executive vice-president in charge of programming for the CBS Television Network. On February 12th I received a letter from the general manager for radio and television of a major advertising agency. It said, in part:

> We have already passed along to your people something of the flareback that came to various members of the sponsor organization and, in turn, was passed along to us.
>
> We know that your series is striving mightily to do things that are different and outstanding so that as a series it will rise above the general level of TV drama. This is fine but since the series is a vehicle for commercial advertisers, it must also be extremely sensitive to utilizing anything, however dramatic, however different, however well done, if this will offend viewers. Creative people, of course, are constantly protesting against being stifled by what they may think are the narrow, limited or prejudiced views of other people, and certainly creative people must be offered an opportunity for the full development of their creative talents—but only under certain circumstances. This cannot be true in the case of a commercial vehicle.
>
> You know that we can never lose sight of the fact that the sole purpose for which an advertiser spends money is to win

friends and influence people. Anything that he might do, however meritorious in one direction, that makes enemies is a bad action and is to be assiduously avoided. As long as this series wishes commercial sponsorship, all of the creative people associated therewith must never forget that not to offend people must be an inviolate rule for guiding their operation. Narrow, prejudiced, ignorant, or what you will, though any part of the population may be, as a commercial vehicle the series must be ever alert not to alienate its viewers. I think you can gather that from the sponsor's point of view this matter is serious. We would like to hope that as a result of this second major flare-up in one season you are taking such steps as may be necessary to insure that no future program in this series violates the public concept of what is right.

Eleven Februaries later Michael Dann, sitting in the same CBS pew, received a letter from a vice-president of a company then sponsoring a major dramatic series. Among other things, he wrote, "Heavy-handed avant-garde types of shows that look at one minute aspect of life do not seem to work very well for us." A paragraph later he repeated, "The introspective, heavy-handed, brooding and moody dramas do not seem to work well for our company."

I have not cited these letters to be derisive, although the syntax of the first and the rhetoric of the second are tempting targets. I have cited them because they are symptomatic of the strains and stresses that occur when business and drama lie down together. They are uneasy bedfellows. Good drama cannot be bland; it makes a statement with all the eloquence and passion the playwright can summon. Good dramatists from Aristophanes to Albee have dealt with the human condition introspectively and moodily. They have been abrasive and contentious. They have made controversial statements. As Charles Alexander Robinson, late head of the Classics Department of Brown University, said of the Greek theater, "the drama inevitably spread advanced ideas through the body politic."

The first sponsor has no interest in the body politic nor in spreading advanced ideas throughout it. Nor should they have. Turbulence and contention are not the climate best suited to persuade you to buy what they have to sell. Unfortunately those ingredients are the raw material today's playwrights find most stimulating, most fruitful. We live in combustible times. Serious writers want their work to reflect these times. They feel impelled to concentrate on their own era, to weigh its values, to pass judgments.

Both stances have validity, a circumstance that doesn't help you or me very much. It means we are not likely to see any dramatic anthology series in the immediate future.

The ideological gap is not the only hazard.

Drama is as costly as other types of shows that gather larger audiences. And the audience for thoughtful drama has its limitations. Television plays dealing with the manners and mores of our times with bite and punch can enlarge that audience, but that is exactly the dramatic texture advertisers blanch at. We are indeed heaping Pelion on Ossa.

Such are the realities for those of us who have been dedicated to the kind of drama this book celebrates. "Ignore reality and it will break your neck," admonished Henry James. The final reality in this context is that we must find other means of providing the kind of bristly fare that gives a play size and thrust.

It seems to me there are two ways this could be done.

One way is to provide high quality movies made expressly for TV. "My Sweet Charlie," the last play in this collection, is an example. It reveals how people of opposite race, color, and heredity can break through their own barriers of prejudice, intolerance, and ignorance. As a theme this doesn't sound like one that would rope in viewers by the millions. But the play was done with such skill, such sensitivity and perception, that it engaged and involved you right at the start and never let go.

One hopes that other creators with comparable talent will turn their attention to the world around us. And, indeed, there are signs that they will attempt that. "Relevance" is a big word in Hollywood these days.

The other refuge for drama that can be remembered an hour after you've seen it is Public Television. In Public TV, one supposes, there would be freedom from queasy sponsors, from the squirrel cage of the rating race and the compulsion to program for all the audience all the time.

Alexis de Tocqueville, commenting in 1832 on the young American Republic, said his main doubt about our system was "the possible tyranny of the Majority." As far as commercial network television is concerned those doubts were well founded. The U. S. television's minority audience suffers from precisely that tyranny. Public Television could be the answer. It isn't now because it limps along on a budget of minimal proportion in spite of its maximum needs and opportunities. Its *NET Playhouse* tries manfully but does not have the funds to mount a weekly series of the first order. It cannot afford writers of the caliber represented in this volume.

While Public Television "makes do" as best it can the British Broadcasting Corporation increases its drama budget by $2,400,000 over the previous year; and the Japanese, as Federal Communications Commissioner Nicholas Johnson has pointed out in his book *How To Talk Back to Your Television Set,* have funded their version of our Corporation for Public Broadcasting at a proportion of their gross national product equal to $2 billion a year in the United States. All of which makes one wonder if such would-be movers and shakers as Thomas Hoving and his National Citizens Committee for Broadcasting wouldn't be wiser to direct their considerable energies to helping CPB rather than assaulting the current network schema. That course is unlikely to be fruitful. They are apt to get mired in the thicket of dollar signs that protects the status quo. The great opportunity lies in creating entertainment for the sizable minority who are intellectually and emotionally undernourished and largely ignored. That, as I have always understood it, was one of the reasons CPB was created—to give viewers a choice. There can be no choice until CPB is given the funds to create one on a full-time basis. No solution to that problem is in sight. And no one seems to be concerned because it isn't.

The sum total of these laments is that commercial network television drama of the sort we have been describing here seems headed for almost total oblivion. That is why the scripts brought together here are important. They demonstrate how high television drama can soar, how poignantly it can articulate the problems of our times, how it can jog minds wrapped in prejudice and habit.

So treasure these scripts and the gifted people who wrote them. It may be a long time before television sees their like again.

Preface

By Richard Averson and David Manning White

As Gilbert Seldes commented, each new communications medium begs, borrows, or annexes the expressive forms of older media. Not surprisingly, television, like the movies before it, borrowed the dramatic form from the theater medium. The *play,* with its enacted and sequential narrative, encompassed within a limited and manageable "stage," seemed so obviously to be the early electronic studio thing.

Admittedly, the art of TV drama in those prehistoric, pre-1945 television days was subservient to the technology of "live" sight-and-sound transmissions. The prestigious 1938 telecast of Gertrude Lawrence in scenes from the play *Susan and God* was primarily a successful engineering demonstration. During the period from May 1939 to August 1940, however, the borrowing of the dramatic form was more earnestly aesthetic: NBC presented a series of regularly scheduled, unrelated, and "one-shot" plays which, in a sense, comprised the first drama anthology. During this prenatal period many of the production techniques, camera movements, and transitional devices now familiar in electronic drama were initiated. The most innovative production of the NBC anthology, *The Farmer Takes a Wife,* used a miniature (of an Erie Canal lock), an off-camera narrator to bridge sequences, and even specially shot film inserts to establish exterior locales.[1]

But it is the peculiar programming nature of television that what it borrows, it soon dominates; and by some twenty years after *Susan and God,* television had largely displaced both the theater and the movies as the supplier of "dramatic experience" to mass audiences.

---

[1] A concise overview of pre-1945 electronic drama is provided by William Hawes in his "Television Drama: The First Twenty Years" (*Today's Speech,* September 1963, 22–23).

The nine dramas selected for this book indicate the content, theme emphases, and creative directions of the "serious" dramatic experiences offered by television during one decade of the medium's history, the Sixties. Notwithstanding the limitations imposed by space and script availabilities, the editors consider the selections collectively representative of the decade's significant drama-anthologies, continuing series, and occasional "special" programs.

Although our prime criterion for choice was, of course, excellence, we were also concerned with achieving diversity in such matters as author, year of broadcast, source (originals and adaptations) and production technique (videotape and film). In reviewing ten years of electronic drama, we soon realized that the laurels to be conferred were more than space and a reasonably priced book would allow. Our hope is that in distributing the accolades among the nine dramas here included, and with the considerations described above operative, we have rendered fair judgment of the decade's accomplishment. Needless to say, we are aware that the selection made reflects our opinion solely.

The editors' decision to focus attention exclusively on the TV drama of the Sixties was not merely because the turn of the decade provided a convenient historical reference point. By the end of the Fifties, two discernible and prolific "waves" of electronic drama had reached their apex and, for whatever reasons, had seemingly spent their creative course. Thus, we regarded the advent of the Sixties as a crucial moment in the evolution of the dramatic form on television. Further, since many of the outstanding dramas of these two "waves" were already available for reading in various collections, we were eager to discover what subsequent riches the new decade might yield.

The two "waves" of electronic drama before 1960 cannot be discussed often enough. The first "wave" comprised the period roughly from 1947 to 1955, during which time appeared such "live" anthology programs as "Kraft Theatre," "Studio One," "Philco Playhouse" and, to which the latter was eventually joined, "Goodyear Playhouse." It has been estimated that for three of these anthologies over three hundred original hour-long plays were written between the years 1950 to 1955 alone.

Cast within the sixty-minute format, the dramatic equivalent to a short story, the dramas of this first "wave" were praised for their sensitive exploration of "small situations" in the lives of their characters. Restricted in plot to a single telling incident, these hour-long dramas emphasized, in Kenneth Tynan's words, "a tremor on the surface of events, a pebble dropped into the pool of everyday living." [2] The plays and their authors are so well remembered: *The Mother* and *Marty* by Paddy Chayefsky; *My Lost Saints* by Tad Mosel; *A Man Is Ten Feet Tall* by Robert Alan Aurthur; *The Strike* by Rod Serling; *Thunder on Sycamore Street* by Reginald Rose; *A Young Lady of Property* by Horton Foote; *The Rabbit Trap* by J. P. Miller, and many others. That the period from 1947 to 1955 has been described nostalgically as the "Golden Age of 'live' TV anthology drama," is indeed understandable.

The second "wave" of electronic dramas before the Sixties, most of them longer plays and usually broadcast live-on-videotape, occurred soon afterward. It was exemplified by such anthologies as the monthly "Producers' Showcase" and the weekly "Playhouse 90"; the uniquely innovative semidocumentary "Armstrong Circle Theater"; "Hallmark Hall of Fame," which had begun in the early Fifties as a half-hour program and was expanded to an hour and one-half; "U.S. Steel Hour," which continued until mid-1962; and "Sunday Showcase" and "Ford Startime."

Of the dramas presented during this second "wave," the editors regard as most notable: *Little Moon of Alban* by James Costigan ("Hallmark Hall of Fame"); the "special" offering *The Moon and Sixpence,* adapted by S. Lee Pogostin from the Maugham novel; *The Turn of the Screw,* adapted by James Costigan from the Henry James short novel ("Ford Startime"); and the presentations of "Playhouse 90" which Hubbell Robinson created—J. P. Miller's *Days of Wine and Roses,* Rod Serling's *Requiem for a Heavyweight,* William Gibson's *The Miracle Worker,* Abby Mann's *Judgment at Nuremberg,* and Horton Foote's adaptation of William Faulkner's short novel, *The Old Man.*

The achievement of "Playhouse 90" is without equal in the history of electronic drama. Indeed, in a cross-country VideoVote survey conducted in 1970 by *Variety,* the program most named, by far, by the responding editors of newspapers, magazines, wire services, and feature syndicates as the Greatest Network Series of All Time was "Playhouse 90."

By 1960 the best of "Playhouse 90" was over, and live-on-videotape anthology drama had virtually disappeared. That an era of TV drama had passed was brought poignantly home to the editors by the television retrospect sponsored by the Museum of Modern Art Film Library in

---

[2] Kenneth Tynan's "The Electronic Theater," in the August 1960 issue of *Holiday,* is probably the finest analysis of TV drama of the late Forties and Fifties.

1962. The looking-backward was entitled *Television U.S.A.: 13 Seasons,* and a portion of the schedule of events was devoted to screenings of kinescopes of such 1947–60 dramas as *The Rich Boy, Marty,* and *A Night to Remember.*[3]

Yet, as we reread the MOMA program notes written by Lewis Freedman in our research for this book, we could not but feel—from our widened time perspective of 1970—that while the retrospect was surely deserved, it was somewhat premature. For we were aware that there was much noble work in the electronic drama of the Sixties, as well as in other TV programming areas, awaiting recognition.

Of the writers who had contributed to the two pre-1960 "waves" of drama on television, only a few were still active in the medium at the turn of the decade. One of them was Tad Mosel, and it seems to the editors particularly appropriate that the first selection in this book, *That's Where the Town's Going!,* is his work. Two happy coincidences surround this selection. One of the leading performers in the live-on-videotape broadcast of this play was an actress closely identified with the drama of the Golden Age, Kim Stanley. Also, the play was a production of "Westinghouse Presents" in the spring of 1962—and it was Westinghouse, we recalled, that had sponsored the early "Studio One."

In theme and characterization, *That's Where the Town's Going!* is vintage Mosel; and, expectedly, the quality of the writing is splendid. Like many of Mosel's plays, this early-Sixties drama coolly examines the frustration in the lives of sad and lonely women. The Silly Sills Sisters may be incapable of tragedy on a grand scale, but they are, in Henry James's phrase, finely tuned "vessels of consciousness," and it is their being so intensely aware of their situation that makes for our interest in them.

"Serious" drama may be comedy, of course, and especially if the

---

[3] At this writing, the program notes for *Television U.S.A.: 13 Seasons* are still available at the bookstore of the Museum of Modern Art.

The editors especially recommend these collections of dramas of the pre-1960 "waves": *Best Television Plays* (1956) edited by Gore Vidal and including his *A Visit to a Small Planet; Television Plays* (1955) by Paddy Chayefsky; *Harrison, Texas: Eight Television Plays* (1956) and *Three Plays* (1962) by Horton Foote; *Patterns: Four Television Plays* (1957) by Rod Serling; *Other People's Houses* (1956) by Tad Mosel; and *Six Television Plays* (1956) by Reginald Rose.

A valuable source of data concerning pre- and post-1960 electronic drama is *The Emmy Awards: A Pictorial History* by Paul Michael and James Robert Parish (New York: Crown Publishers, Inc., 1970).

comedy be satire. Our second selection, Sidney Carroll's *Big Deal in Laredo,* is a Western allegory with a slyly stated moral. But one need not look for the message to enjoy reading this gunless, horseless Texas yarn set against "the biggest poker game that ever came down the pike." *Big Deal in Laredo* inaugurated in 1962 the second season of the generally high-quality "Du Pont Show of the Week," one of the few live-on-videotape original-drama anthologies then on the air. The play was later filmed as "A Big Hand for the Little Lady."

If the editors had had enough space in this book, we would have included another "Du Pont Show of the Week" production, Roger O. Hirson's *The Outpost.* The plot was slight but the characterization superb. At a desert military outpost a colonel, a captain, a sergeant, and a private are psychologically threatened by the perhaps-hallucinatory report of a newly arrived lieutenant that the enemy is approaching. The suspense is carefully mounted as the soldiers await the doom born of their own cowardice and spiritual weakness.

If "live" or on-videotape anthology studio-drama was, for the most part, missing in the Sixties, there was an abundance of filmed anthologies, such as the early "Dick Powell Show," "Alcoa Premiere," "Kraft Suspense Theatre," and "Bob Hope Presents Chrysler Theatre." The latter's productions included several teleplays by Rod Serling—many of which are still broadcast by local stations as "the late show"—as well as William Inge's *Out on the Outskirts of Town.* "Alcoa Premiere" presented a teleplay of some interest to film buffs of the *auteur* variety: *Flashing Spikes,* adapted by Jameson Brewer from Frank O'Rourke's novel of bribery in professional baseball, which was directed by film veteran John Ford. An "Alcoa" drama which the editors found diverting was Alfred Bestor's *Mr. Lucifer,* in which Fred Astaire played a high-ranking devil whose home base was Madison Avenue.

The filmed series, written around a continuous character—a doctor, a teacher, a lawyer, detective, or police chief—clearly dominated the decade's dramatic offerings. Most of the teleplays were melodramas of adventure and suspense, but some outstanding scripts were written for series such as "Route 66," "Slattery's People," "The Eleventh Hour," "The Breaking Point" (especially Allan E. Sloane's teleplay *And James Was a Very Small Snail*), the long-running "The Fugitive," and the durable "Gunsmoke." Melodrama is not necessarily inferior art, as best evidenced by the "entertainment" thrillers of Graham Greene and the existential-horror films of Alfred Hitchcock.

The third and fourth selections in this book are teleplays from continuing filmed series: Arnold Perl's *Who Do You Kill?* from "East

Side/West Side," and Ernest Kinoy's *Blacklist* from "The Defenders."

Although in different ways, the Perl and Kinoy dramas continue into television the tradition of fictional social commentary that marks such American films of the Thirties, Forties, and early Fifties as "I Am a Fugitive from a Chain Gang," "You Only Live Once," "The Southerner" (directed in Hollywood by the French master of social realism, Jean Renoir), "Boomerang," and such street-photographed, documentary-style Louis de Rochemont films as "Lost Boundaries" and "Walk East on Beacon." As in these films, the social problems examined in *Who Do You Kill?* and *Blacklist* are disturbingly indigenous to American society; and although these teleplays were broadcast in 1963 and 1964, respectively, they are perhaps more relevant to the condition in which American democracy finds itself in the Seventies.

As television "problem plays," *Who Do You Kill?* and *Blacklist* are not entirely without precedent in the evolution of electronic drama. In the Golden Age of "live" anthology drama, the plays of Reginald Rose, the creator of "The Defenders"—and to some extent, the plays of Rod Serling—raised a strident voice against social injustices and the Establishment pressures on the individual. But, as one television writer has remarked, the Golden Age was generally silent on such issues as poverty, racism, and intimidation of civil liberties. It was no doubt due in great measure to the investigative daring and critical acclaim of television documentary programs such as "CBS Reports," "NBC White Paper," and the ABC "Bell & Howell Close-Up!" that art and journalism so importantly interfaced in the electronic drama of the Sixties. Indeed, if one broad and distinguishing characteristic of the majority of "serious" dramas of the decade—and of the best and worst of the less-than-"serious" melodramas—might be risked proposing, it was a concern with the contemporary social issues.

That the convergence of art and journalism was always successfully brought off in the Sixties, is another matter. Too often, the convergence yielded mere propaganda. Despite their well-intentioned writers, directors, and players, the Telsun Foundation's presentations of *The Poppy Is Also a Flower* and *Once Upon a Tractor* were lugubrious *agitprop* drama that would have made even a John Grierson blush. "Social consciousness" can be too heavy a message for dramatic art, whether in the theater medium, the movies, or on television. There is always the consideration of the audience's expectation to be entertained, and the joining of persuasion with popularity is not so easily balanced.

To the credit of its creators, "The Defenders" managed the combination skillfully, and this book would be remiss without a representative episode from this extremely successful series. *Blacklist* treats a complex and "touchy" political subject forthrightly and with broad understanding. It is not at all gratifying to recall that the broadcasting media were themselves a part of the blacklisting problem, but with the telecast of Kinoy's drama, they were at least becoming a part of the solution.

Although several individual programs of the "East Side/West Side" series had great dramatic impact, the series as a whole was on an unsure, "unsatisfying" course. Perhaps it was the stark realism of the series that had contributed to its inadequate Nielsen ratings and its being canceled after one season. Or perhaps it was because Neil Brock, the social worker, was, as many critics have suggested, too discomfortingly an antihero, helpless against the human misery that surrounded him. Brock was perhaps too experienced at life, too immobilized by the imagination of disaster to be an authentic *contestatore*—but his essential character re-emerged less than a decade later as the youthful hero of such films as "The Strawberry Statement" and "The Revolutionary."

The editors selected *Who Do You Kill?* as a representative episode of "East Side/West Side" for its bold and humanistic depiction of the American Negro's sorrow in a deaf society. The first television drama to deal with the Negro protest movement, *Who Do You Kill?* won a special award in 1964 from the National Press Club in Washington.

As an historical aside to this discussion of the television "problem play," it is interesting to note that the executive producer of "The Defenders," Herbert Brodkin, was also creatively involved in two other social-confrontation series of the Sixties, "The Nurses" and "For the People." Robert Markell, the producer of "The Defenders," also produced the somewhat *cinéma-vérité* series "N.Y.P.D." (created by Arnold Perl), which occasionally dealt with social issues. Of interest, too, is the social-commentary work of the director of *Blacklist,* Stuart Rosenberg. Rosenberg also directed the film "Murder, Inc." and the film that is often compared in subject matter to "I Am a Fugitive from a Chain Gang"—"Cool Hand Luke."

Three innovations in the television drama of the Sixties deserve mention here.

One was "The Richard Boone Show," a drama anthology of the 1963–64 season which utilized a repertory company of players. There was no continuing "star" of the anthology; the players assumed roles of varying importance in the weekly productions. Until his death, Clifford Odets served as "superintendent" of dramatic materials. Among the teleplays presented by the Boone company were Dale Wasserman's *The Stranger* and Odets' *Big Mitch.*

Westinghouse Broadcasting Company linked television with a Broadway "opening night" in an unusual event on the evening of October 14, 1963. Television viewers of the Group W stations in Boston, Baltimore, Pittsburgh, Cleveland, and San Francisco saw a videotaped version of Robert Noah's *The Advocate* at the same time that it was being performed on the stage of the ANTA theater in New York. The two-and-one-half-hour program included an introductory film sequence of Manhattan traffic, ticket buying, and "lobby excitement"; a six-minute film on famous opening nights that was shown during the first intermission; an interview with Peggy Wood and Stanley Young of ANTA during the second intermission—and a dinner-jacketed Henry Fonda, who was the program's host.

If neither *The Advocate,* based on the Sacco-Vanzetti case, nor the theater-simultaneously-television concept was an unqualified success, the venture was a laudable attempt at a creative and financial partnership between two media of dramatic art.[4]

In 1967 the Sunday-afternoon "NBC Experiment in Television" had its premiere. Although not all of its programs were dramas, "Experiment in Television" often introduced the work of new playwrights. The inaugural program included a realistic and persuasive videotaped drama of a Negro family's struggle against grinding poverty in the Watts ghetto of Los Angeles. The play, *Losers Weepers,* was a first effort by Harry Dolan, a member of the group of Watts Negroes in Budd Schulberg's writers' workshop. The play was directed by Lamont Johnson, who also directed the production of the final selection in this book, *My Sweet Charlie.*

A 1969 teleplay presented by "Experiment" which the editors considered generally excellent, and which also dealt with a racial theme, was Manya Starr's *Color Me German.* That fine Negro actor, the late James Edwards, remembered for the film "Home of the Brave," played the leading role of an American schoolteacher who goes to Germany to find his German-born nephew, also a black and the son of a white German woman.

Television drama has proved to be a creative training ground for

---

[4] The extensive production background of the Group W "Opening Night on Broadway" presentation is described by Herbert Seltz in his "Stage To Television: *The Advocate*" (*Television Quarterly,* Spring 1964, 33–45).

numerous successful directors as well as writers and actors. Many of the directors of the pre-1960 "waves" have, unfortunately, left the medium and have since worked solely in motion pictures. A few of them are Ralph Nelson, John Frankenheimer, Sidney Lumet, George Roy Hill, Robert Mulligan, and Yul Brynner (a 1949 "Studio One" director who went on to "The King and I"). Directors who made feature motion pictures but who continued to work in television during the Sixties include George Schaefer, Buzz Kulik, Fielder Cook, Jack Smight, Paul Bogart, and Leo Penn.

One of the most original writer-directors who began his career in television is Sam Peckinpah, who wrote (from a short novel by Katherine Anne Porter) and directed the fifth selection in this book, *Noon Wine.* Like Peckinpah's feature films "Ride the High Country" and "The Wild Bunch," *Noon Wine* is a Western—but with a vast socio-psychological difference. Simply, but not so simply, the teleplay *Noon Wine* is the story of a less-than-ambitious dairy farmer whose ineffectual and "bad faith" way of life is disrupted by his own act of violence. Only by a supreme and self-realizing movement of the spirit does he "enter into his house justified."

Peckinpah also directed another "Western" which the editors regarded as an alternate selection had the script of *Noon Wine* not been obtainable. This drama is *The Lady Is My Wife,* and was presented by "Chrysler Theatre" in early 1967. The almost surrealistic teleplay, adapted by Halsted Welles from a story by Jack Laird, concerned the rivalry between a proud and wealthy horse breeder and a down-at-heels former Union cavalry colonel for the love of the colonel's unhappy, despairing wife. The most "fantastic" scene in the play, as bizarre as the ending of Peckinpah's "The Ballad of Cable Hogue," was a billiards game whose winner would claim the lady. The game was masterfully staged in a huge Xanadu-like mansion—and was played by the rivals on horseback.

Noon Wine, like our sixth selection, *The Trap of Solid Gold,* was a presentation of "ABC Stage 67." Probably the only significant dramatic offering of the entire season preceding "Stage 67" was the telecast of Arthur Miller's *Death of a Salesman*—and similarly to the 1961 production of Dale Wasserman's adaptation of Graham Greene's novel *The Power and the Glory, Salesman* was a blockbuster. The reported economics of the Miller play are as impressive, at least for TV drama, as the critical ovation and enthusiastic audience response: the production itself cost $450,000 while air time for the two-hour broadcast amounted to another $250,000. The sponsor, Xerox, in this unusual case, paid the airtime cost only; CBS undertook the cost of the production as well as an additional $500,000 for promotion.

Death of a Salesman is not included in this book because it is available in its published prior-to-television stage form. And while the Wasserman adaptation of *The Power and the Glory* was generally sympathetic to Greene's difficult theme, the editors prefer the Denis Cannan-Pierre Bost stage version that was telecast in 1959 on WNEW's "The Play of the Week."

Although "ABC Stage 67" often turned to the variety and even documentary formats, it was primarily a drama anthology. In the fall of 1966 the dramas presented included Murray Shisgal's *The Love Song of Barney Kempinski,* David Karp's *Confession,* and the Truman Capote–Eleanor Perry *A Christmas Memory,* in addition to *Noon Wine. The Trap of Solid Gold* was a live-on-videotape broadcast in January of 1967.

This Ellen M. Violett play, adapted from a story by John D. MacDonald, examines in well developed dramaturgy a sensitive aspect of our contemporary social value system: how to reconcile the individual career aspirations of young executives with the increasingly conformist monolith of the business Establishment. It is perhaps the single most important question facing our business-recruitment oriented universities in the Seventies. Ben Weldon, the bright young husband and father in *The Trap of Solid Gold,* who dreams of being "up there at the top," is the kid brother of the man in the gray flannel suit. (If Ben has been to war, it was to Vietnam, not Italy.) But although he has read his Vance Packard, he has almost too willingly introjected the ideals of a college degree, a home in suburbia far from but close enough to Megalopolis, and Yankee initiative rewarded. After reading this drama of forcibly compromised ambition, one wonders if Ben Weldon will replace his Packard with Herbert Marcuse, and allow his children to demonstrate in the streets.

It is interesting to note that Ellen M. Violett returned to this theme of the individual's goals versus the business Establishment, but with a more youthful protagonist, in her even more timely "CBS Playhouse" drama of 1969, *The Experiment.* Because Miss Violett's work was already represented in our initial selection of plays, and because we had another drama from "CBS Playhouse" in mind, we did not include *The Experiment* in this book.

The much-heralded and widely anticipated "CBS Playhouse" offered its premiere play in January of 1967: Ronald Ribman's *The Private War of Olly Winter,* a drama set against a background of the Vietnam war. The central character of the play was a Negro U.S. Army master sergeant who, in flashback reverie, juxtaposes the events of his childhood against the brutality of battle. The second season of "CBS Playhouse" began more auspiciously with the telecast of Loring Mandel's *Do Not Go Gentle into That Good Night,* which is the seventh selection in this book.

Mandel's play deals with subject matter never before treated on television: the universal concern of old age and family rejection, a problem to which our youth-indulgent mass media pay little attention. Disconsolate after the death of his wife, old Peter Schermann, a carpenter, has let himself be buried, too; he has abandoned all prospect of a further useful life. At the goading of his unsympathetic son, he agrees to being sent to a rest home. Peter soon realizes what the Golden Days haven really is—a halfway house between the living and the dead, a deep-freeze limbo for the unwanted and the socially functionless. His growing rebellion against his fate culminates in his "rage against the dying of the light." The videotaped play was a sterling and memorable event of the electronic drama of the Sixties.

Among the other presentations of "CBS Playhouse" were dramas marking the return to television of three writers identified with the Golden Age: Tad Mosel (*Secrets*), Reginald Rose (*Dear Friends*), and J. P. Miller (*The People Next Door*). The latter drama, of uncompromising social realism, was an examination of the generation gap between drug-addicted teenagers and their bewildered parents. Not entirely unexpectedly, the play was produced by Herbert Brodkin.

The successful and popular "Hallmark Hall of Fame" continued to present drama "specials" throughout the decade, most of which were of the high quality associated with the program since its inauguration in the Fifties. Among the TV originals presented during the Sixties were James Lee's *The Invincible Mr. Disraeli* and *The Holy Terror,* Millard Lampell's *Eagle in a Cage,* and Jerome Ross's *Soldier in Love.* All of these were historical drama, a genre which "Hallmark Hall of Fame" has perhaps overemphasized. With *Teacher, Teacher,* telecast in early 1969, and Rod Serling's *A Storm in Summer,* of the mid-1969–70 season, the program turned to contemporary drama.

The teleplay *Teacher, Teacher,* by Ellison Carroll, is the editors' eighth selection; and like *Do Not Go Gentle into That Good Night* it is concerned with a subject which serious electronic drama had rarely ex-

plored previously. The pivotal character is a mentally retarded young-
ster, a role that was performed in the play's broadcast by Billy Schulman,
himself a retarded teenager. Trying to reach "Freddie" are a former
prep-school teacher—a burnt-out case of a man because of excessive
drinking, and a Negro Air Force combat veteran who finds work as a
handyman. In the fenced-off and isolated estate of an architect, they
share a "community of damage": the boy, damaged mentally; the tutor,
damaged psychologically; and the handyman, sociologically. Each in his
own way is trying to build a new life, and by the end of the play the
three have all learned something of value from one another.

An unpleasant circumstance surrounds this selection—a matter indigenous to television because it is a collaborative communication-art of
many different talents. Displeased with the final treatment of his play,
the author refused to be identified in the broadcast credits for the program. "Ellison Carroll" is, therefore, a pseudonym. But whatever were
the creative compromises made in *Teacher, Teacher,* the editors regard
it as one of the most moving and remarkable dramas ever on television.

In this survey of electronic drama we have noted the increasing use
of film as a production and recording technique to complement "live"
TV or live-on-videotape. And although we have indicated those dramas
that were filmed ("teleplays") and those that were live-on-videotape,
the distinction seems of little importance. "The play is the thing," indeed; and, at bottom, the film shooting-location of Monument Valley
or 92nd Street or the moon—when the first "company" arrives there—
is no less a "stage" or a "set" than an electronic television studio. Film-
reels *and* videotape-reels can give us the dramatic experience of people
playing out their lives in a quest for order and understanding; they are
both reels of the what-is-most-real.

The economic advantage, however, of film in production is of great
importance. Considering the opportunities for wider distribution of
filmed program material to local stations here and abroad, it is eco-
nomically apparent why "live" and even live-on-videotape drama is
rarely seen on television anymore. Further, filmed drama productions
can be shown in theaters, opening even new markets. Three examples
of this in the Sixties may be cited: episodes from "The Man from
U.N.C.L.E." were, after re-editing, released for theatrical distribution
in the United States; three consecutive "Lassie" programs were com-
bined into a feature-length film for showing in European theaters; and
the Truman Capote–Eleanor Perry *A Christmas Memory* and *The
Thanksgiving Visitor,* both seen on TV, were joined to a third collabora-

tive effort into the theatrical feature "Trilogy." Such procedures are not uncommon.[5]

Feature films are, of course, a staple of televising programming, and they were more so in the Sixties. One of their programming assets is that they are a longer form of drama, therefore more capable of holding an audience over a two- or three-hour period of time.

All three of the networks went into the production of feature-length dramatic films in the Sixties. In the case of the CBS Cinema Center and the ABC Pictures Corporation (Palomar) features, the films were shown in theaters prior to their television release. But both ABC and CBS, in addition to NBC, also were involved in the production of features expressly for television "first-run" showing. It is probably this programming emphasis on the made-for-TV feature that was responsible for the decline in occurrence of serious studio drama during the 1960's.

The final selection in this book is the teleplay of a made-for-TV feature, *My Sweet Charlie*. Although the teleplay was an NBC "World Premiere" offering in January of 1970, the editors decided that since it was broadcast during the 1969–70 season—and so close to the formal end of the Sixties—it qualified for our consideration.

Adapted by Richard Levinson and William Link from the novel and stage play by David Westheimer, *My Sweet Charlie* is not one of those ponderously "Important" racially thematic dramas, such as the films "In the Heat of the Night" and "The Liberation of L. B. Jones." If a comparison might be made, it is closer in mood to the gentleness of the film "One Potato, Two Potato." Indeed, if the teleplay is to be considered at all a racial drama, this interpretation can only be based on understated and secondary evidence.

My Sweet Charlie is an "encounter" play, a boy-meets-girl story, if you prefer, of two fugitive young people—and like most of the plays of the Golden Age it is a drama of the "small situation." The Gulf Coast setting of their meeting is a landscape of social hostilities, interpersonal distrust, and bluntly stated racial antagonism—which is the "temporal" difference between the on-the-table realism of this teleplay and the "civilized," but surely equally honest, realism of much Golden Age drama. The Gulf Coast, however, is not the humanistically arid

---

[5] Of passing interest in this regard was the release to European theaters of a kinescope, film-transfer of David Susskind's 1961 videotaped production of *The Power and the Glory* after its showing on American television. Such tape-to-film transferal is often of questionable technical quality; it is better to "shoot" originally on film and then make a videotape duplicate, if necessary.

Zabriskie Point of the Antonioni film of the Seventies: although their situation is tragic, Charlie and Marlene still have that youthful and casual wisdom to find unexpected humor in the serious, and ordinary pleasure in their responsibility toward one another.

It is primarily for its excellence of characterization, expressing without pretense what the editors feel is the essentially optimistic and saving quality of America's young people—a quality which the film "Zabriskie Point" failed to take into account—that *My Sweet Charlie* is included here.

The editors are aware that in this discussion of electronic drama we have neglected mention of an ambitious attempt to restore serious live-on-tape drama to television in the late Sixties; for a not merely historical purpose, it must be noted. This series of occasional drama "specials" was "Prudential's On Stage," and among the plays presented were *Certain Honorable Men* by Rod Serling, *The Choice* by Henry Denker, *Male of the Species* by the British dramatist Alun Owen, and *Mirror, Mirror off the Wall* by David Shaw. The latter was a comedy-fantasy and, in Jack Gould's description, "a dramatic soufflé"—a refreshing change from socially conscious plays.

The decade of the Sixties was not without those "peripheral" dramas which television has offered over the years, and which too often go unnoticed over the electronic-programming dam. Many of these unheralded dramas were presented in such programs as "Camera Three"; the consistently outstanding religious series, "The Eternal Light," and in such local-station programs as "New York Television Theater," broadcast by the noncommercial facility, WNDT. And certainly of interest in the continuing development of the dramatic form on television was the premiere in December of 1969 of "CBS Children's Hour," whose first offering was Jane Wagner's poignant teleplay, *J. T.*

The editors deeply regret that there is no selection in this book representative of "NET Playhouse," the noncommercial television series that was always innovative and of generally high achievement. From "NET Playhouse" we had hoped to include Paul Zindel's *Let Me Hear You Whisper,* but the script was not available to us because of the author's prior publishing commitment. The videotaped play, broadcast in 1969, and set in a sterile research laboratory, tells how a simple scrubwoman tries to save one of the experimental animals, a dolphin who "talks," but only to her. This theme of the striving for "communication" among various forms of life—and the suggestion of all of creation yearning toward consciousness—make *Let Me Hear You*

Whisper something more than a comedy. Indeed, the ultimate consciousness of all matter may well be the divine comedy.

The scripts of electronic dramas, whether presented "live" or on
videotape or on film, are like musical scores: to creatively interpret
and play them, the reader must collaborate with the notations—with
the dialogue, the sound effects, the stage directions, the camera movements and scene transitions. To "completely read" the score of the
scripts in this book the reader must himself be, within his own sensi-
bility, the agile Camera and the sensitive Microphone.

To encourage this creative collaboration, the editors have repro-
duced here the full scripts of our selections as they were written by the
authors, with their notations intact. As such, the scripts reflect somewhat varying writing styles. Our only alterations were in arrangement
of format and were minor. In some instances, perhaps, such notations
as camera shots (e.g., the long shot and the closeup) and scene transitions (the cut, the dissolve, the fade-in and fade-out) may, because
they are *in print,* slow down somewhat the sequence of the plot and the
"story"; but in television drama, the visual "look" as well as the aural
"sound" of the plot are an integral part of our understanding the events
of the plot.

At any rate, the editors do not regard such notations in these scripts
as difficult; we feel certain that readers in this sight-and-sound age have
had sufficient television-viewing experience to collaborate creatively
with the scripts. For those readers who may have relatively fewer clock-
hours in their log of television viewing, we suggest that the scripts be
read in the order of their appearance, since the notations of camera
shots and camera movements become, gradually, more "sophisticated."

Many people have been of generous assistance to the editors in the
preparation of this book. We wish to thank first the authors of the
selections for permission to publish their work—but for their accomplishment there would have been little reason for undertaking this volume. In related matters, we are grateful to Homer R. Heck, of Foote,
Cone & Belding, for his aid in our obtaining permission from Hallmark
Cards to publish *Teacher, Teacher*; and to Reginald Rose, the creator
of "The Defenders," for his own permission to include the Ernest Kinoy
script. Our gratitude for permission to publish goes also to the authors
of the original sourceworks of those selections that are adaptations.

For their agreeing to our publishing these plays, we extend our ap-
preciation to the following producers, personnel representing production companies, and officers of agencies holding various program rights:

Bob Banner; Rose Blacker of Henry Jaffe Enterprises; Fielder Cook; Burton H. Hanft of Paramount Television; Robert Markell; and Valerie Mitchell and Daniel Melnick of Talent Associates/Norton Simon.

We want to express our thanks, too, to the following people at networks and other organizations who gave us various kinds of advice and assistance: Kay Murphy and Ellis O. Moore of ABC–TV; Harry V. Coren, Leslie F. Davis, Nat Gartsman, Ronald Kaiser, and Charles S. Steinberg of CBS–TV; Fred Mahlstedt of CBS Enterprises; Sydney H. Eiges, Barry J. Wagner, and Gene Walsh of NBC–TV; Curtis W. Davis of National Educational Television; Tony Hoffman of Universal Pictures; and Kay Johnson of the University of Wisconsin Center for Theatre Research.

Several people were especially sensitive to our needs concerning the many details and accommodations involved in editing this book, and we hereby acknowledge their kindness. They were Evelyn Burkey and Paul A. Erbach of the Writers Guild of America, East; Naomi ("Nicki") Goldstein of the National Academy of Television Arts and Sciences; Catherine Heinz of the Television Information Office; Peter Cott; and Professor Ronald S. Marquisee of Syracuse University.

Richard Averson
Brooklyn College, CUNY

David Manning White
Boston University

September 1970

Electronic Drama: Television Plays of the Sixties

That's Where the Town's Going!

By TAD MOSEL

Westinghouse Presents
Columbia Broadcasting System Television Network
April 14, 1962

DIRECTOR: *Jack Smight*

PRODUCER: *Gordon Duff*

A CBS–TV Production

THE CAST

WILMA SILLS: *Kim Stanley*

RUBY SILLS: *Patricia Neal*

HOBART CRAMM: *Jason Robards, Jr.*

GEORGE PREBLE: *Buddy Ebsen*

AUNT SOPHIE (*Mute*)

PROLOGUE

FADE IN: THE HALL OF THE SILLS HOUSE.
WILMA SILLS enters from the outside, throws her coat down and hurries up the stairs . . .
CUT TO:
AUNT SOPHIE'S ROOM, which has the closed-in heavy look of a sick room. An aged, dying woman lies in bed, the palm of her hand covering her eyes.
Wilma enters. She adjusts the window shade so that more spring sunlight comes into the room.

WILMA: Aunt Sophie. Summer's practically upon us, and I've been making plans! Do you remember when the whole town used to pack off to Atlantic City? When you were a girl, that was as far as anyone could imagine going. Now do you know where everyone's going? Spain! And I'm going too! Downtown at the travel agency, they don't think I mean it. But I'm going to fool them this year. I'm really going! July the first. You see, I've already decided on the date. There's my whole trip, Aunt Sophie, all worked out! Three weeks in Madrid, two in Barcelona, then on to Majorca—isn't that marvelous?
The old woman has not stirred.
Of course, I'm not sure I need three weeks in Madrid. What would I do with all that time? There are only so many places a woman can go by herself. A man can go anywhere. Maybe I should cut Madrid down to a week. I guess there's still plenty of time to decide. Summer's a long way off. July the first seems miles away.
Silence. Wilma holds out the travel folders.
Would you like to look at these? I'm through with them.
Silence.
Is there anything I can get you, Aunt Sophie?
The hand covering the old woman's eyes merely flickers. Wilma settles back. Another silence.

FADE TO BLACK.

ACT ONE

FADE IN: THE LIVING ROOM.
GEORGE PREBLE at the window. Wilma stands near, scarcely listening.

GEORGE: Since they widened the street out there, Wilma, it seems to come right into your front room, doesn't it? But I'm glad you saved your grandfather's trees. Trees are a selling point.

WILMA: Even when they've been plastered up for years? There's nothing but cement inside those trees.

GEORGE: I wish they hadn't put that filling station so directly across the street. They might have put it on the corner.

WILMA: Excuse me, George.

She quickly goes out of the room.

George opens his briefcase, takes out a pint, and has a swallow. He gets the bottle back into the briefcase before Wilma returns.

WILMA: I thought I heard Aunt Sophie call. She used to have a little bell, but she can't move her fingers anymore. And she never did have a voice that carried.

GEORGE: Is Ruby going to join us?

WILMA: Saturday morning, it's her turn out of the house.

GEORGE: I was hoping she'd be here.

WILMA: We live by turns.

GEORGE: I guess I don't mind being alone with you, Wilma. I've given serious thought to your situation, and I think the best place for you and Ruby to go is out the Brick Road. There's a new development about ten miles out called Shadyside. Of course it's been named with an eye to the future, because right now there aren't any trees. But nice little ranch-type houses—I've got the plans here—and stores, a movie theater—you can see the photographs in this brochure. The whole town seems to be moving out there, Wilma.

WILMA: On your way down here, George, did you pass our postman?

GEORGE: I don't know, Wilma.

WILMA: You came down Western Avenue, didn't you? That's his route.

GEORGE: I wasn't lookin' for him.

WILMA: He's got to come before Ruby gets home.

GEORGE: Don't you want to look at these plans, Wilma?

WILMA: We're not moving anywhere, George. Why, what if one of us married?

GEORGE: Which one?

WILMA: It could happen—like *that.* And what if he wasn't a local man, but someone from the East, maybe? New York City. Then the other would be stuck with a brand new ranch-type house out the Brick Road. Besides, Ruby would never live in anything called "ranch-type." She says bungalow is still a perfectly good word.

GEORGE: But you said on the telephone—

WILMA: Oh. Oh, that was just one of my ideas. Ruby would call it a tangent. I go off on these tangents and call people up.

GEORGE: You may remember, Wilma, you came into my office *after* your telephone call, and you were very serious.

WILMA: It was my morning out, and I remember thinking how marvelous it would be not to come back to this house. So I went to your office to talk about buying a new one. Then I didn't *mind* coming back so much.

GEORGE: I think it would be fair to let people know when you're fooling.

WILMA: Then it wouldn't be real. (*Looks out the window, then crosses to front door*) He's going by! The postman's going right on by! He can't.

GEORGE (*Following her*): I went to a lot of trouble to get this information together, Wilma—but I don't mind, do you hear me, Wilma? I don't mind since it was for you. All right, Wilma? You can come into my office any time you want to, and we'll—sit around. Just drop in, Wilma.

WILMA: Everybody gets at least a circular. Even on Saturday.

GEORGE: Were you expecting something special, Wilma?

WILMA: I'm not going to wait any longer, George. Excuse me, will you, I have to make a telephone call.

She goes to the phone in the living room.

GEORGE: I'll be on my way then.

WILMA: Operator, I'd like to make a long distance call—— (*Covering the mouthpiece*) Thank you for coming, George.

GEORGE: Maybe some day you'll drive out to Moon Lake with me.

WILMA: I thought you realized, George, I'm as good as married.

GEORGE: I guess you're just saying that, aren't you?

WILMA: Is it so impossible?

George goes out of the room. Wilma looks after him curiously, then uncovers the mouthpiece.

WILMA: I'm sorry, operator. I'd like to make a person-to-person call to New York City. Mr. Hobart Cramm. No, I don't know the number. Can't you find out for me? It's the Commercial Club. No, operator, it's a place to live.

RUBY'S VOICE: Wilma?

WILMA: Never mind, operator.

She quickly hangs up. RUBY SILLS enters.

WILMA: You're back early.

RUBY: Everybody's so rude these days that I hurry on home. What was George Preble doing here?

WILMA: He wanted me to drive out to Moon Lake with him.

RUBY: I hope you know he just starts at the beginning of the telephone directory and goes right through, trying his luck. Today he must have gotten to the *s*'s.

WILMA: I've always wished our name began with *A*.

RUBY: A woman would have to be desperate to go alone with George Preble to Moon Lake. Desperate or irresponsible. Which are you, Wilma?

WILMA: I didn't *go*, Ruby. Can't you see I'm still *here?*

RUBY: How is Aunt Sophie? Is she in pain?

WILMA: Why must you always ask if she's in *pain?* Can't you ask if she's better or needs anything?

RUBY: I like to relieve pain.

WILMA: Then you have to like *seeing* it there in the first place.

RUBY: Some day, Wilma, you're going to say the first thing that comes to your mind to someone who's not used to you. I bought her a sleeping mask. (*Holds it up*) The lights from that new filling station blink in her eyes all night. (*Taking two letters from her handbag*) Who do you know in New York City?

WILMA: Is that the *mail?*

RUBY: I met the postman on Western Avenue and thought I'd save him a stop. You have this letter with a New York City postmark.
She takes up a paper knife and starts to slit open the letter.

WILMA: Ruby——!

RUBY: When we were little girls, it was *fun* to open each other's letters— Mother wanted us to.

WILMA: Did she mean for us to go on our whole lives?

RUBY: She wanted us to *share* our lives, Wilma. I think she knew that some day we'd be left here with nothing but each other. I have a letter, too. You may open it. (*Gives Wilma the second envelope*) You open my letter first.

WILMA: It's from *Good Housekeeping Magazine.*

RUBY: I don't think my subscription's run out. Open it.

WILMA: I'd rather open mine.

RUBY: When a family dies out, Wilma, *custom* is all that's left to treasure. You can't break it so lightly.

WILMA: Just this once.

RUBY (*Looking at the letter in her hand*): It can't be that personal. It's typewritten.

WILMA: Everybody's so busy these days that typewriting's accepted as personal.

RUBY: Is there something in here you don't want me to see?

WILMA: I can't tell until I've read it, can I?

RUBY: All right, Wilma. (*Hands her the letter*) And give me mine, please.

She crosses away into the solarium, Wilma following.

WILMA: I'll tell you who mine's from, Ruby.

RUBY (*Opening her communication from* Good Housekeeping): I've my own mail, thank you.

WILMA: Hobart Cramm!

RUBY: Hobart Cramm——? I haven't thought of him in fifteen years.

WILMA: I came across his address the other day. I wrote to him.

RUBY: And that's his answer?

WILMA: It must be!

RUBY: I don't see what can be so personal about a letter from Hobart Cramm. He was just a boy from River Street. He used to help out in the garden, when we had a garden. We all knew him.

WILMA: He was more than that, Ruby. He asked me to marry him once.

RUBY: Hobart Cramm! You never told me that.

WILMA: I'm telling you now.

RUBY: Why didn't you tell me then?

WILMA: We stood on the pier at Moon Lake, and he said, "Wilma, I want you to marry me." Hobie always put things very simply.

RUBY: And what did you say?

WILMA: You'll say it was thoughtless, and I suppose it was. I said, "Hobie, I could never marry a man who wears orange shoes."

RUBY: For once in your life, you said the sensible thing.

WILMA: Do you know what he did? He took off his shoes and threw them as far as he could into Moon Lake. Then he said, "Would you marry a man with no shoes at all?" I laughed, because I thought it was a joke. And he said, "Some day you'll *cry* to marry me."

RUBY: He said what!

WILMA: That's how much he cared.

RUBY: He was crude and deserved to be put in his place.

WILMA: But he's grown into a wonderful man, Ruby. I went into the Welfare Office the other day to see if I could help out in my free time——

RUBY: The *Welfare* Office——! You never told me.

WILMA: That's not the *point,* Ruby——

RUBY: I'm *interested* in what you do!

WILMA: While I was there, they said they'd had this letter from Hobart Cramm, wanting to know who lived in his old house on River Street and if they were as poor as *his* family had been, because he wanted to help them out. Imagine, he wanted to give perpetual care to the house where he was born!

RUBY: I thought people only gave perpetual care to graves.

WILMA: *I* thought it was very *generous.*

RUBY: A monument to himself?

WILMA: *Help* to those *people!*

RUBY: Did he happen to say in this letter if he ever married?

WILMA: I didn't *see* the letter. But I got his address. It's a men's club.

RUBY: So you wrote to him.

WILMA: On Monday.

RUBY: I see. I'm afraid I see the whole thing. I shudder to think what you said to lead him on.

WILMA: I never dreamed I'd have an answer so soon.

RUBY: There it is in your hand.

WILMA (*Holding it out*): You read it first.

Ruby takes the letter and opens it.

RUBY (*Reading*): "Wilma Sills, Two Twenty-one Ohio Street——!

WILMA: Not even "Miss"?

RUBY: "Wilma Sills."

WILMA: It begins like a business letter.

RUBY: "Dear Wilma——"

WILMA: That's better.

RUBY: "What a pleasure it was to receive your cordial letter of the seventh. It is always good to hear from old friends."

She scans the rest of the page.

WILMA: Go on, Ruby!

RUBY: "Sincerely yours, Hobart C. Cramm." That's typewritten. He's forgotten to sign it. And here are his secretary's initials in the corner, in case anyone's to be blamed—if you interpret the *meaning* of the letter. (*Gives it back to Wilma*) It's not exactly what you expected, is it? But Wilma dear, I must say it's what you deserve.

She exits to the hall.

WILMA (*Crumpling the letter*): Ruby, let's move out of this house! I've heard of a marvelous place out the Brick Road called Shadyside——!

RUBY: Why would we want to move out the Brick Road?

WILMA: Because that's where the town's going.

RUBY: The whole town? All 7,872 of them? This is one of your tangents.

WILMA: Oh Ruby, I get to feeling so left behind!

RUBY: Behind whom?

WILMA: Everybody!

RUBY: If you move out the Brick Road, do you think you'll catch up?

WILMA: We'll plant our own *trees!* We'll watch things grow for a change, instead of watching them die!

RUBY: We'll have to watch Aunt Sophie die, no matter where we go. And then you'll have to watch me, and I'll have to watch you.

A silence.

Kim Stanley and Patricia Neal in *That's Where the Town's Going!*

RUBY: Why can't you accept the peace of acceptance. We both know what it is we've *missed*. The great difference between us is that *I* don't *mind*. I'm very contented. *I* wouldn't have written a cheap letter to Hobart Cramm.

WILMA: Sometimes you're so *adjusted,* Ruby, that you're not kind.

RUBY: I don't mean to be kind. I thought we were close. I thought I knew everything about you, as you know everything about me. If there isn't that in this house, what *is* there? We might as *well* move out the Brick Road.

She has crossed out to the living room.

WILMA (*Following*): No. That was just one of my tangents.

RUBY: You don't like to be left behind. I don't like to be left *out.*

WILMA: You know me. I don't always think.

RUBY: It's time you did. We've all let you get away with it too long. Father actually—— Do you know what they think of you in this town? The children have a tongue twister, "The Silly Sills Sister." I hear them daring each other to say it as they run past the house. I'd be ashamed of that if I were you.

She goes out the door.

Wilma uncrumples Hobart Cramm's letter and reads it, absently switching on a radio to a loud, hearty male voice.

VOICE: ——and now, folks, since tomorrow is Mother's Day, we have nothing but moms on our show today! The studio's just full o' moms! The biggest gosh-darn all-out buncha moms you ever saw in your life! Now I have a whistle here, and when I blow it, I want every mom in this studio and every mom listening in, I want every mom everywhere to sing out, "I want my mama!!!"

In the middle of this, Wilma has thrown the letter away and switched on a small portable radio to loud dance music. She stands between the two radios, absorbed.

Ruby comes in and turns them both off.

RUBY: Why do you have to listen to two radios at once?

WILMA (*Going to the telephone*): I like to know what's happening on both stations.

RUBY: You mean you like to drown out your own silly thoughts.

WILMA: Three-eight-six.

RUBY: Who are you calling now?

WILMA: Harvey's Flower Shop.

RUBY: I've already ordered flowers for Mother's grave.

WILMA: I'm not ordering flowers.

RUBY: I should have known you wouldn't think of it.

WILMA: Busy. (*Hangs up*) Ruby. From now on——

RUBY: Will you be in for supper?

WILMA: We haven't even had lunch!

RUBY: *I* can tell you what *I'll* be doing for supper next *year*. It's a good feeling. I like it. I wouldn't have it any other way.

WILMA: I'll be here.

RUBY: We'll play some cards afterwards.

WILMA: You know I'm not good at cards.

RUBY: We'll play a game where you and I are evenly matched. Old Maid.

Wilma closes her eyes.

RUBY: There you go. I was merely trying to make a joke because I know you like to laugh. Instead you take offense.

WILMA: I'm sorry, Ruby. It was a very funny joke.

She phones again as Ruby goes out.

WILMA: Three-eight-six, please. Harvey? This is Wilma Sills. Oh you know me, always on the go. For one thing, I've been taking that course in flower arrangement in my free time—you know, at the high school in the evenings? And I thought with Mother's Day tomorrow I might be useful. Oh. Well, keep me in mind for the *Christmas* rush, will you? Well, Christmas is practically upon us. Then Easter, then Mother's Day again. That's the way the years seem to be going, and we have to go right along with them. All right, Harvey. Thank you. Goodbye.

She hangs up as Ruby appears.

RUBY: Wilma.

Wilma turns.

RUBY: Hobart Cramm is at the front door.

FADE TO BLACK.

ACT TWO

FADE IN: THE DINING ROOM.

Wilma, Ruby, and HOBART CRAMM finishing lunch.

CRAMM: These rooms used to seem so *big!* My dad wasn't an educated man, Wilma, and he could never get the right size of things. But I wasn't an educated kid, so I believed whatever he told me! And he used to lead me past this house, not on the same side of the street, of course, but on the other side, out of respect—where the filling station is now. And he'd say, "Hobie, there's the old Sills house, the biggest house in the whole state!" I can't get over how little it's gotten!

WILMA: Maybe you've just gotten bigger, Hobie.

CRAMM: Do you think it's that? And the old bank building! He was afraid to go inside, even to look! And he'd tell me it was the tallest building in the *world!* I got into a fight with a kid at school when he said it was only the tallest building in this town! I guess that's when I began to *get* educated. I tell you, I never go into a bank without thinking of my poor dad, and it's a very sobering thought. Why here I am, I say to myself, Hobart Cramm from down on River Street, walking right into the biggest bank in the East! And I'm reminded that I'm just a lucky guy from the Middle West.

WILMA: I'm sure will and determination had something to do with it, Hobie.

CRAMM: Not everybody would see that, Wilma.

WILMA: What business did you finally go into?

CRAMM: Shoes.

RUBY: Will you be here for supper, too, Hobie?

CRAMM: No, thank yuh kindly, Ruby. I'm just between trains. Just an hour between trains to catch up on an old girl friend.

RUBY: I won't plan for you then.

She takes the dishes to the kitchen.

Wilma and Cramm cross to the hall and into the living room.

WILMA: Ruby's the one who's good at people. She can always tell why they do things. She says I never can, so I've given up trying and I just ask, point blank, why'd you come here today, Hobie?

CRAMM: You mean, after that letter I wrote you?

WILMA: It was a very *nice* letter——

CRAMM: But you thought old Hobie was high-hatting you.

WILMA: I just didn't think from reading it that you'd ever care enough to stop off between trains.

CRAMM: That letter kind of let you down, didn't it, Wilma?

WILMA: What right would I have to be let down?

CRAMM: You can say so if it did. I don't mind. It let you down.

WILMA: Did you know you forgot to sign it?

CRAMM: What if I deliberately didn't sign it?

WILMA: Without thinking? I do that, too.

CRAMM: How can you do something deliberately without thinking?

WILMA: Did you mean to be rude?

CRAMM: What if I sat there, with the letter on my desk, and said to my-self, "A typewritten signature's good enough for Wilma."

WILMA: I'd say you didn't think much of me.

CRAMM: All this fuss about a signature. The Sills family always put value on *form*, didn't they? It was my secretary's fault, Wilma. I apologize on her behalf. And if the letter seemed—short, it's because the things

I wanted to say are the kind of things a man has to come and say for himself.

Ruby enters.

RUBY: Is everything all right?

She leaves.

WILMA: If you've only got an hour, Hobie, I'll have to work fast! I'm going to interview you! I'm taking a course in journalism in my free time, and I'll bet the newspaper'd *print* an article on *you!*

CRAMM: In your letter you said you had a *job* on the newspaper. In your free time.

WILMA: I practically have!

CRAMM: You also said you had a fine-paying position at the Welfare Office.

WILMA: I keep my hand in.

CRAMM: I thought maybe the old Sills family's in trouble. Financially, that is. Maybe Wilma *has* to work. So when I found myself on this trip, I thought, why don't I stop off between trains and see if there's anything I can do to help.

WILMA: Is that what you came to say?

CRAMM: Does it hurt your feelings?

WILMA: No.

CRAMM: You can say so if it does. I don't mind.

WILMA: But it doesn't, Hobie! You're very generous. You always were generous. I remember the first time you ever spoke to me—I was in fourth grade and you were in seventh. I'm sorry if that means I know how old you are.

CRAMM: It also means I know how old *you* are.

WILMA: The other boys used to call you "Hobo." "Hobie the hobo." They were so cruel. Remember, you used to jingle change in your trouser pocket to show them. And they'd shout "Robber!"

CRAMM (*Jingling change in his pocket*): Nickels and dimes mowing lawns.

WILMA: You still do it! Only they must be fifty-cent pieces now!

CRAMM: I still know the value of a nickel.

WILMA: This one day I was walking home from school, and you came up behind me. It was this time of year, a day like today. But you were carrying an umbrella. Was your mother a worrier?

CRAMM: We couldn't afford to get sick at our house.

WILMA: The boys were yelling at you from across the street, and you suddenly put up the umbrella and held it over me. It was very thoughtful, but I laughed because it wasn't raining! And you stormed off down the street, holding the umbrella over *yourself* in the afternoon sun.

CRAMM: I remember. I guess you're saying the Sills family's never needed help and never will.

WILMA: Oh, I don't know. Ruby's the one who figures things out, and she says we have enough to get ourselves to the grave and a little beyond. Hobie, I don't have any jobs. I just wrote you that so you'd see what a happy and useful life I have.

CRAMM: I guess I misread the purpose of your letter.

WILMA: Did you think I wrote on *purpose* for *help?*

CRAMM: Now I *have* hurt your feelings.

WILMA: No. I have a feeling I've hurt yours.

CRAMM: I'm used to being turned down by you, Wilma.

WILMA: I'm not getting much of an interview.

CRAMM: Why *did* you write to me?

WILMA: Just to say "hello."

CRAMM: Hello, Wilma.

WILMA: Hello.

CRAMM (*Pulling up his trouser legs*): I hope you notice I'm not wearing orange shoes anymore! They still sell very good, though, on places like River Street, where they're considered elegant. Don't apologize at this late date, Wilma. I know how it was with you then. You told yourself, "There'll be another one down the pike! In black shoes! Patent leather, even!" I can tell yuh, Wilma, patent leather's made of plastic now. So much for patent leather.

WILMA: There was another one. Charlie Vine.

CRAMM: Didn't you like his neckties?

WILMA: I was taller than he was and the part in his hair was crooked. I looked down at it and thought, "I don't want to spend my life watching that part widen. I'll wait for a tall one." And when *he* came along, it simply seemed enough that he *had.* I thought I'd wait for the next one.

CRAMM: Like buses. Until finally you were left looking up that long empty pike and you started wondering, "What was ever so wrong with orange shoes? I'll just write to old Hobie. Of course he's just been sitting around all these years, waiting to hear from me. Poor old Hobie, I may even forgive him for being a hoodlum from River Street."

WILMA: You give me too much credit for thinking things out, Hobie.

CRAMM: Still, you see, I didn't really misread the purpose of your letter. (*A silence*) I suppose you're wondering why I never got married. And maybe never will. Because every woman wants to forgive me something. They try to pin themselves on me like a medal. And I'm supposed to salute.

He makes a mock salute.

WILMA: I didn't mean to do that.

CRAMM: Whatever you meant, Wilma, I thought you'd like to have your answer in person.

He calmly looks at his watch.

WILMA: You didn't have to look at your watch. You're not between trains at all. You came here purposely to say what you've just said. And what's more, you've probably been waiting fifteen years to say it.

CRAMM: Do you think I'm the kind of fellow who looks to get even, Wilma?

WILMA: No, I don't. So if you seem to be, this time, it must be my fault.

CRAMM: I really came to tell you I forgive you, *I* forgive *you*, Wilma.

WILMA: That's very generous.

CRAMM: And to have a look at your useful, happy life. If you want to cry, Wilma, go ahead. I understand.

WILMA: I'm thinking of taking Italian lessons in my free time. It's a very useful——

CRAMM: Why don't yuh cry, Wilma? And I *am* between trains. On my way to Chicago. A busy man can't take special time out of his life for things like this, although some women will always think he can.

WILMA: I know I'm not that important to you.

CRAMM: I guess the whole Sills family's not so important any more.

Wilma nods agreement.

CRAMM: You know, I don't really have to be in Chicago until Monday! I could take the train tomorrow night. There are one or two things I've been meaning to do in this town for years—when I had the *free time!* People I want to look up! Mr. Kramer who had the grocery store! He gave me my first job! What a tyrant he was! He must be old by now, maybe ill. I'd like to do what I can to ease his life! I'd like to share my good luck with some of the folks who were in at the beginning. Especially if *their* lives haven't turned out so well. I'd like to give them a boost. Help them up. Maybe tonight we can go out to Moon Lake. Didn't expect me to say that, did you? But I did say it, Wilma. Are you superstitious? I am. Things always happen in threes. And you know what I asked you once at Moon Lake—twice?

DISSOLVE TO:

AUNT SOPHIE'S ROOM.

The old woman does not seem to have moved, except that now she wears the black sleeping mask. It is night. Outside the window, lights blink on and off incessantly.

Ruby sits in a corner, huddling under a tiny lamp, reading aloud.

RUBY (*Reading*): " 'Come here, child,' cried her father as she appeared. 'I

have sent for you on an affair of importance. I understand that Mr.
Collins has made you an offer of marriage. Is it true?' Elizabeth re-
plied that it was. 'Very well—and this offer of marriage you have refused?' 'I have, Sir.' "

*Ruby stares at the page, then closes the book. She looks across at the old
woman.*

RUBY: Are you in pain, Aunt Sophie?

There is no answer. Ruby goes softly out of the room.

CUT TO:

WILMA'S ROOM.

Ruby enters and watches Wilma as she dresses for the evening.

WILMA: Is Aunt Sophie any better?

RUBY: No.

WILMA: Maybe I shouldn't go out tonight.

RUBY: Maybe not.

WILMA: But I'd hate to disappoint Hobie.

RUBY: You're not going to let him bully you into marrying him, are you?
I watched the two of you at supper. He's brought you low and now
he's bestowing himself on you like a presidential citation. And you
seem to be swallowing it. People don't change. Whatever they were,
they just become more so. Hobart Cramm is still a bully and a fake.

WILMA: Aunt Sophie says a woman should take the first man who comes
to the door with his hat in his hand, no matter who he is or what he is.

RUBY: Are you saying that to see what I'll say?

WILMA: That's the conclusion she's come to at her age.

RUBY: I spend two-thirds of my life in that room with her, and I know
she can hardly mumble anymore, let alone say all that. You're simply
ashamed of this tangent you're off on and you're trying to blame it on
poor Aunt Sophie.

WILMA: It's what she would say if she could talk. She wore that sleeping
mask all afternoon. She doesn't want to shut out the lights from the
filling station, she wants to shut out everything, her whole useless life.

RUBY: Promise me you won't marry Hobart Cramm.

WILMA: *Promise*——?

RUBY: You owe it to me in a way.

WILMA: Do I?

RUBY: I've had chances myself. Every woman has, and she's lying if she
says she hasn't. I never told you, of course, but *I* don't keep my secrets out of thoughtlessness, as you do. I simply never told you because you would have laughed.

WILMA: I don't think I'd have laughed at that.

RUBY: I know you. I refused my chances. Because Aunt Sophie needs looking after. And so do you. I'd never have dared leave you to yourself. Heaven knows what would have happened to you.

WILMA: I'm not sure you're being fair, Ruby.

RUBY: You can't leave me alone in this house with a dying woman.

WILMA: I don't know *what* I'm going to do! (*Laughs*) It's very upsetting when you suddenly get what you want.

RUBY: Promise you won't marry him.

WILMA: I *can't* promise you that. I couldn't promise anyone that. Not even Aunt Sophie. But she'd never ask.

RUBY: You spoke without thinking again.

WILMA (*After a moment*): Now I've thought.

She goes out of the room.

DISSOLVE TO:

THE SOLARIUM.

Hobart Cramm, in a lounging posture. Wilma enters. He does not rise.

CRAMM: Imagine someone flopping like this in the old Sills house! Just flopping! Remember the last time we went to Moon Lake we rode the streetcar. Tonight we're going in a taxi.

WILMA: Hobie, I don't think I ought to go with you tonight. Maybe it isn't fair to leave Ruby alone with Aunt Sophie.

CRAMM: I've a notion to call my own doctor, long distance. No, I mean it. In things like this, a man doesn't stop to think of expense. Don't thank me, Wilma, I don't have to be thanked. Maybe we should move her back East with us, if we could convince her it wasn't charity.

WILMA: You're taking something for granted, Hobie.

CRAMM: Still can't believe it, can you? Let yourself believe it, Wilma. It's all true.

WILMA: The only way I know to do things is to plunge right in. Is it all right if I plunge right in, Hobie?

CRAMM: Old Hobie'll catch you.

WILMA: The first thing that comes to my mind to say is, "Yes, I'll marry you tomorrow."

CRAMM: Good!

WILMA: And thank you for asking.

CRAMM: You're welcome!

WILMA: But whenever I say the first thing that comes to my mind, it's wrong, and I hurt someone. So I suppose I should say, "No, I won't marry you." But you'd want a reason, and it must be that I don't love you. But that's the first thing that comes to my mind, so it can't be a *good* reason. It would have been, fifteen years ago, if I'd thought of it then, but at *my* age a woman can't afford to be so romantic. She has to think about things like companionship and having someone to lean on. So I'm back to "yes" again. But then I'd be getting married just for the sake of it. I'm trying very hard to be serious about this and not treat it lightly. You can see how serious I'm trying to be.

CRAMM: I can see.

WILMA: So I'm back to "no" again.

CRAMM: Go on.

WILMA: I seem to be stuck with it this time. My mind just won't go any further. Maybe I just wanted to be *asked,* Hobie. And that's enough. It's enough to know that things *can* happen—that Hobart Cramm from River Street can go into the biggest banks in the East! That Wilma Sills, the silly Sills sister, can have an offer of marriage at *her age!* It's enough to know that. And to watch. And settle back and accept the peace of acceptance.

CRAMM: Any other woman in your *shoes* would give her *soul* to be married.

WILMA: That's a very appropriate pun, Hobie! I must tell Ruby!

CRAMM: I'm sorry I don't speak elegant enough for you.

WILMA: Ruby likes puns! Do you know, she's far more suited to you than I am?

CRAMM: Any other woman in your *position* would *appreciate* the *chance* to get married!

WILMA: To get married, Hobie, or to get married to *you?*

CRAMM: Don't think it was just *you* I wanted, Wilma. A man reaches a point where he wants a wife. That's all. It can be anybody.

WILMA: Poor Hobie. Have they *all* turned you down?

He suddenly slaps her. There is a stunned silence.

WILMA: I guess—even when I try desperately to be serious, I hurt people.

Ruby enters.

RUBY: Aunt Sophie's much worse. Go sit with her, Wilma. I'm going to get the doctor over here.

Wilma goes quickly out of the room. Ruby follows to the living room.

RUBY: Wilma. Thank you.

WILMA: I didn't do anything for you, Ruby.

RUBY: I always make the mistake of thinking you've had a generous impulse.

Wilma leaves. Ruby stands for a moment, then returns to the solarium.

RUBY: So you made your gesture, and what did it get you? Did she laugh? I could have told you she would.

CRAMM: She didn't *see,* Ruby.

RUBY: What? That you're a lonely man?

CRAMM: She didn't see what I was doing for her.

RUBY: She doesn't want things done for her. She's not like the rest of us, who appreciate kindness and generosity. She's like someone from another time, and I don't mean the past, I mean some rude future—at least the way the world's going now—when all thoughtfulness is gone out of life. Did you know she was named for Wilma Deering? Remember her? Buck Rogers' girl friend in the twenty-fifth century. How like Father to give his *pet* a comic-strip name. And how fitting. *I* was named for a poem he used to say:
"Let the man who has and doesn't give
Break his neck and cease to live!
Let him who gives without a care
Gather rubies from the air."

CRAMM: "Him who gives without a care."

RUBY: That's you, Hobie.

CRAMM: Is it?

RUBY: Oh yes. And you should be gathering *your* rubies. I must call the doctor.

Cramm watches as she leaves.

FADE TO BLACK.

ACT THREE

FADE IN: RUBY'S ROOM.
Ruby, in a dressing gown, packing a suitcase. Wilma watches.

RUBY: The wedding will be in the East because it wouldn't be right to have it here, so soon.

WILMA: I shouldn't think you'd *want* it so soon.

RUBY: I think Aunt Sophie, of all people, would have understood.

WILMA: That's not what I meant.

RUBY: Hobie's been marvelous since the funeral. I don't know what we'd have done without him.

WILMA: You don't even like him.

RUBY: What's the matter, Wilma? Are you sorry now that you refused him? Are you the jealous one for a change? You can say so, if you are. I don't mind. You're envious.

WILMA: You sound like *him.*

RUBY: I think Hobie and I are very well suited to each other. Maybe it's not as romantic as it might be, but at my age there are more important things. Hobie agrees. Companionship. Someone to lean on. I'm quite contented. Even happy. I wouldn't have it any other way.

WILMA: You said we were happy as we were.

RUBY: Poor Wilma. You'll never be good at people, will you? If only you could learn to think things through. You see, dear, every woman has to share her life with *someone*—every woman, that is, except you. I've decided you don't need anyone. I suppose you're very lucky. But every woman with *feeling* has to *share* her life. And she reaches a point where it's only sensible to share it with the first person who will let her.

WILMA: I said that and you called it a tangent.

RUBY: Well, it was, wasn't it? You didn't follow through.

She continues packing. Wilma goes out of the room.

          CUT TO:

AUNT SOPHIE'S ROOM, which is now emptied and unlived-in. The bed has been stripped.

Wilma enters and opens the windows, then throws back the mattress across the footboard. She is about to go when she sees the sleeping mask underneath. She takes it with her, out of the room.

          CUT TO:

THE LIVING ROOM.

Outside, at the front door, children are heard screaming: "Silly Sills Sister! Silly Sills Sister!"

Wilma crosses from the hall into the living room and turns on a radio to drown out the voices.

GEORGE'S VOICE (*At front door*): Get away from that fence and stay away! Hear me!

He comes into the living room.

GEORGE: Wilma?

WILMA (*Shutting off the radio*): Hello, George. I have to say goodbye to Ruby first, then we can go.

GEORGE: I just chased some kids away from out front. I told them someone had died in this house.

WILMA: It's all right. Poor Aunt Sophie's forgotten already. Who is there to miss her? Gone without a trace—except this.

She puts the mask to her eyes briefly.

GEORGE: I almost didn't come, Wilma. I know you on the telephone, you're always fooling. But then, I thought maybe this time she isn't. I'll take a chance.

WILMA: I wasn't fooling, George. I want you to take me out to Moon Lake.

GEORGE: What for?

WILMA: We'll go swimming.

She crosses to the solarium. George follows.

GEORGE: This early?

WILMA: We'll beat the whole town to the first swim of the season. I have to have some accomplishment to put on my gravestone. Why all the questions, George? Don't you want to take me?

GEORGE: That's what I'm here for. And you don't have to worry about being *seen* with me, Wilma. I know a place where nobody else goes. A little cove around the bend—it's at least a mile from the pier.

WILMA: Why wouldn't I want to be seen with you?

GEORGE: Because the whole town says if you go out with George Preble, you'll go out with anyone.

WILMA: Isn't anyone better than no one?

GEORGE: If nobody else ever *asks* you, Wilma, it's because you used to turn them all down. They think you're happy the way you are. Oh yes, they have a saying in this town, "Happy as Wilma Sills!"

WILMA: Who do they say is happy as Wilma Sills?

GEORGE: I'll admit they kind of laugh when they say it.

WILMA: And roll their eyes and touch their heads.

GEORGE: But you don't want them saying you'll go out with just anyone.

WILMA: If there isn't any love to be had, George, you get married anyway. And if you can't get married, you take whatever there is. That's the way everyone seems to be going, isn't it? At least everyone *I* know. I might as well go along with them. Don't *you* just start at the beginning of the telephone directory and go right straight through, trying your luck?

GEORGE: I have more luck than most people in this town would admit.

WILMA: That's what I'm saying.

GEORGE: They have no right to sneer at me.

WILMA: What do you do if nobody answers the telephone? Even when you get to the *z*'s?

GEORGE: We don't have any *z*'s.

WILMA: What do you do?

GEORGE: I think I know what you need, Wilma.

He takes out a flask.

WILMA: One thing leads to another. Well, at least we can drink out of glasses.

She goes out of the room.

GEORGE: I'm only trying to cheer you up.

He takes a slug.

RUBY (*Stands at the foot of the stairs*): We're going now, Wilma.

WILMA: What have you got *on?*

RUBY: Still too quick to laugh, aren't you. This dress is a present, Wilma. Hobie picked it out himself. I wouldn't expect you to think it through and see how touching that is, but you don't treat these things lightly.

WILMA: You look as if you've just walked up from River Street. And that's how he wants you to look.

RUBY: I guess no one will ever cure you of saying the first thing that comes to your mind.

WILMA: I'm beginning to hope they won't.

RUBY: Wilma, will you do me a favor?

WILMA: If I can.

RUBY: I have this box of rice here. I took it out of the kitchen cupboard. And as we go out, would you throw some at us? Just a handful. There's no need to waste it. You can put the rest back. After all, I *am* going to my own wedding!

Wilma suddenly hugs her tightly. Ruby responds, and they cling to each other.

RUBY: I know it's silly, but I'm *going* to be silly from now on! Oh Wilma, the *fun* of it! To get out of this house at last! Out of this town! I'm going to be just as silly as I want to be!

Hobart Cramm comes down the stairs with Ruby's suitcases.

CRAMM: Do you know what I'm going to give you for a wedding present, Ruby? A new set of luggage with your name on it! Ruby S. Cramm in big gold letters!

RUBY: We'll see, Hobie.

CRAMM: You'll need it, because I'm going to show you the sights of the world!

RUBY: Thank you, dear.

CRAMM: You don't sound very appreciative.

RUBY: I've just never cared for my name on things, that's all.

CRAMM: Too crude?

RUBY: A little.

CRAMM: Or don't you like the name Cramm? You can say so, Ruby. I don't mind. Don't you like to see the name Sills cut down to an *s*?

RUBY: There is no Sills family anymore. Whoever heard of them? I'll be delighted to have the luggage, Hobie. You'll have to be patient with me at first. I'm not used to such thoughtfulness.

CRAMM: I'm a patient man. (*Kisses her affectionately*) The taxi's waiting. (*Holding out his hand*) Goodbye, Wilma. You'll always be welcome in our house.

RUBY: Hobie's getting me a house.

CRAMM: Just think of that! I don't have to live in a club anymore! And there'll always be plenty of room for you, Wilma, but I don't expect we'll see much of yuh. I know you'd rather be here by yourself.

WILMA: Yes.

SOUND: TAXI HONKS.

CRAMM: Let's go, Ruby, taxis cost money, especially when they're just standing there, not going any place.

RUBY (*At the door*): Oh dear, it's raining!

CRAMM (*Turning back to Wilma, with a laugh of triumph*): It's raining, Wilma! After all these years, it's raining!

He grabs Ruby's arm and propels her out of the house.

Wilma moves to the door, then runs back for the box of rice.

As the taxi starts up, she flings a handful. There is a loud clap of thunder. Wilma closes the door.

GEORGE (*Coming into the hall*): I guess with the rain we can't go to Moon Lake. We can stay right here. Have a good time without going anywhere. Have some of this.

He holds out the bottle.

WILMA: I wasn't going anyway. (*Looking up at the ceiling*) The windows in Aunt Sophie's room are open. If I don't close them, it will rain in. And after a few minutes, it will come through that ceiling. Right there. See the spot? These old houses fall down after so many years.

GEORGE: I guess you got me down here for nothing again.

WILMA: No, George! I've decided to move out the Brick Road to that place you were telling me about! Shadyside!

GEORGE: Have you, Wilma?

WILMA: That's what I asked you here for!

GEORGE: That's not what I came for!

WILMA: I want to see the house plans and the photographs!

GEORGE: You can't just waste a man's afternoon, Wilma.

WILMA: This isn't a tangent, George, I promise you! I'm not fooling this time! I mean it! And I'm going to get a very useful job! It's all settled!

GEORGE: It sure is. Shadyside is built on sand, Wilma.

Wilma abruptly turns on a radio.

GEORGE: There's no place left for the town to go, so they're building it on sand. What kind of useful job do you think you're going to get?

WILMA: Excuse me, George. I want to hear what's happening on both stations.

She turns on the second radio. George watches her for a moment.

She stands between the two radios, absorbed.

GEORGE: Silly Sills sister.

He goes.

UPSTAIRS, *the rain sweeps into a dead woman's room.*

FADE TO BLACK.

BIG DEAL IN LAREDO

By SIDNEY CARROLL

Du Pont Show of the Week
National Broadcasting Company Television Network
October 7, 1962

DIRECTOR: *Fielder Cook*

PRODUCER: *Jacqueline Babbin*

EXECUTIVE PRODUCER: *Fielder Cook*

A Presentation of Edens Productions, Inc., for The Directors Company

THE CAST

MEREDITH: *Walter Matthau*

C. P. BALLINGER: *John McGiver*

OTTO HABERSHAW: *Zachary Scott*

HENRY DRUMMOND: *Roland Winters*

MARY: *Teresa Wright*

JACKIE: *John Megna*

WALLY BUFORD: *Arthur Hughes*

DR. JOSEPH SCULLY: *William Hansen*

DENNIS WILCOX: *Dana Elcar*

SAM: *James Kenny*

JASON CRAWFORD: *Allen Collins*

PETE: *Keith Carsey*

COACH DRIVER: *Paul Sparer*

PROLOGUE

FADE IN: THE BACK ROOM OF THE PALOMAR HOTEL.
LAREDO, TEXAS, 1899.
*DRUMMOND, HABERSHAW, BUFORD, and WILCOX are play-
ing poker. SAM, the owner of the hotel, looks on.*
WILCOX: Bet one hundred.
HABERSHAW: That's about as far as I can go . . . Sam!
SAM: Yes, sir.
HABERSHAW: Hurry up.
SAM: Yes, sir.
Sam exits.
DRUMMOND: I'll just raise that two hundred dollars.
CUT TO:
THE BAR IN THE LOBBY.
JASON and PETE with drinks.
Sam rushes to the bar from the back room.
JASON: Who's ahead? What's happening, Sam?
SAM: Poker, that's what.
PETE: I know that, but who's ahead?
Sam fills two shot glasses.
JASON: Two whiskeys. That's Drummond and Habershaw.
Sam changes the bottle for another and fills two more glasses.
PETE: Two corn. That's for Wilcox and Buford.
JASON: Come on, Sam, tell us what's happening in there!
SAM: What's happening? They're still playing.
*He takes the money Habershaw has given him to the safe; Pete and
Jason follow him.*
PETE: Well, tell us who's ahead, Sam.
JASON: You're the only one they're letting in there! You're the only one
out here with the information—what are you holding back for? You
playing some kinda game? Come on, Sam, who——
Sam takes some chips from the safe.
JASON: That's a pile of money.
*Sam goes back to the bar for the drinks, then goes to the door leading to
the back room.*
JASON: Just tell us who's winning, Sam!
SAM: Drummond's winning.
He enters the back room.
The COACH DRIVER appears in the door of the lobby.

COACH DRIVER: The stage is leaving, gents! Climb in or get left! (*As he walks through the lobby addressing all*) Pick 'em up, Mister, throw 'em on top and climb in . . . first in gets the choice seats, last one in sits with me . . . all aboard . . . don't forget your wife, Mister . . . tha–a–at's right . . . all aboard . . . (*Reaches the bar and gulps a drink*) Who's winning?

PETE: Drummond.

COACH DRIVER: Drummond came out the heavy winner last year. How much did he win, Pete?

PETE: Must've been more'n six, seven hundred, maybe.

COACH DRIVER: Six, seven hundred! You know what you're talking about? That's small change with them boys! Well, the way they're going they might go right on playin' into next year.
Sam enters from the back room.

JASON: Hey, Sam! How much money you figure is on that table by now?

SAM: None of my business.

PETE: Come on, Sam! It ain't no secret, is it?

SAM: I don't know, I ain't in the secret business. I'm in the hotel business. You say you wanted another drink, Pete?

PETE: Well, I—uh—

SAM: You want a drink—you pay for it.
He crosses to the desk.
MEREDITH, MARY, and JACKIE enter through the lobby door. Meredith reaches for their carpetbag.

MARY (*Taking it from him*): You know you shouldn't . . .
They go to the desk.

MEREDITH: How do you do?

SAM: Hi.

MEREDITH: Sign outside says "Hotel." I hope that means you have accommodations for transients.

SAM: If you mean have we got rooms?—we got 'em. Up the stairs. First door to the right. That's the one with three beds. (*Pause*) Three dollars. You can pay when you leave. How long you gonna stay?

MEREDITH: Oh—just overnight, we hope. We broke a spoke in our wagon, and we figure to get it fixed here . . .

MARY: There is a blacksmith in town, isn't there?

SAM: Oh yes, Ma'am. Down the end of the street.
Wilcox appears and puts money on the desk.

WILCOX: Sam . . .

SAM: Yes, Mr. Wilcox. (*Gets chips for the money and gives them to Wilcox*) Thank you, Mr. Wilcox.
Wilcox returns to the back room.

MEREDITH: What's going on back there?

SAM: Poker.

MEREDITH: Oh? . . .

MARY: Come upstairs, Meredith. We're all very tired.

MEREDITH: Must be a big game!

SAM: The biggest, Mister. The biggest.

MEREDITH: How big is that?

SAM: Mister—the four richest men in the territory are in that back room, playing for blood.

MEREDITH: How often does this go on?

SAM: Just once a year. Twelve months they been saving up their blood.

MARY: Meredith.

MEREDITH: Wait a minute, Mary. I only want to——

MARY: Meredith, you promised.

MEREDITH: Now, Mary!

They start upstairs.

MARY: Let's not go through this again.

MEREDITH: I was only asking the man a few questions.

MARY: I saw that look in your eye.

MEREDITH: What look? What are you talking about?

MARY: You know.

MEREDITH: I do not know. And I'd like an explanation of just what you do mean, if you don't mind . . .

They enter the room upstairs.

PETE: They don't come from no place around here, do they? I never seen them before.

JASON: They're dressed like they're going to church.

Habershaw comes to the bar.

COACH DRIVER: How's it goin', Mr. Habershaw?

PETE: You ain't quit the game, have you?

HABERSHAW: Naw. Just stretching my legs.

JASON: We heard Drummond's wa–a–ay ahead in there!

HABERSHAW: He's ahead. He ain't way ahead.

PETE: Game's got a long way to go, huh?

HABERSHAW: That's right.

He drinks, and sees Meredith, Mary, and Jackie at the head of the stairs.

All look at them as they come down the stairs and into the lobby.

JASON: You boys must be gettin' sleepy. Fifteen hours!

PETE: How much is Drummond ahead? About how much?

JASON: What about you, Mr. Habershaw? You ahead, too, or you losing?

HABERSHAW: Shhh!

MARY (*To Sam*): You said the blacksmith was down the street. You didn't say which way.

SAM: South.

MEREDITH: Am I correct, sir, in assuming that you are one of the players in the game?

HABERSHAW: That's right.

MEREDITH: Would you permit a passing stranger to watch the game for a while?

JASON: Nobody that ain't playin' is allowed in that room, Mister.

MARY: We have to get the wagon to the blacksmith's, Meredith! He's got a lot of work to do on that wheel and we've got to be on our way in the morning!

MEREDITH: Mary . . .

MARY: No, Meredith.

MEREDITH: Mary——

MARY: Meredith—you promised!

MEREDITH: Mary, dear—all I want to do is watch! Good grief, you can't deprive me of that! There's no harm in watching—!

MARY: Meredith, I never——

MEREDITH: Mary, dear, listen—you and Jackie drive the wagon down to the smith's. Just let me watch the game a little while. This is fate, Mary—don't you see that?—chancing in on a game like this, in the middle of nowhere—the Good Lord giving me one last chance to simply watch a game of poker! There won't be any poker to watch on the farm, Mary. You know that. Not for a long, long time. Not for—ever. Give me this one last little holiday—please? Just let me watch?

MARY: You just heard the gentleman say they don't allow any spectators.

MEREDITH: Is that a hard and fast rule, sir?

HABERSHAW: If you can persuade the lady, maybe I can persuade the boys to change the rules.

MEREDITH: Mary?

MARY: The blacksmith may be a long time, and I don't want to wait there all by myself.

MEREDITH: Fifteen minutes! Just give me fifteen minutes—then I'll come right over and join you at the smith's. I give you my solemn promise!

MARY: All right. Fifteen minutes. I want you to stay with Papa, Jackie.

MEREDITH: Aw no, Mary!

MARY: Stay with him!

She exits.

HABERSHAW: Fifteen minutes, why not?

PETE: Can't we come in too?

HABERSHAW: No.

Habershaw, Meredith, and Jackie head for the back room.

CUT TO:

THE BACK ROOM *as they enter.*
Drummond, Wilcox, and Buford have been waiting at the table.
DRUMMOND: Well, it's about time! Where you been—the hand's been dealt for ten minutes . . . Otto? Who's this?
HABERSHAW: Friends of mine. I said they could watch.
WILCOX: Now, Otto, you know the rules!
HABERSHAW: I said he could watch. (*To Meredith*) You on the poker wagon, Mister?
MEREDITH: You might put it that way.
HABERSHAW: Your wife make you give it up?
MEREDITH: She asked me to—yes.
WILCOX: Can you open, Otto?
HABERSHAW: A hundred.
He puts his chips in; the others follow suit.
DRUMMOND: Call . . . I'd like to see my wife ask me to quit! Eh, boys? Can't you just see that li'l ol' Genevieve asking me to ree–strain myself from a little friendly game of cards?
WILCOX: All right, Otto. How many?
HABERSHAW: Two.
DRUMMOND: Three.
BUFORD: Three.
HABERSHAW: Where you folks bound for?
MEREDITH: San Antonio.
BUFORD: That's a lo–o–ong way.
MEREDITH: Yes. We—uh—we bought a place up there. Plan to do a little farming.
BUFORD: No such thing as a little farming. Eh, Henry?
WILCOX: Dealer takes three.
MEREDITH: Well, what I mean is, we haven't got a big place . . . uh . . . a big spread. We bought some land just outside San Antonio.
DRUMMOND: You opened, Otto.
BUFORD: How much land?
MEREDITH: Forty acres.
WILCOX: Forty acres! What're you fixin' to raise? Stinkweed?
DRUMMOND: Listen! What are we here for? To talk about San Antonio, or to play poker? One whole year I been honin' my backside to sit in on this here game, and for fifteen hours we've been playing two-bit poker. And what are we doin' now, we're discussin' the stinkweed crop in San Antonio, Texas. Let's play cards! And I mean—cards!

Time we got a little warmed up, ain't it? Time to make it interesting. That's five hundred United States dollars says I got a hand.

HABERSHAW: Is that supposed to be a lotta money?

DRUMMOND: I've got lots more. I come loaded for bear, not chickens.

HABERSHAW: All right, Henry. Put it away. We know you got it. And you know *we* got it.

DRUMMOND: Then let's play for it!

HABERSHAW: You're the one who said it. I'll see you, Henry.

DRUMMOND: All right! Three deuces! Can you beat that?

HABERSHAW: Full house beats it. Don't it? Don't the rules say a full house beats three of a kind?

DRUMMOND: Horse shoes!

HABERSHAW: I don't think so, Henry. I'm not lucky. I'm skillful.

DRUMMOND: Ye–a–ah!

MEREDITH: You bet five hundred dollars on three deuces?

DRUMMOND: I bet the way I feel like it!

MEREDITH: Is this a—private game?

DRUMMOND: Why?

MEREDITH: Can anybody pull up a chair?

JACKIE: Papa!

MEREDITH: Quiet!

WILCOX: Well now, anybody with the price of admission. That's the rule we go by.

MEREDITH: How much is that?

WILCOX: One thousand dollars, cash.

MEREDITH: Oh . . .

DRUMMOND: Your deal. This game is just beginning to get interesting. I didn't say the conversation. I said the game.

BUFORD: You're right, Henry.

MEREDITH: I've got a thousand dollars!

WILCOX: What you say?

MEREDITH: I said I've got a thousand dollars.

DRUMMOND: Well, get it.

MEREDITH: I'll be right down.

He starts out of the room; Jackie follows.

JACKIE: Papa . . . You mustn't take that money! You know what you promised Mama and me——!

MEREDITH: It's all right, son! It's all right! Don't worry! Your mama knows all about it! I—I told her. I'm not taking the money, son. I'm only borrowing it! . . .

JACKIE: Papa!

CUT TO:

THE LOBBY *as they enter and cross to the bar.*

MEREDITH: Here! Step up to the bar, son. (*To Sam*) You got a man's drink for a little fellow? Sarsaparilla?—something like that?

SAM: Sure.

MEREDITH: Well, pour one for the gentleman here! In a beer glass, if you please!

SAM: Sure.

MEREDITH: How's that, old timer? A schooner all for yourself. (*To Sam*) Take care of him. I'll be right down.

He rushes up the stairs.

SAM (*To Jackie*): Step up to the bar, Mister.

CUT TO:

MEREDITH'S ROOM.

Meredith stares at the carpetbag, then pulls out his gold watch and looks at it. He opens the bag and dumps its contents on the bed. He reaches in and rips the lining off the bottom of the bag. Under the lining are four stacks of paper money. Meredith pulls out one of the packets of money and stares at it . . . a broad grin creases his face.

FADE TO BLACK.

ACT ONE

FADE IN: THE LOBBY OF THE PALOMAR.

Jackie is at the bar with Sam and Drummond. Meredith comes down the stairs to them.

MEREDITH (*Gives Sam a packet of greenbacks*): Sam—would you change that into chips, please?

DRUMMOND: Count it.

SAM: One thousand, even.

DRUMMOND (*To Meredith*): Bring the chips in. Come on.

MEREDITH: I thank you, Sam!

JACKIE: Papa!

MEREDITH: All right, all right—come along!

Meredith, Jackie, and Drummond go into the back room.

CUT TO:

THE BACK ROOM.

Meredith takes a place at the table.

HABERSHAW: No limit.

MEREDITH: I assumed as much.

WILCOX: And it's western rules on betting.

MEREDITH: Meaning what?

WILCOX: Meaning you can't tap out if you ain't got enough to bet. You just gotta bow outa the game.

MEREDITH: That's a rough game.

DRUMMOND: It's the game we play!

MEREDITH: I'm in!

DRUMMOND: Then it's your deal, Mister.

MEREDITH (*Shuffling*): Feels good . . . Hi, son! Want to watch? Want to watch your papa buy us another forty acres in San Antonio, Texas? *They play. A montage of several hands.*

MEREDITH: Call.

DRUMMOND: Beat three tens?
He rakes in the chips.

MEREDITH: It's time I get a good hand!

HABERSHAW: Why don't you wait for it? Why do you keep betting on the bad ones?

DRUMMOND: Don't educate him, Otto!

MEREDITH: Like another drink, son?

JACKIE: Papa, when are you going to stop?

MEREDITH: Don't you get tired just sitting there, watching Papa? Why don't you go upstairs?

JACKIE: I'll go upstairs with you.

WILCOX: Whyn'cha pull your chair around here, boy? You ain't gonna learn much watching Papa.

DRUMMOND: Mister, I can see now why your old lady made you quit this game!

MEREDITH: It's a question of averages. The cards are due to break for me.

WILCOX: Famous last words.
Meredith deals from a new deck . . .

HABERSHAW: . . . So you were good to yourself, huh?

DRUMMOND: Oh, he's got himself a hot one this time. Can't you tell? I bet he's got himself two dandy little deuces.

MEREDITH: I open for four hundred dollars.
All call.

MEREDITH: Mr. Buford?

BUFORD: One.

WILCOX: Three.

HABERSHAW: Three.

DRUMMOND: Well now, you know something? I'm just gonna have one li'l ol' card. Any one of four particular ones you got in that deck will do.

HABERSHAW: And you, sir?

MEREDITH: Oh . . . I guess I'll just play these.

DRUMMOND: We–e–e–ell! Whaddaya know!

BUFORD: He's got hisself a big one!

HABERSHAW: Just like he said he would!

WILCOX: Watch out, boy! He may have five deuces!

BUFORD: 'Smatter, boy? It ain't hot in here. I check.

WILCOX: Why sure it is, Wally! Sure it is, if you got four aces. Check.

HABERSHAW: He can't have the four aces. I got 'em. Check.

DRUMMOND: You know something, Mister? Your pat hand don't scare
me a bit. Here's five whites—five hundred dollars! You ain't got
enough left to stay in this pot.

WILCOX: And you know the rules. Remember we said—western style!
Meredith puts his cards in Jackie's pocket.

MEREDITH: You just keep them there, son, till I get back. Don't let anybody see those cards!

He dashes out the door.

WILCOX: You know something? It don't say nothing in the rule book
about leaving the room in the middle of a hand.

HABERSHAW: Long as he leaves the cards here, Denny—long as he leaves
the cards.

BUFORD: Good thing your mama ain't here yet, eh boy? She'd give him a
what-for—huh?

Jackie runs out of the room.

WILCOX: Hey! Hey—come back here, boy! Where you goin' with them
cards?

He chases after Jackie.

CUT TO:

THE LOBBY.

Meredith comes down the stairs as Jackie is running up.

MEREDITH: What are you doing here? Anybody see those cards?

JACKIE: No, Papa.

MEREDITH: I told you to stay in there. (*Goes to Sam and gives him a stack
of greenbacks*) Count it!

SAM: Three thousand dollars!

JACKIE: Papa! . . .

MEREDITH: Well!?! What do you say?

WILCOX: Give him the chips, Sam.

Sam does. Meredith, Wilcox, and Jackie return to the back room.
Mary enters the lobby and starts up the stairs.

SAM (*Calling to her*): You better take your key, Ma'am.

Mary gets the key, then goes upstairs.

CUT TO:

THE BACK ROOM.

MEREDITH: I call your eight hundred and I'll raise you a thousand.

DRUMMOND (*Shouts*): Sam! . . . So the gamblin' man thinks he got himself a hand, huh? Well, I got some information for him! I got one, too!

HABERSHAW: So have I.

WILCOX: So have I!

Sam comes in—prepared.

DRUMMOND: Sam—get that box of chips out of the safe.

SAM: I already got it.

DRUMMOND: I'll take a thousand.

WILCOX: And me.

Sam changes their money for chips, then leaves.
All call.

DRUMMOND: Call and raise five hundred dollars.

They continue playing . . .

CUT TO:

THE BAR.

DR. SCULLY enters the lobby and goes to Sam.

SCULLY: I heard the strangers lost a lot of money in that game.

SAM: Hello, Doc.

SCULLY: How much did they buy?

SAM: Four thousand dollars, Doc.

SCULLY: How much money you figure is in that game?

SAM: More than you and I'll ever see. (*Looks up and sees Mary coming down the stairs*) Shh!

MARY: Meredith! . . . (*To Sam*) Where is my husband? Four thousand dollars has been stolen from my room.

SAM: Nobody's ever been robbed in my hotel, Ma'am. Your husband took that money. He's in there—playing cards with it.

CUT TO:

THE BACK ROOM.

DRUMMOND: Mister, you ain't paying strict attention. You wanna stay in this game, you better go upstairs and get five hundred more dollars outa the sock.

MEREDITH: I have no more money.

HABERSHAW: Now ain't that a shame? After he invested his whole four thousand dollars in the game, he can't even finish it!

MEREDITH: Now wait a minute!

DRUMMOND: Sure! We'll wait two minutes, if you can ante up another five hundred.

MEREDITH: I haven't got it!

DRUMMOND: Ain't that a shame? Well now, boys—

MEREDITH: You can't wash me out of the game like this! You can't do it!

WILCOX: The first rule of the game, Mister, is put up or shut up.

MEREDITH: You've got to extend credit!

Mary enters.

MARY: Meredith!

JACKIE: Mama!

MARY: Meredith!

MEREDITH: Now keep out of this, Mary! Listen, I've—I've got—(*Pulls his watch out*) this!

DRUMMOND: Worth a hundred dollars. You need four more, Mister.

MARY: Meredith, in the name of heaven, what are you doing?

HABERSHAW: He's trying to play poker, Ma'am.

MEREDITH: Listen, I've got a wagon and two horses out there I paid six hundred dollars for!

MARY: No—

MEREDITH: Mary darling, listen—it's not what you think it is! We've got a chance here to make more money than we've ever dreamed of!

MARY: Have you lost the entire four thousand dollars?

MEREDITH: I haven't lost it! Don't you understand? I'm still in the game! Now listen to me—I've got a hand of cards here that comes to a man once in a lifetime—you hear me? Once in a lifetime! Sure I've bet every cent we've got! But I know what I'm doing! With this hand I can't lose! Trust me! You've got to trust me just this once!

MARY: Trust you! Trust you! In heaven's name, how many times have I trusted you? How many days of how many years have I trusted and trusted, and sat, and wept, and waited, while you played with cards that couldn't lose—and you lost, and lost, and lost! You swore!—and I trusted you!—and look at us, Meredith! Look at us! You've thrown away every cent we have in the world!

MEREDITH: I haven't thrown it away! I'm going to win! This time I'm going to win! If I can stay in this game! (*To the men*) What do you say? I'm willing to sell a six-hundred-dollar team and wagon for four hundred! Did you hear me? I'll take a two-hundred-dollar loss on a brand new——(*Stops suddenly*)

MARY: Meredith! What's the matter?

MEREDITH: I——I——

He falls to the floor.

MARY: Meredith! Meredith!

BUFORD: Sam! Jason! Pete!—somebody!!!

They come running in.

Roland Winters, Teresa Wright, Walter Matthau, and Zachary
Scott in *Big Deal in Laredo*.

BUFORD: One of you go get Doc Scully. Get him fast!

MARY (*Holding Meredith*): Water . . . could one of you get him a glass of water?

SAM: Sure, Ma'am; be right back, Ma'am.

He rushes out.

MARY: . . . Darling, darling . . .

JACKIE: Papa! What's the matter with you, Papa? What's the matter?

BUFORD: He ain't breathing very good, is he?

Sam comes in with Dr. Scully.

SCULLY: Water be damned, if you pardon me, Ma'am. (*Tending to Meredith*) . . . Drink this. Go on now, drink it!

MEREDITH: Mary . . .

MARY: Yes, my love—yes?

MEREDITH: You . . .

MARY: What, darling, what do you want me to do?

MEREDITH: You . . .

SCULLY: No time for bedside manners, Ma'am. Your husband is having a heart attack.

MARY: No!

SCULLY: Sam, where's your nearest bed?

SAM: In the storeroom, there's a couch.

SCULLY: All right, boys—give me a hand . . . Gently, gently.

The men carry Meredith into a nearby storeroom. Scully stops Mary from entering.

SCULLY: I'd rather you didn't come in right now, Ma'am. Fewer people in that room the better.

MARY: I'm his wife!

SCULLY: His wife's the last person I want in that room! Be sensible, woman. Do as I say! I'll let you in as soon as I can.

DRUMMOND: Doc, is he gonna be able to finish this hand?

SCULLY: Henry Drummond, for the love of——.

MARY: How can you be so vile?

DRUMMOND: Ma'am, we aim to finish this pot, right now, and if he ain't around to finish it with us——

MARY: What happens?

DRUMMOND: He just naturally loses that money, Ma'am.

MARY: It's every penny we own!

DRUMMOND: I'm sorry, Ma'am.

MEREDITH'S VOICE: Mary! . . . you . . . you!

MARY: What is he trying to say?

SCULLY: I guess he means for you to play the hand, Ma'am.

MARY: Me?

SCULLY: You! Now get out of here, Ma'am.

MARY: But . . .

Scully closes the door of the storeroom in her face.
Mary sits at the table.

MARY: How do you play this game?

FADE TO BLACK.

ACT TWO

FADE IN: THE BACK ROOM.

Mary is sitting at the table with Habershaw, Drummond, Buford, and Wilcox.

WILCOX: You mean to say, Ma'am, that you don't know the rules of the game?

MARY: I've never played a game of cards in my life.

DRUMMOND: Then how in the name of——

HABERSHAW: Quiet, Henry. You mean to say, Ma'am, you don't know anything about poker?

MARY: I have no alternative but to continue to play this game in my husband's place. That money represents ten years of scrimping and saving; it represents all our dreams of a decent future for our child. So I intend to protect it. And you have no alternative, gentlemen.

DRUMMOND: No? What do we have to do?

MARY: You have to teach me the game.

DRUMMOND: Now, lady—look! It takes years to learn to play poker. It's crazy to teach somebody how to play the game when——

HABERSHAW: Hold it, Henry. Hold it. I think the little lady's got spunk, and just for that I think we ought to clean up this situation to everybody's satisfaction.

DRUMMOND: How? In a big fat pig's eye—how?

HABERSHAW: Now here's the way it is, Ma'am. We're all holding cards, see? And we all, each one of us, we think we got better cards than anybody else in the game. You follow me, Ma'am?

MARY: Yes.

HABERSHAW: Now we're each of us so sure we got the best hand in the game, we're willing to bet on it. I got thirty-four hundred dollars on that table, says I got the best hand. Mr. Wilcox here, he's got thirty-four hundred in there, saying the same thing for him. And the same for Mr. Buford here, and your husband, Ma'am.

MARY: Go on.

HABERSHAW: But Mr. Drummond just raised the bet another five hundred dollars. And your husband hasn't any more money. He's got to come up with another five hundred if he wants to stay in the game.

DRUMMOND: Tell her the rest of it! Even if he does come up with the five hundred, it ain't gonna be enough! This pot's gonna get higher. And higher! That's a guarantee!

MARY: My husband was willing to sell his gold watch and chain. I heard him.

DRUMMOND: Then mebbe you heard me say it was worth mebbe a hundred dollars.

MARY: Gentlemen all. All gallant gentlemen.

DRUMMOND: We're gentlemen on Sunday. This is Saturday, and we're playing poker.

Scully, Jason, and Pete enter from the storeroom.

MARY (*To Scully*): What are you going to do?

SCULLY: I've got to move your husband. We're a long way from a hospital, Ma'am. Next best thing in these parts is my house, where my equipment is—— Hurry up, boys.

MARY: Is it serious, Doctor?

SCULLY: Serious isn't the word, Ma'am, I'm sorry to say. The word is critical.

Meredith is carried out of the storeroom on a stretcher.

MARY: Darling . . .

SCULLY: Don't try to talk, man!

MARY: Don't worry, darling!

JACKIE: I'm coming with you, Papa!

SCULLY: Son, you can't be any help to your daddy now. I'm the only one can help him, and I don't want company. Now if you want to be helpful, you stay with your mama. She needs you. All right, you fellows. Get moving—but gently, gently.

Pete and Jason carry Meredith out.

WILCOX: Well, Ma'am. As we were saying.

DRUMMOND: Five hundred dollars, Ma'am, if you didn't hear right the first time.

HABERSHAW: Take it easy, Henry. No need to insult the lady.

DRUMMOND: Ah, now look! Since holy when did you climb up on that big white horse? Just 'cause you got some hot ideas for you and the lady after the game—don't tell me! I know you!—that's your business! But don't go telling me how to behave! I come here to play poker! I didn't come for sweet talk and how–de–do and lah–de–dah!

HABERSHAW: And I didn't come here to listen to you shoot your big fat mouth——

WILCOX: Come on, come!—you two! Bust it up! None of us come here to watch a dog fight, either. Let's stick to the point.

BUFORD: You tell 'em, Dennis!

WILCOX: And the point is very simple. You got five hundred dollars to stick with this game? Or ain't you got five hundred dollars?

MARY: Will you accept my—I.O.U.?

DRUMMOND: Ah now, Ma'am. I'm willing to give you one hundred dollars on the watch and chain, and that's a generous offer. But what else you asking credit on, Ma'am? What's your security? What collateral you offering?

HABERSHAW: Ma'am, your husband mentioned something about owning some land near San Antone. Now if you could put up the deed for that . . .

MARY: We don't own that land! We were going up to buy it! Half of that money was going to pay for that land!

HABERSHAW: Well . . . in that case . . .

MARY: Is there a bank in this town?

WILCOX: Say that again, Ma'am?

MARY: I asked you, is there a bank in this town?

BUFORD: Yes, Ma'am. The Cattle and Merchants. Right across the street.

WILCOX: You going to the bank?

MARY: I am.

WILCOX: For what?

MARY: For money.

DRUMMOND: From the bank?

MARY: Directly across the street, did you say?

DRUMMOND: Lady, maybe you don't understand. If we ain't gonna give you money—credit—how d'you expect to get it from a bank?

WILCOX: Just a minute, Ma'am. I don't like to be, like they say, the lawyer for the devil. But Ma'am, you can't walk outa this room holding them cards in your hand.

MARY: Why not?

WILCOX: Well, Ma'am! It just ain't poker! It don't go by the rules! Anything could happen. I mean, while you're outa the room, you could—uh—

MARY: I could cheat?

WILCOX: Well, I didn't mean——

MARY: Now let me tell you something, all of you. You allowed my husband to participate in this game, knowing full well he had no business to do so. You allowed him to put every cent we have in this world on that table. You may play poker for fun—or whatever selfish thrill it is you find in this beastly game—but I am playing for my life, gentlemen! My life! And I have no intention of putting these cards out of my possession. (*Puts the cards in her purse*) And you will not force me to! Having placed us in this terrible jeopardy, you can be human enough and decent enough to allow this one compromise in your silly rules.

HABERSHAW: I think maybe we can accommodate the lady and still keep everybody happy.

DRUMMOND: How?

HABERSHAW: Easy. One of us goes to the bank with her.

DRUMMOND: You—huh?

HABERSHAW: I'd be honored. May I make one point, Ma'am?

MARY: Yes.

HABERSHAW: You willing to turn your back on them?

MARY: What do you mean?

HABERSHAW: Well, once you leave this room you don't know what they'll do with their cards.

MARY: I trust them.

Mary, Jackie, and Habershaw leave.

WILCOX: Shouldn't we tell her who runs the bank? Shouldn't we warn her——

DRUMMOND: She'll find out.

DISSOLVE TO:

THE CATTLE AND MERCHANTS BANK.
A teller escorts Mary, Jackie, and Habershaw to the office of C. P. BAL-LINGER . . .

BALLINGER (*To the teller*): Back to your cage, man . . . Sit down, sit down. Now then . . . Who are you?

JACKIE: John Bradshaw Marshall.

BALLINGER: This is your son, Madame?

MARY: Yes. Shake hands with Mr. Ballinger, son.

BALLINGER: How–de–do. How–de–do. Have you quit the game, Otto?

HABERSHAW: No, I'm still in it. Just taking a little rest.

BALLINGER: No rest for the wicked, Otto. You know that. Now then, Madame, what can I do for you?

MARY: I've come here to borrow some money.

BALLINGER: Then you've taken the right turn in the road. This is a bank. Our business is lending money. First, Madame, may I inquire the purpose of the loan?

MARY: Mr. Ballinger, you seem to be aware of the poker game going on in the hotel?

BALLINGER: I am. I am. Man would have to be deaf, dumb, and blind not to be aware of the competition.

MARY: Competition?

BALLINGER: Madame, there's more money passes hands in that one annual poker game indulged in by these four upstanding members of our community than passes through our wicket in a month of Sundays. That's high finance going on in that hotel, Madame, and I have a right to call it competition. But what has that game got to do with you?

MARY: For reasons too—too unreasonable to go into here, I happen to be playing in that game.

BALLINGER: This true, Otto?

HABERSHAW: It's true.

BALLINGER: I don't believe it.

MARY: It's true!

BALLINGER: All right. I believe it. I don't approve of it but I believe it. Now then?

MARY: There's a grand total of seventeen thousand five hundred dollars sitting on that table right now.

BALLINGER: You mean—in one pot?

MARY: Yes.

BALLINGER: That must be a new record, Otto.

HABERSHAW: It is.

BALLINGER: Seventeen—seventeen thousand five hundred dollars. Good heavens . . .

MARY: And it's my turn to bet, Mr. Ballinger, but I haven't got—I mean, my husband and I—oh dear, how can I explain it? We've put four thousand dollars into that game, and I've got to stick with it! I won't be forced out of it!

BALLINGER: A commendable display of tenacity and grit. But just how does your desire to stick with it concern me? And my bank?

MARY: It's my turn to bet and I don't have the money to bet!

BALLINGER (*Pause*): Is this your idea of a joke, Otto?

HABERSHAW: No, Mr. Ballinger.

BALLINGER: You sure?

HABERSHAW: Yes, Mr. Ballinger.

BALLINGER: All right. For the moment I believe you. Now then, Madame, you've answered my first question. You wish to borrow money from my bank in order to place a bet in a poker game. Now let us proceed to the second question. Just what collateral do you offer, Madame? On what do you propose to borrow this money?

Mary shows him her cards.

MARY: On this!

FADE TO BLACK.

ACT THREE

FADE IN: BALLINGER'S OFFICE AT THE BANK.
Ballinger is looking at Mary's cards . . .
MARY: It must be a good hand, Mr. Ballinger!
BALLINGER: What?
MARY: Isn't it a good hand? Isn't it a very good hand of cards?
BALLINGER: Don't you know?
MARY: No, I don't. I'm only taking my husband's word for it.
BALLINGER: Your husband's—word . . . ?
MARY: But isn't it a good hand, Mr. Ballinger; isn't it?
BALLINGER: Put those cards away, young woman.
MARY: What?
BALLINGER: Put them away. Otto, this is one of your jokes.
HABERSHAW: Jokes?
BALLINGER: Young woman—woman I've never seen before—tells me
she's involved in the biggest poker game that ever came down the
pike. That one was hard enough to believe. Then she tells me she
wants to borrow money to stay in the game. Pelion on Ossa, Madame! Pelion on Ossa! Quotation from the Greek poets. Means that's
when you piled one mountain on top of another. Then, young
woman, you have the bile and the gall to tell me you don't know the
first thing about poker. Otto, go back to your friends and tell them to
stop laughing. The joke is over! As for me, I'm a very busy man.
HABERSHAW: You—got it—all wrong . . .
BALLINGER: You've got *me* all wrong, Otto Habershaw—at compound
interest! They didn't take the trouble to tell you, young woman, that
C. P. Ballinger is the kind of man who can't tolerate liquor, cards,
and women, reading from right to left. I would appreciate it if you
would remove yourself from these premises and go back to your fun-
loving friends.
DISSOLVE TO:
THE LOBBY as Mary, Jackie, and Habershaw enter.
JASON: What happened?
DRUMMOND: What happened?
All go into the back room.
CUT TO:
THE BACK ROOM.
BUFORD (*Softly*): Did you get the money, Ma'am?
WILCOX: We tried to tell you, Ma'am, before you went over and wasted

your time. You wanna borrow money from C. P. Ballinger, you gotta leave at least a second mortgage.

DRUMMOND: And a pound of flesh! Look, Ma'am, it ain't like me to be rough on you, but if you didn't get the money you might as well let us get on with the game.

BUFORD: If I ain't being too nosey—just what kind of collateral *did* you offer Ballinger?

HABERSHAW: She asked Ballinger to lend her money on the cards.

DRUMMOND: She asked him what?

HABERSHAW: She showed him the hand she's holding and she asked him to lend her money on that.

DRUMMOND: You bullin' me, Otto?

HABERSHAW: Nope.

DRUMMOND: A bank loan—on a poker hand?

Ballinger appears.

DRUMMOND: What interest would you charge me on an inside straight, Ballinger?

BALLINGER: So it *was* a joke, wasn't it? I came over to see for myself.

HABERSHAW (*Shouting*): I told you, Ballinger, I tell you again! It was no joke! The lady meant it! That's what they're laughing at, if you really wanna know!

BALLINGER: Then it's not me you're laughing at?

WILCOX: Be dangerous for any man in this town to laugh at you, wouldn't it, C. P.?

BALLINGER: That it would, sir. That it would. Good thing you recognize that fact.

DRUMMOND: Oh, I don't know, C. P. There's still some of us get along pretty good without you.

BALLINGER: But it's still a good idea to stay on the good side of the money, isn't it, Mr. Drummond? Well, young woman! I must say you've given these people good enough reason to laugh at you! They are all aware of the fact that my religion, my politics, and my banking methods are all very old fashioned. They all know that I built my bank with my own two hands on good old-fashioned principles. I do not lend money on blue skies or rosy promises. Decent collateral, Madame—hard collateral—that's the way to build a bank. And I don't mean soft collateral. You!—Jason Crawford!

JASON: Yes, sir.

BALLINGER: What'd I make you do before I gave you a mortgage on your house?

JASON: You made me fix the cellar.

BALLINGER: Correct! Give me collateral with a good foundation or don't ask me for money! Thirty-six years ago I started lending money over in Larry Bingham's back room. First customer I ever had was a drover named Penney who wanted two dollars on a brindle cow at six percent interest. He said she gave six quarts of milk a day. You know what I made him do? I made him move that cow into my back yard for a whole week!—and I watched him milk it every day!—and sure enough she gave an average of six and one-half quarts a day. So I lent him the money—at six and a half percent. You show me collateral, Madame, you better make sure it's good collateral! Get me a chair. *Jason does. Ballinger sits next to Mary.*

BALLINGER: Thirty-six years I've been lending money on good old-fashioned principles. Thirty-six years I've been examining applications for loans up and down and sideways, and I tell you now, gentlemen, one and all, I've never been offered a finer piece of collateral than I hold in my hands right now!

DRUMMOND: What you say?

BALLINGER: You heard me, Henry Drummond! Keep 'em close to the vest, Madame. Close to the vest! Nobody sees that hand but you and me! Sam!

SAM: Yes, Mr. Ballinger?

BALLINGER: Bring your chips in here. All of 'em!

SAM: Got them right here, Mr. Ballinger.

BALLINGER (*To Jackie*): Son, you hold that—(*Gives Jackie his hat*) I don't like to sweat in a new hat. Blues two hundred dollars, I presume? And was it five hundred you needed to stick, Madame? Now then, let's play some poker, the good old-fashioned way. Let's you and me and the Cattle and Merchants Bank just raise the bet once again. Gentlemen, if you want to stay in this game you'll have to ante up another five thousand apiece. Five thousand? . . . (*To Mary's worried look*) Subside, little lady. Any time anybody shows up with that kind of security, the Cattle and Merchants, C. P. Ballinger, President, is prepared to back them to the limit. Of course, you understand there's an interest charge?

MARY: I understand.

BALLINGER: Seven percent. Make it six.

There is no response to his raise. He rakes in the chips.

BALLINGER (*To Jackie*): Lend a hand, sonny!

MARY: I've won!

BALLINGER: That you have, Madame. That you have. Now then, whose deal is it?

DRUMMOND: I don't care! I'm goin' home!

BUFORD: I'm going with you.

WILCOX: If you don't mind, Ma'am—could I have a look at your cards?

BALLINGER: This is the game of poker. Lady doesn't have to show her hand if she doesn't want to.

HABERSHAW: You should read the rules, Mr. Wilcox. (*To Mary*) It's been a pleasure.

MARY: Thank you.

BALLINGER: The Cattle and Merchants lent you a sum total of fifty-five hundred dollars. At six percent interest that comes to three hundred and thirty dollars. Would you care to pay that off on a monthly basis or in a lump sum?

MARY: I think we can afford the lump sum.

BALLINGER: Good! That's the way to do business. Don't take chances if you don't have to. Now if I may escort you to the desk in the lobby we can change your chips for cash, Madame.

MARY: Would you take care of that for me, Mr. Ballinger? I've got to see my husband . . .

BALLINGER: A pleasure, Madame!

Mary and Jackie exit.

DISSOLVE TO:

THE DOORWAY TO SCULLY'S HOUSE.

Sam and Mary.

SAM: Brought your bag over, Ma'am.

MARY: Oh—thank you.

SAM: How is he, Ma'am?

MARY: Dr. Scully says I'll have to get him to the hospital in McIntosh tonight.

SAM: Can I be any help?

MARY: What? Oh, no—no. The wagon's been fixed and we'll make it all right. But I do appreciate all your kindness to us . . . Sam.

SAM: Been my pleasure, Ma'am. Goodnight.

MARY: Goodnight.

Sam leaves . . . and Mary enters the house.

CUT TO:

SCULLY'S ENTRANCE HALL.

Mary stands with her back to the door a long moment . . . She looks at the carpetbag and smiles. Then she walks down the hallway, and opens a door. She hesitates for a moment—then goes in.

CUT TO:

SCULLY'S DINING ROOM.

THE CAMERA FOLLOWS MARY as she walks to a chair at the head of the table. She sits down, her eyes steadily on something at the other end of the table. After an interval, she rises and walks around the corner of the

*table to where Ballinger sits in the first chair to her right. Ballinger's
eyes are also on the opposite end of the table. Mary puts a hand on Ballinger's shoulder; he reaches up and pats her hand. She comes round and
sits on his lap.*

THE CAMERA PANS *past one empty chair, then to the opposite end of the
table . . . Jackie sits there, peeling a large stack of greenbacks into six
separate piles. He does so with perfect concentration, with all the flourish
of a professional cashier. He finishes the six stacks. Then he rolls up the
first stack, ties a rubber band around it, and pushes it down to Ballinger.*

JACKIE: That's the four-thousand-dollar stake, Mr. Ballinger.

Ballinger nods.

Jackie tosses a second roll to him.

JACKIE: And here's your one-fifth of the profits. Twenty-seven hundred
dollars.

Ballinger nods.

Jackie pushes a roll to Mary.

JACKIE: Twenty-seven hundred for you, Rosie.

Mary nods, smiles.

Jackie shoves a roll to Scully.

JACKIE: Twenty-seven hundred for you, Doc.

Scully accepts it, nods.

Meredith enters.

JACKIE: Just in time; there's *your* twenty-seven hundred, Benny.

MEREDITH (*Grins, turns to the others*): Did I pick the right man? Or did I
pick the right man?

MARY: You picked the right man.

MEREDITH: Okay, Jack. Now let's you and me get going while the going's
good.

BALLINGER: Yes. If anybody should get wind of what really went on tonight, I don't want you in the neighborhood. It would be our third
lynching in two years. (*Laughs*) Would be kind of difficult, wouldn't
it, to try to convince them they lost their money in a perfectly honest
game?

SCULLY: Well, now . . . *honest* . . . ?

BALLINGER: Doctor, we did not cheat them. We bluffed them. The heart
of poker is bluffing. We may have bluffed them with embellishments,
but we did it entirely within the code, the rules, and the spirit of the
game. But I wouldn't try to tell that to the boys in the back room!

MARY: Better take off, Benny.

MEREDITH: Yeah.

SCULLY (*Rises*): I'll go out and check the wagon first. Make sure nobody's looking.

He reaches the door.

BALLINGER: Joseph.

SCULLY: Yes, C. P.

BALLINGER: You performed magnificently tonight. You could have been a great actor. Perhaps you missed your true calling.

SCULLY: Perhaps I did. (*Grins at the wad in his hand*) I like money.

BALLINGER: We are all firmly agreed that what we did here tonight we will never do again—none of us! This story's going to be all over the territory in no time. Any one of us is stupid enough to try it again, he'll be lynched in a minute, and *really* lynched!

MEREDITH: Don't worry. I got enough to hold me. I won't be playing cards for a long time. Jack, I promised your old man I'd have you back at the carnival by Sunday morning in time to go to church. I never broke a promise in my life. (*Goes to Ballinger*) C. P.—thanks. If I run into any good investments, I'll let you know.

BALLINGER: Thank you, my boy. You were a very happy choice, a very happy choice.

Meredith steps close to Mary.

MEREDITH: Rosie, thanks for everything. See you around Galveston, huh?

MARY: Sure, Benny. (*She hugs him*) Remember me to that nice wife of yours.

MEREDITH: I will.

Jackie goes to Mary. They embrace. Then he steps up to Ballinger and slams his hand into Ballinger's. They shake heartily.

Meredith swings the boy up into his arms and carries him to the door.

MEREDITH: I just wanna see your mother's face when you walk into that tent with twenty-seven hundred dollars. *Twenty-seven hundred dollars!!!*

JACKIE: She'll be proud of me, huh?

MEREDITH: Proud? She'll be hysterical! You'll be the *king* of the carnival!

They exit with Scully, closing the door behind them.

Ballinger and Mary are alone. He turns to contemplate the two stacks of money in front of him. Mary stands by, affectionately studying him.

MARY: Sweet revenge, huh, C. P.?

BALLINGER: Thirteen years ago the four of them cheated me on a land deal. Thirteen years to figure out how to beat them, but I did it. (*Rises, beams down at her*) Much as I regret the idea, I think you'd better get going.

MARY: All right, honey. But I'd better change first. It's a long ride on horseback.

She crosses to the staircase.

BALLINGER: I'll see you in Galveston in six weeks.

MARY: I'll be waiting, C. P.

BALLINGER: What do you intend to do with the money?

MARY: You know what.

BALLINGER: No.

MARY: We play big poker in Galveston.

Ballinger hurriedly overtakes her at the staircase.

BALLINGER: Now, Rose, you promised me!

MARY (*Innocently*): What, C. P.?

BALLINGER: You said if I got you a big stake out of this game, you'd give up poker!

MARY: I didn't say I'd give up *poker!* You know I wouldn't do that, C. P.!
She starts up the stairs.

BALLINGER: Rose, you gave me your solemn word!

MARY (*Climbing the stairs*): I did not! I never did!

BALLINGER (*Starting up after her*): Now, Rose . . .

MARY: Now, C. P., let's not start this one again. You know very well I could never give up poker. You might as well ask me to stop breathing!

BALLINGER: Now, Rose . . .

MARY: A girl's got to have a *little* fun! What am I supposed to do all the time you're sitting here in Laredo in your big fat bank and I'm waiting for you in Galveston? I only see you every six *weeks!* What am I supposed to be *doing* all that time? What am I——

Her voice trails off as Ballinger puffs after her.

BALLINGER (*A groan*): Now, *Rosie* . . .

FADE TO BLACK.

WHO DO YOU KILL?

By ARNOLD PERL

East Side/West Side
Columbia Broadcasting System Television Network
November 4, 1963

DIRECTOR: *Tom Gries*

PRODUCERS: *Larry Arrick and Don Kranze*

EXECUTIVE PRODUCER: *Arnold Perl*

Talent Associates–Paramount Ltd.

THE CAST

NEIL BROCK: *George C. Scott*

FRIEDA HECKLINGER: *Elizabeth Wilson*

JANE FOSTER: *Cecily Tyson*

RUTH GOODWIN: *Diana Sands*

JOE GOODWIN: *James Earl Jones*

PORTLY: *Godfrey Cambridge*

MORGAN: *John McCurry*

REVEREND WILLIAMS: *Maxwell Glanville*

DOCTOR: *Dan Morgan*

DR. FRAZER: *P. Jay Sidney*

NURSE: *Doris Belack*

KRIEGER: *Stephen Pearlman*

UNDERTAKER: *Earl Sydnor*

NEIGHBOR: *Cynthia Belgrave*

MRS. MARTINEZ: *Carla Pinza*

FELLER: *Douglas Turner*

WOMAN: *Lenzie Perry*

WAITER: *Rai Saunders*

LAWYER: *Ed Harding*

IVY GOODWIN: *Nancy Olivieri*

PROLOGUE

FADE IN:
EXTERIOR—MORGAN'S BAR   NIGHT
ESTABLISHING SHOT
A small nondescript bar on one of the Harlem avenues.

INTERIOR—THE BAR   NIGHT
THE BLARE OF GOOD LOWDOWN JUKE-BOX MUSIC *greets us.*
SHOTS *show a smoky, fairly busy bar, not lacking in patrons so much as patronage. That is, people nurse their beers, a dime gets squeezed here, and the hard liquor—where the real money is—is not flowing.*
CLOSE SHOT   MORGAN
The owner of the joint, a worried man in his fifties, who is polishing the counter to no purpose. He looks at the semi-deadbeat crowd, then looks over at RUTH as she approaches, enters FRAME, *her back to* THE CAMERA.
> MORGAN: Lot of smoke, but, phew—don't hardly pay to wash the glasses.
> RUTH: Gimme a scotch.

Ruth turns INTO THE CAMERA
Waiting for her scotch and receipt. She is a beautiful, cool, composed woman. Somebody once said she had the gift of laughter. It is always with her. Even in this dismal room which boasts nothing but tables and whiskey and synthetic music.
Ruth is one of the main reasons that men come here to drink. Morgan knows it, and this is reflected in his attitude toward her. The men know it, and this is reflected in the way they watch her move. But Ruth has a special quality— an ability to turn them on and handle this as well. Her job is to sell liquor, and this she does without compromising her other principle, which is to keep men at a distance.
> MORGAN: Well . . . business is picking up.

TWO-SHOT   MORGAN, RUTH   FAVOR RUTH
> MORGAN: . . . That's better.

He pours a shot of scotch into one of those glasses that makes it look like four ounces, then gives her a paper receipt. Without making a federal case, this happens to be the kind of glass they use at Morgan's. For this he gets 65 cents.
FOLLOW SHOT   RUTH

She picks up the drink professionally, puts it on an antique tray, and walks most of the length of the bar. She arrives at a booth where a FELLER is waiting for the drink; but before she gets there, every eye in the place will note her attributes.

Mind you, Ruth does not sashay or wiggle. Her own natural walk does the job. In fact, Morgan has been trying to get her for some time to enhance the uniform she wears (divest is a more accurate word); but Ruth comes to work in her own idea of what a B-girl should wear. And, while not immodest, it would hardly raise an eyebrow. It is the woman within that does the trick. So we watch Ruth go down the aisle. She gets up to the Feller. She holds the drink between her thumb and index finger. She is about to announce the price or at least wait for it, because this is customary, before placing the drink on the table, when——

INTERCUT: TWO-SHOTS   RUTH AND FELLER

FELLER: I didn't just order *a* scotch.

RUTH (*Nicely*): Sixty-five cents.

No argument. The Feller takes out a dollar and hands it to her, nodding "keep the change."

FELLER: What I said was "scotch and sit down."

RUTH (*Good humored*): And what did I say?

FELLER: Never mind what you said.

RUTH: I said—you're sweet, but we go by the rules of the house.

FELLER: This *is* my fourth drink.

RUTH: Not in here.

ANOTHER CAMERA ANGLE   FAVOR RUTH

As she escapes a mild pass—moves on, but is able to pause for the following exchange.

FELLER: How many more I got to go?

RUTH: Mark it on the table, then the boss can't cheat you.

CAMERA ANGLE   ANOTHER PART OF THE BAR

A group of listeners, some of whom laugh; but one of them, "PORTLY," doesn't.

FELLER'S VOICE: Ruthie, bring me a double, *now.*

RUTH: Gotcha.

CAMERA ANGLE

Portly stands in Ruth's way to the bar—not menacing but not quite friendly.

PORTLY: Honey, that happened to me last night, only after I had my fourth I went to sleep—on the table.

RUTH: Now that ain't my fault, Wally.

PORTLY (*Pleased that she knows his name*): Ain't I entitled to a rain ˈcheck?

CLOSE SHOT   RUTH

She ponders this. It is only fair, and so, smilingly, she answers:
> RUTH: One drink, you got your rain check.

TWO-SHOT   RUTH, PORTLY
> PORTLY: I don't believe you.
> RUTH: What are you having, Wally?
> PORTLY (*Winningly, he hopes*): Same as you. Two of them, Ruthie.
> (*Then*) Don't put me on.
> RUTH (*Looking him over, laughing*): Man, do you think I'd lie to
> the size of you?

Portly has to laugh. He sits and waits.

CAMERA ANGLE   AT THE BAR   CLOSE ON MORGAN
He is still waiting for the meat-and-potatoes of the evening, and as Ruth approaches, he expects the typical order: "A couple of beers." But he is surprised.
> RUTH: Double shot of scotch, and two bourbons—(*Slightly sotto*)
> —one for me.

Morgan smiles. He fixes a double scotch, a regular bourbon, and a "house" bourbon, which is one part bourbon and three parts water. This he sets a little apart from the regular drinks. He gives her another paper check. Ruth knows the procedure equally well, puts the drinks on her tray—double scotch, the real shot of bourbon, and her drink. She puts the check in her chest pocket . . .
> MORGAN: That's my girl.
> RUTH: Yes, suh.
> MORGAN: Wally any trouble?
> RUTH (*Smiling*): Ain't nobody any trouble, Mr. Morgan, except . . .
> MORGAN: I know.

Ruth and Morgan's meaning is "The World."

FOLLOW SHOT   RUTH
She works her way back to the Feller. And, as usual, people watch Ruth as she goes. The Feller is waiting for her.

INTERCUT: CLOSE SHOTS   RUTH; FELLER
She is about to serve the double shot to him; he looks up ingratiatingly.
> FELLER: Put her there.
> RUTH: C.O.D. Sorry, rules of the house (*Adding as a joke*)
> . . . and the State Liquor Commission. A dollar thirty.

He starts to pay.
> RUTH: You are the big spender!

CLOSE SHOT   MORGAN
As several men (three) enter, without saying anything, come up to the bar,

and are served beer without any further ado. They drink it, pay for it. They are well-known patrons. This goes on every night. This is where misery gets a small degree of surcease; small smiles all around.

TWO-SHOT   PORTLY, RUTH   FAVOR RUTH

She is holding her drink aloft, seated opposite Portly in a booth.

    RUTH: Drink heartily.

They drink.

    PORTLY: That water do anything for you?

Ruth has to laugh.

    RUTH: Not too much.

    PORTLY: Have a real one. Be glad to pay the price.

    RUTH: No thanks. Too early. And besides.

She says this "besides" with finality. Portly knows what she means and so does everybody else. What it means is that Ruth is getting it where she wants to get it, at home: liquor and love.

    PORTLY (*Just a trace nasty*): I know. Husband, the whole bit. And besides, you don't even really like the stuff.

    RUTH (*Herself revealed*): If you want to get personal, I'll split.

CLOSE SHOT   RUTH

She doesn't get up, but if Portly doesn't change his tune she will. This is quickly conveyed.

TWO-SHOT   RUTH, PORTLY

    PORTLY (*Now kidding*): Hold your horses. Ain't a guy entitled to one wisecrack for his money for all these drinks?

    RUTH (*Smiling*): Just about.

She settles back in the booth, enjoying this man—what woman wouldn't? Because it's straight and it's business and nothing dirty happened, or is about to.

MEDIUM LONG-SHOT   FAVOR MORGAN

As the front door of the bar opens, JOE GOODWIN enters carrying his 18-month-old daughter, IVY (asleep or partially asleep), on his shoulder. His face is not so much wreathed in anger as it is in determination. He has simply made up his mind. This is the end of the line for him tonight. The object of his search is Ruth.

Joe stops near the three beer sippers, and surveys the bar.

CLOSE SHOT   MORGAN

Sees Joe. His reaction is several-fold, but dominant is the desire to avoid loss of revenue, loss of Ruth. So . . .

    MORGAN (*Very friendly*): Hiya, Joey. What, did you bring the baby?

TWO-SHOT   MORGAN, JOE   FAVOR JOE

    JOE: I wanta talk to Ruthie.

MORGAN: Well, she's working, Joey. It's the shank of the evening.

THE CAMERA PANS as Joe walks toward Ruth. Morgan calls after him . . .

MORGAN: Gimme a break. Go in my office, I'll send her in. Don't make a scene.

CLOSE SHOT   RUTH   PORTLY IN FOREGROUND

Without a word, without reference to the man in front of her, she gets to her feet.

REVERSE CAMERA ANGLE   HER POINT-OF-VIEW   JOE

Joe walks into FRAME and stands there looking at his wife.

INTERCUT: CLOSE SHOTS   RUTH; JOE

RUTH: What's a matter?

JOE: Nothin'. The kid ain't been asleep all night.

RUTH (*With double sympathy for her child and her husband*): Lemme hold her.

He gives her the baby. It is an act of bestiality.

JOE: I had it, sweetie. This is the end of the line. This is as far as I go. I don't know what the answer is, but I tell you—you working here, and me babysittin' there—making believe I'm studying, learning something, or I'm going to be something—that's nowhere. Never was.

He starts out.

RUTH: Where you going?

JOE: I don't know, and I don't care.

RUTH: Don't be crazy. I'll go home with you. Right now. Joey, I love you. *Joe!*

He walks out the door.

CLOSE SHOT   RUTH

Walking down the aisle of the bar, simply carrying her baby. And despite the fact that there is a lady with a baby in her arms, that behind continues to attract them, and always will. That's the way things are.

Ruth walks out the door. There will be a SHOT of Morgan hoping she will change her mind. Maybe she'll put the baby to sleep in the office behind the bar. But that doesn't happen.

No tears. Ruth exits the bar.

FADE OUT.

ACT ONE

FADE IN:

EXTERIOR—A STREET IN HARLEM   DAY

ESTABLISHING SHOT   PEOPLE ON THE STREET

An average thoroughfare, like 3rd Avenue or Lexington, just south of 125th Street. There are furniture houses on this block with Discount and Time Payment signs pasted on the windows. The rest of the block is normal specialty stores: hardware, butcher, supermarket, pizza, soft drink, etc.

A nice bright day, Indian Summer, not too many people passing; some intent on their own affairs, some strolling near the windows looking in. Feeling of a leisurely Saturday afternoon.

THE CAMERA PICKS UP: RUTH, JOE, AND IVY

We see them now in daylight, so a description:

They are a young Negro couple in their early twenties. Joe carries his baby daughter, Ivy, with ease and affection, despite the fact that his face is clouded with a degree of bitterness. Joe is a great-looking man: thin, proud, but not without the inevitable stamp of someone who has faced life without a high-school diploma. Joe got as far as the third year of high school, then dropped out to find work. The work he has been able to get is the average job open to unskilled Negro men: rarely better than a rack-pusher in the garment industry, a lavatory tender, an assistant painter in a fly-by-night nonunion shop. Despite adversity, Joe has never lost his fight, his determination to make it—no matter how—and, above all, his love for the two people in the world closest to him: his beautiful wife and his beautiful baby.

Ruth is a lovely, generous, relaxed woman, with a special gift for life. It is this that has helped her through the trials a Negro woman faces, this that makes her popular, that makes Joe love her so deeply. She is less educated than Joe, but she carries herself with a special grace, a special self-respect. Her person, her coiffure, her clothing are always in order—an index of her self-esteem and her desire, at all times, to please Joe.

Ivy is eighteen months old; a vital, healthy, eatable baby. She is no "convenient" child, in the sense that she coos when the script says so, cries when that's called for, and disappears when she might be in the way of "dramatic action." Quite the contrary, Ivy is a baby-baby and we get from her what she wants to give. This is not meant to be improvisational theater, but the script is written so that whatever she does in front of the camera, *we can take advantage of the "accidents" and miracles that any kid will normally perform—and work with them. Just now she is enjoying the contact with her daddy and is holding him close, riding in the crook of his neck.*

But Joe, though enjoying the feel of Ivy, is looking dour. For he and Ruth have been having a fight, which has been going on for months. It's about her job.

RUTH (*Deadpan*): Smile.

JOE: Give me one good reason.

RUTH: Because I'm happy. Because you came home last night. Be-

cause, man, that daughter of yours is three good reasons by
herself.

CLOSE SHOT   JOE

*On this he grins. And coming from the somewhat dour exterior, it is a sun-
light smile. The man beneath the bitterness comes through: big and broad
and warm.*

JOE (*But the smile quickly fades*): You sure know how to snow a
man. But what I said still goes.

TWO-SHOT   JOE, RUTH   FAVOR RUTH

RUTH (*Smilingly*): Honey, soon's you finish that class, get yourself
a money job. Man, your slippers'll be waiting—and your
choice of menu. From filet mignon to collard greens.

JOE (*A relaxed response*): Nut.

CAMERA ANGLE   SHOOTING PAST THEM INTO FURNITURE STORE

*There is a sign in English and Spanish that permits "Easy Time Payments."
(Not prominent, just pasted on the window.)
Ruth turns Joe and Ivy so that they face into the store and delights the child
with her chatter.*

RUTH (*To Ivy*): I don't like that lamp. But I love that couch, don't
you?

CLOSE SHOT   JOE AND IVY

The baby and her father look where Ruth is pointing.

JOE: It's too fancy.

RUTH'S VOICE: Oh, it's pretty.

*Let's hope the baby points; but if she doesn't, then SHOOTING PAST HER
HEAD (FROM BEHIND) she shows interest in the display.*

RUTH'S VOICE: Now I like that table—that's what you call a split-
level—

CLOSE SHOT   JOE, IVY, RUTH

*She takes the baby from Joe to hug. Brings her smack over to the window to
show her:*

CLOSE SHOT   TOY IN THE WINDOW

Let Ruth's hand be in FRAME, pointing.

RUTH'S VOICE: Baby asleep?

CLOSE SHOT   JOE

*Watching, with pleasure, but knowing the truth of their finances, and his own
inadequacy to buy these things.*

JOE: Come on.

THREE-SHOT   RUTH, IVY, JOE

*Ruth turns to Joe with her usual good humor. None of this was a putdown,
but she knows she always has to watch her step with him, that she isn't sham-
ing him.*

RUTH: Just a game . . .
They start walking.
RUTH: I love Saturday. Love it.
CAMERA ANGLE   AS THEY WALK ON
Through the passersby on the thoroughfare, turn a corner—start down a block.

EXTERIOR—SIDE STREET   DAY
ESTABLISH, A STOREFRONT CHURCH
From the doorway of this small, somewhat garishly decorated church catering to the people on the block, emerges first—a small boy, age maybe nine, holding onto one end of a rectangular sign. (The lettering, as yet, not seeable.) Now comes the sign carried on the other end by a taller boy, age eleven. And behind them is REVEREND WILLIAMS, the pastor of the church. Williams carries a ladder, a hammer, and in his teeth—some nails.
ANGLE   WIDER SHOT   INCLUDING PASSERSBY
This is somewhat unusual activity and it attracts a few people, who might otherwise stroll by. There are a WOMAN in her fifties, a well-dressed gent, a LAWYER, one or two others. They know Williams and he them, and the Lawyer greets him . . .
LAWYER: 'Afternoon, Reverend.
MEDIUM SHOT   BOYS, LADDER, AND WILLIAMS
He acknowledges the greeting, but with the nails in his mouth can't do more than smile and nod.
MEDIUM CLOSE-SHOT   WILLIAMS
He mounts the ladder—and motions for the boys to pass the sign up. (We still can't read it.)
CLOSE SHOT   WOMAN
Trying, by holding her head sort of sideways, to read what's on the sign.
LAWYER'S VOICE: What's that all about?
WILLIAMS' VOICE (*With nails in his mouth*): Hold your horses.
FOLLOW SHOT   THE SIGN
Goes up, next to the church entrance. It is partially blocked by Williams' body, and by his action of nailing it into the wooden upright of the door jamb.
LAWYER'S VOICE: I can't make it out.
CLOSE SHOT   THE SIGN
Williams, finished nailing it firmly, steps down and out of FRAME—and we read the carefully lettered sign: "PROTEST MEETING. EVERY MONDAY—8:30 P.M."
CLOSE SHOTS   FACES READING THE SIGN
The Woman with no response; the kids grinning; the Lawyer nodding his head in approval; Williams.

RUTH'S VOICE: Reverend—I got a question.
WE HAVE BEEN ON WILLIAMS as he hears her . . . he turns.
SHOT   RUTH, JOE, AND IVY   WILLIAMS' POINT-OF-VIEW
They have walked down the block and are standing with the others watching.
Joe really couldn't care less about the sign.
WILLIAMS' VOICE: What's that, Mrs. Goodwin?
(*He knows her quite well. No need for any hellos or introductions.*)
RUTH: What's a matter with Tuesday, Wednesday, Thursday, Friday, Saturday, and Sunday? (*A broad grin as she finishes*)
THE CAMERA PULLS BACK TO INCLUDE ALL
The other watchers, especially the Lawyer, think this is true and laugh. Not the Woman—she merely listens.
LAWYER: Got a point there. You can say that again.
WILLIAMS: It's beginning anyhow. Right, Joe?
CLOSE SHOT   JOE
Joe normally wouldn't answer, but he has been asked a question by a man of the cloth; others are listening. So he talks.
JOE: You asking me?
WILLIAMS' VOICE: Why, sure.
JOE: You gonna change *that* by "protesting"——
He mocks the word "protest" in the way he says it; and at the same time he points to a pile of garbage—not ten feet away from the church entranceway.
SHOT   GARBAGE   JOE'S POINT-OF-VIEW
Four cans are filled to the brim, and ringed with bags upon bags, left nearby —an accumulation clearly of several days.
JOE'S VOICE: Garbage laying in front of houses day after day and not picked up.
ANGLE   JOE   INCLUDE WILLIAMS
JOE: Houses that been condemned fifty years ago and still standing——
WILLIAMS: That's the whole idea. Raise a little sand.
JOE: We've been raising sand, man, for a hundred years. Same dirt's here—same one-room traps, same jobs open and no others——
WIDER ANGLE   INCLUDE RUTH, IVY, LAWYER
LAWYER: There's a wind going through this land—young man— from Birmingham to Washington to——
JOE (*Sharply*): Only wind I hear is the flapping of tongues.
The Lawyer is taken aback, looks at him sharply.
RUTH (*Trying to ease the situation. With humor*): Maybe if we flap our tongues together, or flap them louder——
JOE (*Cuts her off*): You gonna change Mr. Charlie? Lemme tell

you something. Mr. Charlie do anything for you—except one thing: get off your back. (*With contempt*) Protest.

WOMAN (*Her experience too*): Amen to that.

Joe, carrying Ivy, having said his piece—starts off. As always, carrying the baby tenderly and lovingly. Ruth stands, as he goes off.

RUTH (*Trying to save face and the situation*): It's a good idea, Reverend. I'm coming one Monday—and who knows? I might just figure out a way to bring Joe too. Bark is worse than his bite . . .

Williams waves at her, pleased; watches . . .

ANGLE   WILLIAMS' *POINT-OF-VIEW*

As Ruth catches up to Joe.

THREE-SHOT   JOE AND RUTH   *IVY ON JOE'S SHOULDER*

RUTH: Wait a second, will you—I'm wearing high heels.

JOE: You believe that——? (*He doesn't say the obscenity but thinks it*)

RUTH (*At first, straight-faced*): Why do I put up with you?

JOE: You don't have to.

RUTH (*Now broadly*): I'll tell you: Because I want to. Because I love my daughter by you. Because I love you. And six more reasons if you want them . . .

Joe sighs. This girl knocks him out—knocks out the bitterness, that is. And so—his face as we first met him, the mask of bitterness back on it—they walk on. This is Saturday and the sun is shining. And they love each other.

EXTERIOR—INNER COURTYARD, HARLEM TENEMENT   *MORNING*

TIGHT SHOT   GARBAGE

THE CAMERA SLOWLY PULLS BACK . . . *a broken bag of garbage fills the screen.*

It is, perhaps, a week old. It does not lie on the earth of the courtyard—which is hidden below—but lies, rather, on top of a melange of antique and old cans, dried-out eggshells, long-ago disintegrated orange rinds, coffee grounds—the accumulation of a decade or more of junk-like garbage tossed out the window by countless successive tenants. Living amid filth, they have thrown their own filth out the nearest exit: the window. And the yard below holds the flotsam.

THE PULLBACK *shows this to be a narrow hexagonal area, bounded by brick walls on two sides and rotting fences on the others. And this we know—whether we see them or not—is the province of that permanent resident of the slum: the rat. (If we find the right location and are a little patient—we shall see the villain of this story. See and hear him.)*

CLOSE SHOT   CELLAR WINDOW   AFTERNOON

It has been covered over by fine-heavy chicken wire, but it is obvious that it will not keep the wandering rodents from going in or coming out.
FOLLOW SHOT   TIGHT   LATE AFTERNOON
A rat's path—darting, twisting—into the house.
TIGHT SHOT   A CELLAR DOOR EATEN AWAY   EVENING
Near the door, A BROKEN DRAINPIPE GOING UP. THE CAMERA FOLLOWS, *TIGHT, up to the second floor.*
(The intention of the preceding four shots, and of the shot that follows, is to show that the rats own the yard from morning to night. But while they "frolic" by day, they eat by night, so that the next shot should be frightening.)

INTERIOR—TOILET   NIGHT
CLOSE SHOT   FLOORBOARDS
They are rotten, riddled with holes.
TIGHT SHOT   WATER PIPES
They drip, leak—offer liquid refreshment for the denizens of the backyard.
TIGHT FOLLOW-SHOT   FLOORBOARDS
Leading away from the toilet—quickly dart down the hall. We almost think we see one. And it is lost in the tangle of open lathwork in the hall: plaster showing, wiring visible—the guts of the house seen for what they are: rotten and rotting and deadly.

INTERIOR—GOODWINS' ONE-ROOM APARTMENT   NIGHT
CLOSE SHOT   THE SLEEPING BABY
Ivy lies in her crib—a cherub asleep. The contrast with what we have seen is sharp; the immediate possibilities apparent. This child sleeps in a rat-infested building. But there is no evidence of this problem in her peaceful rest: Ivy sucks her thumb, or a pacifier, or just lies sleeping. (Optional with the child we use.)

JOE'S VOICE (*Hushed*): I'm going out, I told you.
SLOW PULLBACK FROM CRIB TO A TWO-SHOT   JOE AND RUTH
In the widening of our view, we see the apartment.
Ivy sleeps in a corner of the room, her crib curtained off. Past the curtain is a three-quarter bed (not too large or it would take up half of this tiny room). To one side of the bed is a small bureau: clothes stored within and piled neatly on top. Most are baby clothes, well-worn but clean. At the other side of the bed is an eight-inch sink, a mirror above it. (The toilet is down the hall.)
At the other side of the room is a table and two chairs; next to that—a half-size refrigerator with an illegal two-place electric burner on top of it, and a small lamp (the room's immediate illumination). This is the "living room-

dining room–funroom" part of the apartment. On the table is a TV set (eight years old, but still working), a radio, iron, dishes, knives and forks. Under the mirror and on this table are Joe's shaving outfit, and the lotions, pomades, etc.—the accouterments of female beauty, Ruth's.
A decorative paper shade covers a hanging light bulb—in the middle of the room. It is off now to let the baby sleep. From two pegs hang Joe's clothing, Ruth's dresses. Five people in this room is about all it can take; more than that, it gets to be like the subway.
And yet—this is the miracle of Ruth—the room manages to be un-ugly. Not attractive—how could it be?—but Ruth has invested this room with her own approach to life. Touches do it: a travel poster (a year or two old) brings Paris "City of Light" into the room; a photograph of a skier brings in the Alps and some "air"; a vase of live flowers is on the table. And order: things in neat piles, in well-chosen places, minimizing the terrible closeness. Somehow you have the feeling that this terrible room smells like Ruth, sweet and fragrant, despite everything.
THE PULLBACK ENDS ON: JOE'S FACE AND RUTH'S OUTSTRETCHED ARMS.
THE CAMERA TILTS, *showing her lying in bed, clad in a nightgown, her fingers making little appealing, wavy motions for Joe to come closer, come back, settle down—in her arms.*
(The dialogue is hushed, until it gets away from them.)
> RUTH (*At the end of the day, with all her womanly powers*): Joey, I'm tired and I need you. Stay with me.
INTERCUT: CLOSE SHOTS   JOE AND RUTH
Joe has taken his jacket from the peg.
> RUTH: Sit down. On the edge of the bed. I won't touch you, if you don't want me to. Joooooooey——
This last is a love call and it immobilizes him. He stands, jacket half on, looking at his lovely wife.
> JOE: I told you to quit that job.
She sits up in bed, motions for him—by patting the bed next to her—and slowly he sits. A small smile on her face.
> JOE: I ain't arguing with you. I'm telling you. (*Little louder*) Get out of there.
Ruth turns to see if this has disturbed the baby. It hasn't. She lowers her voice even more as she speaks . . .
> RUTH (*Winningly*): Get that job you studying for. Call me and say, "Honey, quit." And I'll be out of that bar before the phone stops ringing.
Joe gets up on this, moves away from her, cannot face her.
> RUTH: What'd I say? You know I'm not trying to put you down.
A pause.

JOE: I quit the course.

RUTH (*Aloud*): You what?

JOE (*Just as loud*): That's right. I found out if I get that card—it don't matter. I can't get a job.

A CRY: *they have awakened Ivy. Both look over guiltily. There is silence for a moment; maybe she'll go back to sleep. But no: Ivy cries.*

FOLLOW SHOT   JOE

He goes to the curtain, parts it, gently raises his daughter to his shoulder. She is half-asleep. Without even thinking Joe goes into a lovely father-thing, softly singing as he pats her back.

JOE: Pat-a-back, pat-a-back, one, two, three. Joe love the baby and the baby love me.

He repeats it again, and Ivy goes off to sleep. (Or, if Ivy does not go to sleep, fine, let her cry softly—and the scene continues.)

Ruth has gotten out of bed, and joined Joe near the baby. She is in bare feet. She comes close to him. He doesn't respond.

RUTH: You taking that course so's you can——

Suddenly he is not listening to her—but alertly to another SOUND.

JOE: Sssh . . .

RUTH (*Alarmed*): What?

Both strain to listen, and WE HEAR—*the unmistakable sound of a rat in the wall: plaster falls inside the wall as he scampers.*

JOE: Listen to them; it's their house, not ours.

RUTH (*Frightened*): Did you plug up the holes?

JOE: Baby, I did. They make new ones.

They listen: the rat is gone. Ivy sleeps (or is quietly crying).

JOE: He gone. Go on back in bed.

RUTH: Baby, let's go in the hall. We're gonna wake her again . . .

She reaches for a robe and slips it on.

JOE: Ain't nothing more to say.

She has led him to the door and opens it slightly.

RUTH: Please.

JOE: I told you I'm going out.

RUTH: Gimme my bag.

She gestures the table; he gets her bag, hands it to her. And using this she leads him out of the room into the hall.

INTERIOR—HALLWAY   NIGHT

TWO-SHOT   JOE, RUTH   COMING TO THE CAMERA

As they talk, she leads him from the doorway (ajar), toward the hall's one window—above which burns a dim naked lightbulb.

RUTH (*Taking out a bill*): Here.

James Earl Jones and Diana Sands in *Who Do You Kill?*

JOE: I hate it. Taking money from you.

RUTH: Okay, *I* earned it this month; next month *you'll* earn it. What's the difference?

He looks at her, the frustration of emasculation in his face.

JOE (*Nasty*): All the difference in the world. You wouldn't understand.

RUTH (*Showing another side of her*): We leveling tonight? Okay. Then stay off the street. Don't tell me it's a buck. I want you away from the street boys: the ones with the needles and the pot and the heist jobs and all of it. Because strong as you are, they will suck you under. (*Gently now*) That's worth me working in a *sweatshop* till you get on your feet again.

JOE: I ain't getting on no feet. I told you. *There's no jobs.*

She has tucked the money in his pocket. She is very close.

Joe cocks his head queerly—listening.

JOE: You hear something?

Faintly the baby has been crying during the above; now the crying grows louder.

RUTH: Just crying herself to sleep——

But now the CRY *has become a* SCREAM. *Ivy is screaming in agony.* JOE *DASHES DOWN THE HALL, Ruth following, runs into the room.*

INTERIOR—THEIR ROOM   NIGHT

CLOSE SHOT   JOE

At door opening, the SCREAM *is horrifying. It continues throughout the scene. Joe runs toward the crib.*

REVERSE ANGLE   ON THE CRIB

In a leap Joe is across the room. He quickly seizes something, anything—a broom—and beats—at the crib!

CLOSE SHOT   RUTH IN THE DOORWAY

Terror on her face.

CLOSE SHOT   JOE

He picks up the baby (in a blanket), his face aghast. The child has been bitten and is bleeding.

RUTH'S VOICE: Oh, my God!

Joe spins, clutching the child to him, starts out the door. He runs past Ruth. She stands, unable to believe what has happened, unable to utter her feelings.

FOLLOW SHOT   JOE

He runs down the steps, holding his daughter. FOLLOW *him down one flight.*

INTERIOR—THE FLOOR BELOW   NIGHT

ANGLE   RUTH'S POINT-OF-VIEW (ABOVE)

A NEIGHBOR sticks her head out her doorway.
     NEIGHBOR: Big as cats!

INTERIOR—HALLWAY   NIGHT
CLOSE SHOT   RUTH
She has thrown on a coat and some slippers and starts down after Joe.

EXTERIOR—THE STREET OUTSIDE   NIGHT
MEDIUM SHOT   THE STEPS
Joe comes running down the outside steps, crazily, Ivy in his arms. He looks up and down the street. There are no cabs.
CLOSE SHOT   JOE AND IVY
As he peers, the stain of blood spreads quickly, covering part of the blanket— and spreading. He runs out of FRAME.
MEDIUM LONG-SHOT   JOE AND IVY
As he dashes madly down the block, toward the corner, AWAY FROM THE CAMERA.

EXTERIOR—STREET CORNER   NIGHT
WIDE SHOT
THE AVENUE *is pretty much deserted. A cab comes into sight—perhaps 25 feet away. It carries a passenger.*
     JOE'S VOICE (*Screaming*): Hey, stop! Please stop, man! Stop! Hey cab, stop!
The cab goes sailing by. No one within heard Joe.
ANGLE   JOE GETS TO THE CORNER
He stands under the streetlamp, trying to catch his breath, searching for another cab.
CLOSE SHOT   JOE AND IVY
The stain now covers the baby's blanket; has spilled over onto Joe's pants and jacket. He looks up—
THE AVENUE   HIS POINT-OF-VIEW
The headlights of a car come toward him.
REVERSE ANGLE   ON JOE
He steps into the middle of the street, in front of the advancing car, waving his free hand to stop it.
               FAST DISSOLVE TO:
INTERIOR—HOSPITAL; EMERGENCY WARD   NIGHT
TIGHT CLOSE-SHOT   A BOTTLE OF BLOOD
The blood is being given intravenously. We are so close we can read the label on the bottle: "CITRATED WHOLE BLOOD (HUMAN)".
THE CAMERA SLOWLY PANS DOWN AND PULLS BACK—

BROCK'S VOICE: Tell her we'll see her in the morning.

THE PULLBACK is a shock. We see, not Ivy, but a Puerto Rican woman, MRS. MARTINEZ. She lies on the emergency stretcher table, intravenously fed. Beside her are NEIL BROCK, the social worker from the Community Welfare Service, and his secretary, JANE FOSTER. On the other side of the bed is a NURSE, wiping Mrs. Martinez's face.

JANE (*In Spanish*): We'll see you tomorrow. Try to get some sleep, Mrs. Martinez.

MRS. MARTINEZ (*In Spanish*): Tell my husband I forgive him.

JANE (*In Spanish*): Okay. You rest. (*To Brock*) She wants you to tell her husband she forgives him.

BROCK: Okay, Mrs. Martinez. I will . . . (*In Spanish*) I will.

ANGLE   BROCK, JANE, NURSE
Walking away from the stretcher.

INTERIOR—HALLWAY OF EMERGENCY WARD   NIGHT
ANOTHER ANGLE   BROCK, JANE, NURSE
As they walk, a tired white DOCTOR joins them.

DOCTOR: Hello, Neil; how are you?

BROCK: Hello, Doc. You look tired.

The Nurse gestures "next room" and asks:

NURSE: How is the baby?

The Doctor answers with a touch-and-go gesture, twisting his hand back and forth.

DOCTOR (*Professionally*): Too soon to tell. (*To Brock's inquiring look*) Case of rat bite. Eighteen-month-old baby. Severed an artery.

They are walking slowly down the hallway. (It has a dogleg, so they cannot see the waiting room area until they make the turn.)

DOCTOR: . . . Lost a lot of blood. May be infected.

His manner is totally professional; that is, not overinvolved. He says it flat— this happened.

The Doctor walks toward another cubicle.

DOCTOR (*To the Nurse*): I'll see the parents of the child soon as I finish in here. Send Kramer in. For smears.

NURSE: Yes, Doctor.

The Doctor enters the cubicle. Brock looks after him . . .

NURSE: He's had a bad night. The Martinez cutting and a burst appendix at the same time. On top of that—the rat bite. The father ran all the way from his house carrying the child. The loss of blood—that's what's so dangerous.

JANE: Those poor people.

They have walked to the dogleg of the corridor, stop a moment, then turn the corner.

INTERIOR—HOSPITAL CORRIDOR; TURN OF THE CORNER   NIGHT
ANGLE   BROCK, JANE, NURSE
As they come into view.
CLOSE SHOT   JANE
Shocked . . .
    JANE: Are those the parents?
    NURSE'S VOICE: Yes.
REVERSE ANGLE   THEIR POINT-OF-VIEW
On a waiting bench sit Ruth and Joe. Fear has pounded them into a terrible, waiting silence. Joe's face especially is set in fear and hatred. Ruth wears a coat over nightgown and slippers.
    JANE'S VOICE: Neil, I know that girl. That's Ruth Goodwin.
ANGLE   FAVOR JOE AND RUTH
As Jane comes over to them. Brock stands off a little.
    JANE: I just heard, Ruth. I'm sorry.
    RUTH: How is she?
    JANE: I don't know. The doctor will be out in a little while.
    RUTH: I sit here and I don't believe it.
    JANE: You'll know in a few minutes.
Jane touches Ruth in consolation:
Joe has looked at her, merely looked to learn what she knows. Since Jane knows nothing, he looks away. Fierce, unspeaking. He sees Brock, passes over him, and back to himself.
Brock offers Joe a cigarette. Joe doesn't take it, doesn't acknowledge it. Brock offers one to Ruth. She declines with a shake of her head.
ANGLE   FAVORING BROCK
Watching, as the Doctor enters FRAME. *He goes over to Ruth and Joe.*
    DOCTOR: The lab tests aren't back yet. We don't know if there's
        any infection.
    RUTH: Suppose she is infected?
    DOCTOR (*Not hopeful; but honest*): Let's face that when we know.
        She lost a lot of blood, you understand that.
Joe merely looks up at this distant white man, then looks down.
    JANE: They're doing the best they can.
CLOSE SHOT   JOE
He looks up at the faces before him . . .
REVERSE ANGLE   PICK UP DOCTOR, JANE, BROCK
CLOSE SHOT   JOE
And though he doesn't say a word—we know what he is thinking . . .

BROCK'S VOICE (*Expressing the thought*): He didn't say a word, but it was written all over his face: "*Who do I kill?*"

INTERIOR—*BROCK'S OFFICE AT COMMUNITY WELFARE SERVICE   DAY*
TWO-SHOT   BROCK, HECKY
Brock, at his desk, has said this to FRIEDA HECKLINGER ("HECKY"), the director of the agency, who is standing above him.
BROCK: . . . "*My baby was bitten by a rat. Who do I strangle?*"
HECKY: How is the baby?
ANGLE   INCLUDE JANE
Who is putting on an outer coat.
JANE: They don't know yet.
BROCK: I been on the phone all morning— Are you shock-proof? Well listen . . .
Using notes he has made, reaching for them on his desk . . .
BROCK: Department of Health, Bureau of Rodent Control, quote: 300 plus incidents of children bitten by rats in New York City last year. One death.
TWO-SHOT   BROCK, HECKY
BROCK: Who do you kill?
HECKY: I don't know. Who do you kill?
BROCK: That's only the beginning because everyone's in the clear. The landlord was haled into court, given a stiff fine last week. Hired a contractor to clean up the place—but the contractor hadn't completed it yet.
Then in response to Hecky's interrupting look—
BROCK: Wait—Department of Health made a complete report a month ago. Sanitation ordered the investigation—so everyone is off the hook but the rat. And the child is in critical condition.
HECKY: What do you want to do?
BROCK: Scream. Blast in the press. Protest.
JANE'S VOICE (*Almost casually*): There is a protest today, at a church on that block.
HECKY: Let's go to it. Let's yell. Do something.
WIDER ANGLE   TO INCLUDE ALL
Jane has been listening carefully. Now fully dressed she says:
JANE: A couple of white faces in that church meeting would help.
HECKY: Exactly my point— What are you going to do, Jane?
JANE: I'm going over to the hospital. To see Ruth and Joe. She's been there all night and all this morning. I'm going to try to persuade her to take a walk. Go to a movie with me. Anything

to take her mind off—the waiting . . . If she wants to go to the
meeting, I'll take her with me.
*Hecky and Brock, two white people, look at each other; they have both
learned something.*
HECKY: You want company?
A pause. Jane nods her head.
JANE: If you want to.
VOICES ARE HEARD IN SONG—singing softly: "We Shall Overcome."
VOICES: ". . . Deep in my heart I do believe . . ."

EXTERIOR—THE STOREFRONT CHURCH   DAY
ESTABLISH   DOOR OF THE CHURCH
CLOSE SHOT   THE SIGN
*We see again the carefully lettered words: "PROTEST MEETING.
EVERY MONDAY—" and, tacked on just below, the hastily added, hand-
written: "RAT BITE."*
VOICES: ". . . We shall overcome . . ."

INTERIOR—THE CHURCH   DAY
MEDIUM LONG-SHOT   FROM THE REAR OF THE CHURCH
The audience concludes the song.
*Reverend Williams takes his place at the podium, speaks quietly, befitting
the subject . . .*
WILLIAMS: Patience, nonviolent determination, unity—these are
our weapons. The answer to the many great tragedies of slum
living——
REVERSE SHOT   THE AUDIENCE   WILLIAMS' POINT-OF-VIEW
*Most are Negro faces, listening. But there are also Puerto Ricans and a few
whites. And to one side . . .*
FOUR-SHOT   BROCK, HECKY, JANE, RUTH
They are sitting in the audience listening. Ruth is thinking of her child.
WILLIAMS' VOICE: ——of which rat bite is, perhaps, the most terri-
ble—lies in this course of action. We welcome our white
friends. We need them as they do us. For if we are to move out
of these conditions——
CLOSE SHOTS   LISTENING AUDIENCE:
INTERCUT WITH WILLIAMS' TALKING
WILLIAMS: Then we must remember that we have survived and
triumphed through——
SLOW PAN ACROSS BROCK, JANE, AND END ON RUTH
WILLIAMS' VOICE: ——dignity, our ability to roll with the punch,
and the gift of love, of understanding, and the greatest of them

all—the gift of laughter—laughing to keep us from crying. For violence betrays our cause——

JOE'S VOICE (*Breaking into the proceedings*): Ruth!

HEADS TURN *to see——*

CLOSE SHOT   THEIR POINT-OF-VIEW   JOE

At the rear of the church, distraught, looking for Ruth.

JOE: You here?—Ruth?!

CLOSE SHOT   RUTH

She sees his state, starts to get up——

RUTH: Joe.

CLOSE SHOT   JOE

He sees her.

JOE: You better come with me.

CLOSE SHOT   WILLIAMS

WILLIAMS: We are having a meeting.

CLOSE SHOT   JOE

JOE: Man, you crazy. You all crazy. You talking and my kid is laying in the Butcher Shop.

His eyes catch Brock and Hecky, white faces looking at him.

TWO-SHOT   BROCK AND HECKY

MEDIUM SHOT   RUTH AND JANE

Ruth has risen in her seat—faces Joe.

RUTH: Joe, don't——

CLOSE SHOT   JOE

JOE (*Full attack now*): How you gonna change the world when you can't do nothing about my kid?!

WILLIAMS' VOICE: Mr. Goodwin, you——

JOE: I'm talking about the truth here and now. Not some people singing, protesting, praying—for the future.

EXTREME CLOSEUP   JOE'S EYES

Burning with fear and hate.

JOE: This is right now. This second. My kid is dying.

And he storms out.

FADE OUT.

ACT TWO

FADE IN:

EXTERIOR—A ROTISSERIE   DAY

TIGHT SHOT   THE SIGN

It is a neon or hand-lettered sign and reads: "CORNER ROTISSERIE:
Best Ribs in Town."

INTERIOR—ROTISSERIE   DAY
CLOSE SHOT   THE RIBS ROASTING
They are luscious-looking, drip fat into a trough below—we get hungry
watching them.
ANOTHER CAMERA ANGLE   FAVOR THE COUNTER
As the chef sets down two plates of ribs with spaghetti on the counter.
ANOTHER CAMERA ANGLE
The hands of a WAITER and part of his body come into FRAME. The Waiter
carries a cup of coffee in one hand. This he sets down, scoops up the two
plates of ribs (on one arm), picks up the coffee again, and walks away.
THREE-SHOT   BROCK, JANE, AND RUTH
They are sitting in a booth. The women are on one side of the table, Brock
opposite. Ruth finishes drinking a glass of water. She sighs.
> RUTH: I want to go back.
> JANE: You've only been away a half-hour.
> RUTH: They said they'd know by—what time is it?
Brock checks the clock.
> BROCK: About 12:45.
> JANE: By two.
> JANE: Isn't this better than—the waiting room?
Ruth tries an appreciative smile: it doesn't come off.
> RUTH: If only I knew where he was.
> JANE: He'll show up.
> RUTH: You don't know Joe.
CAMERA ANGLE
The Waiter is over with the order. They take their hands off the table.
> WAITER: Two with?
> BROCK (*Gesturing Jane and himself*): The young lady and—here.
The Waiter sets the plates of ribs down.
> WAITER: Coffee?
> RUTH: Thank you.
He sets that down before Ruth.
> WAITER (*To Ruth*): Something else for you, Miss?
Ruth shakes her head.
> WAITER: How about something wet?
> JANE: Beer, please.
> BROCK: Two. Mrs. Goodwin?
Ruth shakes her head again.
> WAITER: Got ya——

And goes.
CAMERA ANGLE   ON THE FOOD BEFORE BROCK
He pauses, then starts to eat.
>   BROCK: Good.

Jane starts eating, too.
THREE-SHOT
>   JANE: You ought to eat something. It's good.
>   RUTH: I couldn't.

She starts sipping her coffee, black.
>   BROCK: How long has he been out of work?

Ruth looks over at him—the baby on her mind.
>   RUTH: I don't want to talk about it.
>   BROCK: I'm sorry. I was only thinking—maybe we could be of help.
>   RUTH (*Now answering him, a trace of Joe's tone in her voice*): He isn't out of work. He can clean toilets in Grand Central any time he wants. Or push a handtruck in the garment district. If he's lucky, run a loft elevator somewheres.
>   BROCK: I know what you mean.

Brock eats—somewhat delicately—self-consciously.
>   JANE: There are a number of job possibilities, Ruth—we'll look into them—

But seeing Ruth's pained expression, she stops.
>   JANE: You'll know at two.
>   RUTH: Thanks. I mean it. But I can't sit here. I've got to go back.
>   BROCK: Mrs. Goodwin, I have to call the hospital anyway. Let me call for you. If there's any change——

The Waiter is back with the beer; he sets down bottles and glasses in front of Brock and Jane. He doesn't pour. He puts down a check and leaves.
ANGLE   BROCK
As he rises, he pushes his beer in front of Ruth.
>   BROCK: Take some. Or it'll go flat.

He is asking, and Ruth looks at him and nods slightly: "Okay." He pours some beer in the glass for her.
ANGLE   BROCK
Leaving the table, heading for a phone booth within the restaurant.
REVERSE ANGLE   BROCK IN FOREGROUND; THE WOMEN BEHIND
He walks out of FRAME. *We see the women talking.*
MEDIUM CLOSE-SHOT   RUTH AND JANE
>   RUTH: What could it be?
>   JANE: I don't know. Honestly, I don't know.

RUTH (*Thoughtfully*): Rabies, maybe. That's what I'm afraid of—
some rats are rabid.
Jane touches her hand.

INTERIOR—THE RESTAURANT PHONE BOOTH   DAY
MEDIUM CLOSE-SHOT   BROCK
*As he talks on the phone. Past him, through the glass walls of the booth, the
women can be seen. Ruth is sipping her beer.*
BROCK: She's an amazing woman. I'd be out of my skull now . . .

INTERIOR—HECKY'S OFFICE   DAY
CLOSE SHOT   HECKY
HECKY (*On phone*): How is she?
INTERCUT: CLOSE SHOTS   HECKY/BROCK
BROCK: About what you'd expect. What about Martinez? Did you
see him?
HECKY: Swore he'd go to the hospital. Thanked me. Thanked you.
Did Joe call you?
BROCK: No. No sign of him.
HECKY: What does the doctor say?
BROCK: No change since she saw him. That was about an hour
ago. I'm gonna call there now.
HECKY: Keep in touch.
BROCK: Did you get Krieger at the State Employment Service yet?
HECKY: Got a call in to him now.
BROCK: Please keep after him.
HECKY: All right.
Brock hangs up. Fishes for another dime. Deposits it, dials.

INTERIOR—THE RESTAURANT TABLE   DAY
TWO-SHOT   JANE, RUTH   FAVOR RUTH
JANE: He'll be through in a minute.
*Ruth has finished the beer Brock poured for her. Jane lifts the bottle, asking
her if she wants more. Ruth nods "yes." Jane fills her glass. Ruth drinks.*

INTERIOR—THE PHONE BOOTH   DAY
CLOSE SHOT   BROCK
He is in the midst of another conversation . . .
BROCK: I know you must be over your head . . .

INTERIOR—HOSPITAL EMERGENCY ROOM   DAY
MEDIUM SHOT   NURSE
The same Nurse we saw before is on the phone with Brock. Behind her—and
during the conversation—there is considerable activity. Another nurse will
show her a chart; Nurse will nod "okay." A male attendant will gesture the
medicine cabinet; Nurse will remove a key from her pocket and give it to
him. A patient will come inquiringly for her; Nurse will gesture for him to
go—that way.

NURSE: No more than usual. Your Mr. Martinez was in.

INTERCUT: SHOTS   BROCK/NURSE

BROCK: Yeah, when?

NURSE: Half an hour ago. Kissed his wife's fingers. Begged her forgiveness. Swore it would never happen again.

BROCK: I'll bet. Until the next time. What about the baby?

The Nurse has to put down the phone to write something on a chart being
held for her.

BROCK: Hello?

Now she picks up the phone again.

NURSE: Sorry. I didn't get you.

BROCK: The baby?

NURSE: No change is all we can report.

BROCK: Has the bleeding subsided?

NURSE: Under control—but there *is* infection. How serious doctor didn't say.

BROCK: I'm with the mother now.

NURSE: Don't be too optimistic. It *could* happen.

BROCK (*Shocked*): No.

NURSE: Don't tell her *that* either. We have to wait for the specialist.

The word "specialist" makes him look in Ruth's direction, as he talks.

BROCK: Have they got a specialist on it?

NURSE: Blood poisoning is a possibility, and with an infant this could mean—let's just wait. We will know by four this afternoon, for sure.

BROCK: Could—the baby——?

NURSE: We'll know at four.

A beat.

BROCK: Is the father there?

NURSE: No. Hasn't been here since she left.

BROCK (*Softly*): Who do you kill?

NURSE: Pardon? Hey, I got to go.

BROCK: Thanks.

CLOSE SHOT   BROCK
He hangs up, sits in thought, looking toward Ruth and Jane.
ANGLE   BROCK
As he emerges from the phone booth and heads for the table.

INTERIOR—THE RESTAURANT BOOTH   DAY
MEDIUM SHOT   JANE AND RUTH
Ruth has been looking at Jane, but now, seeing Brock approaching, she looks toward him—expectantly.
Brock enters FRAME, *sits down at the table.*
> BROCK: They won't know till four o'clock. Otherwise—no significant changes.
> RUTH: What does that mean?
> BROCK: I'm telling you what the nurse told me. They've called in a specialist.

Ruth starts to tremble, puts her face in her hands.
> JANE: She's in the best hands, that's all that means.
> RUTH: I got to find Joe. I got to get out of here.

She is sliding out of the booth. Jane joins her.
> JANE: You want us to come with you?
> RUTH (*Nonresponsive, to Brock*): Maybe he's at the hospital.
> BROCK: He's not. I talked to the nurse.
> RUTH: There's a couple of bars he——
> JANE: I'm going with you. Okay?

Ruth hears her offer for the first time.
> RUTH: Please.

The women start out. Brock quickly looks at the check, drops money on the table. Follows them.
CLOSE SHOT—SLOW PAN   THE TABLE
The beer is half drunk; the ribs only touched; the coffee cup empty.

EXTERIOR—THE STREET; A BAR   DAY
TIGHT THREE-SHOT   JANE, RUTH, BROCK
Ruth is between them. Their backs are to THE CAMERA. *Shielding their eyes against the light, they peer into the bar through the plateglass front . . .*
Ruth is the first to turn INTO THE CAMERA. *No Joe.*
> JANE: Where else can he be?
> RUTH: I know. C'mon.

ANGLE   THE THREE
As they walk AWAY FROM THE CAMERA, *down the street. Slowly.*

EXTERIOR—THE STEPS OF THE GOODWIN APARTMENT BUILDING   DAY
THREE-SHOT   RUTH, JANE, BROCK

They go up the front steps. Ruth is dejected. Brock holds the door open for the women.
ANGLE   BROCK
As he enters the building, and the door closes behind him.

INTERIOR—HALLWAY OF THE BUILDING   DAY
SHOT   BROCK
As he enters and goes past two derelicts.

INTERIOR—THE GOODWIN APARTMENT   DAY
TIGHT SHOT   THE HANGING BULB OF THE ROOM
It is lit.
THE CAMERA PANS SLOWLY DOWN TO THE TABLE
On it is a bottle of whiskey, one-third of it drunk.
MEDIUM SHOT   JOE'S BACK
As he leans over the baby's empty crib.
CLOSE SHOT   JOE
He turns from the crib, his hand falling idly on the broom he used to chase the rat. He takes it in both hands, then, suddenly—with all his force—he brings it down on the bed with fury and frustration.
ANGLE   ON THE DOOR
Joe looks, he hears someone outside.

INTERIOR—THE HALLWAY OUTSIDE THEIR ROOM   DAY
MEDIUM SHOT   RUTH, JANE, BROCK
They stop a few feet from the door—then:
      RUTH: C'mon, let's see if he's inside.
      JANE: Sure.
They hang back as Ruth opens the door—

INTERIOR—THEIR ROOM   DAY
CLOSE SHOT   JOE   RUTH'S POINT-OF-VIEW
He stands looking at her. He has been drinking but he is totally sober. The liquor doesn't work for him.
ANGLE   RUTH AND JOE
She runs into his arms.
TIGHT TWO-SHOT
They hold each other, console each other.
      RUTH: Joey, Joey, Joey——
      JOE (*Simultaneously*): Ruthie——

INTERIOR—THE HALLWAY   DAY
TWO-SHOT   BROCK, JANE

They stand watching; they avert their eyes—but stay there.

INTERIOR—THE ROOM   DAY
TIGHT TWO-SHOT   RUTH AND JOE
They kiss—drawing sustenance from each other. Then . . .
    RUTH: How do you feel?
    JOE: Don't feel nothin'.
    RUTH: We'll know at four.
    JOE: I know.
Now for the first time he sees—over her shoulder—that Jane and Brock are in the hall. He moves toward them—sullen, frustrated.
THREE-SHOT   FAVORING BROCK AND JANE
    JOE: Who they?
    JANE (*Flatly, in his mood*): Hello, Joe.
She and Brock have started to move toward the entranceway.
    JOE: Don't come in, man. This ain't no Protest Meeting. Integrated couples ain't allowed.
Brock eyes him carefully, waits. Jane faces him.
    JANE: We're trying to help—is all.
    JOE (*To Brock*): What for? Why now? You scared or something?
Ruth enters FRAME
Trying to restrain him—touching his arm.
    RUTH: Honeybaby, take it easy.
    JOE: They bring you home? Well . . . (*Sarcastically*) Thank ye kindly, suh.
    JANE: He's gonna try to get you a job.
Joe makes a sour-face appraisal of this—right into Brock's face.
    JOE: When he get me one, he know where to find me.
    RUTH (*To Brock and Jane*): You better go.
    JOE: I don't want you around, man. You dig?
    BROCK (*Softly*): I dig.
    JOE (*Turning on Jane*): And you ought to know better, you black.
    JANE: Know what?
    JOE: Ain't nothing gonna change nothing—never.
    JANE: Not every white man——
Joe almost spits at her in his contemptuous outburst.
    JOE: Whut you know about white men? I work for Mr. Charlie every day of my life. Just living——
    RUTH: Joey, don't——
    JOE (*He can't be stopped*): Lemme tell you something——
His first line is directed toward Jane, now he talks right to Brock . . .
    JOE: You, too, mister. If a white man stick a knife in my back and

some other white man pull it out and stick a bandage on it—
you think I'm gonna kiss his hand?!
Ruth puts herself in front of Joe, between him and Brock and Jane.
She touches Joe gently as she turns to them:

    RUTH: Better go now.

    JANE: Okay.

Brock backs away; Jane with him.

    JANE: If you want us, call the office.

    RUTH: Yeah.

    JANE: A little hope, Joe, a little belief——

CLOSE SHOT　JOE
Furious.

    JOE: Girl, git out of here before I——

He slams the door on them—hard.

INTERIOR—THE HALLWAY　DAY
TWO-SHOT　JANE, BROCK
They look at each other, then start slowly down the stairs.

INTERIOR—RUTH AND JOE'S ROOM　DAY
CLOSE SHOT　RUTH
She is trembling.

    RUTH: Joey. Please hold me.

TWO-SHOT　RUTH AND JOE
His wrath goes as he sees her state. He takes her in his arms—fully.

    JOE (*Into her hair*): You want to go over there and wait?

    RUTH: Don't talk.

He holds her. Then . . .

    RUTH: Oh God, I need you.

    JOE: I love you.

    RUTH: What if my baby——?

THE CAMERA COMES IN *as his mouth covers hers to silence her fears and console her. But the fear is too great: it fills them both. There is no consolation —only two people clinging desperately to each other.*

FADE OUT.

ACT THREE

FADE IN:

INTERIOR—THE GOODWIN ONE-ROOM APARTMENT　AFTERNOON
EXTREME CLOSEUP　A SMALL CLOCK

On the room's table reads 3:05.
CLOSE SHOT   JOE
At the mirror. Fixing his hair (or tie). He is fully dressed. Despite the tension—they will know about the baby in less than an hour—there is a degree of relaxation he has not been able to find before. This is because of what happened in the interval between acts. He and Ruth have slept a little, held each other close, escaped with each other from the terrible truth they must now face.
Joe turns, walks slowly, quietly, toward the bed. He passes the clock, looks at it. Then reaching over, he picks it up, checks it, and puts it down. Now he sits gently on the bed. Next to—
WIDEN SHOT TO INCLUDE RUTH
She is in that twilight moment between sleeping and waking. She looks beautiful, relaxed. Ruth is fully clothed except for her shoes—on the floor beside her—and her dress. Joe kisses her awake.
　　　RUTH: Mmmmm——
Joe takes her in his arms. She hugs him back. Then—
　　　RUTH (*Now awake*): What time is it?
　　　JOE: We got about an hour.
She is off the bed quickly, leaning on him to get up.
FOLLOW SHOT   RUTH   JOE'S POINT-OF-VIEW
As she goes to the mirror, starts combing her hair.
CLOSE SHOT   JOE
Sitting on the bed, looking at her.
The tension is with them despite the words they say to each other. In every phrase.
　　　JOE: You're beautiful.
　　　RUTH'S VOICE (*She is lipsticking*): You're blind.
　　　Joe: You are.
CLOSE SHOT   RUTH
　　　RUTH: Like this?
　　　JOE'S VOICE: Most any way.
　　　RUTH: I'm going over to the bar. I ain't been there in two days.
WIDE SHOT
　　　JOE: Why you going there—now?
　　　RUTH: Don't you know?
He thinks for a minute, nods.
　　　JOE: Something to do until? Better than being early at the——?
She nods her head.
　　　JOE: I'll go with you.
　　　RUTH (*Simply*): I think I'd die without you.

JOE: No need to. I'll be around.

Ruth has finished her toilette. She gestures to Joe, still looking in the mirror.

RUTH: Hand me—my striped dress.

Joe goes to the hook, takes her blue dress, holds it up—

JOE: This one?

RUTH: Mmmm.

He brings it to her and she starts to put it on . . . She makes it—her hair comes out looking pretty and much intact.

Ruth looks at herself in the mirror, touches up her hair a little. Then suddenly—the terror stated:

RUTH: Look at the clock, Joe.

He doesn't have to. He has already.

JOE: Five after three.

INTERIOR—AN OFFICE   AFTERNOON

TWO-SHOT   BROCK, KRIEGER   FAVOR KRIEGER

A proper sign on the wall tells us that this is an official New York State Employment Services office.

MR. KRIEGER is an honest guy working for N.Y.S.E.S. Brock stands across from him, his attitude as yet unformed, but in a moment shaped into anger.

KRIEGER: I just talked to him on the phone. The union's business
        agent.

Brock nods.

KRIEGER: He cannot get into the union unless he qualifies through
        the union's apprenticeship program.

Brock nods again.

KRIEGER: He can't get into the apprenticeship program because
        they don't take Negroes into the apprenticeship program.

Brock hits his hand.

CLOSE SHOT   THE CLOCK ON KRIEGER'S DESK

It shows 3:15.

INTERIOR—A BUSINESS OFFICE   AFTERNOON

CLOSE SHOT   A GLASS DOOR

On which is lettered "STOWE INDUSTRIES—PRECISION METAL WORK."

CLOSE ON STOWE

Standing at the window of his small office. MR. STOWE is a journeyman-owner, a man of skill and talent. Not big business, just a nice guy who has made it in a specialty in the precision-instrument field—a Yankee-type fellow.

STOWE (*Talking to his as yet-unseen guests*): You'll forgive me if I make this brief. I've a meeting at four.

THE CAMERA PULLS BACK TO INCLUDE JANE AND HECKY
At his desk. They have an exchange at the mention of four o'clock. And Hecky will look at her wristwatch.

STOWE: Fortunately, we are a small firm. Operating outside the city. So we are able to survive because we are small potatoes.

HECKY: Mr. Stowe. We have many qualified employees. Some are Negro.

STOWE: I'll hire any man who is qualified, regardless of race, creed, or color.

HECKY: May I inquire how many employees you have?

STOWE: As of this morning—sixty-one. Small but efficient.

HECKY: How many are Negro? If you don't mind my asking?

STOWE: Oh——?

JANE (*Politely*): Colored.

STOWE: Oh—six. Yes. Six.

JANE: May I ask how many of those are in maintenance work, Mr. Stowe?

STOWE (*To Jane; thinks*): Six. I do not discriminate. Never have. Won't.

JANE: It's a common complaint. They just don't qualify.

STOWE: That's about the size of it. You have to view the facts, young lady.

HECKY: Do you have an apprenticeship program?

STOWE: Why, yes.

HECKY: Could a Negro get into it?

STOWE: If he were qualified.

HECKY: Would a man with a certificate from a trade school like this—(*Handing him a card*)—a registered trade school, qualify?

Stowe takes the card and looks at it.

STOWE: This isn't exactly precision instrument.

JANE: But he could learn in the training program with that background.

STOWE (*Honestly, not hedging*): I'm not sure.

JANE: If not, Mr. Stowe—maintenance positions are all that will ever be open.

CLOSE SHOT   STOWE
A decent man, thinking.

STOWE: I get your point.

INTERIOR—HOSPITAL WAITING ROOM   AFTERNOON
MEDIUM SHOT   NURSE IN FOREGROUND; RUTH AND JOE BEHIND
Ruth and Joe are on a bench listening to her.
    NURSE: Do you want something?—I can get you——
Ruth has almost a fine tremor:
    RUTH: No.
    NURSE: Doctor will be out in a minute. Will you excuse me?
Ruth nods her head. The Nurse goes.
ANGLE   THE WAITING ROOM
*As the Nurse leaves; Brock and Jane walk in slowly. They merely stand—
waiting—at a distance.*
MEDIUM CLOSE-SHOT   RUTH AND JOE
*Ruth and Joe see Brock and Jane. Ruth's head begins to shake slightly—in
tension. Joe touches her.*
CLOSE SHOT   JANE
    JANE (*Mouthing the words*): No word yet? We'll wait, too——
ANGLE
Ruth doesn't move; Joe shakes his head "no."
*Jane and Brock come a little closer. Brock takes out a pack of cigarettes for
himself, then offers one to Ruth. She does not even decline. Then he proffers
one to Joe. Joe takes it, lights it himself.*
SHOT   THEIR POINT-OF-VIEW   A DOOR OPENS
As the Doctor emerges, his face a mask.
    DOCTOR: Mr. Goodwin, this is Dr. Frazer——
Joe can't find his voice; he slowly gets to his feet. Ruth sits.
    DOCTOR: ——Dr. Frazer is the specialist.
The Doctor turns toward the door now—
CLOSE SHOT   THE DOOR   THEIR POINT-OF-VIEW
DR. FRAZER comes out; a Negro doctor, distinguished.
ANGLE   INCLUDE FRAZER, JOE, RUTH
    FRAZER (*Gently*): You're the mother?
Ruth's mouth hangs open—she nods her head slightly.
    FRAZER: We did everything humanly possible.
    JOE: Oh my God.
Ruth's head falls onto her chest.
    FRAZER: The child died a half-hour ago.
CLOSE SHOTS:
RUTH; DOCTOR; JANE; BROCK; JOE

FADE OUT.

ACT FOUR

FADE IN:
EXTERIOR—A CHURCH STEEPLE   NIGHT
MEDIUM CLOSE-SHOT
The steeple and its illuminated clock against a cloudy night sky.
SOUND: CHURCHBELLS TOLLING THE HOUR
There will be eleven bells.

INTERIOR—HALLWAY OUTSIDE THE GOODWIN APARTMENT   NIGHT
SOUND: THE BELLS, HEARD IN MUFFLED PERSPECTIVE
As they finish tolling eleven o'clock.
CLOSE FOLLOW-SHOT   JOE
*He is coming up the stairs to the floor of his apartment. He carries a bundle
of groceries. Something like spaghetti sticks out, identifying it. He walks
with a slow measured tread. The tragedy is a day-and-a-half old.*
Joe stops just outside the apartment door, gently pushes it open.
SHOT   THE DOORWAY   FULL ON JOE
As he enters the room—his eyes straight ahead of him—on the bed.

INTERIOR—THEIR ROOM   NIGHT
SHOT   PAST JOE TOWARD RUTH
She lies on the bed, her head turned from him.
>   JOE: I'm back.
Ruth doesn't move.
*Joe puts the bag on the table, starts to remove the groceries: a container of
milk, the spaghetti, bread, margarine. Not much more.*
FOLLOW SHOT   JOE
*As he bends to open the refrigerator, puts away the milk and margarine.
Then, standing, he takes a half-pint of whiskey from his pocket. Sets it down.*
>   JOE: You want something?
The body on the bed does not move.
>   JOE: You ain't had anything since—— (*He stops*) It's a day and a
>   half. Lemme pour you a glass of milk.
*No response. Joe walks to her, touches her gently on the shoulder, hoping she
will turn.*
>   JOE: You're gonna make yourself sick.
She shrugs up her shoulders away from him.
>   JOE: Baby, baby—don't——
He tries to turn her to him. She pulls away.
>   JOE: Baby, I know—but——
CLOSE SHOT   RUTH

*It is this "but," the remote edge of hope in his voice that turns Ruth. She
turns to reject it.*

*The immaculate, beautiful girl has let everything go to pot since the death of
her baby. Tears have long ago stained her makeup and she does not care.
Her hair is a mess. She wears the same dress. It is creased, soiled with cigarette ashes, is hiked-up over one knee in an ungainly way. Her shoes are
thrown on the floor, lie there. The ashtray next to their bed is full to
overflowing. There are several empty beer bottles and an empty half-pint of
whiskey near the bed.*

*Ruth reaches for some tissues and blows her nose. This is no moist, tear-filled
nose-blow, but a dry sound of defeat. She drops the tissue on the floor beside
her. We now see there are many pieces of tissue on the floor.*

>   RUTH (*A flat, dead voice*): But. But what? Kids have died before.
>   It's not the end of the world—

She stops. This is more than sorrow: this is her rejection of the world.

>   JOE'S VOICE: Baby, we got each other. Don't we?

*And dry-eyed, frightening, totally withdrawn, there is a kind of defeat in her
eyes—worse than there ever was in Joe's.*

>   RUTH (*Her flat voice falling away to a whisper*): I ain't going to the
>   funeral. Don't you ask me. I just ain't going.

THE CAMERA *goes into her face.*

INTERIOR—THE STOREFRONT CHURCH   DAY

CLOSE SHOT   A SMALL WHITE COFFIN

It is on a chair. It is small, pathetic, and tragic.

WE WILL HEAR VOICES *talking—and stay on the coffin till the last lines of
the scene.*

VARIOUS ANGLES ON COFFIN

>   UNDERTAKER'S VOICE: . . . It's too long right now, Reverend. We
>   have to bury her today.
>   WILLIAMS' VOICE: I know.
>   UNDERTAKER'S VOICE: The city won't let us wait another hour.
>   Not an hour longer. I could lose my license.
>   WILLIAMS' VOICE: Yes, of course. We were just hoping . . . you
>   know . . . that the . . . the mother would attend.
>   UNDERTAKER'S VOICE: I'm sorry. It's the law.
>   WILLIAMS' VOICE: I know.
>   UNDERTAKER'S VOICE: So we'll do it today. All right?
>   WILLIAMS' VOICE: Yes, sir. We'll hold the funeral today.

CLOSE SHOT   THE COFFIN

INTERIOR—THE GOODWIN APARTMENT   DAY

CLOSE SHOT   RUTH

She is standing with her back to THE CAMERA. *She is out of bed, and is dressed. But when she turns (in a moment) we see that she has put herself together differently. She is no longer neat and attractive, but—a tense spring of a woman, merely attired in clothing. The period of slovenliness has passed and been replaced with a new phase: a woman who does not care. She has been looking at the space where the crib was. It is gone. And in its place there is a small potted plant.*

RUTH *(Turning)*: Why did ya take the crib out?

ANGLE   JOE IN FOREGROUND; RUTH IN BACKGROUND

He listens patiently, tries to answer the same way.

JOE: I thought it would—remind you.

RUTH: Yeah. If I didn't see it I'd never think of it.

JOE: I can bring it back. It's only downstairs.

RUTH: Get it back. What's the difference? Let it stay there.

She reaches in her pocket for a cigarette. Comes up with an empty pack.

RUTH: I'm out of smokes.

JOE: I'll bring some back. I have to go out for a while. About the job.

RUTH *(Bitterly)*: So they hustled you a job.

JOE: Please——

RUTH *(On top of him)*: Don't ask me.

JOE: I wasn't. I swear. I just meant——

RUTH: Weren't you?

JOE: You made up your mind—that's all right by me. You ain't going.

RUTH: What time is it set for?

JOE: This afternoon—at two. It has to be.

RUTH: What does that mean?

JOE: Nothing. Health regulations.

RUTH: Get me those cigarettes and—do it before you go.

JOE: Okay. *(Then)* Ruthie——

For answer, she flops on the bed, picks up a movie magazine, and buries herself in it.

Joe walks over to her, touches her lightly on the shoulder.

RUTH *(Bitterly)*: Poor Liz Taylor.

Joe sits, gently as he can. He takes the magazine from her. First she lets him, then she grabs it back. He lets her take it from him.

JOE: You're gonna drive yourself crazy.

She rolls up the magazine tightly and places it next to her body. It is almost a club.

JOE: Let me help you. Don't stay so far away from me.

Ruth lies where she is, still somewhat removed. Now her hand opens on the magazine; she touches it idly. A little relaxed. And now—WE SEE HER FACE—she is crying.

RUTH: Joey. Help me.

CLOSE SHOTS: RUTH; JOE

INTERIOR—BROCK'S OFFICE   DAY
CLOSE ON BROCK   JOE AND JANE'S POINT-OF-VIEW
They have just come in the door.
Brock is at his desk, taking a bite from a sandwich and drinking something from a container or bottle.
THE SHOT IMMEDIATELY WIDENS TO SHOW
Hecky and Reverend Williams both eating and drinking coffee, with Brock, from a nearby delicatessen. They have obviously been talking, and are in the midst of something worthy—

JANE: We interrupting?

BROCK (AND OTHERS): That's okay. No.

CLOSE SHOT   BROCK
As he sees Joe behind Jane, he rises. He starts to enthuse a little, but stops immediately on seeing Joe's face.

BROCK: I'm glad you came. We have a lead, I think, for a job. I
        wanted to talk.

He stops. Joe's attitude is painful.

CLOSE SHOT   JOE
Just standing there, in the doorway; lost.

CLOSE SHOT   BROCK
He responds by going around his desk to this desperate man.
THE CAMERA FOLLOWS BROCK AS IT PULLS BACK

JANE: It's Ruth.

HECKY: Can we help you?

JOE (*Not bitterly; honestly*): I don't know.

BROCK: Would you like to talk?

JOE (*The same tone*): I don't know.

Williams comes over to him.

WILLIAMS: Would you like me to go and talk to her, Joe?

There is an exchange among Brock, Williams, Hecky, Jane. Its content: Can this man be helped? Who is the best person to try to reach him?

HECKY: I think Neil might be more helpful than anybody else. I
        think it would be better if we left.

Neil smiles a little bitterly at this compliment.
Hecky, Williams, and Jane leave.
SHOT PAST JOE IN FOREGROUND
For a moment, Joe doesn't move. Then, slowly, he crosses to the window.
The men, not facing each other, are trying to talk out the problem.
> JOE (*It is almost a blurt*): I never knew how to laugh about things
> —turn them into their opposite, the way Ruth did.

CLOSE SHOT BROCK
Listening.
INTERCUT: CLOSE SHOTS BROCK; JOE
> JOE: I always been like that. Somewhere along the line it got
> beaten out of me, burnt out. When I was a kid my ole man
> used to tell me: Boy, stop laughing. I'd go swimming. I'd
> laugh. Just the feel of the water. I'd laugh. He'd grab a-hold of
> me: You stop that. Don't let the white folks hear you laughing.
> (*A pause*) I ain't really laughed for years. (*Another pause. He
> looks at Brock*) Ruth's worse than that now.

Brock ponders this for a moment, moves, does whatever works for him in the
situation—then earnestly, simply . . .
> BROCK: I don't know what to say to you, Joe. I don't know what
> anyone can say who——

Brock touches his white skin: arm, face, whatever . . .
> BROCK: ——looks like I look. What white man knows what it's
> like—the life of a Negro? Sympathize. Project. Understand.
> But—*know?*

He shakes his head slightly.
> BROCK: I will say this. I believe women are women, and babies are
> babies—no matter what color they are. And when you lose a
> baby, the only thing that means anything is the love of the
> person closest to you. I think you would tell that to me, too,
> Joe, if my child died.

Joe looks at him. If he could he would shake his hand. Instead, he nods.
Brock offers him a cigarette. Joe takes it. Joe lights both his cigarette and
Brock's.

INTERIOR—THE GOODWIN APARTMENT DAY
ANGLE RUTH, WILLIAMS, JOE
At the table, Ruth is listening to Williams. Joe is on the bed.
> WILLIAMS: For some people religion is a help. I hope it's true for
> you.
> RUTH (*Withdrawn*): Sure. I like the music.

WILLIAMS: Friends are a consolation—for some. For others— doing something works.

RUTH: I like straight bourbon.

WILLIAMS: But finally, I think, love is the only real answer. The love of someone who loves you.

RUTH: There's the boy you got to pity. Stuck with me.

CLOSE SHOT   JOE LISTENING

WILLIAMS' VOICE (*Softly, personally, talking to one person, he goes into his sermon*): Harriet Tubman was a slave. Saw her brothers and sisters killed or sold into deep slavery. Made up her mind to do something about it. So she prayed: Lord change that man's hard heart. But he didn't change. So Harriet made up her own prayer. She said: Lord, I'm done praying with my mouth. I'm going to start praying now, Lord, with my heart and my hands and my feet and my wagon. And she took one hundred souls out of bondage on the Underground Railroad. That was a hundred years ago.

RUTH'S VOICE (*To Joe*): I don't got to go at all—do I, Joey? I heard the sermon already.

THE SHOT WIDENS

As Joe gets up. He has been fully dressed—in black—for the services.

JOE: Reverend, it's time.

RUTH: Why do they have a white coffin, Reverend? Is that supposed to make it nicer? White.

Williams goes.

After Williams quietly shuts the door there is a long pause.

Then Joe walks toward Ruth until he stands very close to her. She looks up, sensing the intensity of his feeling. He speaks to her as simply and as honestly as he can.

JOE: Baby, if you had it—then—I'm finished too. Because, I'll tell you straight, without you, baby, I can't make it. I don't want to.

CLOSE SHOT   JOE

CLOSE SHOT   RUTH

(*No decisive response on her part.*)

INTERIOR—THE STOREFRONT CHURCH   DAY

CLOSE SHOT   THE COFFIN

It is on a chair near the podium of the church.

(*Not a word will be spoken during the "services" nor music heard.*)

MEDIUM LONG-SHOT FROM REAR OF CHURCH

One by one the mourners rise, walk to the front of the church, stop for a mo-

*ment and look up at Joe, who stands next to the coffin. A nod of the head is
all they offer. And leave.*
*In succession they file up: the Woman, Jane, the Lawyer, Brock, the Neigh-
bor, Hecky, Morgan, finally—the last person in the church.*
LONG SHOT   THE EMPTY CHURCH—JOE
Standing next to the coffin.
HIGH SHOT   JOE
He starts out—toward the door, then stops.
CLOSE SHOT   JOE
Looking at—
SHOT   CHURCH ENTRANCEWAY   JOE'S POINT-OF-VIEW
Ruth appears.
THE CAMERA FOLLOWS RUTH
As she walks down—disregarding the coffin—toward Joe.
SHOT   CHURCH ANTEROOM   BROCK, JANE, HECKY, WILLIAMS
Watching Ruth—expectantly.
CLOSE SHOT   JOE
Not knowing what to expect.
CLOSE SHOT   RUTH
Slowly walking. She stops.
TWO-SHOT   JOE AND RUTH
He simply opens his arms to her—and she walks into his embrace.
TWO-SHOT   BROCK, JANE   REACTING
CLOSE SHOT   JOE AND RUTH   THEIR FACES
*He holds her. She begins crying. Tears of relief, wet tears—the full sorrow
that she has been unable to express until now.*

EXTERIOR—THE STOREFRONT CHURCH   DAY
WE SEE   THE PRINCIPALS
As they come out and walk away.

FADE OUT.

BLACKLIST

By *ERNEST KINOY*

The Defenders
Created by Reginald Rose
Columbia Broadcasting System Television Network
January 18, 1964

DIRECTOR: *Stuart Rosenberg*

PRODUCER: *Robert Markell*

EXECUTIVE PRODUCER: *Herbert Brodkin*

Plautus Productions, Inc.

THE CAST

LAWRENCE PRESTON: *E. G. Marshall*

KENNETH PRESTON: *Robert Reed*

JOE LARCH: *Jack Klugman*

MILDRED LARCH: *Brett Somers*

GEORGE VEIGH: *John Baragrey*

MAGGIE DALY: *Maggie Hayes*

MAYOR OSTERVELT: *Michael Higgins*

LOUISE LOFTING: *Neva Patterson*

JUDSON KYLE: *Howard St. John*

ART FINE: *Arny Freeman*

DAVE LARCH: *Robert Drivas*

CHARLES MONARCHIO: *Michael Lombard*

LLOYD HICKMAN: *Herbert Voland*

SWITCHBOARD OPERATOR: *Paula Trueman*

SECRETARY: *Kay Frey*

SHOE SALESMAN: *Mark Weston*

LADY (SHOE STORE): *Toni Tucci*

JANITOR: *Theo Goetz*

PROLOGUE

FADE IN:

INTERIOR—VEIGH'S OFFICE   DAY

A theatrical office, not particularly fancy. Framed stills from George Veigh's previous productions. There is a large bulletin board covered with production data, and a blueprint of studio space. There are several framed awards from various film festivals. On the desk is a stack of actors' pictures.

OPENING SHOT   CAMERA IS CLOSE ON GEORGE VEIGH, in his shirt sleeves, harried and tired.

> GEORGE: What's the matter with Joe Larch?

THE CAMERA PULLS BACK. Now we see the other members of the conference. ART FINE, associate producer, a small but busy and rabbity man with a nose and a mustache, and MAGGIE DALY, casting director, a tough cookie who has been in the business since Philco was a summer replacement.

> MAGGIE: For what?
>
> GEORGE: Bronson . . . he'd be perfect.
>
> ART: Larch? Joe Larch? I don't know him.
>
> GEORGE: He hasn't done much recently . . . you remember him in Pete Kantor's picture . . . he played a detective.
>
> ART: I don't remember . . . (*Starting to thumb through* Players Guide) . . . what would he be under, "Leading Men" or "Characters"?
>
> GEORGE: What do you think, Maggie? Joe's a good actor, he could play it!
>
> MAGGIE: So could Wallace Beery . . .
>
> ART (*His nose buried in* Players Guide): He's dead.

Maggie nods "yes" . . . that's her point.

ANOTHER CAMERA ANGLE

> GEORGE: Look . . . we need somebody who'll do a small part . . . all right, you tell me, why not Joe Larch?
>
> MAGGIE (*Shrugs*): It's your picture.
>
> ART (*Just looking up*): He isn't in *Players Guide.*
>
> GEORGE: Give me one good reason!
>
> MAGGIE: What do you want me to say? I just work here. George . . . this is your first chance for a feature picture . . . I haven't been able to get an okay on Joe Larch for ten years.
>
> ART: Why not?

There is no answer . . . Maggie takes a drag on her cigarette.

> ART: Oh.

Reprinted by permission of Ernest Kinoy and Paramount Television, a division of Paramount Pictures.

94

GEORGE: Maggie . . . times have changed, right?

ANOTHER CAMERA ANGLE

ART: What did he take, the Fifth Amendment or something?

GEORGE: As far as I know Joe was never subpoenaed. Nobody actually said he was a card-carrying Communist.

ART: What did they say?

GEORGE: How should I know?

MAGGIE: Who are you arguing with, George?

He is starting to pace, working up to a decision.

GEORGE: Nobody. He's right for the part . . . okay, then why not Joe Larch?

ANOTHER CAMERA ANGLE

MAGGIE: You going to check with Comus Inc?

GEORGE: Why should I?

MAGGIE (*The shrug again*): They're financing the picture . . .

GEORGE: My contract with Comus is very clear . . . they don't have cast approval.

MAGGIE: All right . . . all right . . . you want me to make him a firm offer?

CLOSEUP   GEORGE

George hesitates now . . . just a beat when faced with the yes and no moment . . . then bulls ahead.

GEORGE: Yeah . . . I want Joe Larch.

CLOSEUP   MAGGIE

MAGGIE: Okay . . . okay . . . okay! (*She makes a note with her pencil*) Where do I find him?

INTERIOR—A SHOE STORE   DAY

CLOSE ON JOE LARCH, an ordinary balding middle-aged man whom you would not take for an actor (which is why George wants him). He is bending down concentrating on something of great importance.

THE CAMERA PULLS BACK to show that Joe is sitting on the little bench in a shoe store, fitting a shoe to a LADY in the chair . . . a litter of boxes beside him . . .

LADY: I don't know . . .

JOE: You've got plenty of room there, I wouldn't want to give it to you any bigger . . .

LADY (*Wiggling her foot*): I don't know . . .

MAN'S VOICE: Joe . . .

ANOTHER ANGLE

Joe turns, another MAN is beckoning from the back of the store. Joe rises . . .

JOE: Excuse me a minute . . .

To save a trip he takes several boxes of shoes back with him as he goes. He passes the partition into the stockroom, the other man passes him on the way out.

MAN: Phone . . .

INTERIOR—*THE STOCKROOM   DAY*
MEDIUM SHOT
Joe comes through the partition, picking up a phone lying on the shelf waiting for him . . .

> JOE: Hello . . . yes . . . speaking . . . (*He turns to the other man who has come back in*) Tommy, get me down a 345T in a five-and-a-half A, will you . . . (*Back to the phone*) Yes . . . George Veigh? Yeah . . . hello, George. Well, yeah . . . it's been a long time . . . that's right. You were the assistant director when I was in . . . closer to eleven years.

The other salesman comes back and hands Joe a shoebox on the way out. Joe juggles it as he continues the conversation.

> JOE: No . . . no . . . I had a couple of things since then . . . but I've been . . . keeping busy. Well yes . . . I think I can come up . . . Fifty-fifth Street? Yes . . . in about an hour. Yeah . . . well I'll be glad to see you, too. All right . . . goodbye, George . . .

Joe hangs up the phone a little dazed . . . then suddenly realizes he has a shoebox in his hand, and starts out with it.

INTERIOR—*JOE'S APARTMENT   DAY*
CLOSE ON MILDRED LARCH, *in her mid-forties, a pleasant, plump, not particularly show-biz looking woman. Mildred is crying. . . .*

> JOE'S VOICE: Milly, what are you crying for?

THE CAMERA PULLS BACK *showing the Larch kitchen and dinette. It is in a small apartment, the kitchen is cramped, the dinette strained to take a table and chairs. Joe's son DAVE is sitting at the table along with Joe. Dave wears a T-shirt. He is about nineteen. Mildred, it turns out, is standing with a pot in her hand facing the table, just having turned from the stove . . . the tears are running down her cheeks.*

> JOE: Look out for the soup . . .

Mildred isn't quite sure what to do with the pot . . . makes a false start and then puts it back on the stove and immediately fishes for her handkerchief.
ANOTHER ANGLE

> DAVE: Are you sure, Pop?
>
> JOE: It was a firm offer . . . I went up to the office . . . and

George just said "Joe, I want you to be in my picture." (*Following up Mildred with concern*) Milly, are you all right?
Mildred turns back now, mopping up with her handkerchief. She is half-laughing and half-crying by now.

TWO-SHOT   MILDRED, JOE

MILDRED: I'm sorry . . . it's just silly . . . but I . . . (*The laugh takes over from the crying now*) Joe . . . after ten years . . .

Joe takes her in his arms now . . .

JOE: It's just one picture . . .

ANOTHER ANGLE   TO INCLUDE DAVE

DAVE: What kind of a part is it, Pop?

JOE (*Still holding his wife*): I haven't read the whole script . . . it's based on a youth program they have upstate in Mill City. (*He is patting Mildred on the shoulder*)

MILDRED: I want you to quit that job . . .

JOE: We'll talk it over . . .

MILDRED: For ten years, Joe, it's been selling encyclopedias, and shirts and shoes . . .

JOE: It's only a guarantee of three weeks . . .

MILDRED: I don't care, you're an actor . . . not a shoe salesman!

DAVE: Do you have to go on location?

JOE: For the exteriors . . . they're shooting them up in Mill City . . . and then there's a studio in Brooklyn for the rest.

CLOSEUP   MILDRED

MILDRED: Joe . . . is it over? I mean finally over?

CLOSEUP   JOE

JOE: I don't know . . . maybe. George Veigh is the producer, but the financing is from Comus . . . that means something!

ORIGINAL ANGLE   TO INCLUDE ALL

Mildred heaves a great big sigh . . .

MILDRED: Thank God . . . Thank God . . . (*Then suddenly she turns back to the stove*) All right, sit down . . . have your soup . . . (*Coming back with the soup pot again*) Now tell me all about it . . . what did he say?

DAVE: Do you get featured billing, Pop?

MILDRED: Did he at least look ashamed after ten years?

DAVE: How much are you getting?

MILDRED: David . . .

A pause . . .

MILDRED: Pass your father's plate.

He does, and Mildred dips out a ladleful of soup.

INTERIOR—A SMALL OFFICE   DAY
CLOSE ON a mimeograph machine running round and round. THE CAMERA
PANS *along in . . . pushing in* EXTREME CLOSEUP *to show the counter device
clicking away in the thousands . . . then on to the other end of the machine
with the paper spewing out into the rack. The hum and rattle of the machine
continues. About now we become aware of a girl's voice. She is reading with
the expressionless drone of a proofreader.*

> GIRL'S VOICE: ". . . Postcards should be written to Mayor Oster-
> velt and your City Council member to protest the presence in
> the High School Library of these magazines presenting clearly
> subversive material . . ."

By now THE CAMERA *has moved to pick up the* GIRL, *a perfectly ordinary
young secretary type, who has a mimeograph stencil before her. She is reading proof, copy is being held by another WOMAN, dumpy and middle aged.*

> GIRL (*Continuing in the flat drone*): "Flash Alert—the Vanguard
> Bulletin has just learned that in the proposed motion picture
> based on the Mill City Youth Program the part of the director
> of the project is to be played by an actor with a record of
> seven separate citations of Communist Front affiliations. His
> name, Joe Lodge . . ."
> WOMAN (*Looking up from the copy*): Larch . . . L–A–R–C–H! Joe
> Larch.
> GIRL: I'll have to correct it on the stencil.
> WOMAN: Go ahead . . .
> GIRL: Joe Larch. L–A–R–C–H!

THE CAMERA *is now leaving her slowly, wandering back to the tail end of the
mimeograph which is vomiting pages at a fast rate into the rack . . . one
after the other.*

> GIRL'S VOICE: "The Vanguard Bulletin calls this situation to the
> attention of all Mill City Members of the National Security
> Vanguard League as a public service."

The sheets are flying out of the mimeograph straight INTO THE CAMERA *like
a blizzard.*

FADE OUT.

ACT ONE

FADE IN:
INTERIOR—HALLWAY OUTSIDE JOE'S APARTMENT   DAY
LONG SHOT

A hall with a stairwell. Dave is just coming up the stairway in a hurry, flings down the hall toward Joe's door. He is carrying two copies of a folded newspaper. He flings open the door.

INTERIOR—JOE'S APARTMENT   DAY

MEDIUM SHOT

As Dave comes in fast, slamming the door behind him. There is the merest entry way and then in the living room itself.

DAVE (*As he enters*): I got two copies at the out-of-town newsstand in Times Square.

By now he is in. Joe is sitting in an upholstered chair, a low chair, possibly a little weak in the springs so he is at a very low height. Mildred is at the telephone . . . her conversation overlaps Dave.

MILDRED: No . . . no . . . my husband isn't home right now.

(*The picture of course shows us that he is.*)

MILDRED: No . . . I don't know when he'll be back. No . . . I don't know anything about it. Maybe tonight . . .

DAVE (*Crossing to his father*): Who's that on the phone?

Joe shrugs he doesn't know . . . as Mildred hangs up, turns back to them.

MILDRED: The newspaper in Mill City . . . (*To Dave*) Well?

DAVE (*Shaking out the paper*): It's on the front page . . .

CLOSEUP   MILDRED

Reaction, steeling herself to hear it.

THREE-SHOT

DAVE (*Reads*): "Charge Red Fronter City Film . . ."

CLOSEUP   JOE

He just sits and closes his eyes.

THREE-SHOT

DAVE (*Reading on*): "An avalanche of mail today descended on Mayor Harold Ostervelt protesting the proposed appearance in a City-approved motion picture of Actor Joe Larch. Mr. Larch was named in 1952 in testimony before a Congressional Committee for membership in several alleged Communist Front organizations . . ."

The telephone rings . . . Mildred looks over at it . . . so do Dave and Joe. Mildred takes the phone off the hook and puts it down on the table.

MILDRED: Go on . . .

DAVE: "The motion picture, to be produced by George Veigh, is to be based on the work of the Mill City Youth Program, and has the official blessing of the City. Mayor Ostervelt, questioned at City Hall, stated that the story was news to him, and that he was looking into it."

Dave stops . . . looks up.

MILDRED: Is that all?

Dave nods "yes."

MILDRED: They just said "looking into it." Maybe it'll blow over.

ANOTHER CAMERA ANGLE

JOE: That reminds me of the vaudeville booker in 1920 who went to Hawaii to wait till the movies blew over.

Mildred turns on him with fury.

MILDRED: Joe, don't make jokes. Please don't make jokes.

JOE: What do you want me to do? Knock my head against the wall? Rend my garments?

MILDRED: Ten years . . . what do they want from you? Who remembered? A tiny little part in a movie and who remembered?

DAVE: It's in the article . . . "The information about Actor Larch was brought to public attention in the Bulletin published by the Mill City National Security Vanguard League for its members."

ANOTHER CAMERA ANGLE

MILDRED: You said George Veigh knew when he hired you . . .

JOE: Sure, but that was before the Bulletin hit the fan.

DAVE: What are you going to do, Pop?

JOE: I don't know.

DAVE: You just going to let some bunch of crackpots run you out of town?

JOE: Dave . . . look, don't worry about it. You've got a class . . . you go ahead . . .

ANOTHER CAMERA ANGLE   FEATURING DAVE

DAVE: What do you mean, don't worry about it? Look, Pop . . . this is your first part in ten years . . . it's a chance . . .

JOE: Dave, you don't understand.

CLOSEUP   DAVE

DAVE: Oh, yes I do . . . I've understood since I was eight years old! The Blacklist . . . The Blacklist! . . . I knew why we moved from Riverside Drive. I knew why you had to borrow money from Grandpa and Uncle Gerry . . . the Blacklist! All right . . . all right . . . I didn't understand one thing, I'll grant you that . . . I didn't understand it then, and I still don't. Why didn't you do something? Why didn't you fight back?

THREE-SHOT

MILDRED: Dave!

DAVE: Mom . . . we're three adults now, right? Go ahead, Pop
. . . tell me now . . . why didn't you fight back?

CLOSEUP   JOE

JOE: There was nothing to fight . . . I was a freelance actor . . .
and then all of a sudden nobody called. I went to my agent
and said "What's the matter?" I was so naïve I actually didn't
know. It was gradual . . . at least with me. Nobody would tell
you . . . but you just didn't get work. I made twelve thousand dollars in 1952, in 1953 I made nothing.

THREE-SHOT

DAVE: But you didn't *do* anything . . . you didn't sue anybody
for libel . . .

JOE: You can't sue the Congressional Record. Somebody got up
in a Committee and said . . . "Joe Larch . . . Joe Larch . . .
Joe Larch . . ." Who should I sue?

DAVE: You didn't even make a statement . . .

JOE (*Starting to get angry*): Dave . . . you were a baby then . . .
you don't know. I wasn't a star. I wasn't important . . . just a
character actor. There were fifteen other men in New York
who could do what I could do. If you made trouble then . . .
if you sued somebody . . . if you got yourself called in front of
a Committee you were dead.

CLOSEUP   JOE

JOE: Even if you could win . . . you were "controversial." "Controversial" . . . that was like leprosy. You walked down the
street ringing a bell so people could get out of your way . . .
"Unclean . . . unclean . . ." (*In the same chant*) "Controversial . . . controversial . . ."

CLOSEUP   MILDRED

MILDRED: Joe . . . it's not a joke!

ANOTHER ANGLE   TO INCLUDE ALL

JOE: Dave . . . you just didn't live then . . . it was like trying to
push back an avalanche. I saw people I knew . . . stars . . .
wonderful actors . . . just buried . . . buried!

DAVE: All right . . . let's talk about *now*, Pop. You going to let it
happen all over again? You just going to lie down . . . you
going to "go quietly"?

JOE: You don't understand . . . Dave, you don't understand . . . !

DAVE: You're damn right I don't understand! A girl in my American Lit class just came back from a week in jail for being in a
civil-rights demonstration. She did something . . . she wasn't

afraid. She comes up to here on me . . . (*Very tiny*) . . . but
she didn't let them walk all over her. Next time I'm going with
her . . .

*In anger, Dave grabs his jacket and slams out of the door. Mildred starts a
step with him . . . turning back she finds Joe has picked up the paper. He
looks up with grim humor.*

ANOTHER ANGLE   FEATURING JOE

> JOE: They've got my credits . . . "Mr. Larch appeared in films in
> 'No Trumpets, No Drums,' 'The City of Night,' and 'The Hur-
> ried Man.' Also, Broadway and Television . . ." (*Putting
> down the paper*) They left out Huberman's Restaurant and
> Fine Arch Shoes for Women and Girls.
>
> MILDRED: Joe, you've got to do something this time . . . it's your
> last chance.
>
> JOE: I haven't even signed a contract with George Veigh . . .
>
> MILDRED: I'm not talking about that . . . I mean David. Did you
> hear him?
>
> JOE: He doesn't understand . . .

CLOSEUP   MILDRED

> MILDRED: Do you want him to have any respect for his father? Do
> you *want* him to "understand"? I don't care about the Black-
> list anymore . . . for you or for me. Do something this time
> . . . for him.

INTERIOR—LAWRENCE PRESTON'S LAW OFFICE   DAY
MEDIUM SHOT

*LAWRENCE is at his desk; KEN, his son and junior law partner, is some-
where about; and Joe is in the client's chair. Lawrence has the mimeo-
graphed Bulletin in his hand.*

> LAWRENCE: Actually, Mr. Larch, this is very carefully worded to
> avoid a libel action . . . you see . . . they quote the Congres-
> sional Record verbatim, and don't characterize any fur-
> ther . . .

By now we have seen Lawrence and Ken and Joe . . .

> LAWRENCE: They don't even suggest that you shouldn't appear in
> the film.
>
> JOE: I know . . .
>
> LAWRENCE: As a matter of fact, it's my impression that the . . .
> (*Checking the Bulletin for the name*) . . . Mill City National Se-
> curity Vanguard League has the services of a first-rate libel
> lawyer. I notice they don't actually call anyone a Communist
> directly.

ANOTHER ANGLE

JOE: They don't have to . . . they get the point across.

KEN: Have you heard anything from Mr. Veigh that suggests he's under pressure?

JOE: No . . . not yet.

LAWRENCE: These charges that were made against you go back to 1952, I believe. Have you ever denied them publicly?

JOE: No.

KEN: Why not?

JOE: They're true.

CLOSEUP   LAWRENCE

Reaction.

ANOTHER ANGLE

JOE: It goes back to the late Thirties . . . the Civil War was going on in Spain . . . there were a lot of committees here . . . you know, to suppport the Loyalists . . . the anti-Franco forces.

LAWRENCE: Yes . . .

JOE: Well . . . I joined one . . . two, actually. One was to protest the embargo, the other was a War Relief Committee. You see, I appeared in benefits to raise money for the committees. Everybody was doing something like that in those days . . . and I thought it was right.

LAWRENCE: And these organizations were later accused of being Communist Fronts?

JOE: Yes . . .

LAWRENCE: But you were no longer a member at that time?

JOE: That's right . . . I just dropped out of the Relief Committee because I was too busy, I had a running part in a radio soap . . . er . . . you know, a daytime serial . . .

LAWRENCE: And the other?

JOE: That was actually out of existence five years before it came up in a Congressional Committee.

LAWRENCE: Did you know there were Communists in the organizations?

ANOTHER ANGLE

JOE: After my experience, I don't like to say who is and who isn't a Communist. I guess there were . . . there must have been. I knew one man who *said* he was a member of the party. He was a cellist.

LAWRENCE: You never repudiated your membership in these organizations?

CLOSEUP   JOE

JOE: No . . . at the time I thought it was right to support the Spanish Republican Government. I still think it was right . . . looking back on it historically.

ANOTHER ANGLE   TO INCLUDE ALL

KEN: And how did this . . . membership come out?

JOE: They had somebody up in front of a Congressional Committee and then they had membership lists, and newspaper articles about benefits . . . and my name was there.

LAWRENCE: And that's all.

JOE: That was enough. The list was reprinted in a private "newsletter" . . . and I just didn't work again.

LAWRENCE: But you weren't called to testify?

JOE: No . . . I wasn't important . . . outside of the business I don't think anybody knew who I was.

KEN: Couldn't you *ask* to testify?

ANOTHER ANGLE

JOE: What for? All I could say was . . . "yes, I *was* a member of the Relief Committee, I *did* appear in benefits . . . and I thought it was right." Where would that help me? I thought it was better to let things lie. (*Reflective*) Of course that didn't work either.

LAWRENCE: And that was the only charge against you?

JOE: No . . . you see, when the Blacklisting started I joined a committee against Blacklisting . . . and then I got named for that!

KEN: And that was the only action you took?

CLOSEUP   JOE

JOE: There wasn't anything else I could do. If you tried to fight you only got pushed deeper and deeper. Some people could "clear themselves" . . . sort of confess publicly and recant and say whatever they did was wrong. But I hadn't done anything I thought was wrong . . . and the truth is I doubt if anybody would have been interested in a small-time character actor, even if he wanted to be "cleared."

THREE-SHOT

KEN: Then why do you come to us now?

Joe looks at Ken, young enough to remind him of Dave.

JOE: I have my . . . reason. It's my last chance.

LAWRENCE: I think you may be a little bit premature, Mr. Larch. Nothing's happened so far except a newspaper headline. One small extremist organization has its members all worked up . . . that doesn't necessarily mean anything will happen.

Joe smiles wearily.
JOE: Mr. Preston . . . I'm not a lawyer, I haven't studied . . . I never went to college. But I am an expert on one subject . . . the Blacklist. Something will happen.

EXTERIOR—CITY HALL IN A SMALL CITY   ESTABLISH DAY

INTERIOR—MAYOR OSTERVELT'S OUTER OFFICE   DAY
CLOSE ON A SMALL SWITCHBOARD
A girl's finger has just knocked down a key . . .
GIRL'S VOICE: Mayor Ostervelt's office . . . no, I'm sorry . . . The mayor has no comment at this time . . . he is studying the matter.
Another light has gone on, the finger flicks another key . . .
GIRL'S VOICE: Mayor Ostervelt's office . . .

INTERIOR—MAYOR'S OFFICE   DAY
EXTREME CLOSEUP of a postcard . . .
OSTERVELT'S VOICE: "As a mother of three, I protest the bringing of a commie actor from New York to smear Mill City with the poison of international Communism" . . .
THE CAMERA has pulled back to show MAYOR OSTERVELT at his desk. He has a wire In-basket filled with postcards . . . he puts the card he has just read into an Out-basket and looks up.
OSTERVELT: Lloyd . . . we got a hot potato on our hands.
TWO-SHOT   OSTERVELT, HICKMAN
Now we see LLOYD HICKMAN, Chairman of the City Council.
HICKMAN: How many pieces you got?
OSTERVELT: Maybe a hundred and fifty. Who is this Larch . . . you ever heard of him before?
HICKMAN: No.
OSTERVELT: Is he a Red?
HICKMAN: I don't know. The first I heard was in the *Times-Courier.* Look, Harold . . . you know where this is coming from . . . Judson Kyle and his Vanguard League.
Ostervelt has been reading another postcard.
OSTERVELT: This one says *I'm* a Communist.
HICKMAN: He can organize a letter campaign at the drop of his mimeograph.
OSTERVELT: That's not the point . . . Louis Harrison picked it up in the *Times-Courier,* didn't he? I've got to make a statement . . . how long can I stall?

HICKMAN: Jud Kyle can't hurt you . . . he's got a membership of about a hundred . . .

CLOSEUP   OSTERVELT

OSTERVELT: Lloyd! What's the matter with you? I've got a municipal budget to get through. It's up twelve percent from last year . . . I got to ask for a two-point rise in the real estate tax-rate. Charley Monarchio is trying to knock out the Youth Program completely . . . (*Throwing up his hands*) This is no time for some kind of Red issue! What did we need a movie for anyway?

TWO-SHOT

HICKMAN: It was your idea . . . remember . . . it was going to come out a month before election?

OSTERVELT: All right . . . all right . . .

HICKMAN: I guess you're right. I can keep a couple of boys on the Council in line, but Charley's going to beat you on the head with it if he can.

OSTERVELT: I don't know . . . how long did it take to get that Youth Program through? It's a good program . . . it's good for the City. We're up for a Pacemaker City of the Year award for it, and Jud Kyle has to have a gall bladder attack and take it out on paper. What does he care if this Joe March acts in a movie . . . ?

HICKMAN: Larch.

OSTERVELT: What is he going to do? Steal the plans to the City sewage plant and send them to Moscow?

HICKMAN: All right, Harold . . . (*A big sigh of reality*) . . . what are you going to do?

OSTERVELT: Call that Movie Man . . . George Veigh . . . tell him I want to see him in a hurry.

FADE OUT.

ACT TWO

FADE IN:

INTERIOR—A RESTAURANT   DAY

*A corner booth . . . George Veigh is there, with Lawrence, Joe, and Ken
. . . START CAMERA CLOSE ON GEORGE.*

GEORGE: The Mayor was very reasonable about it . . . he's in a very difficult position, politically.

By now we see the others at the table.

LAWRENCE: Did he make any direct suggestions about . . . Mr. Larch's employment?

GEORGE: No . . . no . . . as a matter of fact he said he thought the whole thing was a lot of nonsense. He sounded like a very liberal man . . .

JOE: That's nice.

Lawrence gives Joe a look . . .

KEN: Then there's no problem about Mr. Larch?

GEORGE: Well . . . no . . . no. That's part of my arrangement with the City officials. I have complete artistic control . . . they can only make requests for changes in the script on factual mistakes. They have nothing to say about casting.

LAWRENCE: I see.

GEORGE: Now look, Joe . . . I want you to know one thing. I'm going to use you in the picture. I'm going to go right down the line for you . . .

JOE: I know, George . . .

CLOSEUP   GEORGE

GEORGE: Now . . . here it is. The whole trouble is coming from a man named Judson Kyle. He's a retired manufacturer of something . . . the Vanguard League is his hobby. Now he supports it completely . . . spends all his time on it. Now . . . Mayor Ostervelt feels it . . . well, if things could be calmed down the atmosphere might be better for the picture . . . politically. He seemed to think something could be worked out . . . with Judson Kyle.

CLOSEUP   JOE

He is shaking his head sadly out of experience . . .

JOE: George . . . it has been tried before! There isn't any easy way out . . .

MEDIUM SHOT   TO INCLUDE ALL

GEORGE: Does it hurt to try? Look, Joe, we're all in this project together. We all want the picture to be great, don't we?

JOE: Yeah . . . sure . . .

GEORGE: Will it hurt for Mr. Preston to talk with Kyle . . . you know, explain the situation, work things out?

LAWRENCE: I think Mr. Veigh has a point. Most things can be settled sensibly . . . often by a disinterested third party.

JOE: I don't mind . . . fine . . . fine . . . you go ahead, Mr. Preston.

GEORGE: Now look, Joe . . . I don't want you to worry for a min-

ute. I made up my mind . . . this whole thing is a lot of . . .
(*He changes in deference to Lawrence*) . . . it's ridiculous and
it's over! Everybody knows that! It all happened a long time
ago, Joe, and it's over, done . . . forgotten . . .

INTERIOR—JUDSON KYLE'S STUDY   NIGHT
CAMERA VERY CLOSE ON a brandy inhaler, at least as big as a softball.
KYLE'S VOICE: 1952 . . . that was a good year . . . a very good
year . . .
*The brandy is swished around . . . We see KYLE now, a small, wizened,
balding man in his sixties, swirling his brandy.*
KYLE: Very good . . . we cleaned a lot of them out that year . . .
*By now we see something of the room. A small but very pleasant study, pan-
eled, booklined, a fireplace with a comfy fire, painting over the mantel. Jud-
son Kyle is on one huge leather armchair that rather dwarfs him, Lawrence
across from him in a somewhat smaller model. Somewhere hovering in the
background is LOUISE LOFTING.*
KYLE: I think we claimed thirty-seven, shot out of the air. (*He
chuckles a little at his joke and repeats the punchline*) Shot out of
the air . . .
CLOSEUP   LAWRENCE
No particular reaction . . .
KYLE'S VOICE: I believe that's right, isn't it, Louise?
*TWO-SHOT   KYLE WITH LOUISE LOFTING coming out of the background.
She is a competent tough woman in her mid-forties, stout, wearing a white
blouse and dark suit.*
LOFTING: I think so, Mr. Kyle, I'd have to look it up.
KYLE: You've met Miss Lofting . . . my secretary? Since I retired
she helps me with the Vanguard work.
CLOSEUP   KYLE
KYLE: Would you believe it, Mr. Preston, in 1952 . . . I think it
was '52 . . . although it might have been '53, we were able to
get seven thousand letters on five days' notice . . . protesting
the appearance of that woman in Pittsburgh . . . I don't remember her name . . . she had quite a record . . . quite a record . . . Front affiliations. But we got her . . . we got her. I
think it's safe to say that the screen . . . and the airwaves . . .
were relatively clean then. But of course they're creeping
back . . . Wasn't it Jefferson who said . . . "Eternal vigi-
lance . . ."?
ANOTHER CAMERA ANGLE   TO INCLUDE LAWRENCE
LAWRENCE: I think he was referring to the price of liberty . . .

KYLE: Yes . . . yes . . . of course.

LAWRENCE: I wanted to discuss this matter of Mr. Larch . . . I thought perhaps if I explained the circumstances . . .

Lofting moves forward with a dossier, laying it in Kyle's lap.

KYLE (*Reading—grunting*): Hah . . . ah . . . ah . . . ah . . . yes, shocking. Now that's what I mean. Now look here, here is a man with a record. A record! And coming back in a motion picture under official government sponsorship. Well!

LAWRENCE: Mr. Kyle . . . I'm an attorney, and I'm very well acquainted with the statutes protecting us against treason . . . espionage . . . subversion. Don't you think it's more appropriate to handle these matters by law . . . rather than private action?

CLOSEUP KYLE

KYLE: Ah . . . ah . . . ah . . . you see . . . that's the trouble. Now what's the use of a law when They're in courts. They're in the District Attorney's offices. In the Attorney General's office . . . They've reached into the highest courts . . . the highest courts.

CLOSEUP LAWRENCE

A little dismay showing.

LAWRENCE: They?

CLOSEUP KYLE

Now leaning forward, quite intense and sincere.

KYLE: In the diplomatic service . . . the newspapers . . . the radio and the television. They've wormed their way in . . . parasites . . . vermin . . . rats . . .

TWO-SHOT LAWRENCE, KYLE

LAWRENCE: In the case of Mr. Larch. Suppose he were to make a statement . . . perhaps write a letter explaining the charges against him . . .

Lawrence stops as he sees Kyle shaking his head "no," slowly . . .

KYLE: You see . . . they're very clever. They'll swear to anything, you know. They'll lie. Now . . . Mr. Preston, I warn you to be careful. It's a poison and it spreads by contagion. We have cases . . . attorneys . . . who are with Them! There are only two sides, you know . . . you're either for Them, or against Them! Which side are you on, Mr. Preston . . . which side?

LAWRENCE: I'm afraid we're not going to accomplish much in this meeting, Mr. Kyle . . .

He rises . . .

LAWRENCE: Miss Lofting . . .
He starts for the door . . .
    KYLE: They think they'll creep back . . . but we're waiting . . .
    We'll get Them . . . Vigilance . . . eternal vigilance . . .
Lawrence goes out the door.

INTERIOR—HALL JUST OUTSIDE THE STUDY   NIGHT
LONG SHOT
*As Lawrence comes out . . . he closes the door behind him . . . moves down
a few steps to a table where he starts to put on his coat and hat . . . there is
a click of a door behind him . . .*
    LOFTING'S VOICE: Mr. Preston . . .
Lawrence turns. Lofting has come out and is now closing the door carefully.
    LOFTING: May I speak to you for a moment?
Lawrence waits as Lofting comes down to him.
TWO-SHOT
    LOFTING: An amazing man, isn't he?
    LAWRENCE: Yes.
    LOFTING: Great energy . . . and dedication.
    LAWRENCE: Miss Lofting, it's late . . .
    LOFTING: I just wanted to have a word with you on this Larch
        case. You see, Mr. Kyle is an idealist . . . he takes a very . . .
        undiluted position.
Lawrence waits . . . go on . . .
    LOFTING: Now . . . you spoke of a statement . . . a . . . well
        . . . an explanation.
    LAWRENCE: Yes?
    LOFTING: Now in our experience a lot of people get themselves
        mixed up in Front organizations by . . . mistake. They were
        duped . . .
    LAWRENCE: Well . . .
    LOFTING: You see . . . these things can be arranged. Actually I've
        helped a lot of men and women—er—rehabilitate themselves.
        I like to think that's my contribution.
    LAWRENCE: Rehabilitation?
    LOFTING: Well . . . yes . . . After all, if they've seen the error of
        their . . . commie associations it seems only right to give them
        a hand.
    LAWRENCE: Mr. Kyle doesn't seem to think so.
    LOFTING: Well . . . I have a great deal of influence with Mr. Kyle.
        We've usually been able to advise people how to overcome
        this situation.

LAWRENCE: We?

LOFTING: My brother has a consulting public-relations service . . .

LAWRENCE: You think he could help Mr. Larch if he were retained?

LOFTING: I'm sure he could.

LAWRENCE: You're Mr. Kyle's confidential secretary, aren't you?

LOFTING: Yes . . .

LAWRENCE: I suppose he depends on your advice a great deal in his activities?

LOFTING: Yes . . . actually I'm the only full-time paid staff personnel for the League.

LAWRENCE: Well . . . Miss Lofting . . . I will report your suggestions to my client . . . good evening.

INTERIOR—LAWRENCE'S OFFICE   DAY

CLOSE ON JOE

JOE: If I wanted to do something like that, I would have done it ten years ago.

Now we see that Ken and Lawrence are present.

KEN: It's a pay-off. A straight pay-off.

LAWRENCE: There is that faint aroma! But I thought I'd better report it to you.

ANOTHER ANGLE

JOE: You know, Mr. Preston, when this whole thing first started I was angry . . . all day . . . all night . . . angry. I got a good start on an ulcer and I had to go on a bland diet and take probanthine all the time. If someone came to me for a pay-off then I would have taken a swing at him. Then . . . after maybe a year I ran out of unemployment insurance and I was living off my brother and my father-in-law . . . then maybe I wouldn't have been so noble. Maybe I would have said, "Joe, take care of yourself!" But after ten years . . . I'm not tempted.

LAWRENCE: I want you to be absolutely sure. Miss Lofting intimated she could stop the pressure . . .

KEN: I'll bet she can; she started it in the first place.

LAWRENCE: It's not as simple as that. There's Judson Kyle, he's a little obsessive but he's completely sincere. And Miss Lofting didn't invent Spain, or Communist Front organizations, or the cold war.

KEN: Which side are we on? What's the difference whether Kyle is sincere? We ought to find some way of attacking the whole Blacklist head-on.

LAWRENCE: That's not our job. We've been retained to consider Mr. Larch's interests.

KEN: You're not advising him to . . . to pay off this Lofting woman? That's just crawling.

LAWRENCE: I think we'd better discuss this later . . .

KEN: That's the issue, isn't it? Mr. Larch came to us to fight—to show up the whole rotten system of Blacklisting. We can't tell him to pay off a . . .

LAWRENCE: Ken! We are conferring with a client.

JOE: Mr. Preston . . . I understand. I have a boy . . . David. He's nineteen. He didn't understand why I didn't fight. Why don't I wait outside for a minute. (*Then offering a polite excuse*) I . . . I could call my wife.

LAWRENCE: You can use the phone in the library . . .

He is escorting Joe to the door of the library . . . As Joe goes out, Lawrence closes the door and turns back. Ken is waiting for the explosion . . . Lawrence comes back toward him slowly.

TWO-SHOT

LAWRENCE: I don't want you to do that again in front of a client . . .

KEN: What about you? Rapping my knuckles in front of him. Sometimes it isn't easy to be in partnership with your father . . .

LAWRENCE: It has nothing to do with the fact that I'm your father. I don't expect my junior law partner to start an emotional argument like that, jumping in on an issue before we've had a chance to study it.

KEN: What do we have to study? It's rotten on the face of it. If he were a . . . a . . . narcotics addict or something he'd be innocent until he was proven guilty . . . but not with the Blacklist. Nobody has to prove anything . . . all they do is accuse, that's enough! It's a heresy hunt . . . a lynching for unpopular political opinions. Who gave Judson Kyle the right to be prosecutor and judge and jury and executioner . . . ?

LAWRENCE (*Waiting it out*): Are you all through . . . ?

KEN: What do you expect me to be—"professionally objective"?

LAWRENCE: You might be able to help Mr. Larch better if you did.

KEN: Would you really let him give in to that slimy black-mail?

LAWRENCE: That's his decision. I don't give moral advice. It's too easy for us . . . we have nothing at stake and he has.

KEN: All right . . . but this whole thing . . . this Blacklisting . . . that's what's really subversive . . . it's a lot clearer and more present a danger than . . . left-wing politics left over from 1937. Isn't there some attack we can make on the whole situation?

CLOSEUP   LAWRENCE

LAWRENCE: We're not involved with the "whole situation" . . . just Joe Larch. The worst thing we could do for him would be to move too fast . . . to rush into some legal action that can freeze everybody's position. The Mayor hasn't committed himself yet. The City Council still has to pass on final approval for the film.

TWO-SHOT

KEN: That'll be some picnic.

LAWRENCE: George Veigh still says he'll back Larch all the way . . . As soon as he has a signed contract with Mill City, he's in control.

KEN: When does that happen?

LAWRENCE: Tuesday night at the regular Council meeting . . .

INTERIOR—COUNCIL ROOM AT MILL CITY   NIGHT
It has a strange resemblance to a court room, although the Judge's dais and the clerks' tables are replaced with a semi-circular table to accommodate the seven Councilmen . . . there is a press table with one or two reporters. In the Public section is a middling-sized crowd, there are numbers of empty seats. Members of the City Council are standing around, some sitting . . . general chatting, etc. In the audience watching is Judson Kyle, with Louise Lofting next to him. Across the aisle we find Lawrence just as George Veigh comes down the aisle and sits next to him.
CLOSE ON GEORGE AND LAWRENCE

GEORGE: There's a picket line outside . . .

Lawrence looks over . . .
ANGLE   KYLE AND LOFTING   LAWRENCE'S POINT-OF-VIEW
Lofting is whispering in Kyle's ear.

GEORGE'S VOICE: . . . You know, "Keep Mill City American"— that sort of thing.

TWO-SHOT   GEORGE, LAWRENCE

GEORGE: You see that man . . . there, the one waving the
glasses . . .

CLOSEUP   MONARCHIO   ONE OF THE COUNCILMEN'S POINT-OF-VIEW

GEORGE'S VOICE: That's Charles Monarchio . . . He's the opposition. He wanted to cut the Youth Program out of the budget
last year.

TWO-SHOT   GEORGE, LAWRENCE

GEORGE: This whole thing hands him an issue on a platter . . . the
Mayor's in trouble. If they approve my agreement the opposition will claim he's . . . well . . . soft on Communism or
something. If it gets turned down . . . it's a political defeat.

There is the sound of a gavel.

MEDIUM SHOT   COUNCIL TABLE

*Ostervelt has taken his place at the center of the table and is hitting his gavel
. . . the Councilmen finding their places . . .*

OSTERVELT: Gentlemen . . . please . . . order . . . order . . .

Gradual quiet . . .

OSTERVELT: Chair will entertain a motion to dispense with reading
of the minutes of our last regular meeting . . .

There is a grunt from someone making the pro forma motion . . .

OSTERVELT: Hearing no objections it is so ordered . . . Now . . .
first on the agenda, reports from the Departments of Sanitation, Water Supply, and . . .

MONARCHIO: Mr. Mayor . . .

OSTERVELT: Councilman Monarchio . . .

MONARCHIO: With the Council's permission I'd like to suggest we
consider item 5B first . . .

TWO-SHOT   GEORGE, LAWRENCE

George is turning to Lawrence whispering . . .

GEORGE: That's us . . .

CLOSEUP   OSTERVELT

Consulting his papers . . .

OSTERVELT: Five B . . . Well . . . if there are no objections?

There are none.

OSTERVELT: All right . . . 5B. A contract between the City and
George Veigh Productions giving official permission and co-
operation for the production of a Motion Picture based on the
work of the Mill City Youth Program. I believe you all have
copies of the proposed agreement . . . The floor is now open
for discussion . . .

WIDE SHOT

On the council table as Monarchio starts rising to his feet . . . and at the other side Hickman is rising . . .

    MONARCHIO: Mr. Mayor . . .

    HICKMAN: Mr. Mayor . . .

The calls from the floor have come almost simultaneously.

CLOSEUP   OSTERVELT

Looking from one to the other . . .

CLOSEUP   MONARCHIO

    MONARCHIO: Mr. Mayor . . . I have a statement on this matter which I . . .

CLOSEUP   HICKMAN

    HICKMAN: Mr. Mayor, I believe I asked for the floor first . . .

TWO-SHOT   GEORGE, LAWRENCE

Lawrence looks at George questioningly . . . George shrugs . . .

    MONARCHIO: I moved the point on the agenda . . . I have a statement . . .

CLOSEUP   JUDSON KYLE

Leaning forward now with interest . . .

    HICKMAN'S VOICE: I asked for the floor . . .

CLOSEUP   OSTERVELT

Looking from one to the other for a beat . . .

    OSTERVELT: The Chair recognizes Mr. Hickman . . .

CLOSEUP   MONARCHIO

He is sitting down, disgruntled.

    HICKMAN'S VOICE: Mr. Mayor . . .

CLOSEUP   HICKMAN

    HICKMAN: I move the matter of the Motion Picture agreement be tabled . . . for further study.

CLOSEUP   MONARCHIO

Looking up startled . . .

    OSTERVELT'S VOICE: Do I hear a second to the motion . . .

Monarchio has started to his feet as off-camera someone is heard saying "seconded" . . .

    MONARCHIO: Mr. Mayor . . . I have a statement on this serious question and . . .

MEDIUM SHOT   TO INCLUDE OSTERVELT, MONARCHIO

Ostervelt gaveling hard . . .

    OSTERVELT: There is a motion to table before the Council . . . any discussion is therefore out of order . . .

    MONARCHIO: Now wait a minute, Ostervelt . . . I've got a right to ask about . . .

Ostervelt gavels again . . .

OSTERVELT: I'm sorry, Councilman . . . you know your parliamentary procedure . . . a motion to table takes precedence with no debate . . .

CLOSEUP   LAWRENCE
His reaction.
CLOSEUP   OSTERVELT
OSTERVELT: All in favor of the motion to table for further study?
There are ayes . . .
OSTERVELT: Opposed . . .
CLOSEUP   MONARCHIO
MONARCHIO (*With a few others*): No . . .
CLOSEUP   OSTERVELT
OSTERVELT: The motion is carried . . . the matter is tabled. Any further discussion on this item is out of order . . . Now . . . item one on the agenda . . .

TWO-SHOT   GEORGE, LAWRENCE
George is shocked . . . he starts to rise to make his way out . . . Lawrence following . . .
OSTERVELT'S VOICE: ". . . An interim report from the Department of Sanitation on the purchase of five street sweepers, the result of bids submitted pursuant to City Council Resolution dated October twelfth of this year . . ."
During this, Lawrence has tried to follow George out . . . as Lawrence reaches the corridor Louise Lofting comes up behind him.

INTERIOR—JUST OUTSIDE COUNCIL ROOM   NIGHT
MEDIUM SHOT
As Lawrence comes out the door . . . automatically he holds it for the person after him, and then finds it is Lofting.
LOFTING: Mr. Preston . . . very shrewd . . . very shrewd . . .
Lawrence is looking for George.
LOFTING: A very good move for Hal Ostervelt.
Lawrence turns to Lofting.
LAWRENCE: You mean tabling the whole agreement?
LOFTING: Mmmm . . . now no one can hold him responsible for this Larch business. He doesn't have to commit himself. (*Moving closer*) That gives us time. I mean . . . if Joe Larch has the right kind of advice . . . well, by the time it comes up again, we might be able to clear him . . .
LAWRENCE: You mean retain your brother?
LOFTING: Well . . . how do you feel about it?

Lawrence looks at her, the temptation to tell her how he feels about it obviously trying to emerge . . . He restrains himself with an effort.

LAWRENCE: I . . . would be quite interested in telling you how I feel about it, Miss Lofting . . . as a matter of fact . . . I . . . (*He stops dead, recovering*) But that's not what I'm here for. I've reported your offer to my client. He—feels he doesn't want that kind of public relations advice. I find I agree with him . . . strongly.

LOFTING: He's making a mistake . . . Hal Ostervelt wouldn't make a mistake like that. He knows the first rule of politics: "Get the heat off yourself . . ."

Lawrence has turned away.

LONG SHOT LAWRENCE'S POINT-OF-VIEW DOWN THE CORRIDOR

George sitting on a bench . . . shaken . . . trying to light a cigarette . . .

LOFTING'S VOICE: ". . . onto somebody else . . . and let them sweat."

CLOSEUP LAWRENCE

Looking at George.

CLOSEUP GEORGE

He misses once with the match . . . finally gets it. He is shaken, worried, thinking . . .

FADE OUT.

ACT THREE

FADE IN:

INTERIOR—LANDING OUTSIDE JOE'S APARTMENT NIGHT

CAMERA ANGLE

Ken is just coming up the stairwell across the landing to the apartment door. He rings . . . and the door opens . . . Mildred Larch stands in the doorway looking up inquiringly at Ken . . .

KEN: Mrs. Larch? I'm Kenneth Preston . . . Mr. Larch called me . . .

MILDRED: Oh . . . oh . . . I'm sorry. I thought you were . . . I mean I was expecting an older man . . .

KEN: You mean my father . . . he's been out of town today on a case . . . Mr. Larch said it was urgent . . .

MILDRED: I'm sorry . . . come in . . .

She turns into the apartment . . .
MILDRED: Joe . . . it's the lawyer . . .

INTERIOR—THE APARTMENT   NIGHT
MEDIUM SHOT
As Mildred comes in with Ken, Joe is standing waiting for him.
Dave appears in a doorway from the bedrooms . . .
JOE: I'm sorry . . . I didn't mean for you to come to the house . . .
KEN: I got the message that it was urgent . . .
JOE: Well . . . I could have come to your office . . .
MILDRED: Sit down, Mr. Preston . . .
She takes his coat and hat . . . Ken sits down . . . and looks up to find them
all looking at him—Joe, Mildred, and Dave.
KEN: Well . . . what is it?
JOE: I got a call . . . a telephone call at the store. I work in a shoe store, you know . . . I didn't give up the job, it's just as well . . .
MILDRED: Joe . . . !
JOE: It was Maggie Daly . . . she's in George Veigh's office. You know, casting . . . production assistant.
MILDRED: He wouldn't call himself . . . he wouldn't have the common decency to call himself . . .
JOE: Please . . . she . . . let's see if I can remember it . . . she said . . . "Hello, Mr. Larch . . ." and I said "yes" . . . and she said "this is Maggie Daly . . ."
Mildred is getting impatient with the detail . . .
MILDRED: Joe . . . don't give a performance, just tell Mr. Preston . . .
CLOSEUP   JOE
JOE: Well, she said . . . "George asked me to call you" and then she said it flat as if she was reading from notes . . . "There's been a revision of the script and the part now calls for a younger man and you won't be needed" . . . and then she said, "Personally I'm going out now and get a job poisoning orphans, it's cleaner."
MEDIUM SHOT   TO INCLUDE ALL
KEN: She meant they didn't want you for the part?
DAVE (*From his door jamb*): What do you think it means? George Veigh caved in.
KEN: Can he do that . . . I mean accepting it at its face value . . .

can he replace you that way? Are there any Union regulations?

JOE: I didn't actually have a contract.

KEN: You're sure it's because of the Blacklist?

DAVE: No . . . No, Mr. Preston, they suddenly found out they could get Sir Laurence Olivier for Pop's part.

MILDRED: Dave . . . please . . . don't butt in . . .

DAVE: Why don't I go up to that office and just punch him in the nose . . .

KEN: I'll have to talk this over with my father tomorrow morning . . .

MILDRED: What do they want from him? Joe is an actor . . . that's all . . . a character actor . . . that's all he was . . . in movies and television, playing a detective, or a doctor . . . or a butcher . . . small parts. Just small parts . . .

JOE: Milly . . .

MILDRED: Why does it hurt them for Joe to be an actor? What do they do it for? What kind of men are they . . . this George Veigh . . . the Mayor . . . what kind of men are they?

JOE (*Dry*): Very ordinary men . . . (*To Ken*) With her it happens fresh every time! Do you think there's anything we can do?

KEN: I'm not sure . . .

DAVE: Forget it, Pop . . . it's too late. You open at Fine Arch shoes in the morning for an indefinite engagement.

KEN: It isn't over yet . . . there must be some legal recourse . . .

DAVE: Yeah . . . what?

KEN: I . . . I'm not sure yet. I want to . . . talk it over and . . . we'll find some way.

CLOSEUP DAVE

Looking at Ken, shaking his head slowly, cynically . . .

DAVE: Mr. Preston . . . a college education occasionally comes in handy. There is an appropriate quotation from Dickens . . . "The Law? . . . The Law is an ass, an idiot!"

INTERIOR—LAWRENCE'S OFFICE   DAY

CLOSEUP   LAWRENCE

LAWRENCE: Well . . . that's been said before!

THE CAMERA PULLS BACK. *Quickly we see where we are; Ken is with Lawrence.*

KEN: There's got to be some attack on it. You're sure about libel?

LAWRENCE: Absolutely. There's no action possible. They worded

that Bulletin perfectly. The newspaper articles were factual
. . . and Larch admits that what they say is true . . . where's
the libel?

KEN: There must be some precedent . . . people must have taken
some legal action about the Blacklist.

CLOSEUP   LAWRENCE

LAWRENCE: Usually it's for conspiracy . . . when several companies may agree not to hire certain people . . . that can be illegal . . . but that's usually very difficult to prove, and I don't
think the notoriety would do our client much good.

TWO-SHOT

KEN: What are we going to do?

LAWRENCE: I'm going with him to George Veigh's office tomorrow.

KEN: Why?

LAWRENCE: I don't believe that face to face we can't work something out.

KEN: That's what you said when you went to see Judson Kyle.

LAWRENCE: There's a difference. Veigh isn't a fanatic . . . or cor-
rupt. He's a reasonable man. So is Mayor Ostervelt. You
should be able to work things out with reasonable honest men.

KEN: I'd feel a lot better if we had an ace up our sleeves . . . some
direct legal attack on the whole Blacklist . . .

LAWRENCE: All right—suppose you look for one. We can try it
both ways . . . negotiation . . . and attack.

INTERIOR—THE PRESTON LAW LIBRARY   DAY
MEDIUM SHOT
*Ken at the table. He has it covered with law texts and case volumes . . . he
is working on a yellow pad taking notes; a law clerk is sitting opposite him
. . . hands Ken a note from the text he is studying . . .*

INTERIOR—GEORGE VEIGH'S OUTER OFFICE   DAY
CLOSEUP   ART FINE
Sitting behind the desk at the phone, he has Variety *before him, and he is
most uncomfortable, sneaking a look over . . .*
POINT-OF-VIEW REVERSE
*To Lawrence and Joe Larch sitting on the skimpy steel tubing and plastic
waiting-room furniture. Lawrence looks at his watch . . . Joe rises and
crosses to Art . . .*

JOE: Did you tell Mr. Veigh we were waiting?

ART: I . . . Mr. Larch, he's in a very important conference . . .

you know how it is. Couldn't you come back tomorrow . . . ?

ANOTHER CAMERA ANGLE

*As Joe turns back the front door of the office opens and Maggie comes in
. . . she does the smallest of takes and then hangs up her coat . . .*

    MAGGIE: Hi, Joe . . .

    JOE: Maggie . . . this is Mr. Preston . . . he's my attorney.

    MAGGIE: Yeah? Good!

Lawrence has risen (gentleman of the old school that he is).

    JOE: Art says George is tied up in a conference . . . do you think
    you could find out when he'll be through? I hate to keep Mr.
    Preston waiting . . .

Maggie looks at Art . . .

CLOSEUP   ART

As he shrugs imperceptibly . . . he's only doing what he is told.

CLOSEUP   MAGGIE

As she turns back to Joe.

    MAGGIE: Yeah . . . I wouldn't be surprised if he was through just
    about now.

She goes to the inner door . . . opens it and goes in . . .

INTERIOR—VEIGH'S INNER OFFICE   DAY

MEDIUM SHOT

*As Maggie comes in. George is, of course . . . alone, he looks up a little star-
tled as she comes in.*

    MAGGIE: George, you've got company . . .

    GEORGE: Listen, Maggie, get rid of him, will you, I mean what's
    the use.

    MAGGIE: I made your phone call for you, now you see him, you
    fink!

    GEORGE: Don't talk to me that way, Maggie . . .

    MAGGIE: Go ahead, fire me . . . I've got an offer from Herb Brod-
    kin now . . .

She has crossed to the door and opened it . . .

    MAGGIE: Joe . . . Mr. Preston . . . Mr. Veigh will see you now.

*She turns back and smiles sweetly at George . . . who is very discomforted
. . . and leaves.*

ANOTHER ANGLE

Lawrence and Joe come in the door . . .

    GEORGE: I'm sorry to keep you waiting, Mr. Preston.

    LAWRENCE (*His eyes flicking around the room*): I understand . . .
    you were tied up.

CLOSEUP   GEORGE

Jack Klugman, E. G. Marshall, and Maggie Hayes in *Blacklist*.

GEORGE: You understand . . . I mean I'm embarrassed about the whole thing. Now look, Joe . . . you've been in the business a long time . . . you understand. Actually we've been thinking about shuffling the character for a long time . . . a way back even before I talked to you. I could show you the memos from Comus. You know how it is . . . you have to have teenage identification. They've been after me to get a Richard Chamberlain type, you know . . . for the kids . . . so . . . (*He is trailing off after this burst of nervous rationale*) . . . it's being rewritten. That's all . . .

CLOSEUP   JOE
Just looking at him.

GEORGE'S VOICE: You know how it is . . .

CLOSEUP   GEORGE
Starting to sweat a little . . .

GEORGE: It didn't have anything to do with that . . . other business. That's all there is to it . . . (*He looks a little hunted*)

CLOSEUP   LAWRENCE
Waiting him out.

GEORGE'S VOICE: Now look, Mr. Preston . . .

CLOSEUP   GEORGE

GEORGE: . . . there's no signed contract . . . we never actually made a deal . . . but suppose I pay Joe for a week anyway . . . just for his trouble . . .

THREE-SHOT

LAWRENCE: That isn't what we came to discuss . . .

GEORGE: Now look, Joe . . . don't try to make any trouble for me . . . what do you want? What did you bring a lawyer for?

LAWRENCE: We want to talk about this situation . . .

GEORGE: What situation? There's no situation. Joe, I told you we're just rewriting, that's all. It's an artistic decision . . . it doesn't have anything to do with anything . . . Joe . . . just let me alone . . . let me alone . . .

There is a pause for a beat.

CLOSEUP   JOE
Looking at him . . . he answers gently.

JOE: George . . . what are you angry at me for? It was your idea to have me in the picture . . . you called *me!*

CLOSEUP   GEORGE
Suddenly he is crumpled, he slumps in his chair.

GEORGE: Oh God . . . Joe . . . I'm sorry . . . I'm sorry . . . I'm sorry . . . I can't do anything . . . Look . . . you know I wanted to use you. It isn't me.

ANOTHER ANGLE   TO INCLUDE LAWRENCE

LAWRENCE: Who is it that told you you couldn't hire Mr. Larch?

GEORGE: Nobody told me . . . who has to tell anybody? You were at that City Council meeting . . . they tabled my agreement. Did anybody have to tell me why? I got called in at Comus . . . without the City approval I have nothing . . . my financing . . . my distribution set-up . . . nothing!

LAWRENCE: The financing company put on pressure?

CLOSEUP   GEORGE

GEORGE: They didn't say anything . . . they just pointed out that if I didn't have the official approval I didn't have a picture . . . and it's true! They didn't even mention Joe's name over there . . . I did. I said to Jakman over there "Joe Larch is the best man for the part." You know what he said? "We leave all the artistic decisions up to you!" What decisions! Joe . . . I worked four years to put together this package . . . my first feature. Four years . . . from nothing. I put it together from spit and adhesive tape. And if I don't have City approval the four years can go in the garbage can. Does anybody have to tell me anything? What am I . . . a child? Listen . . . I've got a choice . . . I can make my picture without Joe . . . or I can't make it at all!

ANOTHER ANGLE   TO INCLUDE ALL

LAWRENCE: You just infer that?

GEORGE: Infer . . . infer . . . don't give me any lawyer's talk. There it is . . . it's reality . . . it's the world . . . (*A little bitter*) it's show business! (*Then rapidly*) Joe . . . you got no right to ask me to throw away four years like that. What good would it do . . . suppose I said to Comus . . . "If Joe Larch goes I go!" You know what they'd say? "Goodbye and Good Luck!" What good would it do?

JOE: I don't know, George . . .

GEORGE: You'd still be in the shoe store and I'd be right next to you! Look . . . why should I have to sacrifice everything. What did I do? Did I get mixed up in a Communist Front organization? Why should I get torn apart?

JOE: I don't know . . .

GEORGE: Listen, Joe . . . before I had Maggie call you up I suffered. I'm telling you I suffered.

JOE: Well . . . don't worry, George. If it's any comfort to you, next time you won't suffer as much. You'll grow calluses.

GEORGE: Joe, believe me . . .

JOE: I believe you . . . this time you're outraged . . . next time and the next and the next it'll be easier, until it'll just be an inconvenience.

GEORGE: Joe . . . I swear to you . . . if I had that official City approval you would be in my picture and I'd tell Comus to go chase themselves around the block . . . I swear!

JOE: What do you want, George, absolution?

GEORGE: I tried, didn't I?

JOE: You knew this could happen; if you weren't ready to fight why'd you call me in the first place? Why'd you dig me out of that shoe store if you were going to fold up under the first push?

GEORGE: Joe, I tried, didn't I? In ten years who else even tried?

JOE: Sure . . . you have it both ways now, George. You have your picture . . . *and* the nice comfortable feeling that you're a fine liberal man of good will.

GEORGE: Joe, don't be bitter . . .

JOE: I'm not. I'm grateful . . . Anything I can ever do for you . . . if you want a pair of shoes—come in . . . I'll take care of you myself.

LAWRENCE: Mr. Veigh . . . you said if you had official City approval you'd keep Mr. Larch in the film?

GEORGE: Mr. Preston . . . how would it help if I fought?

LAWRENCE: We don't know . . . You haven't tried. You just collapse at the first threat. I suppose there are people with less excuse than you . . . Powerful corporations afraid to challenge tiny pressure groups . . . afraid to admit that the "emperor has no clothes."

GEORGE: Yes . . . yes . . . You're right . . . I'm just one man, that's all . . .

LAWRENCE: Nobody is more than one man . . . I'm sorry, that's pretty sententious. Mr. Veigh . . . you did say if you had official City approval you'd keep Mr. Larch in the film . . . ?

CLOSEUP   GEORGE

GEORGE: Sure . . . sure . . . look, it isn't me! You understand . . . it isn't me! Joe . . . I want you to believe that . . . it isn't me!

FADE OUT.

John Baragrey and Jack Klugman in *Blacklist*.

ACT FOUR

FADE IN:
INTERIOR—THE LAW LIBRARY   NIGHT
MEDIUM SHOT
Ken still up to his ears in books . . . he has one open and he is dictating with some excitement to the law clerk . . .

> KEN: Carnes *v* St. Paul Union Stock Yards Co. 164 Minnesota . . . 1925. Quote . . . "It being the law that a man who has employment and is discharged by his employer solely by reason of the wrongful interference of another sustains an injury for which the intermeddlar is liable . . . There is no substantial difference between the loss of employment and the inability to secure employment when each is caused by the wrongful interference of a third party, for in either case the person injured is prevented from enjoying the fruits of his labor . . ." Now let's see what we can find in New York decisions . . .

INTERIOR—MAYOR OSTERVELT'S OFFICE   DAY
CLOSEUP OSTERVELT

> OSTERVELT: You understand, Mr. Preston . . . I consider this completely off the record . . .

THE CAMERA PULLS BACK and we see Lawrence is with him . . . The Mayor is having his lunch on a tray.

> OSTERVELT: Can I send out for something for you . . . coffee?
>
> LAWRENCE: No, thank you . . .
>
> OSTERVELT: I understand you're representing this Mr. Larch . . .
>
> LAWRENCE: That's right. Mr. Mayor, you seem to have the key to this whole problem . . . Mr. Veigh tells me if he had the City approval——
>
> OSTERVELT (*Waving a sandwich half*): Wait . . . wait . . . let's get one thing clear, Mr. Preston. I never suggested to George Veigh that he—well—get rid of this actor. You understand that?
>
> LAWRENCE: Yes . . . he told me that.
>
> OSTERVELT: I merely recommended to certain Councilmen that the agreement should be . . . restudied.
>
> LAWRENCE: Well . . . it seems everybody got the message. Frankly, sir . . . if Joe Larch's name hadn't appeared in that

Bulletin . . . would the agreement need so much further study?

Ostervelt looks at him . . . bites into his sandwich.

OSTERVELT: It's a dirty business.

CLOSEUP LAWRENCE

Looking up in surprise.

OSTERVELT'S VOICE: The whole thing from one end to the other . . .

CLOSEUP   OSTERVELT

OSTERVELT: Jud Kyle seeing Communists under the bed . . . Louis Harrison at the newspaper who can smell a scandal a mile away . . . Charley Monarchio who's willing to use it . . . and I include myself . . . because I'm too vulnerable to do anything about it. This isn't the first time I've had Kyle on my neck . . . he used to be national in scope . . . well, thank God times have changed and a two-bit vigilante outfit like that can't swing that kind of weight. But he can still raise a bad smell in Mill City and I'm stuck with it.

TWO-SHOT

LAWRENCE: How powerful is he politically?

OSTERVELT: I don't know exactly . . . and I'd just as soon not find out unless I have to.

LAWRENCE: But you act under the pressure?

OSTERVELT (*Very deliberately*): Oh no . . . there are many reasons why that agreement should be tabled for further study. It has nothing to do with your client . . . that's my official position. (*Then unbending*) Mr. Preston . . . when you're out in the open where everybody can take a shot at you you're very exposed. I have to play it safe.

LAWRENCE: Do you really believe the charges against Joe Larch?

OSTERVELT: Yes and no. I understand he did belong to something or other in 1937 . . . but if you mean do I think he's a threat to National Security now? No.

LAWRENCE: Then why not let him work . . . ?

CLOSEUP   OSTERVELT

OSTERVELT: I'm not afraid of him . . . he can't hurt me. But Jud Kyle and Louis Harrison and Charley Monarchio can. I'm not going to take the chance. I've got a job to do . . . that comes first. I've got to run this city, I've got to ram new taxes down the throats of my constituents, and I've got to get reelected. Maybe we could approve that agreement and your Mr. Larch

would be in the film . . . and nothing would happen . . .
maybe . . . but I can't take the chance.

TWO-SHOT

OSTERVELT: You understand, Mr. Preston . . . this is all off the
record . . . officially . . . we just want to restudy the agreement and it has nothing to do with Mr. Larch . . .

Lawrence nods wearily and rises to go.

INTERIOR—THE LAW LIBRARY   NIGHT

MEDIUM SHOT

Ken has a thirty- or forty-page typed document before him which he is
proofing . . . carbons lie on the table before him. Joe Larch is in the chair
across from him reading one of the carbons . . . Ken looks up at him.

KEN: I'm sorry . . . my father said he'd be down from Mill City
by nine . . . he must have run into traffic.

JOE: That's all right . . .

KEN: What do you think of that?

JOE (*Shrugs*): I don't know . . . what is it exactly? A brief?

KEN: A preliminary memorandum . . . I think I've got a different
attack on the whole practice of Blacklisting . . .

He stops—there is the noise of a door opening. Ken and Joe swing around as
Lawrence comes in. He is tired and just taking off his coat. They look at him
expectantly. Lawrence shakes his head "no."

LAWRENCE: Off the record Mayor Ostervelt thinks it's all ridiculous . . . but he has to play it safe. On the record: they just
tabled for further study. I'm sorry, Mr. Larch.

KEN: Dad, I want you to look over this memorandum on a prima
facie tort approach . . .

LAWRENCE (*Checking his wrist watch*): It's a little late . . .

KEN: I think I've got something . . . it's backed up by New York
Decisions . . . Appellate Division . . . (*He hands Lawrence*
one copy of the pages) It's only about forty pages, and I told
Mr. Larch you'd look it over tonight.

Looking at Ken a little wearily, Lawrence accepts the papers.

LAWRENCE: I'll read it in my office.

He goes out . . . Ken looking after him . . .

JOE: Look, Mr. Preston . . . I'm no lawyer . . . what is a prima
facie tort?

CLOSEUP   KEN

KEN: A legal term . . . it means it's a legal wrong on the face of it.
I approach it as a violation of a property right . . . the right to
carry on a lawful business . . . like acting . . . is a property

right . . . here's . . . here's the case citation . . . (*Finding it in
his own copy*) Federal Waste Paper Corporation *v* Garment
Center Capitol . . . a property right . . . "as much entitled to
protection as the right to guard property already acquired."
Look . . . it's this way. George Veigh can decide not to hire
you . . . that's his right. *But* if he is *induced* or *coerced* by some
intermeddlar to refuse to hire you . . . then *your* right has
been infringed!

CLOSEUP   JOE

JOE: "Intermeddlar" . . . that's what they call it in law?

CLOSEUP   KEN

KEN: That's right. Here . . . there's a Supreme Court Ruling on it
. . . (*Riffling through pages*) . . . Truax *v* Raich . . . "The em-
ployee has manifest interest in the freedom of the employer to
exercise his judgment without illegal interference or compulsion." It's a whole new way of looking at it . . . you don't sue
for libel . . . or breach of contract. You serve the intermeddlar himself for damages . . .

TWO-SHOT

JOE: That would be Judson Kyle?

KEN: And the Mayor . . . and Comus Corporation . . . anybody
who coerced George Veigh into not hiring you when he
wanted to. Of course they can claim justification . . . but if we
can show there's malice . . . that is, intent to injure you, then
that defense is watered down . . . Dad will be about an hour
. . . come on . . . we'll get a cup of coffee.

                    DISSOLVE TO:

INTERIOR—THE LAW LIBRARY   NIGHT

MEDIUM SHOT

*Joe is sitting at the table smoking, Ken pacing a little, as Lawrence comes
out of his office carrying the memorandum. Ken turns toward him. Lawrence
comes down to the table.*

LAWRENCE: Where did you find the Oliver Wendell Holmes
quote?

KEN: "Privilege, Malice and Intent" . . . I think it was published
in 1895. Didn't I list it?

LAWRENCE: I might have missed it.

There is a beat.

KEN: Well.

LAWRENCE: It's good law. I haven't checked all the cases, of
course, but . . . it's ingenious. You're well researched. I think

Robert Reed and Jack Klugman in *Blacklist*.

you've met the justification question. And it does attack the Blacklist issue head-on.

CLOSEUP   JOE

Reaction, sitting up straight, surprised at what he hears.

CLOSEUP   KEN

> KEN: I can dictate the complaints tomorrow morning when Helen comes in and we can serve them by Wednesday. I'd like to serve that Judson Kyle myself . . .

ANOTHER ANGLE   INCLUDING LAWRENCE

Ken trails off. Lawrence has put the memorandum down, and is shaking his head "no."

> LAWRENCE: No.
>
> KEN: What do you mean?
>
> LAWRENCE: We can't take it into court.
>
> KEN: Why not? You said it's good law . . . I've got the precedents. We can prove damage.
>
> LAWRENCE: Yes, it's good law on paper. Or in an article in a law school journal, but not in court.
>
> KEN: Why not?
>
> LAWRENCE: Because we can't prove that Judson Kyle's action was directly responsible for Mr. Larch's firing.
>
> KEN: You know it was . . . I know it . . . so does everybody else.

CLOSEUP   LAWRENCE

> LAWRENCE: That's not the point. What everybody knows is true can't always be proven in court. George Veigh will swear he's rewriting the script because of an "artistic" decision. Can we prove that's not true? The Mayor and the Council have the right to reconsider City business. Can we prove it was because of fear of political pressure? Comus has a very simple answer. They've only agreed to finance Veigh *if* he had official City approval.

TWO-SHOT   KEN, LAWRENCE

> KEN: You can't get around cause and effect. Kyle prints his Bulletin, the newspaper blows it up . . . the City puts pressure on George Veigh and he fires Mr. Larch. Cause and effect.
>
> LAWRENCE: Ken, this whole Blacklisting business goes on a vague poisonous fog. Nobody "tells" anybody anything, they don't have to. They "know" . . . they get the message, and you can't prove anything. Nothing is "said" . . . Everything is understood. Your law is good, and we know it's true in our soul, but we can't prove it in court.

KEN: You mean there's no cause of action for Mr. Larch?
Lawrence shakes his head "no."
KEN: They're going to get away with it? There isn't anything we
can do . . .
LAWRENCE: Not practically, no.
ANOTHER ANGLE   TO INCLUDE JOE
Ken turning sharply to Joe.
KEN: Mr. Larch, your boy is right. The law *is* an ass!
*He leaves the library quickly . . . Lawrence looking after him as they hear
the sound of a door slamming.*
LAWRENCE: Excuse me, Mr. Larch . . .
Lawrence has started to move . . .
JOE: Go ahead, I'll have to speak to *my* son when I get home.

INTERIOR—A DESERTED OFFICE-BUILDING LOBBY   NIGHT
MEDIUM SHOT
*There is a night-ledger stand in the middle of the lobby. Ken is at it just sign-
ing out. There is an old man with a big mop and a commercial mop-pail
working away on the terrazzo flooring. The elevator opens and Lawrence
comes out.*
LAWRENCE: Ken.
Ken looks up as Lawrence comes to him.
LAWRENCE: Wait a minute.
KEN: You're going to tell me not to get emotional over cases?
LAWRENCE: No.
KEN: Dad, I worked four days solid on that memorandum . . . I
had two boys up at Columbia law school doing the leg-work.
All right. I believe you. It won't work. It's right, but it won't
work. Then what's the use?
LAWRENCE: Maybe we've been too successful, Ken. Maybe we've
won too often. Maybe that's the trouble. It makes people arro-
gant.
KEN: What do you mean, arrogant?
LAWRENCE: The law is man-made and it's imperfect. There isn't a
neat satisfying ending to every story in life. And that goes for
the law. Sometimes everything just ends up in the air. No climax. No rescue. Not even a good rousing disaster. Just a kind
of nagging trailing-off into life.
ANOTHER ANGLE
He takes Ken by the arm, starting him back toward the elevator.
KEN: I was sure I had it. There had to be a way.

LAWRENCE (*Stopping*): Not necessarily. (*Pause*) We have a nice organized closed logical system of courts and briefs and points of law, but we don't always have the answer. There are injustices in the world, in our country for that matter, that can't be neatly disposed of by a brilliant point of law at a dramatic moment.

KEN: I know . . . I know . . . but . . . (*Still fighting it*) . . . it ought to work!

LAWRENCE: Things don't always happen the way they "ought" to.

The elevator door slides open and Joe Larch comes out . . . stops as he sees them . . .

LAWRENCE: I'm sorry we left you, Mr. Larch.

JOE: That's all right, I better get home now.

KEN: I'm sorry.

JOE: That's all right . . . it looked pretty good there for an hour. (*A little amused*) "Intermeddlar" . . . that's what they call it.

LAWRENCE: We can try it . . . although it would be expensive and I don't think . . .

CLOSEUP   JOE

JOE: I'll take your word for it, Mr. Preston . . . I haven't got the money for a grand gesture that doesn't have much chance of working. You know . . . this whole thing . . . Blacklisting . . . throwing people out of their jobs for their political opinions . . . it comes out of a . . . a sort of atmosphere. People are afraid . . . afraid of Communists . . . Socialists . . . anybody—they're not sure who. Ten years ago it was a lot worse . . . even five. It's still going on . . . not in the headlines as much . . . but there are still actors who can't get jobs . . . teachers . . . maybe newspapermen. You know when it will stop? When enough people start to believe what they *say* they're defending! When people have faith in . . . (*Groping for what*) . . . in . . . well . . . (*Then apologetically because it's so simple*) . . . the Constitution. In . . . freedom! Well . . . goodnight, and thanks anyway.

Turning to Ken he says with simple banality . . .

JOE: Well, you can't win 'em all!

ANOTHER ANGLE

Joe turns and starts right down to the sign-out desk. STAY CLOSE *with Ken and Lawrence.*

KEN: Well, what happens with him now?

LAWRENCE: No climax. No rescue. No neat satisfying ending. We do the best we can with the next case.

MEDIUM SHOT JOE
As he approaches the sign-out table. The old JANITOR has come up.
    JOE: Am I supposed to sign my name here?
    JANITOR: Yeah, right here.
The Janitor is looking at Joe curiously, staring. Joe pauses in his writing, looking up as he feels the stare.
    JANITOR: I seen you somewhere before.
Joe takes, goes back to writing his last name.
    JANITOR: A couple of nights ago, on the Early Show, they had an
        old movie.
    JOE: "The Hurried Man."
    JANITOR: Yeah, yeah, that's it. You took the part of a detective,
        huh? You're an actor, huh?
    JOE: I was . . . once.
    JANITOR: Yeah. (*Looking over to the book*) "Joe Larch . . ." You
        were very good.
    JOE: Thank you.
    JANITOR: Listen, would you do me a favor?
He has fumbled in his overalls and come up with a scrap of paper.
    JANITOR: For my wife. She'll get a big kick out of it. (*He is handing
        Joe the paper. Joe still has the pencil*) Would you give me your
        autograph?
CLOSEUP JOE
As he hears this, pauses a beat.
    JOE: All right.
ANOTHER ANGLE TO INCLUDE JANITOR
He is leaning over Joe's shoulder.
    JANITOR: Just write it to "Selma," huh?
Joe writes, gives the paper to the Janitor.
    JANITOR (*Stowing it away*): She'll get a big kick out of it.
The Janitor is moving with Joe the few steps to the front door. He unlocks it for him, holding it open.
    JANITOR: Thanks a lot, Mr. Larch. Goodnight.
AT THE ELEVATORS LONG SHOT
Lawrence and Ken looking down the lobby toward the door as Joe Larch goes out. As the door closes they turn, go into the elevator, and the door closes on them.

FADE OUT.

NOON WINE

By *SAM PECKINPAH*
From the Short Novel by KATHERINE ANNE PORTER

ABC Stage 67
American Broadcasting Company Television Network
November 23, 1966

DIRECTOR: *Sam Peckinpah*

PRODUCER: *Daniel Melnick*

A Talent Associates, Ltd., Presentation

Hubbell Robinson, In Charge of Production

THE CAST

ROYAL EARLE THOMPSON: *Jason Robards*

ELLIE THOMPSON: *Olivia de Havilland*

HOMER T. HATCH: *Theodore Bikel*

OLAF HELTON: *Per Oscarsson*

BURLEIGH: *Robert Emhardt*

ARTHUR: *Steve Sanders*

SHERIFF BARBEE: *Ben Johnson*

HERBERT: *Peter Robbins*

MR. MC CLELLAN: *L. Q. Jones*

MRS. MC CLELLAN: *Jill Andre*

MRS. BERTHA NORD: *Joan Tompkins*

ACT ONE

FADE IN:

EXTERIOR—TEXAS FARM   DAY

TWO BOYS CLIMB DOWN LADDER from hayloft, run across the yard, un-dressing as they go, and jump into a tank of water.

ARTHUR AND HERBERT PLAY IN WATER, *then look up as they see:*

HELTON COMING UP THE ROAD.

    THE BOYS: Hello.

Helton continues into the yard.

THOMPSON, SITTING UNDER TREES.

    THOMPSON: How do you do, sir.

Helton crosses to him.

    HELTON: I need work. You need a man here?

    THOMPSON: Maybe we can make a deal. I've been kinda looking around for somebody . . . Where'd you work last?

    HELTON: North Dakota.

    THOMPSON: North Dakota. That's a smart distance off, seems to me.

    HELTON: I need work. I can do anything on a farm—cheap.

    THOMPSON: Well, my name's Thompson. Mr. Royal Earle Thompson.

    HELTON: I'm Mr. Helton—Mr. Olaf Helton.

    THOMPSON: Well, sit down, Mr. Helton.

Helton sits.

    THOMPSON: How much you fixing to gouge out of me—how much am I going to have to pay for the privilege of giving you a place to stay and all the food you can eat?

    HELTON: I'm a good worker. I get a dollar a day.

    THOMPSON: Why—for a dollar a day, I'd hire myself out. What kind of work is it where they pay you a dollar a day?

    HELTON: Wheat fields—North Dakota.

    THOMPSON: Well, this ain't no wheat field by a long shot. This is more of a dairy farm. My wife—she was set on a dairy. She likes working around the cows and calves, so I humored her. But that was a mistake. She broke down on me and now I've got to do nearly everything myself.

    But speaking as one man to another, there ain't any money in it. So I can't give you no dollar a day, 'cause actually I don't make that much out of it. I'll give you seven dollars a month and you eat at the table with us.

HELTON: That's all right—I take it.

THOMPSON (*Stands*): Well now, I guess we call it a deal, eh? (*Crosses the yard*). Now you just take over this churn and give it a few swings, while I ride into town on a couple of errands. (*At gate*) Guess you know what to do with the butter if you get it, don't you?

HELTON: I know butter—I know butter business.

THOMPSON: You're a foreigner, ain't you?

HELTON: I'm a Swede.

THOMPSON: I'll be damned. A Swede. Well now, I'm afraid you'll get pretty lonesome around here. I never seen any Swedes in this neck of the woods.

HELTON: That's all right.

Thompson enters the house.

INTERIOR—BEDROOM   DAY

MRS. THOMPSON LIES ON THE BED, *a cloth over her eyes. As Thompson enters, she takes off the cloth.*

MRS. THOMPSON (*On elbow*): What's all the noise—who is it?

THOMPSON: Got a feller out there who says he's a Swede, Ellie. Says he knows how to make butter.

MRS. THOMPSON (*Sits up*): I hope it turns out to be the truth . . . looks like my head will never get any better.

THOMPSON: Don't you worry. You fret too much . . . (*Goes to her*) Now I'm going to ride into town and get a little order of groceries.

He kisses her.

MRS. THOMPSON (*Lies back*): Don't you linger, now, Mr. Thompson. (*Pointedly*) None of my family—my father, my brothers nor my grandfather, none of them ever took a dram in their lives.

THOMPSON: I know—I know—(*Kisses her hand*) Now you get some rest. (*Crosses away*) I won't be long . . . He's out there with the churn—you keep an eye on him . . .

He exits. Mrs. Thompson lies back, places the cloth over her eyes, listening to the distant swing churn.

DISSOLVE TO:

INTERIOR—BEDROOM   DAY

MRS. THOMPSON WAKENS SLOWLY, SITS UP A LITTLE, *removes the cloth shading her weak eyes from the flat strips of late summer sunlight that blaze between the sill and lowered shades, slowly realizing that the swing churn has stopped and that she is hearing a new sound . . . somebody is playing a tune on a harmonica—a pretty tune—merry and sad. She listens for a moment longer, stands, then goes out of the room.*

EXTERIOR—SPRING HOUSE   DAY
THE CHURN IS UNATTENDED, *the music is apparently coming from the hired man's shack over near the barn.*
MRS. THOMPSON ON THE FRONT PORCH, *shakes her head and crosses toward the spring house.*

INTERIOR—HIRED MAN'S SHACK   DAY
HELTON IS SEATED IN THE SHACK, *tilted back in a kitchen chair, blowing away at his harmonica, his eyes shut.*

EXTERIOR—SPRING HOUSE   DAY
MRS. THOMPSON PAUSES AT THE DOOR. *The music never stops. After a moment, she enters.*

INTERIOR—SPRING HOUSE   DAY
THE INTERIOR OF THE SPRING HOUSE IS COOL, *the shadows soothing to her eyes. In the center of the building is a small grotto almost choked with pallid ferns. In the spring pool itself are large pails of milk and butter, fresh and sweet in the cold water. Around the pool are rickety wooden shelves and benches. Leaning over, she looks at:*
THE CREAM THAT HAS BEEN SKIMMED *and set aside; beside it, a roll of rich butter; and on the bench, the wooden butter moulds and shallow pans scrubbed and sparkling. She turns. The barrel is full of buttermilk, and the hard-packed dirt floor has been swept smooth. Mrs. Thompson straightens and smiles, then turns and exits the spring house.*

EXTERIOR—HIRED MAN'S SHACK   DAY
MRS. THOMPSON CROSSES TO THE SHACK *and hesitates in the doorway, looking in, weaving her fingers into an eyeshade, thumbs on the temples, blinking up through tearful lids.*

INTERIOR—HIRED MAN'S SHACK   DAY·
HELTON OPENS HIS EYES, *stops playing and puts his chair down. Mrs. Thompson hesitates a moment, then enters.*
She stops just inside the doorway.

> MRS. THOMPSON: How do you do, sir. I'm Mrs. Thompson, and I want to tell you I think you did real well in the spring house.
> HELTON: That's all right.
> MRS. THOMPSON (*Goes in*): That's a pretty tune you're playing. Most folks don't seem to get much music out of a harmonica.

Helton, except for his moving hand, his open eyes, might be asleep. Mrs. Thompson stares at him, then sees:

FIVE OTHER HARMONICAS standing in a row on a shelf.

MRS. THOMPSON: I see you're mighty fond of music . . . We used to have an old accordion and Mr. Thompson could play it right smart, but the little boys broke it up.

Helton stands.

MRS. THOMPSON: You know how little boys are . . .

Helton crosses to the harmonicas.

MRS. THOMPSON: You better set those harmonicas on a high shelf, or they'll be after them. Boys are great hands for getting into things. I try to teach them, but it don't do much good. (*Then*) They'll be needing something to eat, pretty soon. I wonder what I ought to be thinking about for supper. What do you like to eat, Mr. Helton?

HELTON (*Crosses away and sits*): I eat anything.

MRS. THOMPSON: Well, we usually have cornbread, except on Sundays. I suppose in your part of the country you don't get much cornbread.

Mrs. Thompson turns and leaves the shack. Helton tilts his chair back and begins to play the same tune again.

DISSOLVE TO:

INTERIOR—KITCHEN   EVENING

MRS. THOMPSON IS STANDING AT THE WINDOW watching Helton chop wood. (He is off-camera.)

WILD SHOT THROUGH WINDOW, Helton chopping wood.

MRS. THOMPSON IN APRON AT WINDOW. Thompson enters with supplies.

THOMPSON (*Crosses to table*): Take a good look, Ellie. That Swede sure is grinding out the labor. But I swear he is the closest-mouthed feller I ever met up with in all my days. (*Goes to her*) Looks like he's scared he'll crack his jaw if he opens his front teeth.

MRS. THOMPSON (*Moves to table*): You smell like a toper, Mr. Thompson.

THOMPSON: Well, I'm sorry—but I just had one little toddy—would have been impolite not to.

MRS. THOMPSON: Drunkenness can lead to lies and violence. I wouldn't want to live with either.

THOMPSON: I'm sorry, Ellie. It'll never happen again.

MRS. THOMPSON: Perhaps you could get one of the boys to bring me in an extra load of firewood. I'm thinking about baking tomorrow.

THOMPSON: I'll get it—I'll get it!

He exits.

INTERIOR—PORCH   EVENING

THOMPSON ENTERS THE PORCH, throws a Sen-Sen package into the corner, then crosses to the pump.

ARTHUR AND HERBERT ENTER FROM THE YARD, pounce on the Sen-Sen package.

> HERBERT: What's in it?
>
> ARTHUR: Clean breathers—you drink whiskey, then chew 'em.
>
> THOMPSON (*Crosses to them*): Give that to me! Now both you boys go get some wood! No—wait a minute. I'll get the wood. You get washed up for supper!

The boys mimic their father:

> ARTHUR: "You get washed up for supper."

They go to the water pump.

DISSOLVE TO:

INTERIOR—KITCHEN   DAY

MRS. THOMPSON AT STOVE in apron; boys seated on bench at table. Thompson enters.

> MRS. THOMPSON (*Crossing to table with platter*): Arthur, call Mr. Helton for supper.
>
> ARTHUR: Saaayy—Helton! Supper's ready—you big Swede.
>
> MRS. THOMPSON: That's no way to act! Now you go out there and ask him decent.

She takes off her apron. Arthur looks at the front porch:

HELTON AT THE DOOR.

> THOMPSON: Come on in, Mr. Helton. Sit right there.

Helton sits opposite the boys. Mrs. Thompson sits.

> MRS. THOMPSON: Lord, for all these, and thy other blessings, we thank thee, in Jesus' name. Amen.
>
> THOMPSON: Amen.

They all start to eat.

> THOMPSON: Well, Helton, what do you think about the weather? Is it going to rain or is it going to snow?—or are we just going to dry up and blow away?

Mr. and Mrs. Thompson exchange looks and continue eating.

> THOMPSON: Funniest thing you ever saw, happened today. Old Judge Sims has a beer-drinking goat, and they poured so much into him that he butted the mayor, then whirled around, and watered the square to the point where they had to call out the shovel brigade to stop the flood from washing out Franklin's Mercantile.

Thompson laughs.

ARTHUR: Last time you said it was the Courthouse that was hit by the flood.

THOMPSON: That was a different day.

ARTHUR: And maybe a different goat.

Arthur looks at his father and they laugh.

MRS. THOMPSON: Mr. Helton, you're not eating enough to keep you up to your full powers, if you expect to go on working the way you started today.

Helton hesitates, wipes his plate up clean with a piece of bread, stuffs his mouth full, and moves toward the door.

MRS. THOMPSON: Good night, Mr. Helton. (*Rises*)

HELTON (*From porch*): Good night.

ARTHUR: Gude not.

HERBERT: Gude not!

Mrs. Thompson tries to hush them.

ARTHUR: You don't do it right. Now listen to me. Guude Nottt.

The boys laugh.

MRS. THOMPSON: Now you stop that! He can't help the way he talks. (*Sits*) You ought to be ashamed of yourselves, both of you, making fun of a poor stranger like that. How would you like to be a stranger in a strange land?

HERBERT: I'd like it. I think it'd be fun.

THOMPSON: That's enough. (*To Herbert*) You're going to get sent to school next year, Herbert. That'll knock some sense into you!

HERBERT: I'm going to get sent to the 'formatory. That'll knock some sense into me!

THOMPSON: Oh? Who says so?

HERBERT: Sunday School teacher.

The boys laugh.

THOMPSON: Get to bed, you two. Get now—before I take the hide off you!

The boys exit.

MRS. THOMPSON: It's no use picking on them when they're so young and tender. I can't stand it.

THOMPSON: My goodness, Ellie—I wasn't picking on them.

MRS. THOMPSON (*Rises*): As a teacher I learned that yelling and pounding and violence do not help a child develop good manners and propriety.

THOMPSON: Yes'm.

MRS. THOMPSON (*Crosses to sink*): I hope Mr. Helton will be a good example for them, even if he can't be made to talk.

She goes to the table.

> MRS. THOMPSON: To tell you the truth, I think it's a mighty good change to have a man around the place who knows how to work and keep his mouth shut.
>
> THOMPSON: Means you can do all the talking, eh?
>
> MRS. THOMPSON: Means he'll keep out of our business. Not that we've got anything to hide. (*Gets her apron*) Only thing is though, he don't eat hardly enough to suit me. Like my grandma used to say, it's no use putting dependence on a man who won't sit down and make out his dinner.
>
> THOMPSON: To tell you the truth, Ellie, I always thought your grandma was a terrible old fool. She'd just say the first thing that popped into her head and call it God's wisdom.
>
> MRS. THOMPSON (*Clearing the table*): My grandma wasn't anybody's old fool. She knew what she was talking about when she said, the first thing you think is the best thing you can say.
>
> THOMPSON: Oh, really? (*Rises*) Well, suppose you just try speaking out—(*Crosses to her*) in mixed company the first thing you think. Suppose you happen to be in church thinking about a hen and a rooster, eh? I reckon you'd shock Brother Martin right off the pulpit.

He pinches her rump.

> THOMPSON (*Sits*): No more meat on you than a rabbit. Now I like 'em cornfed.
>
> MRS. THOMPSON: Mr. Thompson—sometimes I think you're the evilest-minded man that ever lived.

She pulls his hair

> MRS. THOMPSON: That's to show you how it feels, pinching so hard when you're supposed to be playing.

He hugs her.

DISSOLVE TO:

EXTERIOR/INTERIOR—FARM   DAY

MONTAGES—ANGLES OF:

HELTON WORKING—Plowing, milling, hoeing, moving, gathering eggs, cutting wood, cleaning up trash, building fences, slopping pigs, etc.

THOMPSON IS SOMETIMES WITH HIM, watching, commenting—seldom helping out. Mrs. Thompson spends a great deal of time watching them.

> THOMPSON'S VOICE, OVER THE ABOVE ANGLES: I guess one of my problems has been that I have a deep conviction that running a dairy, and chasing after chickens, is woman's work. I'm probably wrong, but that's my feeling and I'm stuck with it. I can plow a furrow, cut sorghum, shuck corn, handle the team,

build a corn crib as well as any man. But slopping hogs . . .
slopping hogs is not for Royal Earle Thompson . . . and
cows! Cows! Coming up twice a day to be milked, standing
there sadeyed . . . and them calves.

Pull at that rope till their eyes pop out, and still they break
their necks trying to get at the teat. Now I don't change the di-
apers on my kids, so why should I try to wean a calf?

And chickens—cackling, clucking, hatching out, always in the
wrong places . . . Getting stepped on by the livestock, those
that ain't already dying of the roup and wry-neck . . .

INTERIOR—*SPRING HOUSE   DAY*
HELTON IS SEPARATING *the butter from the milk and forming it into moulds.*
Thompson is sitting and watching him, chewing his tobacco.

THOMPSON (*Rises*): Buying and selling—that I can do. (*Crosses to
Helton*) Why, you know that I can take this fresh butter and
the eggs and the fruits in their proper season and I do a right
smart job of selling. That's a man's work. So this next year you
just keep working like you been, while I just keep on running
the place like I been.

HELTON: That's all right. I'm a good worker.

THOMPSON: That you are—and I'm going to raise you to ten dollars a month.

HELTON: That's good.

Thompson exits.

DISSOLVE TO:

EXTERIOR—*PIG PEN   DAY*
THE BOYS ARE SHOVELING *manure into a wheelbarrow. Helton works beside
them.*

MRS. THOMPSON CROSSES TO FENCE, *carrying a garden basket.*

MRS. THOMPSON: It's a beautiful day. You boys go and play until
lunch time.

*The boys drop their pitchforks and run off, whooping and hollering and mak-
ing faces at Helton.*

MRS. THOMPSON: Mr. Helton, you know that my husband and I
are both pleased with your work these past years . . .

He doesn't react.

MRS. THOMPSON: Well, sometimes, Mr. Helton, I do believe that
you have a grudge against the world and I sometimes don't
know what to make of it—but I feel it is not Christian of me
not to ask you to hear Brother Martin at the Mountain Baptist

Church, and I want to extend an invitation and tell you how
happy we would be if you would join us next Sunday.

Helton stares, leaning on his pitchfork.

HELTON: I got work!

*Turning from her, he goes back to work. Mrs. Thompson hesitates a moment
and then walks away.*

THE BOYS FOOLING AROUND HELTON'S SHACK *watch her, then duck inside.*

INTERIOR—HELTON'S SHACK   DAY
THE BOYS *are in the shack.*

DISSOLVE TO:

INTERIOR—PANTRY   DAY
MRS. THOMPSON AT THE WINDOW. *She stops, looking off at:*

EXTERIOR—YARD   DAY
HELTON, STANDING NEAR HIS SHACK, *shakes Arthur. Beside him, Herbert
stands meekly.*

EXTERIOR—PANTRY   DAY
MRS. THOMPSON TURNS, *starts toward the door, as . . .*

EXTERIOR—YARD   DAY
HELTON DROPS ARTHUR, *grabs Herbert and shakes him.*

EXTERIOR—PORCH   DAY
MRS. THOMPSON STEPS TO THE DOOR, *stops, and steps back inside as Helton
lets her youngest go. The boys run for the house.*

INTERIOR—PORCH AND KITCHEN   DAY
THE BOYS BURST THROUGH *the door, past their mother.*

MRS. THOMPSON: What were you doing?

THE BOYS (*Exchanging looks*): Nothing.

MRS. THOMPSON: Nothing now, you mean . . . (*Then*) Well, I have
plenty for you to do. (*Crosses in*) And so will your father when
he hears about this.

DISSOLVE TO:

INTERIOR—HELTON'S SHACK   NIGHT
THOMPSON IS LISTENING TO HELTON *who has two harmonicas in his hands.*

HELTON: Your boys—play, make game with—(*Extends the harmonicas*) Not for games or plaything! For music—my music—
no good now!

He throws them on the floor, takes three others.

HELTON: This—these belong Olaf Helton—for music!
Mr. Thompson picks up the harmonicas, exits.

INTERIOR—KITCHEN NIGHT
THE BOYS SEATED ON BENCH. Mrs. Thompson in apron at stove, crosses to
table with cornbread.
THOMPSON ENTERS, SLAMS DOOR, and stands looking at boys.

THOMPSON: He said they'd been fooling with his harmonicas,
Ellie. Blowing in them and getting them full of spit and dirt
and they don't play good!

MRS. THOMPSON: Now we've got to do something so they'll always
remember they shouldn't ever go into Mr. Helton's things.

THOMPSON (*Crosses in*): I'll do something—I'll tan their hides for
them! I'll take a calf rope to them if they don't look out.

MRS. THOMPSON: You had better leave the whipping to me, Mr.
Thompson. You haven't got a light hand enough for children.

THOMPSON: That's just what's the trouble with them now. Rotten
spoiled! Botherin' Mr. Helton—who never done nothing but
help—help all of us!

Mrs. Thompson goes to the stove.

THOMPSON: I'd knock them down with a stick or stone—anything
that came to hand!

MRS. THOMPSON (*Turns to him*): I don't hold with that way of raising children, Mr. Thompson, and you know it.

THOMPSON (*Crosses around table*): Well, now what have you got to
say for yourselves?!

Silence from the boys.

THOMPSON: I ought to break your ribs and I've got a good mind to
do it!

MRS. THOMPSON (*Goes to the boys*): Mr. Thompson—

Silence from the boys.

THOMPSON (*Sits*): A boy fifteen years old acting like he's five—
that's what you're doing. You know that, don't you?

ARTHUR: Yes, sir.

THOMPSON: The next time I catch either one of you hanging
around Mr. Helton's shack, I'm going to take the hide off both
of you.

THE BOYS: Yes, sir.

Mrs. Thompson crosses to the table and sits.
The parents stare at the boys. Boys are eating, look at their mother, look at
their father, look down.
The parents start eating.

Peter Robbins, Olivia de Havilland, Steve Sanders, and
Jason Robards, Jr., in *Noon Wine*.

THOMPSON: They're so mean and ornery that it's a wonder he
   don't just kill them off and be done with it.
The boys look at each other, start eating again.
   MRS. THOMPSON: Mr. Helton hasn't come for his supper. Arthur,
   go tell Mr. Helton he's late for supper.
Arthur looks at his father, rises, and crosses to the door.
   MRS. THOMPSON: And you tell him nice, now.
Arthur exits.

INTERIOR—THE SHACK   NIGHT
*HELTON SITS AT A SMALL TABLE, the light of the lamp yellowing the two har-
monicas on the table in front of him. There is a knock on the door and he
turns slowly.*
Arthur steps into the doorway.
   ARTHUR: Supper is ready, Mr. Helton——
Helton doesn't answer.
   ARTHUR: Mother would like you to come and eat now if you wish,
   and so would father . . .
Helton stares at him.
   ARTHUR: ——and so would Herbert—and so would I.
Helton looks at him, then at his harmonicas. Finally he nods.
Arthur exits.
*Helton sits for a moment longer, listening to the boy's footsteps. He starts to
pick up the harmonicas, stops, and blows out the lamp.*

FADE OUT.

ACT TWO

FADE IN:
EXTERIOR—FARM   DAY
MONTAGE:
HELTON LOADING CHEESE ON WAGON, *Thompson watching.*
BOYS WORKING *in corn patch, Helton working beside them.*
MRS. THOMPSON WATCHING HELTON *paint the house.*
HELTON CARRYING SUCKLING PIGS *to the wagon.*
THOMPSON SHOWING OFF *his new salt-and-pepper suit.*
HELTON—HAIR, FACE, AND SHIRT SWEATY—*chopping wood.*
                    DISSOLVE TO:
EXTERIOR—SPRING HOUSE   DAY

THOMPSON SITTING UNDER TREE.
HATCH DRIVES UP in his rig.
HATCH SURVEYS the farm.
THOMPSON WATCHES HIM.

HATCH: Is this Mr. Thompson—Mr. Royal Earle Thompson?

THOMPSON: That's my name.

HATCH: My name is Hatch, Mr. Homer T. Hatch, and I've come to see you about buying a horse.

THOMPSON: Well, I'm afraid you've been misdirected. I haven't got a horse for sale. Usually if I have anything like that to sell I tell the neighbors and tack up a little sign on the gate.

Hatch laughs and crosses to him.

HATCH: I always say something like that when I'm calling on a stranger because I've noticed that when a fellow says he has come to buy something, nobody takes him for a suspicious character. (*Sits, laughs*)

THOMPSON: Well, that's all lost on me because I never take a man for a suspicious character until he shows himself to be one. Until that happens, one man is as good as another as far as I'm concerned.

HATCH: Well, I ain't come neither to buy nor to sell. The fact is, I want to have a little talk with you and it won't cost you a cent. Yes, sir, Homer T. Hatch is my name and America is my nation. I reckon you must know my name.

THOMPSON: No—don't think I know the name—

HATCH: Don't know the old Hatch family? Well, we came over from Georgia fifty years ago. Been here long yourself?

THOMPSON: Just my whole life and my pa and grandpa before me. Grandpap emigrated in 1836.

HATCH: From Ireland, I reckon?

THOMPSON: From Pennsylvania! What makes you think we came from Ireland?

HATCH (*Laughs*): What I always say is that a fellow's got to come from somewhere, ain't he?

THOMPSON: What I always say is that this is the slack season and we're laying around a little. Nonetheless, we have our chores to do—(*Puts his feet up and works the churn*)—and I don't want to hurry you, but if you've come to see me on business, maybe we'd better get down to it.

HATCH: I'm looking for a man named Helton, Mr. Olaf Helton from North Dakota. And I was told I might find him here.

THOMPSON: Well, Mr. Helton is right here and he's been here now going on better than three years. He's a mighty steady man and you can tell anybody I said so.

Hatch laughs.

THOMPSON: If you want to speak to Mr. Helton now, I'll round him up. (*Rises*)

HATCH (*Stops him*): I'm in no special hurry.

Then from around the house comes the music of Helton's HARMONICA.

HATCH (*Rises*): I know that tune like I know the palm of my hand. (*Crosses around tree*) That's a kind of Skandahoovian song—it says something about starting out in the morning feeling so good you can't hardly stand it, so you drink all your likker before noon. All the likker, understand, that you was saving for the noon layoff. The words ain't much, but I understand it's a pretty tune. It's a kind of drinking song.

THOMPSON: Well, he's been playing that same tune off and on for better than three years right here on the place.

HATCH (*Laughing*): And he was certainly singin' it as well ten years before that in North Dakota. He used to sit up in a straitjacket and sing it when he was in the asylum—in a strait-jacket—couldn't hold no harmonica then.

Mrs. Thompson enters the yard from the house, in background.

THOMPSON (*Turns to him*): What's that you say?—what's that?

HATCH (*Facing him*): Why shucks, I didn't mean to tell you.

THOMPSON: You mean to tell me they had him in a straitjacket? In a lunatic asylum?

HATCH: They sure did. That's right where they had him from time to time. In that white jacket, and he was perfectly content so far as you could see, singing that song of his.

They both sit.

HATCH: Then one night he just disappeared, left, you might say—went. (*Laughing*) And here he is—all settled down and playing the same song.

THOMPSON: Well, he never acted crazy to me. He always acted like a sensible man. He never got married for one thing, and he works like a horse. Saves his money and he don't drink or swear. If he's crazy, why I think I'll go crazy myself for a change.

HATCH: That's good! I hadn't thought of it just like that. Let's all go crazy and get rid of our wives and save our money, huh?

THOMPSON (*Rises*): No, that ain't exactly what I had in mind . . . Let's move around to the back—there's more breeze there.

Hatch rises and follows him, with Mrs. Thompson watching them.

They cross around the house to the back yard. Mrs. Thompson goes into the house.

THOMPSON: What I meant was that my wife's been kind of an invalid now, going on for almost fourteen years. It's mighty tough on a poor man having a sickness in the family. (*Almost proudly*) She had four operations, one right after the other. They didn't do no good—she's a mighty delicate woman. She's got trouble with her eyes, too.

HATCH: My old woman had a back like a mule, could have moved the barn with her bare hands if she took the notion. I never had much for a woman always complaining. I'd get rid of her mighty quick. It's just as you say, a dead loss keeping one up.

THOMPSON (*Crosses to stump*): Well, that's not really what I had in mind. You see—well, my wife's a mighty reasonable woman, but I wouldn't answer to what she would do if she found out we'd had a lunatic on the place all this time.

Hatch laughs.

THOMPSON: I might have got upset myself at such a thing once, living with a lunatic, but now I defy anything to get me lathered up! (*Sits*)

Hatch offers him a tobacco plug. They exchange plugs, chew, and return their plugs.

HATCH (*Sits*): Amazing how different two men's ideas of good chewing tobacco are—for instance, mine is lighter colored because there isn't any sweetener in this plug.

THOMPSON: Well . . . a little sweetener don't do no harm as far as I'm concerned, but it's got to be mighty little. A man near here named Williams, John Morgan Williams, who chews a plug, well, sir, it's as black as your hat and as soft as melted tar and fairly drips with molasses. I don't call that a good chew.

HATCH: Such a chew would simply gag me. I couldn't begin to put it in my mouth.

THOMPSON: Well, I just barely tasted it myself as you might say. I took a little piece in my mouth and spit it out again.

HATCH: I'm dead sure I couldn't even get that far. I like a dry natural chew without any artificial flavoring of any kind! Artificial flavoring is just put in to cover up a cheap leaf and make a man think he's getting something more than he is getting. Even a little sweetening is a sign of a cheap leaf.

THOMPSON: I've always paid a good price for my plug! I'm not a rich man and I don't go around setting myself up for one, but

I'll say this—when it comes to such things as tobacco, I buy the best on the market!

HATCH: Sweetening, even a little, is a sign of—

THOMPSON (*Rises*): About this Mr. Helton, I don't see any reason holding it against a man because he went looney once or twice in his lifetime, and so I don't expect to take no steps about it, not a step.

HATCH: I suppose there's some people who would just as soon have a loonatic around their house as not. But back home in North Dakota we don't feel that way. I like to as seen anybody hiring a loonatic there—especially after what he done!

THOMPSON: "After what he done." (*Crosses up; turns to Hatch*) "After what he done"? . . .

HATCH: Oh, nothing to speak of, just went looney one day in the hay field and shoved a pitchfork right square through his brother when they was making hay. That's all he done. Nothing to get lathered up about.

THOMPSON (*Crosses in*): Well, I don't deny that's news. Yes, sir, news. (*Sits*) But I still say something must have drove him to it.

HATCH: His brother was going to get married. He borrowed Helton's harmonica to give his bride a serenade one evening and lost it, a brand new harmonica. Brother wouldn't buy him a new one, so Mr. Helton just ups, as I says, and runs his pitchfork through his brother.

THOMPSON: Well, he does think a heap of his harmonicas.

They listen to Helton's harmonica.

HATCH: I like that part about getting up so gay you just go ahead and drink up all the likker you got on hand before noon— (*Turns to him*)—in those Swede countries a man carries a bottle of wine around with him as a matter of course.

Thompson rises and crosses up.

HATCH: The fact is, this Helton here is a dangerous escaped loonatic, and the fact is, last twelve years or so I musta rounded up twenty-odd escaped loonatics, amounts to quite a little sum in the long run—the reward—but that ain't the point. (*Rises and goes to him*) The point is, I'm for law and order—I don't like to see law breakers and loonatics at large. You agree?

THOMPSON: Well, circumstances alters cases, as the feller says, and now what I know of Mr. Helton, he ain't dangerous, as I told you. (*Sits*)

HATCH: He ain't? Well I say he is and the law is solidly behind me!

Hatch picks up an axe and chops wood.

HATCH: I might never have caught him, 'cept about two weeks ago his old mother gets a letter and in that letter was a check on an old bank in town for four hundred fifty dollars. Said he was sending her a few little savings just like that . . . Well, naturally with that check to cash and everything, I come to know. (*Chops*) You could have knocked me down with a feather.

THOMPSON: Yeah, well, that must have been a surprise all right.

Hatch crosses with chopped wood.

HATCH: Yes, siree, well the old woman . . . half blind now, was all for taking the first train out, but I put it up to her square how she was too feeble, so I'd do it—for my expenses—and bring her back all the news about her son . . . She gave me a new shirt she had made and a big Swedish cake to bring him but I must have mislaid them along the road somewhere. (*Laughing*) It don't really matter, though. I'll bet he ain't in any state of mind to appreciate them.

THOMPSON (*Rises*): And now, what are you aimin' to do? That's the question.

Hatch sinks the axe home in a log, takes out handcuffs, and crosses to Thompson.

HATCH: Well, I came prepared for a little scuffle but I don't want no violence if I can help it. I figure the two of us could overpower him.

THOMPSON (*Moves away*): Well, I want to tell you I think you've got a mighty sorry job on your hands. You sure must be hard up for something to do and now I want to give you a good piece of advice. You just drop the idea that you're going to come here and make trouble for Mr. Helton. The quicker you drive that hired rig away from our front gate, the better I'll be satisfied.

HATCH: Now just a minute! Maybe you'd like it better if I looked for help to your neighbors, 'cause you're set on harb'ring an escaped loonatic who killed his own brother.

THOMPSON (*Crosses up*): But I've been trying to tell you all along the man ain't looney now! He's been with us for near four years. He's been like one of the family, the best standby a man ever had. (*Turns to Hatch*) You're crazy, you're crazier than he ever was. You get off this place or I'll handcuff you and turn

you over to the law. You're trespassing! Get out of here before
I knock you down!!

HATCH: Try it, try it, go ahead.

Thompson steps forward—the sun hot in his eyes, then hesitates, looking at:
THE LONG BOWIE KNIFE *in Hatch's hand, its point held forward—then next
to his own leg Thompson sees:*
THE AXE, ITS BLADE SUNK DEEP IN THE LOG; *then he turns as:*
HELTON COMES AROUND THE CORNER OF THE HOUSE *on the run, then as if
seeing Hatch for the first time he stops.*
HATCH DRIVES AT HIM, *the knife in one hand, the handcuffs in the other, the
blade going toward Helton's stomach—and then the axe is out of the log, in
Thompson's hand, his arms coming over his head as he steps forward—the
flat of the axe swinging toward Hatch.*

INTERIOR—PORCH   DAY
MRS. THOMPSON STEPS ONTO THE PORCH THEN STOPS, *hearing a* SOLID
CHUNK. *She hesitates for a brief moment, then exits the porch.*

EXTERIOR—YARD   DAY
HELTON RUNS OUT OF THE YARD *into the field, running stooped down.
Mrs. Thompson moves around a corner of the house watching him, then
turns and looks at:*
THOMPSON, SUPPORTING HIMSELF *by leaning on the axe handle, shaking
Hatch by the shoulder. Hatch is doubled up on the ground, with the blood on
the ground beneath him.*
Thompson, without taking his hand from the man's shoulder, turns:

THOMPSON: He killed Mr. Helton, I saw him do it. I had to knock
him out, but he won't come to!

MRS. THOMPSON: Why—yonder goes Mr. Helton.

She points.
Thompson pulls himself up and looks at:
HELTON—RUNNING ACROSS THE FIELD.
MRS. THOMPSON SITS AGAINST THE SIDE OF THE HOUSE *and slowly begins to
slide forward on her face.*

MRS. THOMPSON: The boys are fishing. Fishing at Halifax. Thank
God the boys are not here.

*Thompson stares at her as the distant figure of Helton disappears beyond the
field. Then he looks at the dead man at his feet as we:*

FADE OUT.

ACT THREE

FADE IN:
EXTERIOR—COUNTRY ROAD   DAY
*THOMPSON AND SHERIFF BARBEE RIDE UP the road toward the farm, followed
by the coroner in a wagon driven by a deputy.*
> BARBEE: How'd your missus take it——
> THOMPSON: She took it hard.
> BARBEE: Damndest thing I ever heard of. That Hatch fella coming
> better'n fifteen hundred miles to settle a score with your hired
> man . . . what's his name . . .
> THOMPSON: Helton——
> BARBEE: You sure he got him?
> THOMPSON: He got him. He put that blade right up in Helton's
> stomach then sliced up—couldn't have run far hurt like that.
> BARBEE: Well, we'll find him—alive or dead. I've got half the
> county looking for him right now.

Then Barbee follows Thompson's glance at:
MRS. THOMPSON SITTING ON A LOG. Thompson pulls up, turns to the sheriff.
> THOMPSON: Sheriff, I'd appreciate it if you'd just ride on with the
> others. You'll find him next to the wood pile. I'll just take my
> missus with me and follow along.
> BARBEE: Why can't she just ride in the wagon with the coroner?
> THOMPSON: Well, if it's all the same to you, I'd just as soon she
> went with me.

*Thompson pulls to one side. The sheriff rides on past, followed by the coroner
and the deputy.*
*Mrs. Thompson, wearing her smoked glasses, looks up as they pass. Thomp-
son steps off his horse, crosses, takes her hand.*
> THOMPSON: Come on, Ellie, we're going home.

Mrs. Thompson rises.
> MRS. THOMPSON: How's Mr. Helton?
> THOMPSON: They ain't found him yet.
> MRS. THOMPSON (*Moves*): ——I hope they never do.
> THOMPSON (*Follows*): It don't make any difference, Ellie. He's hurt
> so bad it don't make any difference.
> MRS. THOMPSON: Poor man, a stranger in a strange land.
> THOMPSON: Ellie, there's something I've got to mention to you.
> When the Sheriff asks you, I want you to tell him you saw it
> happen. You saw him jump Mr. Helton with the knife and you
> saw me—(*Turns to her*) I want you to say that you saw me de-
> fend Mr. Helton's life.

MRS. THOMPSON: You're asking me to tell a lie, Mr. Thompson.

THOMPSON: Well, it ain't a lie. That's what I did do. If I'd just moved a little quicker, I might have saved his life. (*Crosses to horse*) Damn man coming in to cause trouble and murder.

MRS. THOMPSON: But he didn't do murder . . .

THOMPSON (*Going to her*): Well, do you think I did?

Mrs. Thompson turns away.

THOMPSON (*Turns her to him*): Ellie, you answer me——

MRS. THOMPSON: I will say what you want me to, Mr. Thompson. But I will tell a lie for I didn't see it happen. I saw him lying on the ground and you with the axe and Mr. Helton running. But I'll say what you want me to. I'll lie if that's what you want me to do.

THOMPSON: It's not what I want you to do—it's what you have to do. (*Then*) But it ain't a lie!

She turns and walks up the road toward the farm.

MRS. THOMPSON: What is it exactly you want me to say, Mr. Thompson?

He tries to catch up.

DISSOLVE TO:

EXTERIOR—THOMPSON YARD   DAY

MR. AND MRS. THOMPSON AND THE SHERIFF *stand in the middle of the yard as the coroner and the deputy cover Hatch's body with a tarp and carry it to the wagon.*

MRS. THOMPSON: . . . That's what I saw, Sheriff. Mr. Hatch moving with the knife, then Mr. Helton stepped in front of Mr. Thompson and as he did, Mr. Thompson took the axe and tried to stop him from hurting anybody.

BARBEE: That's good enough for me, Missus Thompson. I don't see no reason to take your husband in. It looks like a clear case of self-defense. But there will have to be a trial.

Hatch's body drops into the wagon.

MRS. THOMPSON: Why will Mr. Thompson be tried? If it's self-defense?

BARBEE: There's always got to be a trial in a case like this, Missus Thompson. In a case where there is a killing.

MRS. THOMPSON: He will be tried then—for killing?

BARBEE: He'll be tried for murder, Missus Thompson—that's the law—that's what has to be.

Mrs. Thompson crosses to Sheriff Barbee.

MRS. THOMPSON: You tell me when you find Mr. Helton—you hear? Tell me how he is. I want to know.

Jason Robards, Jr., and Olivia de Havilland in *Noon Wine*.

She goes into the house.
Thompson turns to the sheriff.
THOMPSON: It's hard on a woman.
BARBEE: Yeah, a killing always is——
Arthur and Herbert, motionless against the wall of the house, look at their father silently. . . . Thompson hesitates, turns, and moves away toward the barn.

EXTERIOR—MONTAGE   DAY-TO-NIGHT
A SERIES OF ANGLES:
HELTON RUNNING THROUGH FIELDS, UP A MOUNTAIN, DIVING UNDER A FENCE, RACING THROUGH TREES

EXTERIOR—WOODED AREA   NIGHT
HELTON SLEEPS EXHAUSTED, against the side of an old barn. Apparently he had eluded the posse; then he sits up, crouching, as a ring of twenty or thirty men (some carrying torches) slowly move toward him. He stands, picks up rocks, throws them—driving the men back; then:
BARBEE AND FOUR OR FIVE DEPUTIES rush him. He fights savagely, picking up a club, knocking two or three deputies down. Others jump him, but for a moment it appears he is going to break loose. Then a clutching hand tears his clothes and:
TWO HARMONICAS FALL ON THE GROUND. As he bends to pick them up, he is grabbed, handcuffed by one wrist. Then he suddenly breaks away and lashes out, and a posse member, hit by the swinging cuffs, drops. Then:
A FARMER, MC CLELLAN, SWINGS HIS RIFLE in an arc and it catches Helton in the back of the head. He staggers forward, straightens, cries out, his eyes blind and weeping in the night, then crumples.
BARBEE'S VOICE, OVER THE ABOVE SHOTS: He acted like a mad dog. We didn't mean to harm him, but he was crazy as a loon. He picked up rocks and tried to brain every man who got near him. Then he came after us with a club and after we finally got a handcuff on him, he almost killed a man with it. We had to be rough, Mrs. Thompson . . .

EXTERIOR—YARD   DAY
MRS. THOMPSON IN ROBE AND THOMPSON IN PANTS AND LONG-JOHN TOP are listening to Sheriff Barbee, who is on horseback.
BARBEE: . . . Nobody likes killing a looney, but we got to protect ourselves.
Mrs. Thompson doesn't answer.

BARBEE: Well, you asked me personal to tell you what happened, Mrs. Thompson, so I did—that's how it happened.

MRS. THOMPSON: I thank you, Mr. Barbee. (*Crosses up*)

THOMPSON: But I can't understand how a man that badly cut could do all them things——

BARBEE: Well, he wasn't cut. There wasn't a mark on him, 'cept where his head was broke.

Mrs. Thompson turns back.

MRS. THOMPSON: What did you say?

BARBEE: I said there was a mark on his head, but there was no sign of any cut anywheres on his body.

Mrs. Thompson crosses back down.

THOMPSON: But—I saw the knife . . . (*Then*) You see, I was there.

BARBEE: Well, I know you was there, Thompson, but it don't make no difference what you saw—there wasn't no marks on that man's body of any knife.

Thompson sits.

BARBEE: Have you got yourself a lawyer yet?

THOMPSON: No.

BARBEE (*Turns to go*): Well, I'd give that some thought if I was you.

He leaves.

Mrs. Thompson moves to the house.

INTERIOR—LAWYER BURLEIGH'S OFFICE   DAY
BURLEIGH SEATED, THOMPSON PACING.
Burleigh rises and crosses to him.

BURLEIGH: Now you keep calm, cool, and collected. Your wife can sit in court and she'll be a powerful argument with the jury. You just plead not guilty and I'll do the rest.

THOMPSON: But you don't understand, Mr. Burleigh.

BURLEIGH: Mr. Thompson, sit down.

Thompson sits.

Burleigh goes to him.

BURLEIGH: I understand that stranger hadn't any right to come to your house on such an errand! (*Sits on desk*) Why that wasn't even manslaughter you committed, so now you just hold your horses and keep your shirt on. And don't say one word without I tell you to! You just remember, Mr. Hatch came down to settle an old score with Helton, a personal score as far as you knew. You didn't know nothing about Helton being crazy all along. Just remember you don't say nothing less I tell you.

You just answer "yes" or "no." You understand, Mr. Thompson?

THOMPSON: Yes.

Burleigh leads him to the door.

THOMPSON: But you see, Mr. Burleigh, I never even thought of killing anybody, much less Mr. Hatch. They tell me there was no knife mark . . . not a scratch anywhere——

BURLEIGH: Well, those things happen. Maybe it looked that way to you 'cause of the way he was standing——

THOMPSON: Maybe . . .

Burleigh closes the door.

INTERIOR—COURTROOM DAY

THE TRIAL IS OVER. SPECTATORS ARE LEAVING.

The Thompson family is standing at the defense table.

Two more people, MRS. HECTHORN and MAN, come up to the Thompsons.

MRS. HECTHORN: You did fine, Ellie—just what you had to do.

MAN: Worked out well, Royal Earle.

They leave.

MRS. BERTHA NORD turns at the door and shouts at Thompson.

MRS. NORD: I don't care what the jury said——. My brother was a lawman who came down to take an escaped looney back to the booby hatch. (*Pointing to Thompson*) And that man killed him because he didn't want to spoil a good thing. He didn't want to lose a poor fool who did a hundred dollars' worth of work every month for less than ten.

The deputy hurries her out the door.

Thompson sees Burleigh crossing to the door.

Thompson goes to him.

THOMPSON: Hold up there, Burleigh—you did fine, but you know I never had a chance to talk . . . You know—like the man says—I never even had a chance to explain what happened . . . and I remembered while the jury was out—some things that had slipped from my mind before. (*Then*) You see, I don't think the people ever understood what an ornery little louse that Mr. Hatch was . . .

BURLEIGH: I don't think we have to worry about that anymore.

THOMPSON: Well—I should come down to see you tomorrow—sort of explain what really happened.

BURLEIGH: Mr. Thompson, you got off just like I predicted, didn't you?

THOMPSON: Why—yes, sir, I did, and I surely thank you for all your help—but——

BURLEIGH: Well then, you just send me your check, Mr. Thompson . . . I don't think we need to talk further about the matter!

He exits. Mrs. Thompson and the boys cross to door.

THOMPSON: Hold up there, boys. I want you to be up early in the morning. I want old Jim hitched to the buggy by six o'clock.

MRS. THOMPSON: What on earth for——?

THOMPSON: Because we're going to see every one of our neighbors, and we're going to tell them the truth. (*Crosses down*) They never let me talk at this trial. They just asked me questions and I just answered "yes" or "no." I never did get to the core of the matter. But I'm going to start tomorrow. (*Goes to her*) I want you there with me, Ellie. I want you to tell them what you saw.

MRS. THOMPSON: Just as you say, Mr. Thompson.

She exits. The boys follow. THE CAMERA HOLDS ON THOMPSON.

FADE OUT.

ACT FOUR

FADE IN:

EXTERIOR/INTERIOR—MONTAGE   DAY/NIGHT

A SERIES OF ANGLES AS THE THOMPSONS VISIT THEIR NEIGHBORS.

THOMPSON: Now—I never killed Mr. Hatch on purpose.

ALLEN: Pleased to hear that.

MRS. ALLEN: We knew it.

THOMPSON: I was trying to save Mr. Helton's life.

HECTHORN: Of course, only thing you could do, Thompson.

THOMPSON: But I never had a chance to tell it at the trial.

MRS. HECTHORN: What a shame.

THOMPSON: If you don't believe me, you can always believe my wife. She won't lie.

MRS. THOMPSON: That's right. I saw it—it's just as he says . . . that's right.

MRS. HECTHORN: It must be terrible for you, Ellie.

HECTHORN: You're a brave woman, Mrs. Thompson.

MRS. PETTITT: Thank you for stopping by.

THOMPSON: No—I'm telling you the truth! You heard my wife! *Thompson lifts his fists, fighting air.*

EXTERIOR—THE MC CLELLAN YARD   DAY
MR. AND MRS. THOMPSON *in the buggy.*
Watching them is JIMMIE LEE.
THOMPSON: Is your Mamma and Papa at home?
The boy doesn't answer.
THOMPSON: Tell them Mr. and Mrs. Thompson want to see them.
The boy turns and shouts into the front door:
JIMMIE LEE: Momer—popper—come out hyeah . . . the man that kilt Hatch has come ter see yer.
The Thompsons look at the boy.
McCLELLAN steps out of the door.
MC CLELLAN: Light down, Missus Thompson. The old woman's washing, but she'll git here shortly.
Mrs. Thompson slowly descends from the buggy, crosses to the rocking chair on the porch, and sits.
Thompson follows.
MRS. McCLELLAN comes out of the house.
MC CLELLAN: These folks have come to pay us a visit.
Mrs. McClellan nods.
THOMPSON: Well, as I reckon you happen to know, I've had some strange troubles lately, and—as the feller says—it's not the kind of trouble that happens to a man every day in the year, and there's some things I don't want no misunderstanding about in my neighbors' minds, so——
Thompson almost hits McClellan as he turns.
THOMPSON: I killed that man Hatch in self-defense. I was trying to protect Mr. Helton. My wife will tell you. Ask my wife, she won't lie.
MRS. THOMPSON: It's true . . . I saw it . . . it's just as Mr. Thompson says.
MC CLELLAN (*Crossing to Thompson*): Well, now that sholy is too bad. But I kain't see what we've got to do with all this here, however. I kain't see no good reason for us to get mixed up in these murder matters. I shore kain't. Whichever way you look at it, it ain't none of my business . . . However, it's mighty nice of you-all to come around and give us the straight of it. Fur we've heerd some mighty queer yarns about it . . . mighty queer. I golly you couldn't hardly make head ner tail of it.

MRS. MC CLELLAN: Everybody goin' round shootin' their heads off!
But you better know we don't hold with killing. The Bible
says——
MC CLELLAN: You shet yer trap or I'll shet it fer yer—now it looks
to me——

Mrs. Thompson stands, crosses to the buggy.

MRS. THOMPSON: We mustn't linger—we've lingered too long now.
It's getting late, and we've got far to go.

*Thompson glares at the McClellans for a moment, then follows her, helps her
into the buggy.*
McClellan laughs softly—then his wife joins him, and . . .
*The Thompsons drive away in their buggy, listening, without expression, to
the laughter.*

MRS. THOMPSON: This finishes it, Mr. Thompson. I'm just not
going to do this anymore.
THOMPSON: But we've got to make people believe in the truth,
Ellie——
MRS. THOMPSON: Whose truth, Mr. Thompson? Don't you know—
don't you remember—how it was—with Mr. Helton. Don't
you know what he did for us— Don't you know how he managed things—so good. Did you know that, Mr. Thompson?
How he managed? . . . Why couldn't you argue with that
Hatch and get him off the place? Why did you have to ruin the
boys' lives and have Mr. Helton killed like some poor mad
dog?
THOMPSON: Well, Ellie, I keep hoping—I keep hoping you might
say, "I remember now, Mr. Thompson, I really did come
around the corner in time to see everything." I keep hoping
one day you'll quit saying it's a lie . . . For I—I truly trust to
God it is not.
MRS. THOMPSON: There was a time when I thought we had neighbors and friends; there was a time when I thought we could
hold up our heads. There was a time when my husband hadn't
killed a man and made me lie for him and I could tell the truth
to anybody about anything.
THOMPSON: Well—I'm sorry you feel that way about everything.
(*Trying to be strong*) But it's going to change, Ellie.
MRS. THOMPSON: I hope so, Mr. Thompson, but now life has become all one dread . . . (*Then, crying*) There's no place for me
to go. Oh, Sweet Jesus, I just don't know how to go on living
anymore . . .
THOMPSON: Now just don't you worry. Things will be all right.
We'll work it out, Ellie. We'll live with it, and we'll whip it!

He looks at her, trying to smile.

DISSOLVE TO:

INTERIOR—THOMPSON BEDROOM   MOONLIGHT

MR. AND MRS. THOMPSON LIE IN BED.

> THOMPSON'S VOICE: Maybe, everything about my killing that Hatch was wrong from start to finish—but dammit, I did—maybe not the right thing—but the only thing I could do . . .

SUPERIMPOSE: silent portions of the Hatch/Thompson scene.

> THOMPSON'S VOICE: But did I have to kill him? Well, by God, I never saw a man I hated more. When I first laid eyes on him, I knew in my bones that feller was just here for trouble . . . but why didn't I just tell that Hatch to get out before he ever got in? . . . Hell, why didn't I do a lot of things . . . ?

> THOMPSON (*Aloud*): You asleep, Ellie . . . ?

She doesn't move.

SUPERIMPOSE: more silent portions of the Hatch/Thompson scene.

> THOMPSON'S VOICE: All I had to do to get rid of him peacefully was to tell him—well, maybe I had to hit him—or just grab him and put those handcuffs on him and turn him over to the sheriff for disturbing the peace—maybe they'd have just locked him up—fined him a little something . . . what could I have said? (*Beat*) But what about that knife? (*Then*) No—but if I hadn't killed him, nothing would have happened to Mr. Helton . . . Oh, God——

SUPERIMPOSE: SHOTS of Helton and Thompson together.

> THOMPSON'S VOICE: Helton would be playing his tune right now . . . about feeling so good in the morning—about drinking up all the wine, so he'd feel even better . . . and that Hatch would be safe—in jail, maybe——

SUPERIMPOSE: scene that climaxes with the killing of Hatch.

> THOMPSON'S VOICE: Ready to listen to reason, maybe—and repent his meanness . . .

> THOMPSON (*Aloud*): . . . the dirty, yellow-livered hound—coming around . . .

He sits up.

> THOMPSON (*Aloud*): . . . ready to persecute an innocent man, ruining a whole family that never harmed him!

He gets out of bed, yelling.

Mrs. Thompson sits up—

> MRS. THOMPSON: Don't!—Don't! Don't! Don't!

> THOMPSON: Arthur! Herbert! Bring a light!

Thompson goes to her.

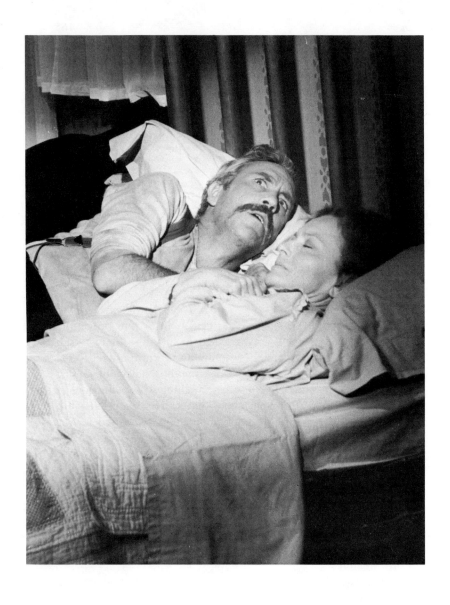

Jason Robards, Jr., and Olivia de Havilland in *Noon Wine*.

THOMPSON: Ellie! (*Shouts*) Get in here!
The boys rush in, Herbert with a lamp.
Arthur pushes his father out of the way.
ARTHUR: She's scared—she's scared to death! (*To his father*) What
did you do to her? (*Then*) You touch her again, and I'll blow
your heart out.
THOMPSON: Why, Arthur——
HERBERT: Ma! Mama, don't die!
MRS. THOMPSON (*Sitting up*): I'm all right. Now don't you worry
around, Herbert—I'm all right.
The boys glare at their father.
Thompson crosses to his clothes, starts dressing.
THOMPSON: Well, I reckon I'll just ride over and get the doctor.
Don't look like this fainting is a good sign. (*To the boys*) Now
you just keep watch till I get back . . . And don't get any no-
tions in your head—I never did your mother any harm in my
life, on purpose.
He goes to the door, looks back.
THOMPSON (*Trying to smile*): You know how to look after her.

INTERIOR—KITCHEN   NIGHT
*THOMPSON ENTERS THE KITCHEN, takes a thin pad of paper and a pencil
from the shelf where the boys keep their school books, picks up a lantern,
reaches in the cupboard and pulls out his shotgun, then walks out of the
house without looking back.*

INTERIOR—THE SPRING HOUSE   NIGHT
*THOMPSON ENTERS, LIGHTS THE LANTERN, hangs it above him, sits. He be-
gins to write . . .*
THOMPSON: I, Royal Earle Thompson, do solemnly swear that I
did not take the life of Homer T. Hatch on purpose. I did not
aim to hit him with the axe, but only to keep him off Mr. Helton. I have told this all to the judge and the jury and they let
me off—but nobody believes it. I'm not a cold-blooded mur-
derer, like everybody seems to think. If I had been in Mr. Helton's place, he would have done the same for me. My
wife . . .
He stops, blacks out the last two words, then continues to write . . .
THOMPSON: It was Mr. Homer T. Hatch who came to do wrong to
a harmless man. He caused all this trouble, and he deserved to
die. But I'm sorry it was me who had to kill him.
He signs his full name, folds the paper, puts it in his outside pocket.

Lifting the shotgun, he cocks it, then sets the butt of the shotgun along the ground. It is awkward as he is trembling, hardly able to breathe.

EXTERIOR—FARM   NIGHT
AS THE SOUND OF A SHOTGUN BLAST *echoes across the field.*

INTERIOR—BEDROOM   NIGHT
THE BOYS, BRINGING A GLASS OF WATER AND A CLOTH *to* Mrs. Thompson, *stand frozen.*
Mrs. Thompson *turns her head slightly, as if listening for it to be repeated, as we:*

FADE OUT.

The Trap of
SOLID GOLD

By ELLEN M. VIOLETT
From the Story by JOHN D. MacDONALD

ABC Stage 67
American Broadcasting Company Television Network
January 4, 1967

DIRECTOR: *Paul Bogart*

PRODUCER: *Bob Markell*

Bob Markell Productions, Inc.
EXECUTIVE PRODUCER: *Hubbell Robinson*

THE CAST

BEN WELDON: *Cliff Robertson*

GINNY WELDON: *Dina Merrill*

MR. MALLORY: *Conrad Nagel*

HAL CRADY: *James Broderick*

ED BARTLETT: *John Baragrey*

J. J. SEMMINS: *Dustin Hoffman*

PEG CRADY: *Joan Darling*

GERALDINE DAVIS: *Ruth White*

LATHROP HYDE: *Barnard Hughes*

GEORGE BLESSING: *Robert Gerringer*

STAN GEARLING: *Richard Kendrick*

KAY BARTLETT: *Carole Mathews*

CHRIS WELDON: *Jason Gero*

VEE WELDON: *Heidi Rook*

PROLOGUE

FADE IN: INTERIOR—AIRPLANE.

CLOSEUP OF BEN'S HAND, HOLDING A DRINK.

BEN'S VOICE: If we had only had time to sit down quietly and think things through, it might have been different. . . . Our paradise at 88 Ridge Road, just an hour from New York City, seemed to have everything: strength, love, ambition, and a future. So it was a shock when we finally began to realize that Paradise had become just a little conditional. We might have seen where we were heading . . . if we'd only had time to think things through. . . .

DISSOLVE TO:

THE LIVING ROOM OF BEN'S HOME.

BEN; GINNY, his wife, and ED and KAY BARTLETT are playing bridge.

ED (*Bidding*): Five diamonds.

BEN: Bye.

KAY: Seven spades.

GINNY: Bye.

ED: Bye.

BEN: Bye.

Ed lays down his trump. Ginny leads. Ed puts down his hand. Kay plays a trick. All ad lib until the game is over.

KAY: Game and rubber. Time to go home. (*To Ginny who is adding the score*): You should have led Ben's suit, dear. Instead of the singleton.

GINNY: I sort of got that feeling. Eighteen sixty, Ben.

BEN (*Rises, takes out his wallet, then puts it away*): Have to give you a check, Ed.

He goes to the desk to make out a check for $18.60.

CLOSEUP OF HIS BANK BALANCE: $42.63.

ED: Fine . . . (*Moves to the bar tray*) I'll have one for the road.

Kay rises; Ginny follows her to help her with her coat.

KAY: Ginny, try to make the bridge tournament more often—you've paid the club dues.

GINNY: You know how it is the first couple of years in a dream house. You don't want to move.

KAY: Ought to mix in a new community, though. *C'mon, Ed.*

GINNY (*Calling to the children*): Chris! Vee! Come say goodnight.

ED (*Going to Ginny*): Glad old Ed talked you into being neighbors?

Reprinted by permission of John D. MacDonald, Ellen M. Violett, and Bob Markell Productions, Inc.

Ginny nods, smiling.

ED: Mr. Mallory wants the best talent at National moved up fast. Ben's going to leave the old department head behind someday, aren't you, Ben?

BEN: Not at the bridge table.

He hands Ed the check.

ED (*Takes it; smiling malice*): You can't win 'em all.

CHRIS and VEE run in. Chris's right arm and hand are in a cast. Ad lib goodnight business.

KAY: Goodnight, everybody.

ED (*To Ben and Ginny*): Y'know—old Ed envies you! Yessir, if I say it myself. You kids have it made!

CLOSEUP OF A FAMILY TABLEAU: BEN, GINNY, CHRIS AND VEE.

FADE TO BLACK.

ACT ONE

FADE IN: THE FAMILY TABLEAU, dispersing as Ed and Kay Bartlett leave.

BEN: Want to know a joke?

GINNY: The one about the wife who played the wrong card?

BEN: Funnier. It'll kill you. (*Hands Ginny the checkbook*) Our bank balance.

GINNY: Enough to get you through the week without borrowing?

BEN: Not a prayer!

GINNY (*Looking at the checkbook balance*): Well, that's the last time we take on old Ed's wife in a friendly little game. You know she's the champion of that club tournament.

BEN: I know who isn't.

CHRIS: The Bartletts stay too long.

VEE: He smells funny when he breathes.

BEN: So would you if you lived on a diet of vodka and tomato juice. (*Showing the empty bottle*) One for the road!

GINNY: At least we can deduct the liquor.

BEN: Right now I'd rather drink it.

GINNY: I guess this shoots the raise I was going to ask you for next month.

BEN: Don't guess. Be absolutely confident. It does.

GINNY: Fifty dollars?—thirty? Settle for twenty-five——

BEN (*Kisses her*): Where does that allowance go?

GINNY (*Arranging glasses at the bar*): Darling, I throw it away. Isn't that what I'm meant to do? Throw it away in the supermarket—all up and down the aisles. Throw it away on sitters, the yard man, gas and oil for the car. And when the children need new clothes—every ten minutes—that's really a good throwing-away day!

BEN: Okay, big spender. But no raise. Insurance is due in December——

GINNY: But so's Christmas.

VEE: What about Christmas?

BEN: It's coming.

CHRIS: Did you ask Dad about you-know-what?

GINNY: Not yet. It's late now. Both of you go up and wash your face and hands.

CHRIS: I've only got one hand.

The children exit.

BEN: What about the "you know what"?

GINNY: Chris has his heart set on an electric train.

BEN: Electric train? Ouch! Okay—but nothing for you and me.

GINNY: Oh, no—oh, Ben——

BEN: We really can't afford it.

GINNY: Don't let's take all the fun out of it. Please—ten dollar top?

BEN: Five. And no cheating this year.

He sits on the ottoman; Ginny sits beside him.

GINNY: All right. Ben—what happens to us and money?

BEN: I don't know. But we must be doing something wrong.

GINNY: No, seriously. I really am careful. And you make a good salary. But it's as if you'd never been promoted.

BEN: Well, a lot of new overhead came with the promotion and this address on Ridge Road—plus mortgages, taxes, club dues, and the bank loan—plus Chris's arm.

GINNY: We have it made all right. Only we can't pay for it. I'll go wash up.

She rises; he stops her.

BEN: Hey—it was the right move, Ginny. The only move from a business standpoint.

GINNY: I know. Mr. Mallory wants the best talent moved up fast!

She goes into the kitchen.

BEN: Just a question of taking in all the slack till we get going.

GINNY'S VOICE: Right, skipper! About that slack—where is it?

Ben crosses to the card table. He grabs a pencil and a scorepad and starts figuring the cost of cigarettes.

CUT TO:

EXTERIOR—THE TRAIN STATION.

Ben and Ginny have just driven up in their car; Ginny is in the driver's seat. As she switches off the ignition Ben gives her a cigarette.

GINNY: Did you hear that? Motor's funny . . .

BEN: What? Oh . . . guess it's time you took it by Tony's to be serviced. *He lights her cigarette.*

GINNY: You're not smoking!

BEN: All morning. Observant girl. I've got a kind of hacking cough . . .

GINNY: What hacking cough?

BEN: You didn't notice that either?

GINNY: I can't notice something that doesn't happen. Not turning into a hypochondriac, are you?

BEN: No. I am just kicking a habit that was becoming a crutch——

GINNY: Well, you certainly needed to cut down. I'll kick it with you!

BEN: Both of them? The one you don't inhale in the morning—*and* the one at night?

GINNY: Yes . . . that's not much help. But darling, if it's an economy move, you're under pressure already.

BEN: Economy move? Would I go through this to save a few bucks—? *Ed Bartlett approaches the car.*

BEN: There's old Ed!

Ben and Ginny wave.

ED: Morning, kids! Ben . . . join me in the club car?

BEN: Glad to.

Ed goes by.

GINNY: He doesn't say that often! He does that every Monday morning when you have progress meetings and he wants to pick your brain. *The train arrives at the station.*

BEN: Here's old unreliable.

He gets out of the car and starts toward the platform.

GINNY (*Calling after him*): Get a pipe in town if it's too rough!

BEN (*Turns back*): You always did like the pipe type, didn't you?

GINNY: I like what I have.

Ben kisses her, then walks away down the platform.
Ginny watches him go. She turns the ignition key. A grinding noise— then nothing. She tries again—then reaches to get out of the car and re- call Ben. Something on the dashboard catches her attention:
CLOSEUP OF THE OIL LIGHT BLINKING.

GINNY (*Leans back*): Oh no . . .

                                        CUT TO:

BEN'S OFFICE AT NATIONAL.
Ben is seated at his desk. HAL CRADY comes in with coffee.

HAL: Coffee before progress, genius!

Ben goes to Hal's desk and they sit.

BEN: Do I need that! Thanks——

HAL: Don't tell me—I can guess. It was a perfect Sunday . . .

BEN: You and Peg should have driven out.

HAL: Life's too short. What'd you drop to that riverboat gambler Ed's married to?

BEN: . . . Cigarette money.

HAL: Ed likes to get you hung up in games you can't afford—you know that? And he isn't tuned out like Mallory. Ed remembers the pinch! Wasn't that long ago he was making your money. And dreaming big dreams that aren't going to pan out now.

BEN: What do you want from Ed, Hal?

HAL: What I want from Ed is to let me live my life—so I don't end up with his. Let me pay my nice controlled rent on my run-down West Side apartment. Park my second-hand car on alternate sides of the street——

BEN: Peg parks your car.

HAL: Let me send my three noisy children to P.S. Nothing with the rest of the delinquents. But suburb me no suburbs. Don't keep nudging how much Mr. Mallory would like it if I joined you in the country club set. Mr. Mallory isn't going to pay me enough to handle the first mortgage! Man, that status route is a real grind!

BEN: It's the only route at National.

HAL: Want to bet? I just found another way. Somebody I know in show business put me onto a CPA called J. J. Semmins—(*Pulls out a card from desk drawer*) in the West Forties. A nothing office, but if you bring the records, Semmins can set 'em straight. So I know the opening to go for. A regional managership in some nice town west of the Hudson River—where you start at thirty thousand dollars, peak at forty——

BEN: And stay there! They never bring a regional manager back where the action is. It's a dull routine job——

HAL: I'll take up a hobby . . . like breathing unpolluted air, deeply.

BEN: Will Peg settle for that?

HAL: Fats? What's she care as long as she gets eight squares a day? And the thrill of loving me.

The secretary buzzes.

BEN: C'mon . . . progress time.

They move toward the office bullpen.

HAL: My wife's on to me. She knows there isn't enough money to pay me for the politics you'll have to go through to make top brass.

BEN: It's not just the money that keeps me pressing.

HAL: Status turns you on a lot?

BEN: About as much as it does you— No. I guess it's the times when you get an idea that you know is right and it ends up influencing policy. So that, for just a moment you can see what it must be like to be up there and have the power to make things happen.

HAL: Poor genius, you're hooked. You love your work!

CUT TO:

THE PROGRESS MEETING.

MALLORY is at the head of the conference table. One of the other executives present is STAN GEARLING, National's treasurer.

ED: And as treasurer, Stan agrees that money's too tight—it's no time for a firm essentially concerned with instrument manufacture to expand into computers or anything else. We'd have to enlarge Hal's staff . . .

There is a murmur of agreement from the others around the table.

ED: Which makes it a fairly unanimous negative.

MALLORY: Not quite. Ben, we certainly know you're here today . . .

Laughter.

MALLORY: . . . But we haven't heard from you.

ED: I sounded Ben out in the train this morning. He registered a mild dissent. But he's been too busy to study the full picture.

BEN: I just looked into this Chicago proposition which we could go into on a relatively small scale. Make it a sort of pilot operation. And rather than see National end up on the sidelines of a field with this kind of future, I say take that limited risk.

ED: It's a field where we have no experience.

GEARLING: We'd be overextending.

MALLORY: Now wait a minute, gentlemen—there's a large profit opportunity here. Ben . . . this so-called Chicago project . . . Would you be willing to take on the extra work load—say for six months—on the understanding we'd go all the way with you if you make the pilot operation show real progress?

BEN: I could have it underway before I go home tonight.

MALLORY: I really feel that Ben's got a point. We'll go forward on a limited basis. . . . Thank you.

The executives rise to go.

Hal crosses to the door with Ben.

HAL: Try wearing a hair shirt, too! Six months of overtime . . . You should get a raise for that.

BEN: It'll happen. Get in on this!

MALLORY: Oh, Ben!——

BEN: Sir?

MALLORY: You left your pipe.
Ben returns to the conference table.
MALLORY: In heaven's name, why don't you get yourself a decent briar? One of these—(*Shows Ben his pipe*) I have an excellent tobacconist about two blocks up on Fifth.
BEN: With due respect, I'm not about to invest twenty-five bucks in this habit until I'm sure I've kicked the old one.
MALLORY: You can do anything you make up your mind to do, Ben. You're that kind of man . . . (*Sits against the edge of the table*) Ben . . . may I count on your discretion?
BEN: Of course.
MALLORY: You know my retirement is due in seven years. Well, I'm tired—I'd like to make it nearer five. If I can find the makings of the right alternative. And over and above National's senior officers, I'm watching and considering you.
BEN: I'm honored, sir.
MALLORY: But there's nothing like putting my money where my mouth is—so I won't keep it a secret—we're including you in the Christmas bonus set-up, as of this year.
BEN: Well . . . that's great.
Mallory rises, and walks Ben to the door.
MALLORY: Since it's unexpected money, maybe you should spend it unexpectedly . . . even foolishly. Only young once!
BEN: So my wife tells me.
MALLORY: Lovely girl, Virginia. Alice and I were most impressed with her party last month. She's a credit to you, Ben—deserves a surprise!
CUT TO:
BEN AND GINNY'S BEDROOM.
Ginny is seated at the dressing table. Ben is on the bed watching TV and eating.
GINNY: It was too complicated to explain on the phone. Anyhow, I never understand what Tony's talking about so I wrote it down. It seems the car had an oil leak. A rock got flipped up by the wheels or something. And (*Reads*) "the drain plug was sheared off the bottom of the pan." The motor froze.
Ben turns off the TV.
GINNY: I knew it was a bad idea to go into this now . . . (*Crosses to the bed and sits*) Replacing the motor would take weeks and cost seven hundred and thirty dollars—cash, which we haven't got. But Tony would allow us seven hundred on a trade-in— But we don't have to do that. He's got a used station wagon——
BEN: *A used car?*

He takes the tray to the bureau.

GINNY: It's in excellent condition. Tony's for it and so am I!

BEN: It's not for us! The first morning we were seen driving to the station in that second-hand car, it would be all around . . . everybody would know . . . even Mallory would hear about it . . . Ben Weldon's slipping, can't manage, his wife's extravagant——

GINNY: Get to Mallory first, with the truth. It's an accident, that isn't covered by insurance . . . Tell him about the rock hitting the whosis——

BEN: It's not the sort of problem Mallory wants to hear from the executive he's hoping will replace him! That's today's good news. From the horse's mouth.

GINNY (*Goes to him and hugs him*): Mr. Mallory said it . . . in so many words! Oh Ben!

BEN: That's all it'll be—words—if we start letting the front down. We've got to play the little game by the Ridge Road rules. C'mon . . . dream about the day you won't have to play bridge with the Bartletts.

He turns out the light.

GINNY: I'm dreaming about expensive Christmases.

They get into bed.

BEN: Mallory's for it. Says we shouldn't be so reliable all the time.

GINNY: We aim to please. We let the oil leak out of the shearing plug.

BEN: Out of the pan, honey, after the plug was sheared off.

He turns the bed-light off.

GINNY: That's what I said.

                              DISSOLVE TO:

THE LIVING ROOM; CHRISTMAS MORNING.

Ben, Ginny, Chris, and Vee are playing with the electric train.
Chris is working the switch.

BEN (*To Chris*): Hey, sport—you're not a southpaw. Why not try using your right hand?

GINNY: The doctor said you should exercise, darling. As much as you can.

CHRIS (*Continuing to use his left hand*): This is okay.

BEN: The cast has been off for a week, Chris. Got to start sometime.

VEE: He's scared to try!

CHRIS: I am not—!

VEE: You are too!

CHRIS: Mind your own business!

GINNY: No fights Christmas day. Come on. Let's give the train a rest for a minute. We can watch Dad open his present.

VEE: Yours too. (*Gives Ginny and Ben their presents. To Ginny*) You go first.

CHRIS (*To Ben*): Mom wraps them better than you do.

BEN: Better than my store does. That's not a big deal, remember?

Ginny opens her present; she lifts a figurine from the wrapping paper.

GINNY: Oh, it's very pretty . . .

VEE: What is it?

BEN: You're supposed to turn it on that stand.

Ginny does, and a tune starts tinkling.

GINNY: Ah—a music box. (*Kisses Ben*) I love it!

CHRIS (*To Ben*): Open yours.

GINNY: A story goes with that . . .

Ben opens his present. In a case is a briar pipe on a stand—an exact duplicate of Mallory's.

GINNY: Wait till you hear how it happened. Mrs. Mallory invited me to lunch while I was shopping last week. She told me how you wanted a pipe like Mr. Mallory's—and Ed let me in on the secret about your bonus!

BEN: Including how much it was?

GINNY: Well, no . . . but it sounded like a big deal . . . thousands.

BEN: No, more like fifteen hundred. We owe every cent . . . on the car, on the bank loan—doubled and redoubled.

GINNY: I'm sorry.

She crosses to the coffee table; Ben follows her.

CHRIS: What about?

BEN: Nothing, nothing . . . (*To Ginny*) Want to know a good joke? It's on me.

GINNY: I could use a good joke.

BEN: Don't get mad, though—it's Christmas. That pipe costs almost exactly what I saved—on two packs of cigarettes a day for forty-five days.

GINNY: Ben Weldon! That was why you did it!

BEN: That's what's funny! Laugh with me!

GINNY: Honey . . . I ought to make you keep it. But I'll take it back.

VEE: Doesn't he like his present?

CHRIS: What's the matter with it?

He picks up the pipe—then drops it.

VEE: Chris . . . look what you did!

Ben and Ginny turn as Chris faces them, almost in tears.

CHRIS (*Showing them his hand*): It wasn't my fault. I couldn't help it. I can't make the case close. It just won't do anything, Dad! It just won't!

Ben and Ginny rush over to comfort him.
CLOSEUP OF THE PIPE ON THE FLOOR—THE CASE IS BROKEN.

FADE TO BLACK.

ACT TWO

FADE IN: THE OFFICE OF J. J. SEMMINS.
SEMMINS is examining Ben's financial records.
SEMMINS: You keep nice records . . . but it isn't doing you much good.
BEN: Hal Crady said you could fix that, Mr. Semmins.
SEMMINS: We'll see . . . So, you make twenty-three thousand, five hun-
    dred a year. Seventy-one hundred comes right off the top for Uncle,
    the governor, payroll deductions, and your company's cooperative
    pension plan. Can you borrow the nine thousand you got in there?
BEN: For a real disaster. Technically. But it's frowned on—I'm supposed
    to manage on my salary.
SEMMINS: So take away seventy-one and we're talking about sixteen four.
    You've borrowed to the hilt on your life insurance policies, so now
    we're talking about thirteen eight. Got to send this two hundred a
    month to your mother?
BEN: No other relatives. But she lives simply out in Indiana with a com-
    panion. Her house is paid for.
SEMMINS: Now wait a minute—if you got her to sign it over, brought her
    East, you'd save twenty-four hundred a year for openers. And with
    your overhead, you need it! In fact that, plus what you'd clear on the
    sale of the property, might pull you out.
BEN: I know . . . I've thought of it. She's old . . . weak heart. But she'd
    hate being uprooted—she loves that house. I couldn't do that!
SEMMINS: So in the meantime, we're talking about eleven four. Now if
    you owned *your* house—but two ten a month mortgage; call it one
    fifty heat, light, phone, electric; six hundred town and county taxes—
    call it five grand a year. Lot of house!
    Ben gets a cigarette from his coat.
BEN: My firm takes a strong attitude about status. When I got my last
    promotion, moving to the suburbs was part of the deal.
SEMMINS: So now we're talking about sixty-four hundred. Your wife runs
    the show on forty-eight. Leaving sixteen for car payments, your
    clothes, commutation, entertainment, club dues—you can't knock off
    the club?
BEN: We never use it—but when the men our firm does business with
    come up——

SEMMINS: Uh-huh. You also have interest and payments on your bank loan. Legal. Medical—high for your boy recently. Temporary?

BEN: That's one of the reasons I made this appointment. We're not sure.

SEMMINS: So now we're talking about nothing. Less. Zero minus X. (*Turns in his chair and faces Ben*) What do you want from me?

BEN: Well . . . I thought maybe . . . a fresh eye . . . some new angle . . .

SEMMINS: You got no rabbit in this hat, Mister. And I'm not a magician. Hundreds of you bright organization guys have this . . . The big shots you work for made theirs so long ago they think you're getting a king's ransom. Expect you to swing today's prices and the tax bite and show off for 'em while you're at it! So you sweat to break even. And if you crack it's your fault. Nobody will ever feel sorry for you. Go anywhere in the country and beef about not making it on twenty-three grand and you'd have 'em rolling in hysterics. You and I know the sad story . . . but it won't sell.

BEN: Frankly, I'm looking for an answer—not sympathy! If you were me and you had to stick it out somehow, what would you do?

SEMMINS: Hit the top chinch Monday morning for thirty-five grand. That's what it's costing you. Get it from him. Or shop around.

BEN: I'd have to once I stuck my neck out! But it's not worth the risk. My edge is at National—where I've proved myself. And they won't jump anybody but top brass twelve thousand!

SEMMINS: So grab your pension savings and run. Open a gas station in Florida. Other guys have. They live longer.

BEN: Maybe they don't have my reasons. Look—I can *be* top brass in a few years. At a lot better than thirty-five thousand. Doing the job I was meant to do. It isn't a pipe dream. They want me up there——

SEMMINS: But not yet. That's how they keep you in the game, isn't it? You sit at the big spender's poker table with twelve bucks, folding every hand, waiting for a royal flush. And while you're waiting, they ante you to death.

Ben rises and gets his coat; Semmins crosses to him.

BEN: Thank you anyhow.

SEMMINS: I wish you well. Listen—I'm for you. Something's got to give, that's all. If something happens and you lose just one of these loads you're carrying . . . and your nerve holds out——

BEN: Don't worry! It will.

SEMMINS (*Holding out Ben's records*): So when you're lucky, we'll settle up. That much I can do for you, Mister. I won't bill you. I haven't the heart.

CUT TO:

BEN AND GINNY'S BEDROOM; MORNING.

Ginny is packing Ben's clothes.

BEN (*Bringing clothes from the closet*): I'm not arguing—I'm asking!

GINNY: You're taking a tone. I wish you'd see Chris's doctor yourself.

BEN: How? I've got meetings all morning—the four o'clock flight to Chicago——

GINNY: And last night you were too late. There's always something.

BEN: Ginny, tell me calmly—Chris has to see this therapist, for who knows what a crack, how many times, and then maybe have the operation anyhow?

GINNY: I don't know yet—but we should try everything to spare Chris more surgery.

BEN: I agree. I'm for that.

GINNY: Your main concern seems to be the cost——

BEN (*Going to bureau for his attaché case*): Well, it's all got to be paid for somehow. Insurance only covers so much—and borrowing more on that note at the bank won't be easy. I was told to bring in a balance sheet this time. And you—for some reason.

GINNY: Right now I frankly don't care. My mind's on Chris. (*Holds up Ben's dinner jacket*) What's the dinner jacket for?

BEN: Oh . . . one of the engineers said something about a party in Lake Forest Saturday. (*Watching her*) I don't know what we're fighting about, do you?

GINNY: Yes I do . . . This—the right luggage. The right suits with the right labels! The plush hotel you're going to. The lovely meals you'll be buying everybody——

BEN: It's not for me—it's on the expense account——

GINNY: It's money—what I need for Chris! Maybe if you're going to travel first class, you should start thinking first class for your family!

BEN: Ginny, that's so illogical!

GINNY: The only thing that should matter now is the use of that child's hand——

BEN: Well, what do you think I've been worrying about for weeks?

GINNY: Computers! Going to Chicago—— Ed Bartlett sniping at you——

BEN: All right, dammit, I've got a couple of other problems—like earning a living—— (*Grabs the bag; crosses to his jacket and puts it on.*) Just hold this thought—my son gets the best. And that comes first! (*Then putting his bag down*) This is plain silly.

GINNY (*Going to him*): It's me . . . I panicked . . . I'm sorry.

BEN: We're both under the gun . . . Just don't give up—huh?

GINNY: No! We'll always pull together.

BEN: That's my girl—we'll keep pulling . . .

They embrace.

BEN: Just a rough spot. But luck changes. You listen to me—we have it almost made. And we'll make it. Something always gives, Ginny—something will happen.

CUT TO:

BEN'S HOTEL ROOM IN CHICAGO.

CLOSEUP OF BEN SIGNING THE LUNCH CHECK *for the waiter; it amounts to $37.00.*

Ed Bartlett and GEORGE BLESSING are talking.

ED: So while I'm in Chicago I thought I'd better horn in on Ben's meeting. Make sure your people were clear that our attitude is speculative on this computer venture. Before everybody invests a lot of effort——

The waiter leaves as a bellhop appears at the door with a telegram.

GEORGE: But we understood from Ben that Mallory was prepared to go all the way if you showed progress.

BEN (*Crossing to the door to accept the telegram*): Within six months, George. And we know we can do that, Ed.

ED: You have a lot of less experimental projects on the home front, Ben.

BEN (*At door*): I'm prepared to come to Chicago every weekend if necessary to pull this off. Anyway, George will be in New York next week. You can see Mallory, find out just how enthusiastic he is.

ED: Oh well, of course we're behind Ben—not throwing cold water, just indicating our conditions——

GEORGE: Naturally. You want proof before you develop a whole program.

ED: Yes—that's our understanding. Isn't it, Ben?—Ben?

BEN (*Holding the telegram*): I'm sorry. We'll have to call this weekend off.

ED: Something happen?

BEN: Yes. Something happened. My mother died.

ED: Oh Ben, our sympathy . . . Know how you feel . . .

GEORGE: Sorry.

ED: Never seems so at the time, but with the very old, it can be a blessing.

BEN: Yes . . . I suppose . . . Thank you . . .

CUT TO:

MARTHA WELDON'S PARLOR.

GERALDINE DAVIS, *the dead woman's companion, enters through the front door, followed by Ben and Ginny.*

GERALDINE: Well, it was a nice ceremony. Simple—but I'm sure that's how she would have liked it. May I get you some tea?

GINNY: I don't think there's time.

BEN: We have to see Mother's lawyer before we leave. But there's something we'd like to talk over first.

GERALDINE (*Sits*): Well certainly, Mr. Weldon.

Ginny sits on the sofa; Ben stands behind her.

BEN: To begin with I want you to know how grateful I've always been you were here, Geraldine.

GERALDINE: It worked two ways. Martha couldn't manage enough for me to put anything by. But she was more my friend than employer.

BEN: Yes . . . I understand. And I know that won't make it any easier—looking for another place. So your convenience is to be a condition of selling this house. And after the lawyer's paid off the funeral expenses, Mrs. Weldon and I want him to arrange a small token——

GINNY: We wish we could do more.

GERALDINE: Oh no, please! Your mother planned all along to make things up to me. I mean it's for Judge Willis Gebbert to tell you the terms of Martha's will, but she showed me a copy—she was that anxious to have me stay on . . . with some peace of mind.

BEN: I'm sorry. I didn't know she'd made a provision.

GERALDINE: She probably felt it wasn't worth mentioning in a letter. An old place like this wouldn't seem of much moment to a couple with a home in a fashionable suburb. My, wasn't Martha proud when you moved! Why I tell you, knowing how well you were doing just made up for everything—even the business trips when you couldn't take the extra time to come see her. Or maybe the money—but she felt so beholden for that little allowance you sent her to eke through on. Mostly though, she just talked about your success. My son's an executive on Madison Avenue in New York. That's how she always put it. But when it came time to think of the security of others—well, I guess I'm the one who seemed more in the same boat with her. So you rest easy—your mother left me this house for my lifetime. I'm taken care of. (*Rises*) Think I'll just make myself a cup of tea . . . unless there's something else you wanted to talk over?

BEN: No. I'd say that about covers it.

GINNY: Well, I wouldn't. What's done is done, Geraldine. But there's been a little misunderstanding about Mr. Weldon's situation—Mr. Weldon was not trying to impress his mother with his situation. He was just trying to keep her from worrying.

GERALDINE: Anyway, I think I understand, Mrs. Weldon. Everybody has problems. About those funeral expenses you mentioned though . . .

I expect you'll be taking that up with Judge Willis Gebbert your-
selves. I wouldn't want to presume . . . not being real family.
She smiles; exits.
BEN: When I think of the guilt that's been eating me up——
GINNY: Guilt!
BEN: Who knows—maybe this is better . . .
GINNY: What have you got to be guilty about? Not these cruel lying
things she said!
BEN: No . . . before . . . when the telegram came. When I took it out I
just saw the first line. *Your mother suffered another heart attack*—and
I thought here we go, this tears it. Hospital bills, nurses, doctors,
dragging on—this'll do it, now we go under. Then I got the thing un-
folded . . . and read the rest. Regretting to inform me she had died.
And it was . . . as if she wasn't my mother . . . I'd never known her
. . . didn't understand about death. I only knew I was off the hook.
In the clear. Something happened. No more two hundred dollars. I
could sell this house . . . Ginny—I'd never been more relieved in my
life.
GINNY: No . . . that was shock, the pressure! You're not like that!
BEN: Maybe I'm getting there. You seemed to think so the other day.
Ginny goes to him and kneels beside him.
GINNY: I was wrong—I didn't mean that——
BEN: I don't know. Ginny— It's as if I'm losing my capacity for feeling.

FADE TO BLACK.

ACT THREE

FADE IN: AN OFFICE AT THE BANK.
*Ben and Ginny are discussing their financial situation with LATHROP
HYDE.*
HYDE: Not quite what I hoped. Heavy on the debit side. Those bills——
BEN: We've had some family troubles recently.
HYDE: But on the credit side—not enough equity in the house, none in
the car. And used furniture's hardly worth listing, is it?
GINNY: We're proud of our furniture! We saved, for one good piece at a
time . . .
HYDE: But in a house with children . . . well. About the only asset that
holds up is your nine thousand in the pension fund. You can borrow
that—wouldn't need us.
BEN: I'd rather continue our association.

HYDE: Oh, I'm afraid another extension——

BEN: No, I meant . . . a new note. I'd like to borrow five thousand to retire this one—pay the bills.

HYDE: Another *one-hundred-eighty-day* note, Mr. Weldon?

BEN: I can allot two hundred a month now——

Hyde doesn't seem to hear.

BEN: I can allot two hundred a month now——

HYDE: Doesn't add up to five thousand dollars in a hundred and eighty
days. Even if you made regular payments this time. It's against bank
policy for us to loan money on an open note—unless it can be repaid
in the time stated.

BEN: Am I to understand this bank considers me a bad risk?

HYDE: That's an unfortunate expression.

BEN: I'd say it's an unfortunate attitude!

HYDE: I'm sorry. We have too much money out on promises. We're
changing our policy as far as you people are concerned.

BEN: What's that mean? *You people?*

HYDE: Why, you rising young executives, Mr. Weldon, who keep rising
up here from New York City. Moving into homes you can't always
afford, living a little beyond your incomes. House poor, car poor,
club poor, party poor—Why, if one little recession brought you down
we'd be left holding the bag. Shareholders and officers in this bank
who've lived modestly in Ridge Center for generations. Doesn't seem
quite sound. Thrift's not such a dirty word, Mr. Weldon—in the old
days a lack of thrift was said to show a want of character——

GINNY: That's not fair——!

HYDE: Not being personal, Mrs. Weldon. Just reading figures. Almost
twenty-five thousand a year coming in—and nothing to show for it?
Except that pension money the company grabs first—which makes a
good show for the bosses.

BEN (*Rises*): Mr. Hyde, you're welcome to your opinion of me. But I'm
sorry you found it necessary to drag my wife into this today.

HYDE (*Stands*): But her name's on the note too. Along with the due date.
Which falls in thirty-nine days . . . ?

BEN: Thanks. We got the message! Come on, Ginny.

They leave Hyde's office.

GINNY: Ben—where do we go from here?

BEN: Right now—the station.

GINNY: What if the new doctor decides about Chris today——?

BEN: We'll talk tonight.

GINNY: We can't—we're entertaining Mr. Blessing tonight——

BEN: *Not now, Ginny!*

CUT TO:

A TABLE IN A SUPPER CLUB.
Ben, Ginny, Hal and PEG CRADY, and George Blessing.
The waiter brings Blessing a drink.

BLESSING: What's this?

PEG: The double you ordered.

BLESSING: Oh—I'll get to it, pal.

The waiter withdraws.

BLESSING: Now about that hit we sat through. Stinks—right?

HAL: We didn't want you to leave town not knowing.

BEN: Mallory's orders. Hot ticket!

BLESSING: Beats me—people paying those prices to hear one tune for two hours—and look at some ugly woman in rags!

PEG: It was a Cinderella story. She perked up in the second act.

BLESSING: Didn't get any younger, did she? I corked off by then . . .

PEG: You blended right in with the brass.

BLESSING (*Laughs; puts his hand on Ginny's knee*): Now here's somebody could have kept me awake. I ask you—is this what a star ought to look like? Is this class?

HAL: Star. Class.

BLESSING: Bet you heard that before.

GINNY: Not recently, Mr. Blessing——

BLESSING (*Puts his arm around Ginny*): George! George and Ginny. Got that squared away in the frog restaurant!

GINNY: Ben, it's late—the sitter!

BEN: Right. I'll get the check.

BLESSING: No—whole other drink here— Oopsie daisy——

He knocks the drink into Ginny's lap; general reaction.

HAL (*Coming around the table*): Party's over, George . . . Better line you up a cab.

BLESSING: Alcohol can't hurt anything. (*Rises; fumbles for a tip*) Waiter's my pal. Hold on.

BEN: None of that! Tab's ours.

BLESSING: Pal's mine.

He drops a ten-dollar bill on the table.
Ben and Hal get on each side of him and steer him toward the door.

PEG (*Sitting next to Ginny*): Fun guy. You're awful quiet tonight—even before the dress. Ginny! What's the matter?

GINNY (*Staring at the ten-dollar bill*): Money. Want to know something lovely about me, Peg? If you weren't here, I'd take it.

PEG: Well, don't let me stand in your way—I'll split it with you. Crazy man—leaving a ten-dollar tip. I bet he doesn't pull that when he takes his wife out in Chicago.

Ginny suddenly starts to cry.

PEG: Oh no, don't let it get you down—Ginny dear!

CLOSEUP OF BEN as he sees Ginny crying.

CUT TO:

THE BEDROOM.

Ginny is showing Ben the stain on her evening dress.

BEN: That'll come out, won't it?

GINNY: No . . .

She hangs the dress on the closet door, and sits on the bed.

BEN: Just alcohol . . .

GINNY: I got a note the last time I sent it to the cleaners: "Forget this dress. We have. Lots of luck. The Morris Brothers."

BEN (*Sits beside her*): Well don't worry. We'll have to get you another evening dress somehow.

GINNY (*Going to the dressing table*): Or get your firm's clients another geisha!

BEN: What's that crack?

GINNY: Figure it out!

BEN: Look—I know how upset you are——

GINNY: Oh, you haven't a clue!

BEN (*Crossing to her*): If it'll ease your mind about that bank hassle, I checked with a few loan companies today. They'll take a chattel mortgage on the furniture——

GINNY: And on and on and on we go! For how long at how much interest? While that nine thousand dollars sits in your pension fund, impressing everybody.

BEN: We've been over that.

GINNY: Explain it to me just one more time, Ben. Now—with your company's spending power so fresh in my mind! Just why is it you can't walk into the office tomorrow and take what's yours?

BEN: I'm supposed to be too good and too sharp and too tough to need it!

GINNY: You mean infallible.

BEN: I can't let them know I'm bleeding!

GINNY: What if you bleed to death—won't they catch on?

BEN: *I'm not letting go!* That's how it is! You want to talk turkey? I don't know anyone my age with my potential who wouldn't grab my place, debts and all!

GINNY: Good luck!

BEN: From where you sit! But out in the cold arena, I have an edge. And I'm keeping it. Because way up at the top of the pyramid, the men who really have power are making book on whether I'll last the distance . . .

Dina Merrill and Cliff Robertson in *The Trap of Solid Gold*.

or weaken, switch, go for the quick salary bump, foul up . . . Well, I didn't make the rules. And when I get there I'll change them. But I am getting there. Even if my banker doesn't dig it—my accountant doesn't dig it——

GINNY: And your wife doesn't dig it.

BEN: You're different. I'd counted on you.

GINNY: But even without me—the point is to get there!

BEN: *I belong there, Ginny!*

GINNY: Then I'm wrong—I'm the one who isn't big league stuff. And I don't want to be. The price is too high. I didn't make the rules either —I just see what they're doing to you. Changing you into the kind of man who doesn't even know what's happening to his marriage—or his children, and doesn't want to know.

BEN: That's not true. Because I'm busy and work hard, does that mean I don't love my family?

GINNY: You tell me! Did you forget I was seeing Chris's doctor today? Or did you just not care enough to ask?

BEN: What happened?

GINNY: What do you think happened? Have you looked at your son's hand recently? Yes, he needs another operation!

                                         CUT TO:

MALLORY'S OFFICE AT NATIONAL.

Mallory is seated behind his desk; Ben is standing. On the desk are Ben's financial records.

MALLORY: *Thirty-five thousand dollars?*

BEN: The figure was recommended by a crack CPA after he looked these over . . . they show a sort of pattern. Even without the emergencies——

MALLORY: Oh Ben, you know better. I have no wish to pry into personal concerns. Things are always tough at this stage of the game. (*Leans back*) Think my wife and I had an easy time of it? The macaroni years, that's what Alice still calls them.

BEN: This isn't a matter of Ginny budgeting—it's beyond that!

MALLORY (*Rises and goes to Ben*): Now, Ben. You have a lovely family and a fine home. But it's up to you to run the show, set an example. I know the lean years are harder on the woman—no wonder they sometimes egg a man on to make a mistake in judgment. But we can't give in to that, Ben. (*Puts his arm on Ben's shoulder*) So you go home tonight and tell Virginia you gave it a good college try, but the old man wasn't buying. Make me the villain. And, Ben, as far as our relationship is concerned, we'll forget this. It never happened.

BEN (*Turns to him*): I'm sorry, I can't. It's not Ginny. It's me. There's a limit—a breaking point.

MALLORY: I'm more disappointed than I can say to hear you admit it.

BEN: It took some doing. But I'm in debt so deep I can't get out, not next year, or the year after. I have to send twenty-dollar checks against my mother's funeral expenses. Bargain about my boy's operation. On the kind of salary I make these things are degrading . . . damaging . . . It's costing me my self-respect.

MALLORY: Really? I should think our conversation before Christmas might help with your image.

BEN: It's because of that I'm here. You indicated a special interest——

MALLORY: In confidence, Ben—in strictest confidence if you'll recall! There are twenty other men on your salary level in this building. How do you think they'd react?

BEN: Then no raise—there's another solution. I could get off the status hook—unload the house. Too much goes into keeping up a front I don't need.

MALLORY: National has needs, however! Or do you consider we're just here to be milked? You're in this income bracket precisely so you can reflect credit on us——

BEN: Then somebody should figure out another bracket, sir! Because the way it's set up it's a trap—it's not enough. It doesn't work.

MALLORY: *You're referring to your future opportunity here as a trap?*

BEN: My future here means more to me than anything but my family——

MALLORY: But not enough to wait for it! Nobody waits any more—you all have to get it now!

BEN: I'm not after a mink coat for Ginny. I'm just looking for a way to make a decent living. And I've got to find it. Somewhere.

MALLORY: You mean elsewhere?

BEN: No. Only as a last resort.

MALLORY: I regret it's in your mind. (*Turns away*) I've felt so strongly you belong here in the National family. I'm sorry.

BEN: All right . . . I never asked for a favor before. But in view of the contribution I've tried to make to this company, please look at these figures. (*Holds out paper*) It's the only fair way to make a decision.

MALLORY: Except by tradition. And traditionally the salaries here are matched to the job, not the man. However, since you put it on a personal basis, leave them with me . . . (*Crossing to the door*) All right, Ben . . . Until next Wednesday at ten. A week should be adequate for your special problem.

BEN (*Following him to the door*): Thank you.

He starts out, taking a cigarette from his pocket.

MALLORY: I see you went back to the old habit . . .
BEN: Why yes . . . that's right. I did.
Mallory closes the door.

CUT TO:

THE OFFICE BULLPEN, *as Ben comes out of Mallory's office.*
He crosses to Stan Gearling.
BEN: Good morning, Stan.
GEARLING: Good morning, Ben.
BEN: I'd like to borrow the balance in my retirement account.
GEARLING: The whole amount?
BEN: How soon can I get it?
GEARLING: Why . . . it has to clear through the trust that handles the
    fund. About three days . . . ?
BEN: That'll be fine. Thanks.
    He moves away.
GEARLING: When will you . . . well . . . be putting it back in, Ben?
BEN (*Stops*): When? Before I retire, Stan. Before I retire.
    He walks slowly away.

FADE TO BLACK.

ACT FOUR

FADE IN: THE STATION.
Ben and Ginny are sitting in their car, waiting for the train.
Ed Bartlett goes by, waving briefly.
GINNY: Not a very big hello.
BEN: Can't have everything. Let him keep the club car . . . Be sure to
    bank that nine-thousand-dollar check.
GINNY: What time are you going to see Mallory?
BEN: Ten o'clock.
GINNY: Will you call me afterwards?
BEN: If there's any news—real news.
GINNY: I still don't see what else we could have done.
    Ben doesn't answer.
GINNY: Oh it's not fair—if he negates your whole career! I know it's not
    my fault, but I sure feel as if it were.
BEN: It's not your fault! It was my decision!
GINNY: I just never thought I'd be one of those women——
BEN: You're not. Now look, Ginny—nothing Mallory says today or any
    day should make that much difference to us. There aren't that many

good marriages around. Don't let's rock the boat any more. It's not our style. We've always had something special going.

GINNY: We have, haven't we?

They sit for a moment.

The train pulls into the station. Ben leaves her, looks back at the car, and walks down the platform.

CUT TO:

MALLORY'S OFFICE.

Mallory is seated; Ed Bartlett is standing near the desk.

Ben enters.

MALLORY: Come in, Ben! We think we have found a solution!

ED (*Crossing to Ben*): Wish I'd known this sooner. Had no idea the scrape you kids were getting yourselves into!

MALLORY: I let Ed in on our little problem, more as a friend than your immediate superior. Glad I did. You tell him, Ed—your idea!

ED: Well, it's so obvious—I don't deserve special credit. Gil Walker sent in a formal request for early retirement—so there it is—the perfect opening!

BEN (*To Ed*): Denver . . .

MALLORY: You'd be regional manager of the entire Southwest. Fine promotion, Ben. Great experience on the administrative level, for anything that might open up—in that line. Not quite the salary you mentioned. Starts at thirty thousand, I believe. But you peak very fast at forty——

ED: And you'd have nothing like the overhead you're carrying here—no side expenses or extra entertaining.

BEN: I'm sure I wouldn't.

ED: Well then—let's cheer up a little. Listen—I don't like to lose good neighbors either, but if it means snowing you kids under with these figures!

BEN: I wasn't thinking about that. I was wondering . . . about the computer project.

MALLORY: Oh, yes . . . that's a concern.

BEN: I've gotten a pretty good start on it, Mr. Mallory. And Chicago's not far from Denver. It seems to me . . .

MALLORY: That wouldn't be the consideration really. You see, a district manager has so much local responsibility . . . There isn't the leeway for travel, initiating other ventures . . . and from our point of view, it doesn't seem too practical—undertaking that kind of policy experiment—so remote from the policy area. Which is still here with us wage slaves in the home office, you know.

ED: So let somebody else take over that worry, Ben! That's the kind of extra burden we're trying to spare you.

BEN: It was never a burden. It was the part of my work that made all the rest of it worthwhile.

MALLORY: Almost worthwhile. But I'm well aware you're the only man here who'd even have tried . . . for those reasons. (*Turns to Ed*) Write it off. National may just have to wind up on the sidelines in that area. One of those casualties.

BEN: That's a great disappointment.

MALLORY (*Sincere, and sad*): For both of us . . . Stamina, Ben, takes a lot of stamina to make it all the way in big business. But a man does what he feels he has to do. And when it's done, he lives with it.

CUT TO:

THE LIVING ROOM.

Ben, Peg, and Hal enter.

PEG: I wish you'd at least tell us——

BEN (*Going to the bar*): It would take the fine edge off the celebration. (*To Hal*) Here . . . open 'em.

Hal crosses to the bar.

PEG: He can only drink one at a time.

HAL: Since when?

PEG (*Joining them at the bar*): Those are the wrong kind of glasses. Ginny won't like it. I know how women feel about surprise parties!

BEN: Not this surprise.

Ginny enters.

GINNY: *What is going on?*

PEG: Oh nothing . . . just us folks . . . pouring champagne again.

GINNY: Ben! What happened?

PEG: He snapped, dear. I tried to slip him into a phone booth to warn you but they threw me into the back seat of the car.

HAL: Got a big picture of us throwing her?

GINNY: Ben, if you've been fired, just tell me.

BEN: Not only have I not been fired . . . You were right all the way, Ginny. All I had to do was ask. We won—a promotion, a new life, and a six-thousand-dollar raise for a start!

All cheer. Ben raises his glass.

BEN: To the wife of the new District Manager of the entire Southwest!

GINNY (*Running to him*): Oh darling, darling, I thought we'd had it!

BEN: The Weldons . . . not likely! Now here's the drill. We put this house on the market. I fly out there, locate a new one. We get Chris squared away immediately so he'll be all recovered for the move. And that's it. We're on our way!

GINNY: I can't believe it. (*To Hal and Peg*) Can you believe it?

HAL: Keep drinking. Everything falls into place.

PEG: Before the group passes out—what's for dinner?

HAL: Oh—there she goes again!

PEG: Once more, Hal Crady, and it's over.

Ben takes out money and drags Ginny to the door.

BEN: To the supermarket, girls. A porterhouse steak for six——

GINNY: Not for this party! I'm going to call the fancy butcher who makes deliveries. I've never even talked to him.

PEG: C'mon, call from the kitchen. So we can do something really imaginative about dessert.

GINNY: Using a champagne base?

PEG: Don't we always?

The girls exit, giggling.

Ben crosses to the bar.

BEN: Want a real drink?

HAL: I'm fine . . .

BEN (*Pouring a drink*): Ed Bartlett begged out of bridge on Sunday so we have some vodka. Great weather vane, Ed.

HAL: No hard feelings, old buddy—but that looks like my rosy future you're walking off into. Isn't that my job you just got yourself?

BEN: Sorry about that.

HAL: Joke, Ben . . . Big deal . . . there are plenty of districts—enough to go around.

BEN: Or maybe they'll give you mine when they bring me back to the home office . . .

HAL: What?

BEN: When they bring me back.

HAL: Sure . . . that's how it'll probably work out.

BEN: Sure . . . one of these years.

HAL: I hope I'm not butting in—but what's the story? What's with the old drive? What happened to the big dream?

DISSOLVE TO:

INTERIOR—AIRPLANE.

Ben, Ginny, Chris, and Vee. Chris is looking at blueprints.

CHRIS: What's a family room mean?

GINNY: It's a room you two can mess up and nobody will care.

VEE: We didn't have that on Ridge Road.

GINNY: The place Dad's gotten us in Denver is bigger and nicer.

CHRIS: You said the old one was your dream house.

GINNY: It was, darling . . . but dreams change.

CHRIS: Will you have a room to mess up?

VEE: Grownups don't need one, dummy!

Dina Merrill in *The Trap of Solid Gold*.

CLOSEUP OF BEN'S FACE as we hear . . .

HAL'S VOICE: What's with the old drive? What happened to the big dream?

DISSOLVE from Ben's face to the conference table . . . Ben is seated with the other executives. A spontaneous hand of agreement greets Ben, and he rises to the applause.

BEN: Thanks for that. I'd like to assure the officers of this company the only immediate changes I plan concern policy. First: as to status requirements . . . Starting today I no longer want the talents of able men discouraged by insisting on expensive conformity. What National will stand for from now on is performance!

SLOW DISSOLVE back to the interior of the plane as we hear . . .

BEN'S VOICE: Performance in the office. And on the job. I would like all the executives at this meeting to think in creative terms—to start feeling directly responsible for policy.

GINNY'S VOICE: . . . Ben . . . Ben—the stewardess!

GINNY (*Rousing him*): Ben—suppertime.

BEN: Oh . . . sorry.

The stewardess offers him a tray.

GINNY: You were miles away.

BEN: Thanks . . . I'm not hungry. (*Wards off the tray and holds up his half-full glass*) What I could use is another one of these. Not going overboard—just relaxing.

GINNY: Don't be silly, darling; why shouldn't you? You're not Ed Bartlett . . . You're missing something. . . .

BEN: I'll eat later.

GINNY: Ben . . . what were you thinking about so hard?

BEN: Oh . . . nothing . . . not really thinking . . . You know . . .

GINNY: Star gazing . . .

Ben nods.

GINNY: Well, if it's about our beautiful future we don't have to dream any more . . . I mean, it's happening already—it's here!

BEN: Yes. That's right . . . no reason to dream any more.

CLOSEUP OF BEN'S FACE as we hear . . .

BEN'S VOICE: But when you get close to the top—get a glimpse of what it looks like—and then have to come down, you know that all your life —when you read about others who made it—you will wonder what it would have been like to be "up there."

FADE TO BLACK.

Do Not Go Gentle Into That Good Night

By LORING MANDEL

CBS Playhouse
Columbia Broadcasting System Television Network
October 17, 1967

DIRECTOR AND PRODUCER: *George Schaefer*

THE CAST

PETER SCHERMANN: *Melvyn Douglas*

HELOISE MICHAUD: *Shirley Booth*

GEORGE: *Warren Stevens*

DR. GETTLINGER: *Lawrence Dobkin*

JOSEPHA: *Claudia McNeil*

EVELYN: *Lois Smith*

PHIL: *Gene Blakely*

MARGARET: *Martine Bartlett*

YOUNG ROSE: *Mildred Trares*

ARTHUR SELIG: *Art Smith*

MARIAN: *Amanda Randolph*

DR. KELLER: *Karl Swenson*

MRS. STONE: *Mary Jackson*

MRS. ERMISH: *Nydia Westman*

LARRY MC DERMOTT: *Val Avery*

WALLACE SLOCUM: *Jacques Aubuchon*

ROBERT RAGLE: *Don Beddoe*

MRS. FLAGLER: *Madge Kennedy*

MARY DEVLIN: *Almira Sessions*

LAURA CHAPMAN: *Sara Taft*

ACT ONE

FADE IN: A STATION WAGON COMES DOWN A SNOWY ROAD in an old village residential area and pulls to the curb in front of the old looming frame house built by Peter Schermann.

CUT TO:

GEORGE SCHERMANN, Peter's 45-year-old son, who is inside the house and watching at the window. Seeing the car approach, he calls to his wife, EVELYN.

GEORGE: He's back.

Evelyn, sitting in the dining room at a table set for company, rises and goes toward the kitchen. There is bitterness in her voice.

EVELYN: The meat's all dry.

CUT TO:

THE CAR AT THE CURB. The car doors are open now. MARGARET, Peter's daughter, is standing on the snow while PHIL, her husband, comes around to help the old man out of the rear seat. PHILLY, their son, runs ahead of them toward the steps leading to the house.

The old man, PETER SCHERMANN, says nothing.

Phil helps Peter up the high wooden steps. Margaret hurries past them. The old man climbs so slowly . . .

We see the entrance into the house, the stairs, and the heavy gothic newel and rail leading up to the long front porch, screened in summer and now open and crusted with ice. The white paint is peeling.

Margaret enters the front door.

PHIL: Hold the door. Hold the door.

MARGARET: Come on, Dad. Phil, get him out of the cold! (*Then, calling to Philly, who has entered in a rush*) Philly! Boots off first! Come back!
Inside, there is a long center hall which goes straight to the back door of the house. At the far end of the hall the kitchen goes off to the left and a rear bedroom goes off to the right.
Philly has raced down this hall and is now squealing with BETH and SCOTT. Evelyn is approaching from the door to the kitchen. George, upstairs, has not yet appeared.

SCOTT: They're here! They're here!

MARGARET: Philly, get back here. Boots off!
Philly comes running back past Evelyn in a great hurry to reach his mother, perform the demanded chore, and get back to his cousins. Margaret removes his boots.

PHILLY: The trains are up!

Beth runs up to Peter and Phil.

BETH: Hi, Pop.

Evelyn chases her away.

There is now a knot of people at the front door. Margaret is helping Philly remove his boots. Phil, still holding Peter tightly by the arm, is helping him through the doorway. Beth and Scott crowd in to be close to Philly. Evelyn brushes the water which clings to the heavy blue overcoat Peter wears. The children are gleeful. All the others are tense.

EVELYN: What a mess, Pop.

PHIL: I'll tell you the roads are treacherous. Where's George?

EVELYN: Upstairs.

MARGARET (*Finishing with Philly's boots*): There. Get out of here.

BETH: Come on.

The children rush down the hall.

MARGARET: And take that coat off!

As Phil puts his own coat in the closet, Margaret turns her attention to the old man who, partly by his silence, remains our focus of attention. She helps Evelyn remove Peter's coat.

MARGARET: His hands are ice.

EVELYN: Did you enjoy yourself, Pop?

PHIL (*Shouting up the stairs*): George?

The women get Peter's coat off. He wears a coat-sweater underneath. Margaret moves him to a chair and he sits.

MARGARET: I'll get his galoshes off.

Evelyn stands watching Margaret, who has gotten to her knees on the wet floor in order to remove Peter's overshoes.

PHIL (*Calling upstairs*): George, your city kin are here! The roads are a mess. (*To Evelyn*) Sorry to be late, Ev, the roads are just treacherous. Holding dinner, I hope.

EVELYN (*Still watching Margaret and Peter*): George is all tired out. Doing accounts. Wasn't feeling too well.

PHIL (*Calling up again*): Georgie!

George comes down the stairs. He looks drawn and pale. He moves, however, with determined steps.

GEORGE: OK, Phil. Dad, how do you feel? (*He reaches the bottom step. He goes to Peter, whispering to Evelyn as he passes her*) All right, I'm here. (*To Margaret*) How is he, Meg? (*To Peter*) How was it, Dad?

PHIL (*To Evelyn*): I hope the dinner didn't dry out or anything, but we started on time.

EVELYN: Yes. The roads are treacherous.

*She walks away, down the hall, toward the kitchen. Phil follows after
her.*

PHIL: Cars off the shoulders all over the place. Like dead horses.

MARGARET: Phil! There's a suitcase in the car.

PHIL: Ye Gods.

*He grabs his coat and rushes out. George kisses Margaret sincerely on
the cheek, takes the wet galoshes she holds up to him and puts them
under the hall table.*

GEORGE (*Not looking at Peter*): Good to have you home, Dad.

PETER (*After considering it*): Why?

GEORGE (*Starting to help Margaret with her coat*): Let me——

MARGARET: Take Dad.

*George loops an arm under Peter's, helps him rise, and they move off to
the left of the hall into the living room.*

GEORGE: Come on, Dad, get in the warm part of the house. I was going
to light up a real fire but the wood is wet and the smoke's no good for
you.

PETER: Shouldn't let it get wet.

GEORGE: Well, we missed you round here, that's for sure. How was it at
Meg's? I'll bet her kids ran you ragged, huh? I talked to the man who
—he's a doctor, too—who runs that home, Dad . . . I know you'd
like it . . .

PETER: I'm tired, George. Let me sit down.

*George assists Peter in sitting on a straight-backed upholstered chair
which we might sense is Peter's habitual seat. George, freed, exhales
deeply and looks down at his father.*

GEORGE: Are you hungry? It'll be a while. Ev was figuring you'd be here
an hour ago . . . You want to rest a while on the bed? I've got to light
a fire or something . . . find some cellar wood . . .

PETER: You can leave me . . .

Peter looks around the room.

*The room is suddenly bare and unpainted, as it was many years ago when
the house was almost ready to be inhabited. A sawhorse stands in the
room, and a rough unfinished credenza. ROSE, Peter's young wife, looks
at him with admiration. She wears a cape on her shoulders.*

YOUNG ROSE: More than I dreamed, Mr. Schermann. A house like this
can stand a thousand years . . . you're so kind to me . . . but you
talk to me so little . . .

PETER: I can build, Rose . . .

Suddenly he sees a new image.

PETER: Rose?

Rose, now a very old woman, sits in a rocker. She looks near death.

OLD ROSE: Always tired, Peter. Why am I always tired?

We are back to the present. Peter sits looking across at the rocker. It is empty and still.

GEORGE'S VOICE: You can't just sit here . . .

Peter looks up at George, then back to the rocker.

GEORGE: You can't just sit here . . .

PETER: I made your crib. I built . . .

At the front door, Phil bustles in carrying a small suitcase.

PHIL: I'll put it in his room.

He hears George pleading with Peter, and moves down the hall.

Phil brings the suitcase to a room off the hall on the right, the middle bedroom, Peter's room. The furniture is outsized and simple . . . a bed, a chest, a stiff-backed chair alongside the radiator by the window, and a small corner table with a cleared-off porcelain-enamel top of a kind familiar in old kitchens.

Phil swings the suitcase lightly to the bed and steps back into the hall. He hangs up his coat, then walks to the back bedroom and opens the door. The three children are inside, Philly still wearing his hat and coat. They are all sitting on the floor and playing with a set of electric trains.

PHIL: Hey, that's pretty good.

He squats by the children and watches the train.

PHILLY: It isn't smoking . . .

SCOTT: It ran out . . .

BETH: It looks smoking to me . . .

CUT TO A CLOSE SHOT at floor level of the train as it comes straight for THE CAMERA. The train turns abruptly just before hitting the lens and starts the curve around the oval. THE CAMERA PANS slightly to follow the train around the turn. As the train begins to retreat from the camera on the highball back, the camera ends its pan and catches Beth's laughing face in FRAME as she presses her head to the floor. She shared the funny terror of pretending the train was going to crash into her eyes.

SLOW FADE TO BLACK.

FADE IN: THE DINING ROOM. It is much later that night.

Before the massive rectangular table, an argument is in progress. George, Phil, and Margaret are settled in the room. Evelyn, drying dishes which are stacked in the kitchen, commutes between the kitchen and the dining room through the connecting doorway. During the scene she is continually picking up a wet dish, drying it, exchanging it for another wet dish, repeating the procedure.

The dining-room table is cleared of all dishes except coffee cups and

saucers. Margaret wears an apron, as does Evelyn, but she's too in-
volved in the argument to work.
We begin the scene with a CLOSEUP OF MARGARET.

MARGARET: He's entitled to better than that from us, George. Why do
you want to rob him? Has he been that bad a father to you?

GEORGE: Rob? How? Why am I——? Did I ever say that? Does that
have anything to do with it? I want the same things you want!

EVELYN (*To Margaret*): Are you keeping him? Why did you bring him
home?

MARGARET: *You* said bring him home.

EVELYN: Unless you want him to move in with you.

GEORGE: Don't accuse me, Meg, unless you're ready to take on the responsibility.

PHIL: George, she's——

MARGARET: You know I can't.

GEORGE: You can't?

MARGARET: No, I can't.

GEORGE: Then God, will you stop? Will you stop with me?

PHIL: What is this? Feeding time at the zoo?

GEORGE: She's accusing me of not loving him! Why should I be defending? I love him as much as you do . . .

MARGARET: You want to ship him off to an institution, not me——

GEORGE: This place is a home, it's not an institution! I went to different
places, I wouldn't . . .

MARGARET (*Continuing without pausing*): I have a five-and-a-half room
apartment, that's five rooms, five rooms. For two adults and three
children. We just can't handle a bigger rent. You have nine rooms in
this house, rent free . . .

GEORGE: You want my tax bill?

MARGARET: Oh, George! This is his house, built with his own hands, like
this table! It was such a damn happy place . . . He built it for Mom;
he has—nine rooms; you have yourselves and two children and you
can't find room for him!

GEORGE: Look at him, Meg! There's nothing left of the man who built it,
and he's agreed, he said I could look for a home . . .

EVELYN: When are we supposed to have a life of our own? (*She holds out
a hand to silence George, who is about to speak*) Do you think that man
is happy now? By what right—listen, George has paid taxes and up-
keep on this house for ten years. George does the repairs, the work,
the deed is in his name! Plus running the agency! But we've never
had a home here, and it may sound cold, but when do Peter's children come into their own? When is the man I married going to be the

head of this household? Your father—and I love him, too, I do—sits like a cancer, sits in his workshop like a lump, a stone, a cancer, just sits, can't cope with the children . . . Beth and Scott just get on his nerves, he frightens them, and you sit up in Boston and say he's not going to be put in a home? Well, he *is* going to be put in a home, yours if you want, or someplace where there are other old people and trained nurses and doctors and . . . I'm sorry. I'm sorry, I'm done. *Evelyn, struggling with tears of frustration, goes into the kitchen. We watch her as we hear from the other room . . .*

MARGARET'S VOICE: Sending him to die! Sending him to die!

GEORGE'S VOICE: Will you look at this brochure, Meg? Look, will you?

THE CAMERA remains focused on the kitchen. And as the discussion goes on in the other room, we . . .

DISSOLVE TO:

THE INTERIOR OF THE BACK BEDROOM. The sounds of the discussion are audible, but not fully intelligible. In the bedroom, the three children are sitting on the daybed. They are whispering and giggling to each other.

PHILLY: Then you'll be able to play in his shop all the time.

SCOTT (*Happily*): Yeah. If they let us.

PHILLY: I guess he's going to a hotel, huh?

SCOTT: You ever been in a hotel?

PHILLY: No, a motel.

SCOTT: No, no, a *mo*tel-*ho*tel.

Scott and Philly both giggle at this. Beth smiles and says in mock amazement . . .

BETH: A *moo*-tell *who*-tell?

The children giggle again. Philly slips out of the bed and crawls on the floor.

BETH: Hey, where you going?

PHILLY: C'mon . . .

Scott leaps out of bed to follow Philly, who has reached the train transformer and turned it on. The train lights blink on and the engine begins to move. Beth watches.

BETH: If they hear us . . .

No response from the boys, so Beth joins them.

PHILLY: I love those headlights . . .

DISSOLVE TO:

PETER'S ROOM.

The discussion is still going on in the background. Peter's suitcase is on the arms of the chair and is almost empty. The small corner table now is crowded with bottles, cans, and tubes of medications. The bed, disar-

rayed, has been slept in, but Peter is not here. The door to his room is open. We see a light coming from the shop in the basement.

                                    DISSOLVE TO:

THE INTERIOR OF THE SHOP. *While very distant, the voices can still be heard. The shop is illuminated by a single lamp. A workbench in the center of the room is piled with odd pieces of furniture framework, including an upturned chair which is missing a leg. Silent power machinery fills part of the room. The walls are lined with cabinets. Carefully kept tools are in chests resting on shelves.*

Peter, in pajamas that seem too large for him, is coming down the stairs. He knows, with the faint sounds of the argument still whispering through the house, that he will be leaving this house. He crosses to a counter and removes a metal cash box from a drawer. He opens the box and takes out a small oval picture of a young woman . . . young Rose . . . head and chest portrait set in a heavy silver frame. Peter puts it in his pajama pocket. He starts out, stops to look at the upturned chair. He picks up the missing leg, blows dust off it, looks at it remotely, then puts it down. He moves to another work table. The tool chests on this table are also covered with dust. One chest is open and a couple of tools have been left out on the table. He picks up a tool and places it inside the chest.

                                  SLOW DISSOLVE TO:

THE LIVING ROOM, *as Margaret, Phil, and George enter from the dining room, still carrying on the argument. Margaret holds the brochure, and she's crying. Phil is shaking his head.*

PHIL: All right now, sweetie, it isn't called for.

GEORGE: Oh, Meg, Meg, I want him to be happy. Well, he will be when he's with his own kind.

MARGARET: I thought we were his own kind, we're his children.

GEORGE: That doesn't help. He's not living. (*He is being very gentle, and the tremor in his voice is beyond his control*) He fell apart when Mom died, he stopped working, and that was it, Meg . . . for ten years there's been no family, we just torment the man. He's so old. We're not his kind, now. OK? Am I right, Meg? Won't you say I'm right?

MARGARET: This morning before we left he asked me who was going to mourn him.

GEORGE: If you had the room, Meg, would you take him? He told me he'd go to wherever we decided, so how about it? (*Pause*) All right.

MARGARET: But you're the one who's sending him . . . to an institution.

GEORGE: No! Make an unpleasant decision once in your life, will you?
Margaret looks at him, tense, torn, defeated. There is acquiescence as she finally opens her mouth to speak. At the point where we would hear her "yes," we . . .

CUT TO:

PETER, CLOSING THE LAST TOOL CHEST AND SNAPPING THE LOCK.
We see Peter sigh . . . he, too, is resigned.

CUT TO:

THE DINING ROOM OF THE GOLDEN DAYS HOME.

The room is half filled. There are only the desultory and subdued sounds of eating . . . virtually no conversation. MARIAN, one of the cooks, is serving dessert. Peter is just finishing his meat course. The only other diner at his table is a white-haired man seated across from him, watching him. A latecomer enters and begins to argue with an interloper seated in his usual place. The new entrant, MR. MASTERS, is palsied.

MR. MASTERS: You're sitting in my chair.

At Peter's table, the white-haired man, ARTHUR SELIG, dabs his mouth with his napkin, then rises. He moves around the table toward Peter.

ARTHUR: Since I have eaten a whole meal with you it would be nice that we know who we are, and I am Arthur Selig. S–E–L–I–G.

PETER: Peter Schermann is my name.

ARTHUR (*Sitting beside him*): Now if they ask me I can say I ate with Peter Schermann.

PETER: Selig . . .

ARTHUR: Mmm hmm . . . You'll find it's very quiet. Everybody is dreaming. Sometimes, however, it's not so quiet, when there's a fight.

PETER: Who fights?

ARTHUR: Who fights? Some lady don't like the food, it isn't cooked like at home, some man says another man, his roomie, takes his handkerchiefs, something like that, the set is too loud, the set is too soft, some lady don't like to take so many baths, it happens. Who's your roomie?

PETER: Mr. L. Collum.

ARTHUR: Collum. He won't last long, that man.

PETER: I think he's ill . . .

ARTHUR: One of these nights. I don't know why, they always go at night.

The cook, Marian, appears at Peter's side.

MARIAN: You the new gentleman, sir?

PETER: Yes?

MARIAN: I'm Marian, one of the cooks, it's my pleasure to serve you. Is the food satisfactory in every way?

PETER: Is this the big meal?

MARIAN: Afternoon dinner, yes, sir.

PETER: I eat the big meal at night. Could I have the heavy dinner at night?

MARIAN: Just a moment, sir.

She pads away. Arthur waits until she's out of earshot. He shakes his head.

ARTHUR: You won't get it.

PETER: I was told . . . just if I would ask . . .

ARTHUR: You won't get it.

DR. KELLER and Marian come walking from the hall to the table where Peter and Arthur sit. Keller is a medium-sized and well-groomed German, with a cheerful manner that defies shattering.

KELLER: Father Schermann, you remember me? I am Dr. Keller.

PETER: Yes.

KELLER: I can explain about the meals . . .

PETER: I was explaining to this lady that in my home the big meal——

KELLER: You see, the experience of our trained people is that the heavy foods served in the evening interfere with the nighttime slowing down of the digestive processes . . . the digestive processes. And so we find that growing accustomed to the afternoon meal as the substantial meal is most satisfactory. You see? And is the food good, do you find?

PETER: The taste was all right, was fine, but——

KELLER: Thank you. Marian, Father Schermann can have his dessert now.

And Keller is gone. Peter looks at Arthur, who allows himself a sympathetic smile.

Across the room, a tall short-haired woman in a tailored blouse, and skirt . . . a pencil clipped on a chain to her collar . . . is moving among the diners. At each table she bends over and speaks softly. She is MRS. STONE.

MRS. STONE: We should write letters home this afternoon. Don't you think so? (*She moves to another table*) Mrs. Ermish, we should write a letter home this afternoon, don't you think so?

MRS. ERMISH: Uh . . . yes . . .

Mrs. Stone leans across the table where MRS. LANG and Mr. Masters are eating.

MRS. STONE: We should write letters home this afternoon. Don't you think so? Mr. Masters, when Marian is free she can write for you. It'll be nice.

MRS. LANG: Could she write mine?

But Mrs. Stone has gone to another table.

MRS. STONE: We should write letters home. Don't you think so?

She moves to Peter's table. Peter is now eating a dish of pasty rice pudding Marian has brought him.

MRS. STONE: Mr. Schermann, I'm Mrs. Stone, I'm the Activities Chairman and the general counselor and the chief cook-and-bottle-washer, so you just bring any problems to me and we'll smooth them out for you. I'm also a trained nurse, if you have any health problems, there's not a thing to be embarrassed over. Thank you. Letter writing, Mr. Selig.

She moves on. After a suitable pause, Arthur fixes a baleful glare at her retreating figure.

ARTHUR: She's a problem smoother all right. Behind me against the wall is a spinet piano, you see it?

PETER: The mahogany?

ARTHUR: You know pianos?

PETER: I know woods.

ARTHUR: I'm no musician, but at one time I could play the piano not masterly but well, yet when I ask Mrs. Problem-Smoother to allow me the use of that piano I get a nice smooth "no." A piano locked up is a deaf mute, Mr. Schermann. You won't mind if I don't call you "father." A deaf mute.

Peter looks carefully at the piano.

PETER: I can make one, I've made the cabinetry. I made one for my wife . . . I like to listen . . . but to play a musical instrument, they're all locked to me . . .

ARTHUR: You could be Ignace Paderewski and the piano would be locked. No, excuse me, and thank you for talking. My ears are almost dried away from the quiet here.

Arthur starts walking away. Peter rises and follows him. As Arthur passes the piano he lets his hand trail over the closed keyboard cover. When Peter passes the piano, he pauses just to let a splayed thumb test the corner of the piano top.

The two men walk into the hall which separates the dining room from the parlor. There is a staircase leading up. Arthur puts his hand on the newel post and waits until Peter reaches him.

ARTHUR: What kind of wood is this, if you know wood?

Peter looks at the post, nodding his head, appreciating the workmanship. He handles it.

PETER: This is a fine black walnut newel post, well made but loose at the bottom. Feel it?

Peter leans over as far as he dares to watch the base of the post as he shakes it.

MRS. ERMISH comes out of the dining hall and moves directly to Arthur Selig.

Melvyn Douglas in *Do Not Go Gentle into That Good Night*.

MRS. ERMISH: Mr. Selig, I just thought—today, I think, is one of my granddaughters' birthdays. I think . . . I think today.

ARTHUR: Celebrate. Put in a call.

MRS. ERMISH: Yes. I think I'll write a letter.

She moves into the lounge. Peter watches her, then looks at Arthur, who is looking back at the piano.

PETER: What is the reason? Why is it locked?

ARTHUR: Are they afraid my fingers will break? When I played as a lad, 18 or 19, for the silent films, the silent screen, my fingers were mercurial, they were lightning on the keyboard. I was a manufacturer of ladies' handbags, which my son now owns and operates, which I was so tired and never happy about, Mr. Schermann . . . my friend, we sometimes used gumwood for wooden handles, you know gumwood?

Peter nods.

ARTHUR: Yes, sir. Yes, sir, I could play very well . . .

PETER: You ought to play it, then.

ARTHUR: Open the lock. Open the lock, carpenter.

Peter wanders back to the piano. Mrs. Stone sees Peter enter and walks to him.

MRS. STONE: Is there something I can do, Mr. Schermann?

PETER: I . . . uh . . . there's a man here I met. He plays the piano. I think he's a Hebrew. He wants to play the piano . . .

Mrs. Stone has stiffened somewhat, she knows what's coming.

MRS. STONE: Mr. Selig, you mean?

PETER: I think everybody would enjoy——

MRS. STONE (*Overriding him*): We'll have to arrange that. It might be very nice. I'll see about it.

She moves away and Peter starts for the stairs.

PETER: Yes. Fine. Mrs. Stone?

MRS. STONE: Yes.

PETER: This newel post is loose.

He is moving up the stairs.

Mrs. Stone now knows that Schermann will be a troublemaker.

MRS. STONE (*Moving back to him*): We'll have to fix it. But . . . (*She waves at the "All Guests Use Elevator" sign*) We prefer that you use the elevator.

PETER (*Looks at the sign, then back at her*): For guests.

MRS. STONE: Yes.

PETER: But this is my home now.

Mrs. Stone stares hard at him; then her face tightens into a smile. After a moment, Peter starts toward the lounge and Mrs. Stone moves away. But as Peter looks into the lounge ahead of him, the room seems like a museum exhibit. He stops and looks.

THE CAMERA PANS the lounge. At the beginning we see several recognizable inhabitants of the home. But as THE CAMERA moves laterally we begin to see mannequins set in daydreaming poses, and by the end of the pan the mannequins are faceless. The final movement of the camera is a speeded up sweep in the same direction as the pan, finding young Rose standing before her dressmaking form, basting together the cut panels for a dress on the form.

YOUNG ROSE (*To Peter*): Mr. Schermann, the fabric's going to make a beautiful dress, come and see . . .

Old Peter looks at the lounge with narrowed suspecting eyes.

Arthur has been watching Peter.

ARTHUR: You'll find here you spend more and more time dreaming. Then it's all dreaming. Then it's nothing. If you're lucky, you're in somebody else's dream.

Peter thinks about this. He understands.

PETER: You mean, if someone mourns you . . . ?

Peter turns and moves to the stairs. He pauses. He remembers, then slowly goes to the elevator and presses the button.

FADE TO BLACK.

ACT TWO

FADE IN: A CLOSEUP OF A PORTABLE MOVIE SCREEN, set up in the dining hall, reflecting a gaudy Busby Berkeley-type musical film of the early Forties. A man in white tie and tails is dancing crazily in front of a chorus of sequin-spangled breasty Hollywood dolls to a bad fast tune, vintage, "Lady of the Evening."

THE CAMERA MOVES back and through the dining hall. It is night. The tables have been pushed into the corner near the piano. The chairs have been set in rows, and the old people sit watching but hardly comprehending the film, bored by it. One or two people are asleep. One old man leers at the screen in a caricature of lust. Two old women talk to one another, heads down. THE CAMERA CIRCLES the room and ends its DOLLY in the hall where the elevator entrance is. A few steps down the hall, outside of the open door to Dr. Keller's office, Arthur stands. Inside Keller's office, Peter talks with Keller.

PETER: There must be times when a musical instrument can be played.

KELLER: It is difficult to understand. That is to say, we have performances here on a regular basis by entertainment people. That's what the piano is for. Your children are paying for that piano, Father

Schermann. (*Confidentially*) There are frankly senile people here. They will pound on the instrument all day. Like children. Mr. Selig is arthritic and would find it painful to play. And difficult. And if we allowed him, how could we deny others? The rules are for everybody. They must be. Go into the dining hall and watch the film, Father Schermann. (*Keller snaps off the desk lamp, puts his arm around Peter's shoulders and moves him toward the door*) We also have band concerts in the summer from the high school. Well, much to be done and miles to go before I sleep.

Keller disappears down the hall. Peter moves slowly to the waiting Arthur.

ARTHUR: I assume the problem is all smooth.

PETER: You ought to play the piano.

ARTHUR: Well . . . (*After a moment, he, looking vaguely into the dining hall, inclines his head toward the rows of chairs*) We might as well . . .

Arthur walks slowly into the dining room and takes a seat. Peter follows, even more slowly. Peter sits just one seat in from the end of a row. He looks at the screen. There are tears in his eyes.

FADE TO BLACK.

FADE IN: IT IS AFTERNOON IN THE GOLDEN DAYS HOME. *Peter is asleep on his bed, his back against the headboard or frame, his eyes closed. Mr. Collum is on the other bed, asleep. Peter's fist is clenched. He flexes the fingers of one hand, and in the flexing we . . .*

DISSOLVE TO THE HAND OF YOUNG PETER. *It holds a small wooden toy. We are in the kitchen-like area of the Schermann home. Young Rose sits at a table, feeding an infant (Margaret), who sits in a wooden high-chair. Rose looks up at young Peter, over whose shoulder we see her accusatory expression.*

YOUNG ROSE: No, he won't know you, he doesn't know me, but something must get through if you talk to him, hold the boy's hand, Peter, you don't want him to—suppose—he could die, you don't want him to die without his father to mourn him, do you, Peter?

PETER: Rose, I'm sure—why believe—?

YOUNG ROSE: Meg, *don't spit, don't spit!* (*She wipes the baby's mouth, then turns angrily to Peter*) The poor little boy has been lying like that for two days and where have you been? Building something? Building him a coffin instead of being a father?

PETER: A toy . . .

YOUNG ROSE: Why haven't you made him a coffin?

Old Peter is startled by the sharpness of her reply. Again there are tears in his eyes, as he sits on his bed in his room. Peter waves a hand in front

of his face to erase the memory just experienced. Collum, still asleep,
rolls restlessly on his bed. All motion seems slow, there is almost no
sound, a cottony silence, and a light distant ticking. Breathing can be
heard. Peter tries to clear his head. He looks around. He leans back and
closes his eyes . . .
Young Rose reaches out to take the toy from young Peter's hand. Now
she smiles.

YOUNG ROSE: What have you made for him? A toy? May I see it? (*She*
takes it from him, examines it lovingly, moves the movable parts) The
arms move. (*She looks up at Peter*) I'll give it to him. It's so skillfully
done . . . I know he'll love it . . .
Old Peter smiles, satisfied with the way he has rearranged the past. His
eyes are still closed as he hears . . .

YOUNG ROSE'S VOICE: Where have you been? Building something?
Old Peter is disturbed. Defeated. The truth of the past reasserts itself
. . . we see the memory again.

YOUNG ROSE: Building him a coffin instead of being a father?

PETER: A toy . . .

YOUNG ROSE: Why haven't you made him a coffin?

OLD PETER: I don't know what to do, Rose . . .

YOUNG ROSE: Do *something,* Peter, don't just give him up, please, please
do something . . .
Old Peter is fully awake, fully disturbed. He presses the call button.
                                CUT TO:
THE KITCHEN. *Marian talks with JOSEPHA, a heavy but alert Negress,*
in a white uniform, white stockings, and brown-and-white space shoes.
Josepha's arms are full of folded towels. The call-board indicator shows
the ring from Peter's room. Josepha leaves at once.
                                CUT TO:
PETER'S ROOM. *Josepha enters and goes immediately to check Mr. Col-*
lum.

PETER: Josepha?
Peter, sitting on his bed, is holding tightly to the headboard. In the other
bed, Collum is still asleep and breathing hoarsely.

JOSEPHA: Yes, Mr. Schermann?

PETER: Is Mr. Selig in his room? Which is Mr. Selig's room?

JOSEPHA: He's down the hall and at the end of the turn, toward the back.

PETER: Thank you. Would you sit down there?

JOSEPHA: That's your chair.

PETER: But you sit in it.

JOSEPHA: No, sir.

PETER: Please Josepha, I . . . I want to talk.

JOSEPHA (*After a moment*): What? (*But Peter doesn't answer, so she finally sits in the rocker and rocks back and forth, smiling*) My, this is nice. *Slowly, Peter gets off the bed and goes to his chest of drawers, removes from a drawer the still-wrapped silver-framed picture of his wife. He unwraps it and holds it out to Josepha.*

PETER: Look at this . . .

JOSEPHA (*Takes the picture, studies it*): My, a lovely lovely lady. This is Missus Schermann?

PETER: Yes . . . Josepha, you know the mahogany piano in the dining room?

JOSEPHA: Yes, sir. I know it.

PETER: What would it take to get it unlocked?

JOSEPHA: Unlocked? Well I don't know. You can't get the key? You can't get them to unlock it?

PETER: No.

JOSEPHA: Well I don't know about that.

PETER: That's a silver frame. It was made in 1799.

JOSEPHA: My. A long time ago.

PETER: Look at the back. The back slides open and the picture lifts out. Take the picture out, Josepha.

She hesitates.

PETER: Take it out.

JOSEPHA (*As she removes the picture*): Something written on the back of it? (*As she examines the removed photograph*) No.

PETER: Do you think you could get that piano opened, Josepha?

JOSEPHA: I don't know.

PETER: Suppose you give me the picture and keep the frame . . .

JOSEPHA: I don't know, Mr. Schermann. You best take this all back.

PETER: Give me the picture. Keep the frame. What do you think?

Josepha stands up slowly. She has been deeply hurt by the bribe, considering herself to be conspicuously incorruptible. She looks at Peter for a long time, hands him the photograph, drops the frame in her pocket.

JOSEPHA: Well, sir. We'll see.

Peter takes the picture and Josepha walks stiffly from the room. He watches her go. He rewraps the photograph in the handkerchief, replaces it in the drawer, and goes out of the room and down the hall toward Arthur's room.

Peter has turned the corner at the end of the hall, and now looks at the name cards on the doors until he finds the right door. He knocks. It is opened by Arthur, who wears a faded silk bathrobe over his clothes.

ARTHUR: Welcome. Welcome.

PETER: Would you come downstairs with me, Mr. Selig?

ARTHUR: Do we see enough of downstairs or do we not? But I'll ask you to come in here and visit . . .

PETER: Downstairs . . .

ARTHUR (*Searching Peter's expression*): What? The scheme? The piano?

PETER: I talked to her . . .

ARTHUR (*Suddenly bursting with energy and excitement*): All right. All right. Just let me get ready. Just a minute.

Arthur hurriedly removes his robe and straightens his shirt . . .

CUT TO:

THE DINING ROOM. *Mrs. Stone walks through the dining room and out of sight. Josepha stands in a corner of the dining room talking to Marian in low tones. Both women look at Mrs. Stone and stop talking while she passes. Mrs. Stone casually returns their gaze.*

A moment after Mrs. Stone has gone from sight, Marian goes back to the kitchen. Josepha walks to the front stairs. She looks blankly toward the lounge. Arthur and Peter sit near the front hall, in the lounge, and both look at Josepha questioningly. She nods "no" ever so slightly, walks up the steps. Arthur is still eager and nervous.

ARTHUR: How did you do it? This is wonderful. I'm shaking.

On the television screen behind them we can see a chase with comic animated animals. The music is distinctly agitato.

CUT TO:

THE KITCHEN, *where Marian takes a key from the keyrack.*

Then she steps into the hall, looking carefully along the hall at the closed doors of the offices. Then she walks slowly and carefully along the hall into the dining room and to the piano. She takes the key from her pocket and unlocks the keyboard cover, then returns the key swiftly to her pocket. Casually, she turns and walks back to the kitchen.

THE CAMERA TURNS *to see Josepha come down the stairs from the landing to nod at Peter and Arthur. Josepha then returns to the landing, where she leans against the wall to watch and listen. From her point of view we see Peter and Arthur cross the front hall and enter into the dining room. They cross directly to the piano. Peter tries the keyboard cover, lifts it back.*

Arthur stares at the keyboard, rubbing his hands to warm them. He puts his fingers in place on the keys, but does not press down hard enough to make the hammers strike. Peter pulls a chair behind Arthur. Arthur sits down, looks up at Peter with tears of joy in his eyes, and then looks at the keyboard and starts to play. He plays "To a Wild Rose" from MacDowell's "Woodland Sketches." He plays very badly. He is straining and sweating to remember, to move his fingers fast enough.

Peter, totally unaware that the playing is really bad, smiles at Arthur. On the stairs, Josepha listens. She starts to nod her head to the slow plodding rhythm, the playing stumbles, she sadly turns, goes upstairs shaking her head "no."

ARTHUR: I'm . . . out of practice . . .

PETER: No, no . . .

Several other people gather around the piano.

MR. MASTERS: Can he play "Evening Star"?

ARTHUR: I'm away out of practice . . . I'm sorry . . .

MRS. ERMISH: I could play "Für Elise" . . .

Arthur stops playing, takes his hands off the keyboard.

PETER: Please. Play more.

Mr. Masters hobbles away.

ARTHUR: Peter . . .

PETER: Very nice . . .

ARTHUR: No.

Arthur looks down hopelessly at his hands.

MRS. ERMISH: When my fingers weren't so crippled up I played so well, I played "Für Elise," I played "Marche Militaire" . . .

PETER: Play more, Mr. Selig, please.

But Arthur looks at his hands, defeated.

PETER: Won't you finish it? It's music . . .

Arthur tries to complete the piece, and it disintegrates at the conclusion. Arthur puts his trembling hands on his knees. The keyboard cover suddenly moves down over the keyboard. Arthur looks up to see Mrs. Stone smiling down at him.

MRS. STONE: That was very nice, Mr. Selig. Thank you for playing for us. Did you find the piano open?

ARTHUR: Yes . . . I just found it open.

PETER: I opened it.

MRS. STONE: You opened it?

PETER: I know about locks, Mrs. Stone. I opened the lock.

MRS. STONE: With what, Mr. Schermann?

PETER: I opened it.

MRS. STONE (*With unflagging friendliness*): With what, Mr. Schermann?

PETER: With a wooden kitchen match, Mrs. Stone, which I found on the floor near the elevator.

MRS. STONE: You must be very skillful. It's admirable. May I see the match? Where is the match now?

PETER: It's in my pocket, Mrs. Stone. Do you want to reach in and get it?

Mrs. Stone finally blushes. After a moment of dead silence, she turns her smiling face to beam at Arthur.

MRS. STONE: Some day you will have to play for us again, Mr. Selig.

*She stands guarding the piano. The two men walk away. Then, she turns
and walks into the rear hall past the elevator, scanning the floor.*

*Then she enters the kitchen. Marian and JOHN, the assistant cook, are
busily at work shredding cabbage. Mrs. Stone looks at the large board on
the wall where the keys of the house are labeled and hung. She takes the
piano key, looks angrily at Marian and John, and strides toward the dining hall.*

*The moment she's gone, Marian and John relax. Marian has a head of
cabbage which she picks up and slams down onto the chopping board
with an obvious meaning. John smiles at her.*

JOHN: That's a fine head of cabbage. That's a fine head of cabbage.
The two cooks laugh gleefully.

CUT TO:

PETER'S ROOM. *Peter and Arthur sit quietly. COLLUM for once, is not
in the room. Arthur is on the verge of tears.*

ARTHUR: The Vitascope Theater. Ten cents. In nineteen ten. A salary
there wasn't. Yes. A slide would come on . . . "Music by the nimble
fingers of Arthur W. Selig."
Peter has been watching Arthur with a growing horror and anger.

PETER: It was good, it was fine . . .

ARTHUR: It was terrible.

PETER: No, please . . .

ARTHUR: It was terrible. My fingers . . . I thought they were still . . .
I'm a baby . . . I'm so old I'm a baby . . .
*Peter looks at the helpless Mr. Selig, and at that moment Josepha,
wheeling the helpless Mr. Collum in a wheelchair, enters the room. Collum's expression is one of frozen anger.*

JOSEPHA: We've had a nice walk. Mr. Collum wants to bed down again.
Well, we had some excitement, didn't we? Mr. Schermann, I put the
picture frame in your drawer. It's in your little drawer.
She begins to prepare the bed to receive Mr. Collum.

PETER: No, that was for——

JOSEPHA: Well I give it back, I don't take no payolas, Mr. Schermann. I
kept it awhile to see if I needed it downstairs, which I didn't, and
don't give it to no one, Mr. Schermann. You put your wife back in it.
(*She starts lifting Collum from the chair*) Here we go . . .
*Peter and Arthur watch as Josepha picks up Collum and deposits him in
the bed and tucks him in.*

ARTHUR: We're babies . . .

PETER: No . . . Josepha, he ought to play the piano every day.

JOSEPHA: I can't help again, Mr. Schermann. They'll let us go.

ARTHUR (*At the same time as Josepha speaks above*): I'm too old . . .

PETER: Tell them they should do something about the newel post, downstairs. Tell them to get someone . . . it's loose. Someone to fix it.

CUT TO:

*A CLOSEUP OF THE CARPENTER'S TOOLBOX as it is placed on the floor by
LARRY McDERMOTT, a 35-year-old handyman wearing coveralls.
THE CAMERA PULLS BACK to reveal Dr. Keller and McDermott at the
newel post.*

KELLER: . . . these old people hold on to anything for support, and
something could happen.

MC DERMOTT: I could slap a brace on it . . .

KELLER (*Hoarsely, as he leaves McDermott*): Don't let anyone pick up a
tool. Shortcut to a lawsuit . . .

*Dr. Keller goes back to the kitchen. McDermott steps forward and tests
the firmness of the banister. He takes off his jacket and gets down on his
knees to examine the molded edge of the stair. He reaches up to shake
the post back and forth. Suddenly the post is firm. McDermott looks up
and sees Peter, holding the top of the post firmly with one hand.*

PETER: You'll have to start in the basement.

MC DERMOTT: That's all right. I'll fix it.

PETER: I'm union.

MC DERMOTT: Good.

PETER: My name is Peter Schermann.

MC DERMOTT: It's all right, Pop.

PETER (*Reaching into the toolbox*): That's right. You pry the trim and I'll
go down in the basement.

MC DERMOTT (*Grabbing Peter's hand*): Don't touch the tools, just sit down
somewhere and watch.

PETER (*Still staring at the tools*): I know every joint in a house like this.

MC DERMOTT: Sure . . .

*McDermott looks at the post. He never gives his direct attention to Peter.
He is searching his pockets. He finds a pencil, and rummages in the toolbox for an L-iron brace.*

PETER: Do you have some fillets? I think it has to be wedged again, the
wood on the stringer is a little spongy.

MC DERMOTT: I'm not going to build a new staircase. I'm just going to
screw down a good tight bracket. That'll hold it till the house falls
down.

PETER: Bracket?

MC DERMOTT: Right here. An L-iron. That's all it needs.

He shows Peter the bracket he intends to use.

PETER: This isn't some loft ladder, this is a stair . . .

MC DERMOTT: I know, I know. Just let me do it, will you?

He puts the bracket against the wood, and with his pencil scribes the screw holes.

PETER: Are you really a carpenter?

MC DERMOTT: I sure am.

PETER: Listen to me, I know how this stair is built, and if you don't, I'll tell you. It's constructed, it goes through the sub-floor and down along the joist. It needs repair, but you don't jam a piece of iron in up above . . . black walnut leans to cracking . . . here . . .

McDermott is about to hammer the first screw-hole. Peter interferes, grabbing the hammer.

MC DERMOTT: I just want to make it safe.

PETER: Learn your trade first.

MC DERMOTT: Let go.

PETER: You don't do that.

MC DERMOTT: Mister, let go. (*Calling*) Dr. Keller!

PETER: You sit down. I know——

MC DERMOTT: Dr. Keller!

He begins to slowly push Peter back toward the lounge.

PETER: You won't hammer up that stair. I won't let you do that . . .

MC DERMOTT: Dr. Keller! (*Softly but firmly, intensely*) No. I won't do that. I'm just going to tighten that post with a bracket, now you stay away, let go of that hammer . . .

He is prying Peter's fingers from the hammer shaft as Dr. Keller runs into the room. Some of the old folks are crowding around. McDermott has trouble with Peter's grip. Peter and McDermott are challenging one another.

KELLER: What is it? Father Schermann . . . (*To McDermott*) Why did you give him the hammer?

MC DERMOTT (*Wresting away the hammer as Keller steps between him and Peter*): Wait a minute.

PETER: I could do that.

KELLER: I can't allow you to.

PETER: That man is no carpenter! Let me fix that staircase.

KELLER: Father Schermann, this man is a fine carpenter, the stairs will be fixed, let him do his job . . . You're done with that, Father Schermann . . .

PETER: Be still!!

KELLER: You can relax——

PETER: Be still!

KELLER: You're an old man. It's time you rest.

PETER: Rest! What do you know about me? You close off—I'm not dead yet . . .

KELLER: Father Schermann . . .

PETER: I'll leave this place!

KELLER: I can't allow——

PETER: I will leave this place!

KELLER: We will talk to your son——

PETER (*Turning to Keller and the crowd*): I will leave this place!

KELLER: You will *not*, sir.

PETER: Can you stop me?

Keller, furiously angry, stares at Peter. During the pause Keller regains his control.

KELLER: You are upsetting everyone.

PETER: I hope so! . . . I hope I upset *you*, Keller . . . because I . . . I am going to walk out of here! It was my agreement to come! Canceled! No! (*He has started up the stairs. He turns back to them*) I'm going to be gone!

Peter gets to the landing, then part-way up the second series of the steps. He leans against the wall, trembling with anger, but eyes full of fear.

FADE TO BLACK.

FADE IN: THE INTERIOR OF THE HOLLY VALLEY HOME FOR THE AGED. *Peter, in other clothing, is walking down the corridor.*

The different tone of this place is almost immediately apparent. Here there is life and spirit and a clean comfortable atmosphere. The old people are active and talkative. Only a slight and inescapable institutional flavor remains. The neatly uniformed nurses and volunteers are friendly but just a shade brisk. No false emotion, no patronizing, rather the other way around. We will learn after a while that there is a warm lack of meticulousness and an irreverence for regulation which reflect the character of the director.

Peter looks around as he walks down the ramp from the second floor. He approaches a bulletin board labeled "Activities." As he stands reading, several others stop to read the notices. Peter watches as one man, WALLACE SLOCUM, pins up a notice, while his companion, ROBERT RAGLE, looks at the board. Slocum sees Peter, calls to him.

SLOCUM: Enamel frying pan, seven-inch. Long wooden handle, no burning, four-fifty.

Peter nods "no" as he turns to enter the glass doors of the game room. There are a number of game tables . . . ping-pong, billiards. There are green couches and chairs with chrome frames. There is a television set, turned on to one of the late-afternoon teenage dance parties. Several old couples are dancing. Peter watches as a song ends and a commercial for some complexion-clearing ointment comes on (back-to-back with one of those free-swinging-hair shampoo jobs). A woman who had been dancing energetically comes straight for Peter. She is in her late sixties, but she looks fifty. Solidly fleshed and trim with carefully tinted gold hair and a vivacious manner. Her name is HELOISE MICHAUD.

HELOISE: Can you dance?

PETER: No.

HELOISE: You can't? (*Meaning "too bad"*)

PETER: I don't think so . . .

HELOISE: We could find out. I dance all the time. I love to dance. My name is Heloise Michaud. Your name is . . . ?

PETER: Peter Schermann. This is my first day . . .

HELOISE: I guessed that, I know who's new. You're a fine-looking man, Mr. Schermann, why don't you try and dance with me?

PETER: I don't believe I'm ready yet for that.

HELOISE: We've got to be modern, sir. If we're not up-to-date, we're discarded. Wouldn't you like to try? Take me, I won't break.

PETER: I'm not . . . modern.

HELOISE: Be modern!

PETER: I like to hold on to things.

HELOISE: That great man, Albert Einstein, said that possessions were stones that would drag him down.

And, as music starts up again . . .

HELOISE: There's the music, hear the rhythm? Come, come, hear the rhythm, keep up with the world, Mr. Schermann.

PETER: Thank you, no.

HELOISE: You've got time to change your mind.

PETER: That's right. Who knows?

HELOISE: Very right. I accept. Who knows? (*She turns, smiling, to Slocum, who is entering with Ragle*) Mr. Slocum, I'm yours.

RAGLE (*To Peter*): Play pool?

PETER: No.

Peter watches for a moment as he wanders through the room. He exits from another door into another corridor. As he stands looking around, DR. GETTLINGER approaches with a businessman in tow. Gettlinger is a disheveled and energetic man of 45, with a firm speech and a quiet voice. He is always harried but never confused.

GETTLINGER: . . . was hoping to get a larger slice from the United Fund, but we're getting squeezed instead. (*He hardly stops moving as he speaks to Peter*) Mr. Schermann, hope you're getting on. Anything wrong, come to the office, chances are I can help you. (*As he walks on he resumes his*

conversation with the businessman) Understaffed, underequipped, under-
financed . . .
Peter opens the door indicating "Crafts." The sound of machines is heard
instantly. Peter steps into a large room. There are looms, ceramics equip-
ment, potter's wheel and kiln, workbenches, and some small electric wood-
working machinery. On a shelf are a number of paper and cardboard funny
hats. Just a few people are here. Peter is unprepared for the familiar odors of
sawdust and a glue-pot. MRS. FLAGLER is the volunteer worker in charge.
PETER: Is this . . . for anyone?
MRS. FLAGLER: Yes it is. I'm Mrs. Flagler. Did you want to try something? You can build. You can weave, paint, ceramics, jewelry, those
hats are made for our hat contests . . . have you ever done anything
you'd like to try?
PETER (*Staring at the woodworking tools*): I worked with wood.
Mrs. Flagler leads Peter to the wood box where odds and ends of various
kinds of wood are jumbled together.
MRS. FLAGLER: Here's our wood box, small pieces. We can get lumber,
too. We have pattern books, if you like. What would you like to make?
Peter is sorting through the box. He comes up with a piece of 4 × 4
about 15" long.
PETER: This isn't pine.
MRS. FLAGLER: What? . . .
PETER: This is cherrywood.
Mrs. Flagler leads Peter to a workbench where tools are laid out.
MRS. FLAGLER: I'm afraid you've got beyond me. These are wood tools
. . . that's an unlikely piece. What can you carve out of that, do you
suppose? Statuette?
PETER: This could be many things. A small box, the start of a chair. The
start of a chair. For a child.
MRS. FLAGLER: I wouldn't of thought of that. Show me.
Peter looks at the woman, then looks at the wood. He reaches out, picks
up a metal straight-edge and a compass with a pencil attached. He scribes a
tapered line along one face of the 4 × 4, and then uses the compass to mark
identical points for the same line on an adjoining face. He scribes the second
line. He picks up a small plane, examines and adjusts the blade, and places
it on the wood. He bears it along the edge of the wood between the two
scribed faces. He looks at the effect thus produced. He doesn't seem aware of
Mrs. Flagler's presence. She watches, impressed, as he starts planing the
wood with an increasingly rhythmic and easy motion. Peter's own expression
is tense at first, but gradually eases into quiet confidence.

DISSOLVE TO:

PETER'S HANDS *as they continue to manipulate the plane and/or other tools.*

DISSOLVE TO:

PART OF A CHILD'S CHAIR, *already made, sitting on a workbench in the crafts room. In the background, a more assured Peter is giving carpentry instruction to Wallace Slocum. Weeks have passed in these dissolves.*

PETER: Now you know the Mitred-and-Splined is one way and the Dovetail is another?

SLOCUM: Yes . . .

PETER: Now what other? . . .

SLOCUM: There's the Lap Dovetail, too. Is that what you mean?

PETER: All right. The Lap Dovetail is half-blind, you see it from one side . . .

SLOCUM: The other side it looks just butted together.

PETER: Now what's this?

He holds out the empty drawer so Slocum can examine the way the side panels join the front face.

SLOCUM: This is just a Mitre. That's all, just a Mitre joint.

PETER: That wouldn't be very strong, would it?

SLOCUM: Nothing to grab.

PETER: All right. (*He takes the drawer apart, revealing a dovetailed joint lapped on both sides*) This is a Blind Dovetail. It's lapped on both sides.

SLOCUM: Ahh . . . secret . . .

PETER: Yes, some people call it a secret . . . (*He crosses to the small-scaled chair he has been making*) Now see this . . . Beth's chair . . .

SLOCUM: That a grandchild?

PETER: Beth, yes, I made the little drawer for the chair for whatever things . . . see how neat and clean at the edge?

Peter slides the drawer into its runners.

DISSOLVE TO:

MARGARET, SITTING IN A CORNER OF HER SMALL APARTMENT-SIZED KITCHEN. *A two-year-old girl (Deb) is on her lap, a four-year-old boy named Buzzy is running around wildly. Philly sits reading a book. Margaret is trying to talk coherently on the telephone.*

MARGARET: Doctor, I don't understand . . . Deb, Deb, *please* . . . Doctor, you *did* talk to him?

PHILLY: Buzzy, cut it out!

MARGARET: Did you tell him we were planning on driving down this——

PHILLY: Mom, I'm going to kick him . . .

MARGARET: Buzzy . . . Then what did he say? Buzzy, you're going to get it. They wait till I'm on the phone—Yes, I don't—We're his family, if I thought you were turning him against his own family. . . . Well, why is it he won't even speak to us on the phone? Why do I always end up being given to you? He's my father. . . .

FADE TO BLACK.

FADE IN: PETER'S BEDROOM. *It is now furnished with many pieces of furniture he has made while at Holly Valley. Peter sits on his bed, reading a letter. The coffee percolator is bubbling on the stove.*

ARTHUR'S VOICE: Dear Mr. Schermann, my friend. It is a quiet afternoon here. The warm weather is very nice. Mrs. Stone wanted to write this letter for me, but I wouldn't let her. Excuse penmanship, but that old devil arthritis is on me. I miss you these many weeks, Mr. Schermann. I am having a good rest.

Peter puts the letter down without finishing it, but he has read it many times before. He rises, looks around, places another cup and saucer on the table near to his own, stuffs the letter in his sweater pocket as he exits the room.

As he approaches the game room, Dr. Gettlinger hurries past him, saying to Peter as he goes . . .

GETTLINGER: I want to talk to you . . .

Peter stops, but Gettlinger rushes past, and after a moment, Peter continues walking.

He arrives at the game room. He stands looking in at the several old people—at least one in a wheelchair—watching television. Among them is Heloise Michaud. She is knitting and paying scant attention to the program. She looks up at Peter through the glass. They look unwaveringly at one another for several moments. Peter tries to smile at her, but it doesn't work out too well. She, however, smiles back. After a moment, Peter turns away and starts back.

HELOISE: Too famous to talk?

Peter turns to see that she has come out of the game room, standing just outside the doors.

PETER: I'd like to talk. (*He takes a step or two toward her*) Why do you say famous?

HELOISE: I remember you, Mr. Schermann. Oh, I hear you make wonderful things. I'm Heloise Michaud. We met before.

PETER: Yes, we did. What are you knitting?

HELOISE: A throw. I'm not very good.

PETER: My wife did it, and quilts and rugs . . . I'd like to offer you a cup of coffee.

HELOISE: In the village? Not this late.

Peter begins walking toward his room, expecting her to follow. But she doesn't, and when he turns, she is standing where she was.

PETER: No. Not in the village. My coffee.

Heloise begins walking after Peter, who turns and continues. She is a few steps behind him.

HELOISE: Who taught you manners, Mr. Schermann?

Peter stops and waits for her to catch up with him.

PETER: I always have coffee cooking. Since the room has that stove . . .

HELOISE: I'm very fussy about coffee . . .

They walk a bit.

HELOISE: I didn't know carpenters knew about cooking.

PETER: Oh, yes. Cook glue.

HELOISE: What?

PETER: You cook your glue. You always have a glue-pot cooking . . . for furniture-making. For cabinet work . . .

HELOISE: You don't use it from the little bottles . . . ?

PETER: Now you've just got to hope I didn't get my recipes mixed . . .

Heloise smiles as the two walk along together. Peter does not look at her, but doggedly straight ahead.

MARY DEVLIN and Robert Ragle step out of the lounge just as Peter and Heloise are passing.

HELOISE: Mary! Hello, Bob . . . I have a coffee date!

Peter keeps on walking. Heloise stands talking very softly but excitedly to Mary, a woman who is always whispering comspiratorially and who has a slight tremor.

MARY: Ha ha. Who? You got a date?

HELOISE: Schermann, you know? He's a carpenter . . .

Peter stops out of earshot, turns and looks for Heloise. She sees him looking and comes quickly to his side. They continue walking . . . turning to the ramp . . .

HELOISE: If she would only take care of herself. But, you know, it's hard to learn to comb your hair with the other hand . . . she doesn't try . . .

They reach the door to Peter's room. Heloise looks in at the percolator.

HELOISE: How long has it been at the boil?

PETER (*Taking the percolator off the stove*): Enough.

He arranges the cups and saucers on the table.

HELOISE: Let me do the honors.

Peter takes spoons, a jar of powdered cream, a box of sugar, from the oven.

PETER: I have sugar . . . this powdered cream . . .

Heloise takes over. Peter sits back and watches her hands pour the coffee. We see the hands very closely. We see Peter, watching silently. Peter

Almira Sessions, Shirley Booth, and Melvyn Douglas in
Do Not Go Gentle into That Good Night.

reaches out for the cup Heloise is handing him and THE CAMERA *brings us back to her. She is happy, and smiling at him. She looks around.*

HELOISE: Is this some of the furniture you've made?

PETER (*With growing enthusiasm, building*): I can show you. I did make some of these pieces . . . and I've been teaching Slocum . . . you know, Wallace Sloc—he gets something from it, I don't know . . . these chairs, but of course I was just getting back to it . . . this one I made from some culls in the woodbox . . . Mrs. Flagler was surprised, to put it mildly . . . but then, a whole life, Miss Michaud. This chest here . . . this will be a lamp, lamps is a new thing, I didn't do that except to turn spindles and finials for a man who put them together . . . wiring is a whole other skill, its own logic, you have to have a head for it. This is a frame for a raffia stool . . . Mrs. Flagler is going to have some lady do the weaving . . . now this, this is a chair for my granddaughter Beth, this wood comes from the wild black cherry tree . . . wait and see how I bring up a shine in it . . . Rose is dead, she died . . . I made the coffin and I just ran down, I just ran down. But it doesn't last, even marble doesn't last, and Rose didn't last. I don't know what to do . . . I don't know . . . you get tired of habits . . . (*He pushes at the stool, dismissing it*) habits . . . she was tired, she died. You run down.

There is a pause. Heloise understands that she has seen what is almost always hidden.

HELOISE: Music, Mr. Schermann. Beauty. Laughing. Independence. I've never married. I regret that, but I do have a fine, fine time.

Another pause.

HELOISE: This is very nice.

PETER: What do you do for that fine time?

HELOISE: Independence. When I want to walk into the village, I do so.

PETER (*Probing*): To do what?

HELOISE: I shop. I was once a buyer in a department store. Now, I shop.

PETER (*Still unconvinced*): Yes . . .

HELOISE: You haven't gone to the village? A movie house, there's a park, there's a botanical garden . . . I walk, I enjoy seeing the children, the windows . . .

PETER: You know people there?

HELOISE: I've made acquaintances . . . I like people, I'm young and I like people. Don't you?

PETER: Who?

HELOISE: Oh, Mr. Schermann . . .

PETER: Why are you here?

HELOISE: I'm retired . . . when you reach a certain year, it's compulsory.

PETER: It's a long way to fall . . . I don't know.

HELOISE: All the past is prologue.

PETER: I've been working very hard.

HELOISE: At things, Mr. Schermann. Possessions are stones on your feet . . .

PETER: You seem like a very wise lady . . .

HELOISE: How are your feet?

PETER: I don't think I'm ready yet for dancing.

HELOISE: I'm starting you with a walk to the village.

PETER: This late, Miss Michaud?

Heloise moves out of the room. Peter rises and moves after her. As he steps into the corridor he sees her a few paces ahead of him. Dr. Gettlinger is walking down the hall toward them.

GETTLINGER (*To Heloise, pointing to her hair*): That's a new color, isn't it? (*He stops to talk to Peter*) Spoke to your daughter Margaret today. Peter? Have you written them? Called them?

Peter has also stopped, and a way down the corridor, Heloise turns to watch from a distance.

PETER: I wrote a card.

GETTLINGER: They don't understand.

PETER: I wrote a card.

GETTLINGER (*Looks at his watch*): Hell. (*Looks at Peter*) Make peace. It's simpler.

PETER: When I find it, I'll make it.

GETTLINGER: Give us a chance.

PETER: I'm doing that.

GETTLINGER: Peter . . . we'll talk. (*Looks at his watch*) I . . . oh, hell. *Gettlinger rushes on. Peter looks over at Heloise. He starts toward her. She walks on ahead of him. He stops.*

PETER: Manners? Manners?

Heloise turns to Peter, smiles, holds out her hand. He walks to her and the two walk down the corridor together and turn to the ramp.

FADE TO BLACK.

ACT THREE

FADE IN: THE HOLLY VALLEY HOME.
There is energetic activity in the corridors. It is morning, and the residents have been busy for several hours putting up decorations for a Visiting Day. Streamers hang from the ceilings. Home-made paintings and posters are on the walls. A decorating crew (including Bob Ragle and directed by

LAURA CHAPMAN, an 80-year-old in a wheelchair) is at work. Laura wears a home-made comic hat on her gray hair.
A JANITOR (BERNIE) with a dolly-load of folding chairs is walking toward the lounge. Dr. Gettlinger, coming out of the lounge, almost crashes into him.

JANITOR: Now she says she wants more in the lounge . . .

GETTLINGER: Bernie, set them up in the lounge, right where the others are—and get that dolly out of the way before you run someone down. Have you seen the housemistress?

JANITOR (*As he starts pushing the dolly into the lounge*): No, sir.

GETTLINGER: No, naturally not . . .

Gettlinger turns, almost running into Peter and Heloise as they come down the hall. There is more force in Peter's manner now, more confidence. He wears no suit jacket, but rather a pullover sweater.

GETTLINGER (*To Peter*): Chairman, I haven't seen such organization since the army. Have you seen the housemistress?

PETER: No, doctor . . .

Gettlinger walks up the ramp. Peter and Heloise move to Laura and Ragle, as Laura beckons them.

PETER: It's just the right color, Laura . . .

LAURA: Oh, Peter. I have a crew putting up travel posters. You let me know how you like them.

PETER: I will.

LAURA: Got your hats?

PETER (*As he starts away*): I don't make funny hats . . .

Heloise smiles at Laura and moves after Peter as he continues down the hall.

CUT TO:

THE INTERIOR OF A CAR BEING DRIVEN BY GEORGE. He is driving through the outskirts of a fairly small town, the same morning. Evelyn is beside him, and Beth and Scott are in the back seat.

EVELYN: I want best behavior.

SCOTT: Will they give us lunch?

GEORGE: They better . . .

EVELYN: Why didn't you eat breakfast?

BETH: Will he remember us?

GEORGE: Of course he will . . .

EVELYN: And if you see people—in wheelchairs, with crutches, ill people or . . . you don't stare, you remain polite . . .

She is thinking of what to add to this as we . . .

DISSOLVE BACK TO:

HOLLY VALLEY. Peter and Heloise open the doors of the game room and move inside. Here, an exhibit of arts and crafts has been set up. Slocum, in charge here, is arranging a few pieces of carefully made furniture. On a long metal table covered by a cloth is a display of rugs, ceramic objects, basketry, and small wood objects such as scrolled-out nameplates.

Slocum turns as Peter enters with Heloise. Slocum is wearing a small green foil party hat with paper fringe.

HELOISE: Where are the rugs?

PETER: Here, let me help you.

SLOCUM: Peter, how does it look?

PETER: Fine. You going to wear that hat?

SLOCUM: Sure . . .

PETER: Now is this how you want it? You're sweating . . .

SLOCUM: I ate too much. How does it look?

PETER: Where's the bench you made?

SLOCUM: I didn't bring it. Where's the chair you made for Beth?

PETER: I'm going to surprise her with it today . . .

HELOISE: Wallace, does it all have to be spread about so much that there's no room for dancing?

PETER: Why not?

SLOCUM: Next to yours, my bench looks slip-shod. I don't want anything slip-shod representing me.

HELOISE: Can we move everything closer together?

PETER: It was your first. I've made so many things. I shouldn't have anything on display. First things belong on display, first things have great value. We'll put your bench here and take mine away.

SLOCUM: No . . . No . . . (*He sits down weakly*) Who knows, maybe you can sell something. I have no family coming. Peter, the next time you see me eating like a pig will you break a plate over my head?

HELOISE: Take something.

Mary Devlin, holding a stack of framed letters, has entered.

MARY: Peter . . . Mrs. Wilcox sent me to you. Now listen, Schermann, I demand some room for my letters and she won't put them with the paintings, she sent me to you.

PETER: We can hang them on a wall, we can try and do it here . . .

MARY: Well, let's hang them. Schermann, let's hang them . . . This is President Johnson, this is President Eisenhower, this is Senator Green, he was a dear man, here's Nehru . . .

HELOISE (*Overlapping*): Where are we going to dance?

Mrs. Flagler appears at the doorway.

MRS. FLAGLER: Mr. Schermann? I think yours have come . . .

CUT TO:

THE LOUNGE. *From this point on during Visiting Day, increasing num-*

bers of the old people will be wearing comic hats, most handmade. Here in the lounge, the Janitor is setting up additional folding chairs to augment the usual furniture. Several older men are setting up music stands in one corner against a window wall. A few visiting families can be seen. And coming into the lounge from the main entrance directly opposite are George, Evelyn, Scott, and Beth.

BETH: Are they going to play music here?

GEORGE: It looks like it.

SCOTT: Can I investigate around?

EVELYN: You better stay close, honey.

BETH: It's a big place, isn't it?

EVELYN: Yes, it is . . .

Beth and Scott walk up to an old man who is tuning his violin. The man, wearing another funny hat, turns and smiles at the children and holds out the violin for them to look at. Scott plucks at the strings and is pleased with the sounds they make. George, still standing at the lounge entrance, sees Peter approaching with Heloise in tow.

GEORGE: There he is . . .

George and Evelyn go up to meet Peter.

GEORGE: Dad . . .

EVELYN (*At the same time*): Hello, Father . . .

PETER: George, Evelyn, this is Miss Heloise Michaud. I want you to meet her because she's a good person and a friend . . .

GEORGE: Very pleased . . .

EVELYN: Hello, uh . . .

HELOISE: I'm your father's dancing partner . . . well, he doesn't care much for dancing, but I cook meals for him sometimes and so he does me the favor of dancing . . .

PETER: Where are the children? You brought them . . . ?

GEORGE (*Waving at the lounge*): They're in there. You look great.

PETER: Feel great!!

GEORGE (*To Heloise*): This is the first time he's let us visit . . .

EVELYN (*Taking Peter's hands*): Father, it's nice to see you. I mean it.

PETER (*Looking at her*): I know. (*He turns to Heloise*) Heloise, you've got to meet the children.

Peter moves into the lounge, looking for Beth and Scott. Heloise is with him as he calls. Scott sees him and is hesitant to run toward him the way Beth does . . . and even Beth hesitates a moment before embracing him, as he squats to receive her. Evelyn and George, watching at a distance, speak softly to one another.

EVELYN: Who's she?

GEORGE: I hope he doesn't make a fool out of himself . . .

EVELYN (*Observing George*): Are you angry about something?

GEORGE: I only said . . . (*Then taking her arm and guiding her toward Peter and the children*) What's the use . . . ?

DISSOLVE TO:

THE GAME ROOM: LATER IN THE DAY. *Heloise and Evelyn speak to one another while Beth plays ping-pong with an older boy and Scott acts as umpire. As Heloise and Evelyn talk in the foreground, Mrs. Flagler lectures in the background to a group of visitors. While Mrs. Flagler speaks the following words, Beth and the boys argue about the score of the game.*

MRS. FLAGLER: The looms are quite professional and it's surprising that such little experience is needed to make the most beautiful rugs, and it's also very good for the agility of the fingers and hands and arm . . . Ceramics, too, of course. Weaving, and here is a display of letters with leading world figures you may wish to look at closely . . .

At the same time, also in the background . . .

THE BOY: It's my serve.

BETH: I only served four times.

THE BOY: Five.

SCOTT: Five.

BETH: Some brother.

While, close to THE CAMERA . . .

HELOISE: You have two lovely children, Mrs. Schermann.

EVELYN: It's quite nice you keep so busy . . .

HELOISE: Yes. I think so. Your father-in-law sets a fine example for us.

EVELYN: Do you have a family here today, Miss . . . (*She reads the nametag and mispronounces*) Miss Michaud?

HELOISE: French-Canadian name. No. Only a brother lives in California and that's a long way away, so I am an individual, by myself, so far. *Beth hits the ping-pong ball off the table. Scott runs to pick it up.*

SCOTT: I got it.

HELOISE: I recognize much of Peter in the boy.

EVELYN: Well, they're very spirited, they play pretty rough. It used to bother him, you know, the noise. You know. He'd shout at them . . .

HELOISE: Peter?

EVELYN: Yes . . . that was one of the problems, and then . . . well, I suppose he's told you . . .

HELOISE (*After a pause, questioningly*): Yes . . . ?

EVELYN: You know . . . told you why . . . he left . . .

HELOISE: No. He speaks very little about his former home.

Evelyn, without knowing precisely why, is embarrassed and upset.

CUT TO:

PETER AND GEORGE IN THE WORKSHOP. One or two others, and perhaps a small boy, move around looking at the equipment. There is a reasonable amount of privacy for the father-son conversation.

PETER: What they're short here more than anything is a band saw. Mrs. Flagler, who supervises the shop, has been afraid of a large machine but I've almost convinced her, and I'm on the Resident Council now and I've proposed it. We'll get it . . .

GEORGE: Very good. Now where do you get the funds?

PETER: We have what's called a Sheltered Workshop . . . we do a few simple cuts for two local factories . . . a window-sash plant and a toy company . . . they give us a few cents an hour . . . it's not out of your pocket.

GEORGE: That's not why I asked. How does the union like it, your undercutting . . . ?

PETER: They don't——. They want us to sit on our hands. Pottery kiln, supplies back there. So this is the shop. I'd like to take you to my apartment, upstairs. I've made a chair for Beth, and I'm going to make a desk——

GEORGE (*Examining equipment*): They keep you busy . . .

PETER: If you come upstairs, you can take it out to the car, surprise her with it . . .

GEORGE (*Doesn't know what is referred to*): What . . . ?

PETER: The chair, the first thing I did . . .

GEORGE: If there's one thing we don't need——

PETER: A chair for Beth . . .

There is a moment of embarrassment.

GEORGE: Is it scaled down? Is it a child's chair? Small?

PETER: A little scaled down. Has a drawer.

GEORGE (*Unconvincingly*): Well. She'd love it, I know. If I can fit it in the car, fine.

PETER: If you don't need it, don't take it.

GEORGE: No. I want it. I'm sorry. We can't seem to get together on anything. We have no argument. Evelyn and I are so glad you're active and satisfied. You've found a good home here, and we can all be glad about it.

PETER: I don't know that I've found a home, son, I'm trying. You like this place? This is where you want me to be?

George doesn't answer.

PETER: Down the hall is the hydrotherapy room which I can show you . . .

Peter turns and walks away from George, who follows him.

DISSOLVE TO:

MRS. FLAGLER, STANDING IN THE LOUNGE *in front of the several elderly musicians. She addresses the assembled residents and guests . . .*

MRS. FLAGLER: Some of the hats are masterpieces, I'm just glad I'm not the judge. But the hat committee will circulate and examine each one, and after the singing we'll have the finalists up here. Now we're very proud of our Holly Valley symphony here, so if you have any favorite songs just ask for them and they'll play if they know them . . . how about now, to get started, "For Me and My Gal," that's an old one. *With prompting from the musicians, the singing gets off to a rough but full-throated start.* AS THE CAMERA MOVES *among the people we see that many hold coffee cups, cake plates, milk glasses, etc., or have set them down near at hand. The Schermann family is all together. Scott is sleeping on a chair, Beth is happily singing without sure knowledge of the lyric, Evelyn mutters the song, George works strenuously at a spirited rendition. Peter and Heloise sing calmly. We see many, many ludicrous hats on residents. The hat committee circulates.*

When THE CAMERA *reaches the back end of the lounge (where it meets the hall), it* PANS *to look down the length of the hall. Dr. Gettlinger is walking slowly toward the lounge . . . the first time we have ever seen him walk slowly. He is disheveled, tired, and very disheartened. He walks slowly to the edge of the group of singers who are sitting on chairs or on the floor. He looks intently around the room. He walks to where Ragle is sitting, bends over, whispers to him. Ragle rises, goes to Peter, whispers to him. Peter rises, and walks with Ragle to join Dr. Gettlinger.*

MRS. FLAGLER (*After one chorus of the song*): Good. Now, once more, and remember, harmony is encouraged.

The singing starts again. Peter, Ragle, and Dr. Gettlinger walk a short distance down the hall to a more quiet area. Then, Gettlinger stops and turns to the other two men.

GETTLINGER: Wallace Slocum doesn't have any family here today, does he?

PETER: Not that I know of . . .

RAGLE (*At the same time*): No.

GETTLINGER: Well, I'm sorry to take you away from things. Mr. Ragle, you know his family, don't you?

RAGLE: Met them once . . .

GETTLINGER: And Peter, since you're chairman of this thing and friendly with him . . .

PETER: He said he ate too much . . .

GETTLINGER: Yes, well he's dead. What he thought was heartburn was the onset of a coronary occlusion. There's no point in broadcasting this, but I'd like you to tell me which of his children is the stronger, Mr. Ragle . . .

Ragle begins shaking his head, bewildered.

GETTLINGER: . . . and Peter, you go back to your family if you wish, but later I'd like your help as Resident Council representative, if you would.

Gettlinger looks at both men sadly, then turns and starts down the hall. Ragle follows him, funny hat and all.

Peter is alone. He goes back to the edge of the lounge, stands and listens.

MRS. FLAGLER: Well, wonderful. What's next?

VOICE FROM THE CROWD: Tipperary.

MRS. FLAGLER: Request, request, "It's a Long Way to Tipperary." That's a good one . . .

The violinist establishes the key and Mrs. Flagler begins to sing. Soon the guests are singing enthusiastically. The hat committee, taking notes, still circulates. Peter walks to his family and puts a hand on Heloise's shoulder. He bends over and touches Evelyn's hand, then George's.

PETER: Goodnight. Goodnight. Thanks for coming. (*Touches Beth's cheek*) Goodnight, Beth.

EVELYN: It is late——

PETER: I have some work . . .

GEORGE (*Reaching for him confused*): The chair, if you——

PETER: Another time, I have something to do.

Peter has straightened up. He turns and walks out of the lounge and down the corridor, while the singing continues. Heloise watches him go with curiosity. George and Evelyn begin gathering themselves for the trip home. Peter, as he gets farther from them, begins to walk more confidently. He is now on surer ground . . . he could not be at ease with his children. It disturbs him.

CUT TO:

GETTLINGER'S OFFICE. *Gettlinger is sitting behind his desk and talking on the telephone. Ragle sits against the wall, listening.*

GETTLINGER: . . . The certificate has been signed, Mrs. Graham . . . No, not if you object . . . Certainly . . . Then I'll talk to . . . Once again, I want to express my—yes, of course. Goodbye. (*Exhales as he hangs up*) That's that. Come in, Peter. You can sign the disposition and the Council Report . . .

Peter, who had been standing at the door, enters the room.

PETER: I went to his room first. The mattress is rolled up, all his things are gone.

GETTLINGER: Yes.

PETER: So fast. This afternoon he lived in that room, now it looks . . . no trace that he was ever there.

GETTLINGER: Certainly.

Gettlinger rubs his forehead.

PETER: Do you send everything to his family?

GETTLINGER: What?

PETER: Everything he's accumulated . . . he did some paintings . . . he made a bench . . .

RAGLE: They pack it away.

GETTLINGER: The usable clothing goes to the thrift shop. Anything else that's usable goes to the Salvation Army or St. Vincent de Paul.

PETER: What does the family take?

GETTLINGER: They take wings. Nothing. Relief. A twinge or two of sorrow or conscience and then zzzip, that's all.

PETER (*To Ragle*): What did you take?

RAGLE: I don't want anything.

PETER: A close friend . . .

RAGLE: Yes, but now he's gone. People die here.

PETER: I know that.

RAGLE: What do you want from me?

PETER: Well . . . he made a bench. I'd like it.

GETTLINGER: It's yours. The children don't want reminders, Peter.

PETER: But this was his home. I would think . . . something should be left to show he lived here. Isn't that right?

RAGLE: Death is one thing we don't have to be reminded of.

PETER: Is this what you call a home? Is this what everybody wants? It's not real. Hats! What do I say to my children? What do they say to me? If you can erase a person so quick then this is no world! This is a sealed box for old people who die. And disappear! Who work and make things that also disappear!

GETTLINGER: All right . . . Sign the forms.

PETER: When you live in the world, your absence is felt. It's suffered. Nobody mourns here. Wallace Slocum? Oh, yes. He was in 3-B!

RAGLE: You're mourn——

GETTLINGER (*At the same time*): The world doesn't want to mourn, Peter. They want to be happy.

PETER: I've heard that word too much.

GETTLINGER (*Snapping*): So have I.

PETER: It doesn't exist.

RAGLE: Well everyone tries to be happy . . .

PETER: Anyone who is always happy is already dead. That's no secret. Living in happiness is not like living in Duluth, once you're there you're there. What are we, cripples? If we can't have sorrow? Slocum! This afternoon he was alive, he made something!

No one says anything.

PETER: Happiness comes along with things. It's like the heat when you rub your hands together. It doesn't last. You can't look at it, you can only catch it now and then at the side, out of the corner of your eye. Comes from the working. In the living. I thought I knew . . .

GETTLINGER: Well, here you can work.

PETER: Busy work.

GETTLINGER: Legitimate——

PETER: No, no it's not. If it can disappear like that . . . (*Snapping his fingers*) What meaning can it have?

GETTLINGER (*Exploding with anger*): Meaning? You want it all? You can't get it! What do you know about it? That other home you were in was a good place, was good! I've seen the real places, I worked as a state investigator, every day of my life I saw places where the stench alone will stain your clothes, where helpless people are crusted with filth, where I had to nod at blue wrists and ankles where they'd been tied to beds and chairs, where the food was slop, certify places where no matter what questions you ask they don't look at you and they say "nobody beat me," that's the business I'm in! They are waiting rooms for death, every one of them, this one, too. This place is the best! The best there is! But it's a waiting room. It's not a home. It's for the sick and the unloved and the unwanted and the insufferable, and it's the best there is. You're in a good greenhouse. The real world is a place where you hang around longer and are wanted around less. Don't blame the man if he doesn't want to be reminded! Take the bench! (*Pause*) I'm sorry.

RAGLE: Make the best of it.

Peter just glares at them.

GETTLINGER (*Takes another pause*): Who wants coffee? Does anybody? *Nobody wants coffee. Not even Gettlinger. He sits.*

DISSOLVE TO:

GEORGE, AT THE TELEPHONE IN THE HALL OF HIS HOME. He's very upset.

GEORGE: It's worse than that, Meg. I got a letter from a lawyer, too . . . some shyster, I don't know, he wants the deed back, he wants the land title back, he's coming back.

Evelyn, listening unhappily, walks down the hall to Peter's room.

GEORGE: I think they made him senile there . . .

Evelyn opens the door and looks inside Peter's room. It is filled with discards—including the living-room chair that was Peter's. She still hears . . .

GEORGE'S VOICE: . . . No, I'm not talking about committing him, I—no, wait, all right, Meg, no, maybe he should be committed, maybe that's the best thing . . .

CUT TO:

PETER'S ROOM AT THE HOLLY VALLEY HOME.
A box is on Peter's bed and Peter is carefully packing the handicraft objects he has collected. His suitcase is also on the bed, open but packed. Peter works silently. Sitting nearby, very unhappy as she watches, is Heloise.

HELOISE: You haven't been here six months. That isn't enough time to give us.

PETER: I've lost too much time.

HELOISE: They won't know how to take care of you and you'll be sick . . . you'll get sick . . .

PETER: I won't get sick. (*Pause*) If I get really sick, I'll come back. (*Pause*) But if I'm going to be struck down, it will come for me the way it comes for an animal in nature. Struck down. I won't linger like somebody's pet.

HELOISE: You've given much to me, Peter. Some vitality, some meaning, and also some love.

PETER: Anger, I hope. (*He crosses back to the box*) You'll find another dancing partner.

HELOISE: They don't want you back. This is a guarantee. They don't want you at all.

PETER: I know.

HELOISE: Will you take this from a woman who sees everything from outside, everything to do with families, I have seen all my life and I know? From me. Now. You have no family. None. You think I'm making jokes? Peter. The blood ties . . . are untied. Husbands, wives, daughters, sons, aunts, uncles, brothers, sisters, grandchildren, they don't exist. Our generations are independent, independence is the goal, it's what they preach about, it's in the schools, in the life, independence for all, responsibility . . . to none. You have no family. A house, where you'll be like a picture on the wall.

PETER: My home.

HELOISE: Houses and people are not built to accept three generations. Hardly two.

PETER: I built it.

HELOISE: Elephants don't have wings, clocks don't run backwards. Stay here.

PETER: A rolled-up mattress isn't enough of a last moment for me . . . you've got to be in the world to be alive.

HELOISE: You mean something here . . . especially to me.

Peter finds a small jewel box he has made, and he holds it out to her.

PETER: This is for jewelry or things . . . take it and remember me. Or dance and forget.

Shirley Booth and Melvyn Douglas in *Do Not Go
Gentle into That Good Night.*

HELOISE: I'll take it, Peter. Thank you. But I have to dance, and if I forget, at least I'll be happy. I'll dance. (*She rises and goes to the door*) It's so important that I do it.
Slowly, she walks out into the hall.
FADE TO BLACK.

FADE IN: THE LIGHTS COME ON AS PETER SNAPS THEM ON IN HIS BASEMENT WORKSHOP AT HIS REAL HOME. He steps down into the workshop. George, Evelyn, and Margaret follow him into the room as he walks from bench to bench, examining the furniture, the half-made pieces, the tools. Beth comes down a moment later, just behind the adults, and joins them.

BETH (*As she enters*): Will we still be able to play down here, Pop?
PETER: I think so. But over there, near the customers' door, not too close to the power tools. (*To George*) And a sign goes out in front at the road.
GEORGE: How much money do you think you'll make?
PETER: I don't know. Do you know? Tell me. How much money will I make?
GEORGE: I don't know.
PETER: Oh. I thought you did.
GEORGE: It isn't necessary for you to work.
PETER: The most necessary. Margaret, give this your woman's eye and tell me what it needs. Curtains? Any particular kind of fixing, decoration?
MARGARET: It could use some.
PETER: Would you make a list for me?
MARGARET: I'll try.
Peter looks at them. After a pause he speaks softly to them as he turns to pick up the same legless chair we saw at the beginning of the play.
PETER: That's all I have to say. You don't have to stand around.
MARGARET: I'll make that list. I can stitch up some curtains . . . before I leave . . .
Margaret, George, and Beth start away. Evelyn hangs back from the others and watches them exit. Peter knows she is standing there, and he begins to sing softly to himself some inane melody he might have heard from one of the television dance parties. Then he stops.
PETER: Yes, Evelyn? Do you have some ideas for this place?
EVELYN: Do you sincerely want to drive us out?
PETER: Drive you out, no, no, no, Evelyn. I want to live—no, I want *you* to live with *me*. I don't want to drive you out. You may go if you want. I hope you'll stay.

EVELYN: I have two children. They make noise. They run—

PETER: Now that I'll be making noise down here it might not matter. I understand, Evelyn. I'm no problem-smoother, there are still problems. I make problems, I know how many were my fault. But I think . . . a dead person resents the living around him. Now I want to be alive, too.

EVELYN: George is head of his house.

PETER: I'm head of *this* house.

EVELYN: Two heads of ——

PETER: I'm the head of this house and of this family.

George returns, looking for Evelyn. He walks up to her but she doesn't see him.

EVELYN: You can't split authority and——

PETER: I didn't say split authority, did I?

GEORGE: Well when do I come into my own? When am I a man? I'm forty-five, I have the responsibility for my wife, for two children, for you, too . . . do I come into my own?

PETER: Yes.

GEORGE: When?

PETER: When you wrestle it from me. When I can't fight for it any more, or when I'm dead. And I wouldn't count on one without the other . . . Son, cars are made with wheels in front and wheels in back. And the back wheels never catch up to the front wheels. There never comes a time when you start being my father. While I'm alive, I will be the father, you will be the son. Never any other way. If you want to fight me for it, all right. Maybe it's natural for you to try, but I won't stop fighting. I do not stand aside, I do not give up, I do not relinquish my place to you. At this point I don't know how you feel about me. You may not know, yourself. Now you'll find out. That's a problem for you, isn't it? Now, you see that chair? Half done. Everything fell to pieces here when your mother died . . . and I let myself be buried, too. I'm going to put a leg on the chair. You can watch if you like. I'm starting right now.

Peter rolls up his sleeves, picks the chair up off the table and revolves it in his hands, looking it over. Evelyn leaves. George watches.

GEORGE (*After a while*): You're an old man. You look pretty silly.

PETER (*While he works, not looking up*): Only a cabinetmaker. What's silly about that?

GEORGE: We'll see, Dad.

PETER: Mmm hmmm.

Peter continues working.

SLOW DISSOLVE TO:

ARTHUR SELIG'S ROOM, AT THE GOLDEN DAYS HOME.

Melvyn Douglas, Warren Stevens, and Lois Smith in *Do Not Go Gentle into That Good Night*.

Josepha stands at Arthur's shoulder, reading him a letter. Arthur listens in a kind of sleepy impassivity. He could almost be a still photograph.

JOSEPHA: "I have come . . . to my own home. I struggle. I hope you are well, even better than well. Next month . . . some time soon . . . I hope to visit and tell you all my adventures. I mention your name a hundred times and think about you. I think about the piano, too, and I tell you to struggle."

(*She pauses*) He mentions the piano . . .

ARTHUR: Piano? What piano?

JOSEPHA: He says he's coming here to see you soon. Now won't that be nice? Here's your letter, Mr. Selig.

Josepha puts the letter in Arthur's hand, and leaves him.

WE SEE PETER, BUSILY AT WORK IN HIS WORKSHOP . . .

FADE TO BLACK.

TEACHER, TEACHER

By ELLISON CARROLL

Hallmark Hall of Fame
National Broadcasting Company Television Network
February 5, 1969

DIRECTOR: *Fielder Cook*

PRODUCER: *George Lefferts*

EXECUTIVE PRODUCER: *Henry Jaffe*

Henry Jaffe Enterprises, Inc.

THE CAST

HAMILTON CADE: *David McCallum*

CHARLES CARTER: *Ossie Davis*

F. NILES PUTNAM: *George Grizzard*

FREDDIE PUTNAM: *Billy Shulman*

JOEY (CARTER'S NEPHEW): *Anthony Jones*

WOMAN: *Sally Cook*

PROLOGUE

FADE IN:

EXTERIOR—GATE DAY

WE ARE LOOKING THROUGH AN IRON GATE *from the inside of a driveway of a two-plus acre estatelet in suburbia toward the drive that leads from the road. A convertible is just pulling up. It is a somewhat seedy car. Similarly seedy, with the air and the garb of a faded Ivy Leaguer, is the man behind the wheel: HAMILTON CADE. He blows the horn. Nothing happens. He blows again. Nothing. He climbs out of the car.*

Cade is young, handsome, and careworn. He affects a houndstooth jacket that has seen better days, Daks that have been too often pressed, with perhaps even the line showing faintly where they have been de-cuffed for the more up-to-date cuffless style. The jacket's elbows have suede patches that are stained, and some of the stitching has come loose. There is something a bit wrong about him, a touch of peevishness and insecurity as he gets out of his car and walks toward the gate. Though nobody is looking, he adjusts his scarf.

CADE CHECKS THE GATE; IT IS LOCKED. *Shaking it has no effect. He is puzzled. He goes to the gatepost on which is a metal grille, the outlet of an intercom. Above the grille is a plaque: "F. NILES PUTNAM, A.S.A."*

Below the nameplate there is a pushbutton with the legend, "TALK." Cade, with the air of "How dare they do this to me," shrugs, pushes the button. From the grille, a voice:

    PUTNAM'S VOICE: Putnam here . . .

    CADE (*Talking into the intercom*): Hamilton Cade . . .

    PUTNAM'S VOICE: Come on up to the house.

A BUZZER SOUNDS; Cade pushes the gate: it opens. Then as Cade returns to his car . . .

    PUTNAM'S VOICE: Close the gate after you.

    CADE: Of course . . .

CADE DRIVES THROUGH, *stops, pushes the gate, which swings but does not quite "catch."*

    PUTNAM'S VOICE: All the way, please.

Irritated, Cade climbs out of the car, closes the gate properly, returns to the car, drives off.

AS CADE'S CAR PROCEEDS ALONG THE DRIVEWAY *we see a modern but quite modest house. We catch a glimpse of a trampoline.*

On the trampoline is FREDDIE, 13, small for his age. He is jumping up and down. No tricks—no expertise—just going up and down Cade watches the

boy as his car passes the area, but Freddie does not acknowledge his presence.
THE CAMERA GOES IN ON *Freddie, who continues to go up and down, methodically, compulsively. He goes into* SLOW MOTION . . . A PLANE IS HEARD OVERHEAD. *Freddie jumps off, looks around and up for the plane. As he looks up we notice that the buttons of his shirt are done wrong; that is, he has one buttonhole too many and one button too few. He looks up with a vacant expression. But as the plane sound fades away, he lifts his arms to the sky, his fingers outstretched and grasping hopefully the empty air.*
But his expression is changeless.

FADE OUT.

ACT ONE

FADE IN:
INTERIOR—PUTNAM'S STUDY   DAY
A COMBINATION LIVING ROOM AND ARCHITECT'S STUDIO: *drawing board, desk, dazor lamp, blueprints, a cork wall on which are architectural projections. As Cade comes in,* PUTNAM *is on the phone. His voice is heard off-camera as Cade looks around the room.*

PUTNAM'S VOICE: Listen, do you have to call me from London to tell me about this? . . . Well, I knew—I knew all that last week . . . How can you change it when you haven't even called me to talk about it? . . . Look, the specifications call for pre-stressed concrete—impossible. It's absolutely basic to the total conception. It's not a group of individual structures—it's a completely interrelated complex! . . . Unquestionably. Test borings before the hard weather sets in. Look, we've gone over the logistics a dozen times—now do they want design—or do they want glass boxes? . . . Fine. Fine. Next week— . . . Again? It's the third time you've changed the schedule on me! . . . No, no, I can make it. It's just that—all right. I'll confirm by cable. And I'll expect to hear from you in London. . . . No, no, I'll pick them up at the airport. Goodbye.

He hangs up. He is tense, edgy. He turns to Cade.

PUTNAM: Well, they've changed the schedule on me again. Now I have to fly the day after tomorrow.
CADE: How long will you be gone?
PUTNAM: A minimum of three weeks . . . more likely a month.

*Putnam goes to the sideboard where two decanters of whiskey stand. He
pours himself a drink, turns to Cade.*

> PUTNAM: Would you care for a drink, Mr. Cade?

> CADE: No . . . thank you.

Putnam sips his drink.

> PUTNAM: Sure you won't join me?

> CADE: Quite sure.

*Putnam puts down his drink and ignores it. He has been testing Cade. Cade
knows it.*

> PUTNAM: I have a commission in the North of England . . . it's an
> entire community—from the ground up. Designed around a
> college.

> CADE (*Indicating a drawing*): Yes, I see you did the science build-
> ing at Hollenbeck.

> PUTNAM: Just part of the design. I'm free-lance—when you're on
> your own, you hope for the big one. (*Pause*) This English thing
> is my big one.

Putnam indicates the drinks again.

> PUTNAM: Sure you won't join me?

Cade really wants a drink.

> CADE: Ah . . . yes, yes, I will.

*Putnam watches him narrowly. But Cade, going to the liquor, does not make
himself a drink. Instead——*

> CADE: I'll have some tonic . . . Thank you.

Still, he isn't fooling Putnam, who glances at Cade's letters in a folder.

> PUTNAM: I don't really need these . . . what with your letter . . .
> and some asking around. These recommendations aren't very
> recent. . . .

> CADE: They—ah—do go back a bit, yes. You see, I—I taught
> Hillsgrove Academy five years . . . then Colebrook . . .

Putnam cuts Cade off——

> PUTNAM: Hillsgrove five years, Colebrook three years, Westford
> Academy six months . . . the schools get less impressive and
> your stay gets shorter. You're like an actor carrying around
> old reviews. What happened?

> CADE: I'm an excellent teacher, Mr. Putnam.

> PUTNAM: Ivy Leaguer, Phi Bete, started at the top—worked your
> way down. Westford Academy six months. Why did they fire
> you, Mr. Cade?

> CADE: I resigned.

> PUTNAM: You were *allowed* to resign. Why?

CADE: I had a nervous breakdown. I was going through a rather painful divorce at the time——

PUTNAM: You were teaching less and drinking more.

CADE: That's all over now.

PUTNAM: I know, or you wouldn't be here. What I'm really interested in, Mr. Cade, is why you started to reverse your career . . .

CADE: Oh—I don't know. I—ah—I was depressed by kids from rich homes.

PUTNAM: You were giving them A's and B's to keep your job and they were wiping out on the college boards.

CADE: You've done a very thorough investigation.

PUTNAM: I've designed buildings for two of these schools. I know a few of the Directors.

CADE (*Putting the letters back into his briefcase*): Well, yes, you have me at a disadvantage.

PUTNAM: Why did you answer my ad?

CADE: It seemed like an ideal situation for a man with my—history. I need a one-to-one relationship. Away from the pressure of large classes. Prep school boys can be quite cruel, you know.

PUTNAM: I know. I used to be one.

CADE: Yes. I could tell by your approach.

Putnam laughs rather cruelly.

PUTNAM: How long have you been out of the sanatorium, Mr. Cade?

CADE: Six months. . . . To answer your question as to why I applied, your ad did say "an exceptional child" . . . and I need the job, Mr. Putnam. But I am also an exceptionally good teacher. I would have liked the challenge of an exceptional child—it would have allowed me to regain a little confidence.

Putnam motions Cade to wait while he pushes a button on the "console" on his desk. It has several buttons on it. In a CLOSEUP *we see their nomenclature. One says "gate," one "lights," one "bell." As he pushes "bell," a bell rings outside the house . . .*

EXTERIOR—TRAMPOLINE   DAY

WE SEE FREDDIE JUMPING *on the trampoline. He is not immediately conscious of the bell.*

It continues to ring . . .

Freddie stops jumping and heads for the house.

INTERIOR—STUDY   DAY

CADE: Where's he been to school?

PUTNAM: Right here. There hasn't been a school invented that's
right for him.

*By now Freddie has arrived at the house and entered the study. Seeing Cade,
he comes to Putnam and leans against him shyly.*

PUTNAM: This is Mr. Cade, Freddie. Shake hands with Mr. Cade,
Freddie.

*Freddie goes to Cade, puts out his hand. Freddie does not shake—it is Cade
doing all the shaking. Cade all but knows . . .*
*Freddie pulls his hand from Cade's and turns to fiddle with a dazor lamp.
Making it bend up and down on its elbow joint.*
Putnam watches Cade, who watches Freddie.

PUTNAM: All right, Freddie.

Freddie continues playing with the lamp.

PUTNAM: All *right,* Freddie!

*Physically he removes Freddie's hand from the lamp and gives him a turn so
he is facing him.*

PUTNAM: Hey, go wash your hands and face. Use soap.

Freddie dutifully goes off, but stops in the entranceway . . .

FREDDIE: I saw the airplane. Up up up. Down down down. And it
went away.

He exits.

CADE: Your ad said "exceptional child."

PUTNAM: The word "retarded" does not attract many applicants.

CADE: How old is he?

PUTNAM: Freddie's thirteen. As for IQ, he functions somewhere
on the seven-year level. But no trouble. No trouble at all. . . .
Eats anything you put in front of him. Toilet trained. Dresses
himself. Answers the bell. Does what you tell him to do—if he
can do it. As for learning—he's a challenge. A real challenge
to any teacher——

CADE: Well, how many teachers answered your ad?

PUTNAM: You're the ninth.

CADE: And they all turned you down?

PUTNAM: I turned them down. My son is very precious to me, Mr.
Cade.

CADE: I need a job, Mr. Putnam, but I'm not qualified. I've never
been trained to work with retarded children.

PUTNAM: Okay, I'm sorry to put you through all this.

CADE: You've only put me through five minutes.

Freddie enters. He shows his hands to Putnam.

PUTNAM: Hey, good boy.

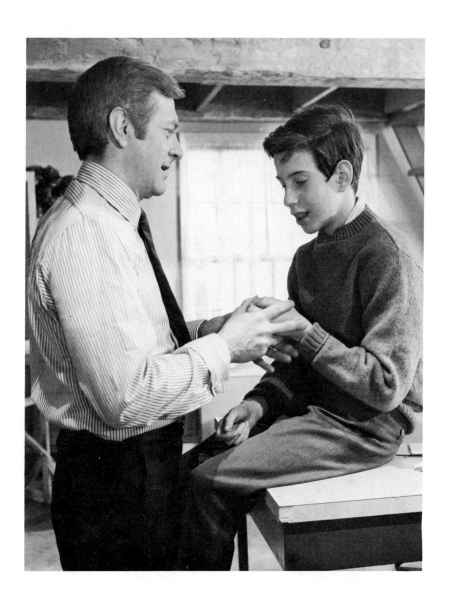

George Grizzard and Billy Shulman in *Teacher, Teacher*.

Freddie shows his hands to Cade.
> CADE: Hmmm. Good and clean.

Cade turns to Putnam, who is now back behind his desk. Freddie hovers around Cade. He examines and fingers the patches on Cade's jacket-sleeve.
> FREDDIE: What's that?
> CADE: That—ah—that's leather . . .

Putnam watches narrowly, as if testing Cade's reactions, as Freddie touches one of two pens in Cade's jacket-pocket.
Cade takes the pen out and hands it to Freddie. Freddie examines it. Cade reaches out—it is a push-button ballpoint—and shows Freddie how it works.
> CADE: Here, let me show you—you do it like this. You see, you
>   push it.

Freddie fiddles with the pen and succeeds in making it work. His face lights up.
> FREDDIE: I did it.

He sets about pushing the end of the pen, making the point go in and out, in and out. Cade shoves a piece of paper toward Freddie.
> CADE: It's for writing. Can you write?

Freddie nods.
> CADE: Show me.

Freddie makes a meaningless scrawl.
> FREDDIE: See?
> PUTNAM: Testing, Professor?
> CADE: Teaching.
> PUTNAM: He can't write. Or read. And nobody can teach him.

Freddie scribbles all over the paper. As he does so, Cade shakes his head ever so slightly "no," and begins to put his papers into his briefcase.
> PUTNAM (*After a pause*): Say goodbye to Mr. Cade, Freddie.

Freddie turns and dutifully puts out his hand to shake. But he holds the hand with the pen in it behind his back.
> PUTNAM: And give Mr. Cade his pen.

Freddie keeps his hand hidden.
> CADE: That's all right. You can keep it, Freddie.
> PUTNAM: Freddie, say thank you to Mr. Cade.

But Freddie, without the automatic prompting, jumps the gun on Putnam:
> FREDDIE: Thank you.

Cade is about to rise when Freddie, without warning, throws his arm around Cade's neck and hugs. Thrown off guard, Cade responds almost automatically with a hug; then all pretense and aside gone from his face, he kisses Freddie's forehead.
> PUTNAM: I think you ought to take the job.
> CADE: Based on what?

PUTNAM: What I just saw.

CADE: I'm not in the habit of kissing children.

PUTNAM: Have you had any?

Cade shakes his head "no."

PUTNAM: Will you take the job? Cade, I'm not kidding anybody. I need you. I've built this world for Freddie and it takes everything I can earn to keep it going. I've had five housekeepers in the last seven years. I've just hired a handyman. God knows if he will stay. (*Pause*) I don't care if all you can teach him is C–A–T!

CADE: I won't settle for that.

PUTNAM: I think you will. What do you say?

CADE (*After a pause*): I say *yes.*

Cade, briefcase in hand, moves toward the door of the study. Putnam is with him, stops him.

PUTNAM: You come through for me—and I'll pull every string I can to get you back in Hillsgrove. No Shakespeare, no algebra—just the bottom line. You teach him two plus two or how to write his name and you're back in business.

CADE: I don't believe in bottom lines, Mr. Putnam. I'll take him as far as he can go.

PUTNAM: Take him as far as you like—but no farther than that front gate.

CADE: Why not?

PUTNAM: For one thing, he hasn't set foot outside of it since his mother died. For another, this is all the world that Freddie needs.

CADE: Six acres?

PUTNAM: He makes it here or nowhere. Here, nobody laughs at Freddie—and nobody pities him . . . or me.

EXTERIOR—HOUSE   DAY

CADE AND PUTNAM HAVE COME OUT OF THE HOUSE *and are watching Freddie on the trampoline.*

CADE: Does he spend all of his time on that trampoline?

PUTNAM: Yes, and your job will be to get him off it.

Cade walks toward his car.

PUTNAM: I'll open the gate for you.

Putnam returns to the study.

Cade has been watching Freddie on the trampoline. As the boy goes up and down, Cade gets an idea. He pushes the button on the dashboard of his car that operates the convertible top. It goes up and down. Up and then down.

Freddie gets off the trampoline and crosses to the car, fascinated.

> FREDDIE: It goes up and down.
>
> CADE: Yes—so you like things that go up and down, do you? Hey, come on, why don't you come for a ride with me down to the gate.

Freddie gets into the car beside Cade.

> CADE: How old are you?
>
> FREDDIE: Thirteen.

Cade drives down the driveway with Freddie . . .

AS CADE STOPS THE CAR AT THE GATE, the buzzer sounds. Freddie hops out and opens the gate. Cade drives through and stops the car on the other side. He gets out and walks back to Freddie on the other side of the gate, which isn't fully closed yet.

> CADE: Freddie, Freddie. How would you like to go see the place where the airplanes go up and down?

Freddie takes a step closer.

> CADE: . . . And maybe even a fire engine with a ladder that goes way way up. . . . All you have to do is step outside the gate. I know a merry-go-round—a merry-go-round with horses you can ride. Horses that go up and down and up . . .

He beckons to Freddie.

> CADE: Come on, Freddie. It's easy. Just one step and you're right outside in the world. Come on, and show your Daddy you can do it . . . do it for me—do it for your teacher. . . . Come on.

Freddie is tempted. . . . His face reflects the strain and the fear. . . . He almost makes it. Then he freezes, afraid. He slams the gate shut.

> CADE: It's all right, Freddie. We'll do it some other time. . . . Maybe.

Cade climbs into his car. He drives off.

Freddie stands behind the gate and watches him go.

DISSOLVE TO:

INTERIOR—HALLWAY OF THE HOUSE   DAY

TWO DAYS LATER . . . PUTNAM AND CADE are in the hallway. Putnam is dressed for travel. Cade wears a different tweedy jacket. They are carrying Cade's bags.

They enter a room from the hallway.

> PUTNAM: Now this will be yours. (*He sets the bag down*) It's right across from Freddie's room. I've left a list of how-to's on my desk, also some phone numbers you might need.
>
> CADE: You said there'd be a handyman.
>
> PUTNAM: Yes— Well, the agency said he'd be here this morning,

probably after I leave. He'll stay over the garage. They say he
can cook, do the gardening, repairs, just about everything.

CADE: I didn't know they came that way anymore.

PUTNAM: You'll be in charge. If he doesn't work out, call the
agency—get somebody else.

They go out into the hall.

Putnam opens a door . . .

PUTNAM: This is my room . . . there's another phone in there . . .

Then, indicating another door . . .

PUTNAM: That was my wife's room.

As they go on . . .

PUTNAM: Freddie doesn't even remember her. Seven years of
housekeepers, practical nurses, homemakers, college kids. . . .
If I'd put in a turnstile, I'd make money. . . . This is Freddie's
room.

*He opens the door to Freddie's room. We look in from the hall. It has none
of the indicative clutter of the "normal" 13-year-old. The things are on a kindergarten level—stuffed animals, etc. Pasted on the ceiling are gold and silver stars of all sizes, over a child's bed on which Freddie is fast asleep, sucking his thumb.*

Cade looks up at the stars as they enter the room.

Putnam raises a shade.

PUTNAM: When he was very little, we had a game. We cut these
out together. And I used to hold him up to touch the stars. As
he got older, he lost interest—he hasn't asked for that in a long
time.

Putnam goes over to Freddie and gently stirs him.

PUTNAM: Freddie . . .

Freddie awakens.

PUTNAM: Good morning. Do you remember Mr. Cade, Freddie?

He helps Freddie sit up.

PUTNAM: He's going to stay and be your teacher while Daddy's
away.

Freddie remains in bed. Putnam is sitting on the edge of the bed.

PUTNAM: . . . And it's just about time for me to go.

FREDDIE: In an airplane?

PUTNAM: That's right. . . . You be a good boy, now and I'll—
bring you presents from London . . . and I'll write you postcards.

FREDDIE: You come back.

(*It is a simple order.*)

PUTNAM: I promise.

FREDDIE: When?

PUTNAM: Soon. The minute I know, I'll let *you* know.

Putnam crosses the room to where Cade is standing by the door.

PUTNAM: Sometimes . . . I don't think he knows me from the milkman. That's what makes it so damned——

FREDDIE: Daddy?

Putnam goes to him. He tries to betray emotion to protect himself and not upset Freddie.

FREDDIE: Goodbye.

Putnam breaks and sweeps the boy into his arms. Freddie is merely surprised at the gesture. For all we know, Putnam, his back to THE CAMERA, *is weeping. Not Freddie.*

FADE OUT.

FADE IN:

EXTERIOR—DRIVEWAY   DAY

WE OPEN ON *CHARLES CARTER, a solid middle-aged Negro in clean work clothes.*

We see a sign on his station wagon: "CARTER HOME SERVICE. ESTATE WORK—PAINTING"—etc.

Carter's tire has blown out. He stands with his hands on his hips, ruefully studying a flat rear tire. Carter opens the back of his wagon, revealing valises, lawn mowers, rakes, etc., etc., a tool chest, and hauls things about to get at his jack.

CARTER: Just what I need. Everything's at the bottom.

As he comes up with a small, old-fashioned jack, Freddie turns up, watching. Carter inserts the jack-handle into the jack and operates it.

Carter sees Freddie.

CARTER: Well, hi!

Freddie makes his shy little hello-wave as Carter, operating the jack-handle to make the jack-handle lower, goes toward the flat.

CARTER: You live here?

Freddie nods.

CARTER: Cat got your tongue?

Freddie frowns, then points his tongue out and looks down to see if it is still there. Then he shakes his head "no." Carter laughs.

CARTER: Has your father got a heavy-duty jack in his garage? Something bigger than this?

FREDDIE (*After a pause*): What's a jack?

CARTER: What's a jack?

He operates the up-and-down mechanism.

CARTER: This is a jack.

FREDDIE (*Coming closer*): Make it go up and down.
CARTER: I'm trying—how about you helping me?
FREDDIE: Can't.
CARTER: No such word as can't.
He kneels down to Freddie's level.
CARTER: C'mon . . . you just do what I do.
Carter puts the jack-handle lug-end on one of the wheel lugs, loosens it— then puts Freddie's hand on the handle. He guides Freddie's hands as the boy loosens the lug, which comes off.
CARTER: That's got it.
FREDDIE: Make it go up and down.
CARTER: One thing at a time.
But Freddie reaches for the jack-handle. Carter gently pulls his hands away —then takes the boy's face in his hands.
CARTER: What's your name, son?
FREDDIE: Freddie. Make it go up.
CARTER: How old are you, Freddie?
FREDDIE: Thirteen years old.
Reaction, Carter. He knows now.
FREDDIE: *Please.*
CARTER: All right—we'll do it together. You and me.
Carter starts to put the lug-wrench on another lug, but now Freddie cups Carter's face in his hands. He studies Carter's face.
FREDDIE: What's your name?
CARTER (*After a moment*): Charley.
FREDDIE: How old are you?
CARTER: Oh . . . old enough to know better . . .
FREDDIE: Will you stay here?
CARTER: Uh-huh.
FREDDIE: And play with me?
CARTER: Uh-huh.
Carter can only shake his head up and down. Then, together, they set to work, Carter guiding Freddie's hands.

INTERIOR—FRONT HALL OF THE HOUSE   DAY
FREDDIE LEADS CARTER into the hallway. Carter lugs a heavy B-4 bag and a tool chest.
FREDDIE: Teacher! Teacher! Teacher!
Cade comes out of the study.
FREDDIE: Teacher! Teacher!
CADE: Oh! Mr. Carter? My name is Hamilton Cade.
CARTER: Nice to meet you . . .

They shake hands.

CADE: I see you've already met Freddie.

CARTER: Oh. Yeh . . . he helped me change a tire.

FREDDIE: I made it go up and down.

CADE: I wondered what kept you. . . . Well, it'll be the three of us. I hope you're a better cook than I am.

CARTER: Steaks and chops are about it.

CADE: Yes. Well, I'm sure we'll manage.

He sees Freddie playing with a knife.

CADE: Freddie, put that down.

Freddie puts the knife down and examines Carter's tool chest.

CADE: Stop playing with that.

Freddie ignores him.

CARTER: Oh . . . that's all right. There's nothing in that box he can hurt. He's a good kid——

CADE: Yes. Well, he's a little slow. I supposed you noticed.

CARTER: I don't know about that—I showed him how to handle a jack. He could be taught.

CADE: Yes—well, that's what I'm here for.

Freddie has removed a big Yankee screwdriver while they are speaking. He holds it up.

FREDDIE: What's that?

CARTER: A Yankee screwdriver. It goes up and down.

FREDDIE: Show me.

Carter kneels down to make himself Freddie's height and shows him how it works.

CARTER: All right, this way. Put your hand right here—this hand up here—down it goes—down.

We see Cade. . . . His face reflects the beginnings of insecurity, even jealousy.

As Carter holds the tool out to Freddie, Cade takes it, replaces it in the chest.

CADE: Well, I don't want him to hurt himself. Freddie, you take this to Mr. Carter's room.

FREDDIE: I want to play with Charley.

CADE: Freddie.

CARTER: Go ahead, Freddie, move out. We'll play later.

Freddie starts out with the tool chest.

CADE: Hurry up.

Cade starts to lift Carter's B-4 bag off the table.

CLOSEUP   THE BAG

On the bag, in faded black letters, we read: "CARTER, CHARLES, CAPT. USAF."
The two men exchange a look. Then Cade hands the bag to Carter.
CADE: I'll show you to your room. Captain.

INTERIOR—KITCHEN NIGHT
THE KITCHEN IS ROOMY AND MODERN. *At the table, Freddie and Cade are eating. Carter, wearing an apron, serves each of them a sizzling lambchop.*
CARTER: Freddie, chops á la Charley.
He serves one to his empty plate and sits down with the others.
CARTER: How do they look? Hmmm—good?
FREDDIE: Cut my food.
CARTER: Cut my food, please.
FREDDIE: Cut my food, *please.*
Cade starts to cut Freddie's food.
CADE: That's better.
CARTER: I bet you could do that yourself.
Cade shoots him a look.
CARTER: Maybe get Mr. Cade to teach you how.
Cade finishes. They eat. Carter pours a glass of milk for Freddie. He offers some to Cade. Cade shakes his head.
CADE: How's the room?
CARTER: Just fine.
CADE: You know we're going to have to do something about laundry.
CARTER: I'll take it down to the village to my sister.
CADE: How long have you lived here?
CARTER: A few weeks. My wife died. I came to live with my sister and her son. I didn't have a profession so I decided to start a business of my own—very useful.
CADE: You were in the Air Force, though.
CARTER: Nine years.
CADE: What sort of work did you do?
CARTER: Bomber pilot.
CADE: What made you leave?
CARTER: I found out they used real bombs.
CADE: I would have thought a fully-qualified pilot . . .
CARTER: There is very little demand for black commercial pilots, Mr. Cade. Right now, this suits me just fine. . . . Nothing like a man—ah—being in business for himself.
For a moment they are busy eating.
CARTER: How did you come to get into child psychology?

CADE: I'm not a psychologist.

CARTER: Oh.

He is willing to let it go at that, but Cade goes on compulsively——

CADE: I'm a teacher. I took my major in the humanities . . . the humanities and education. And a minor in psychology.

Carter makes a generalized gesture indicating the surroundings, then a significant inclination of his head toward Freddie.

CARTER: All that educational clout—and this—?

Cade recognizes the needle, but is holding back . . .

CARTER: I mean, there's such a shortage of teachers . . . I would think a man like you could just write his own ticket.

CADE (*He has regained his self-control*): Yes—well, in a sense, I have. As you said—to be in business for one's self. I did teach for a while . . . Colebrook and Hillsgrove . . .

CARTER: Good schools.

CADE (*More assured*): Yes. But I, ah . . . got fed up with the educational establishment, the institutional complex . . .

Carter nods, not buying a word.

CADE: I find this much more rewarding. The one-to-one relationship . . . the flexibility, the—ah—freedom to move at one's own pace, the pupil, teacher . . .

CARTER: Uh-hm.

CADE (*To Freddie*): Before you leave the table, you say excuse me.

Freddie looks to Carter.

CARTER: That's right, Freddie.

FREDDIE: Excuse me, excuse me.

CADE: All right—off you go and play . . .

Freddie leaves.

CADE: As I was saying—no rigid classroom structure . . . no—timeclock tyranny . . . and above all—the challenge.

He looks at Carter.

CADE: Yes . . . the challenge.

He says it directly to Carter—but straight and sincere, not realizing that he has clued Carter in completely.

CADE: The greater the challenge—the more the personal satisfaction. Not for the school—but for the teacher.

CARTER: Hmmm.

Carter lifts a platter, gestures as if to ask "Would you like more?", but Cade declines. Carter helps himself to another chop and begins to eat it with evident relish.

INTERIOR—CADE'S ROOM   NIGHT

CADE IS UNPACKING BOOKS *and putting them on shelves. Along with Shake-*

speare, collections of poets, drama, etc., he takes out some brand-new elementary teaching materials—first-grade readers, kindergarten workbooks, etc. He takes out a flask, looks at it, puts it aside.

FREDDIE'S VOICE: Teacher, teacher! Teacher, teacher! Teacher, teacher, teacher, teacher! Teacher!

Cade hurries to Freddie's room . . .

FREDDIE IS STANDING IN THE CENTER *of the room, as Cade comes in. Freddie lifts his arms.*

FREDDIE: Stars? Stars? Stars, stars, stars.

Cade looks up to the stars on the ceiling. Freddie is doing the same thing with his hands and fingers, reaching and clutching, as he had done with the airplane.

CADE: Freddie? Freddie, listen! . . . No. You're a big boy now, Freddie—you're a big boy . . .

FREDDIE: Stars—stars—stars—stars—stars.

Cade finally lifts Freddie up so he can touch the stars with his fingertips.

CADE: All right—touch the stars.

FREDDIE (*Whispers*): Stars, stars, stars, stars——

FADE OUT.

ACT TWO

FADE IN:

INTERIOR—FREDDIE'S ROOM   DAY

FREDDIE IS PLAYING *with plastic boxes, trains, tunnel.*

Cade enters with teaching cards.

CADE: Good morning, Freddie.

FREDDIE: Good morning, Teacher.

Cade moves some of Freddie's stuffed animals aside and sits across from Freddie at his child-sized table.

CADE: Ah—what do we have here—ah hah—a tunnel.

Cade sweeps the clutter of trains and tunnel into a box.

CADE: Well, that's enough playing for now. C'mon, help me put them in here. . . . Time for our lesson—now then, now then, let's see what we can remember. Now here we're going to have some pictures again this morning.

Cade holds up a card: on it is a picture of a boat, and underneath the picture the word "boat."

CADE: Here we are, now what's this?

FREDDIE: I don't know. I like pictures.

CADE: This is a boat. Now then—this is the picture of a boat and
this is the word for "boat." . . . This is the picture of a boat
and this is the word for "boat."

Cade covers the picture, leaving the printed word visible.

CADE: What's this?

Freddie just looks.

Cade holds up a card of a boy.

CADE: What's this picture?

FREDDIE: Boy!

CADE: This is the word for "boy."

He points to the word underneath the picture.

CADE: What is this word?

Freddie just looks.

CADE: Now, Freddie, we know what words are, don't we? Do you
know what a *word* is, Freddie? A *word* is something that we
make work for us. We *use* words to write with. Well, there's a
word for everything——

Cade shows him a card with "Daddy" on it.

CADE: This is the word for "Daddy." There's a word even for
where your Daddy's gone. Now—where's your Daddy gone?

FREDDIE: My Daddy's far away.

CADE: That's right. He's gone to London. This is the word for
"London." . . . This is the word for "Daddy."

Cade draws it out . . .

CADE: This is "London." . . . this is "Daddy."

Freddie grabs the card.

FREDDIE: That's not my Daddy! My Daddy's far away!

He throws the card.

CADE: Pick it up. . . . Sit down—now then, we'll start again——
This is the word for "London"—this is the word for "Daddy"
—this is "London" and this is "Daddy"——

Freddie snatches the card and throws it across the room again.

FREDDIE: That's not my Daddy— My Daddy's far away.

CADE: Pick it up—hurry up—c'mon!

Freddie runs out of the room.

DISSOLVE TO:

INTERIOR—GARAGE WORKSHOP   DAY

*CARTER IS BUILDING A CARRY-ALL BOX for tools. He is about to screw one of
the sideboards into place. He sets the board in place and picks up a Yankee
screwdriver. He adjusts the ratchet.*

Freddie enters.

CARTER: Hi!

Freddie grabs at the screwdriver.

FREDDIE: It goes up and down!

CARTER: Sure. But that's not all it does. Give me a hand.

He guides Freddie's hand and shows him how to drive a screw.

CADE: See? It does the work for you.

FREDDIE: I want to do it again!

CARTER: No—let's not do it again. Let's do something different. We're making a tool box.

Carter turns to the bench and picks up a board for the other side of the box. He takes a folding ruler from his pocket.

CARTER: See? This goes up and down too.

Carter unfolds the ruler. Freddie grabs it and starts to open it. Carter stops him.

CARTER: It tells you how long a thing is. You know what *long* means?

He measures Freddie with the ruler.

CARTER: Awright? See, you're that *long,* right?

He lays the ruler along the board.

CARTER: Now I want to find twenty-four on here because I want to make it twenty-four inches.

FREDDIE: What's *inches?*

CARTER: Every one of these little marks here is an inch. It's that much. . . .

He indicates with two fingers.

CARTER: And every one of these big marks are feet.

Freddie looks down at his feet.

Carter smiles.

CARTER: No—that's a different kind of feet. But don't let it bother you. We're going to mark off twenty-four inches on this. You take the pencil. . . . Come on this side——

Carter makes a line, using a T-square.

CARTER: . . . That's it. Now we're gonna saw that line—right— turn the board this way.

He gets a saw and guides Freddie's hand. They saw the board together.

CARTER: That's got it!

The board is sawn through. Carter holds up the board and then fits it to make the other side of the tool box.

FREDDIE: We're doing it!

CARTER: We sure are.

Carter feels a third presence in the workshop—he looks over his shoulder and sees Cade watching them.

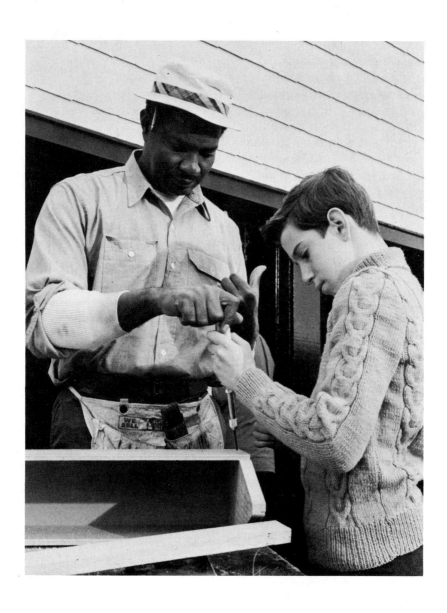

Ossie Davis and Billy Shulman in *Teacher, Teacher*.

CARTER: Oh! Hello, Mr. Cade. (*To Freddie*) Say hello to your teacher.

FREDDIE: Hello, Teacher.

Carter proceeds working on the tool box.

FREDDIE: My Daddy makes houses.

CARTER: So he does.

FREDDIE: I'm gonna make a house.

CARTER (*After a bit*): Oh no.

FREDDIE: Oh yes!

CARTER: First you are going to learn to use tools. Then—*we're* gonna *build* a house.

Carter turns to Cade behind him——

CARTER: The three of us——

Cade says nothing.

DISSOLVE TO:

INTERIOR—FREDDIE'S ROOM   DAY

THE CAMERA PANS SLOWLY *across crudely drawn pictures of houses.*

CLOSEUP   ONE OF FREDDIE'S PICTURES

We see Freddie's hand. . . . He is trying to write the word "house" on it. He fails and scribbles all over it. . . .

AS THE CAMERA PANS THE ROOM *we hear . . .*

FREDDIE'S VOICE: House.

CADE'S VOICE: Good.

FREDDIE'S VOICE: Crane.

CADE'S VOICE: Crane.

FREDDIE'S VOICE: Crane.

CADE: Right. Now we go back to the beginning—okay, we'll do it again. Everything we did before, we'll do again. Now then——

INTERIOR—PUTNAM'S STUDY   DAY

CADE HAS TAPED SIGNS *to most things in the room in an effort to teach Freddie to identify objects and learn the spelling of the words.*

Cade moves from one object to the next as Freddie identifies them——

CADE: What does this say?

He points to a "word card" on the chair.

FREDDIE: Chair.

CADE: It's a chair—right. Now—(*Pointing to the card*)—what's this?

FREDDIE: Chair.

CADE: Chair, right—now you're reading it, aren't you. It's a chair.
. . . Now this——

FREDDIE: Window.

CADE: Window, right—the window.

Cade stands next to the fireplace.

CADE: Now what's this?

FREDDIE: Bricks.

CADE: Right. Read this (*Indicating another card*)——

FREDDIE: Fire.

CADE: Fire—right. And this——

FREDDIE: Lamp.

CADE: Right. . . . Here?

FREDDIE: Steps.

Cade is now at the opposite end of the room.

CADE: Louder.

FREDDIE (*Louder*): Steps.

CADE: Good—very good. Now what about this?

FREDDIE: Table.

CADE: This is a table. . . . Now you're reading. . . . Let's make
sure you're reading.

*Cade crosses to the table where Freddie has been sitting. There are word
cards on the table as well as teaching "props"—flowers, a lemon, a knife,
etc. Cade holds up the flowers.*

CADE: Now what are these?

FREDDIE: Flowers.

CADE: Right. Now show me the card for "flower." Read it.

Freddie holds up the wrong word card.

CADE: All right—put it down. I want you to read the card, Freddie. . . . Now, what's this?

FREDDIE: Lemon.

CADE: Right. Lemon. Now read the card.

*Freddie cannot read the card and again chooses one he thinks may be right.
Cade is becoming more frantic with each wrong card.*

CADE: I want the card for "lemon." What's this?

Cade holds up the knife.

CADE: . . . Look at it.

FREDDIE: Knife.

CADE: A *knife* with which we cut the lemon. Now show me the
card for "knife."

Freddie again chooses the wrong word card.

CADE: Now listen, I want you to *read* the cards. *Knife,* Freddie,
knife!

Cade grabs the word card.

    CADE: *This* is the *card* for "knife."

Freddie takes the card from him.

    CADE: All right. Put it down.

Cade starts over again.

    CADE: Do it once more. . . . Now here are the flowers. Show me
        the card for "flow . . ."

Freddie's attention span is exhausted.

    CADE: Freddie, I want you to learn these things.

*Freddie starts to stand up and Cade takes his arm. He is a little desperate
now.*

    FREDDIE: Why?

    CADE: Because I want you to be able to write; I want you to make
        the words work for you——

    FREDDIE: I make nice pictures.

    CADE: Yes, you do.

    FREDDIE: I make nice pictures.

    CADE: Yes—I know you do . . . but making nice pictures isn't
        using words. Words can help you. When you go out into the
        world—the words can help to keep you safe.

Freddie just looks at Cade.

    CADE: And if you learn the words, you can learn to read books;
        and if you can read books, you need never be alone. Books are
        wonderful friends. Freddie—your Daddy will be home soon
        and . . .

No response.

    CADE: . . . It would make your Daddy very happy if you could
        make the words work for you . . .

He gives up and lets Freddie go.

    CADE: All right, Freddie. That's enough for today. Go out and
        play.

Freddie starts to leave.

    CADE: Here, put your shoes on.

*But Freddie starts to put the shoes on the wrong feet. Cade stops him. Cade
is losing control out of frustration. He jams the right shoe on Freddie's right
foot, then holds Freddie's right hand up in front of his face, saying——*

    CADE: Right, right, right. Put your *right* shoe on your *right* foot.

Freddie fumbles.

    CADE: Well, try . . . go on.

*Freddie stares at him a moment—and takes off. Cade is left alone, discour-
aged and shaken.*

INTERIOR/EXTERIOR—CARTER'S WORKSHOP   DAY
CARTER AND FREDDIE ARE DISCUSSING the "house" they are building.
>   CARTER: Freddie, Freddie—now what are we gonna do today—?
>   FREDDIE: Build a house.
>   CARTER: Build a house. What kinda house?
>   FREDDIE: A wooden house.
>   CARTER: What's the roof on the house?
>   FREDDIE: A wall . . .
>   CARTER: Hold this—here, hold this.

He hands Freddie a board.
>   CARTER: Where are we gonna put this?
>   FREDDIE: On the side.
>   CARTER: Which side——
>   FREDDIE: A wall.
>   CARTER: Which wall—the right wall or the left wall?
>   FREDDIE (*Guessing*): Right wall——
>   CARTER: Right wall—exactly—right—go to the house—show me
>   the right wall . . .

*THEY WALK DOWN THE HILL OUTSIDE THE WORKSHOP to where their almost
completed "house"—a hut—stands.*
>   CARTER: All right—inside.

Freddie enters the "house," Carter follows him.
>   CARTER: All right—show me the right wall.

Freddie goes to the left.
>   CARTER: Not left, Freddie—that board goes on the right—don't
>   you know what the right is? Huh? Come here.

Freddie comes over to Carter.
>   CARTER: I'm gonna fix it so you'll always know what the right is.

*Freddie looks at him. Carter takes a roll of friction tape out of his pocket.
He tears off an inch and sticks it on Freddie's right shoe.*
>   CARTER: Pull up your foot—there you are. Now you can always
>   tell. That one is right.
>   FREDDIE: I like you, Charley.

Carter takes Freddie's face in his hands.
>   CARTER: I like you, too, Freddie.
>   FREDDIE: I don't like Mr. Cade.
>   CARTER: Uh-uh—I don't like to hear you talking like that. Mr.
>   Cade's a good man. Maybe he's just lonely—like you're lonely
>   for your Dad.
>   FREDDIE: Oh.

He looks sad.
>   CARTER: Come on—we've got a house to finish building! Right?

FREDDIE: That's right!
He looks at his shoe with the tape.
FREDDIE: Right, right, right!
CARTER (*Indicating the board*): All right—put it here. Here's the
nail—now—right, right, right——
DISSOLVE TO:
INTERIOR—FREDDIE'S ROOM   DAY
CADE AND FREDDIE ARE STANDING OVER A GLOBE. Cade is moving a toy air-
plane across the globe.
CADE: . . . And your Daddy went in an airplane to London.
Show me London. . . . No. Here, put your finger up there.
That's London.
FREDDIE: London . . .

INTERIOR—FREDDIE'S *"HOUSE"*   DAY
FREDDIE IS SITTING in the completed hut. He smiles up at the sign he has
made. It says: "MY HOUSE."
DISSOLVE TO:
CLOSEUP   A CALENDAR
WE SEE *the date . . . the third day of the month.*

EXTERIOR—*FRONT OF THE HOUSE   DAY*
FREDDIE RUNS DOWN THE DRIVEWAY to the front door. In one hand he
carries a batch of letters, in the other hand he has a big over-sized postcard
with a picture of London Bridge on it.
He runs in the front door. . . .
FREDDIE IS INTO THE DOWNSTAIRS HALL.
FREDDIE (*Calling*): Teacher . . . teacher . . .
He drops the mail on the stairs and runs upstairs with the postcard in his
hand. . . .
CADE IS AT THE DESK IN FREDDIE'S ROOM laying out the day's lessons.
He hears:
FREDDIE'S VOICE: Teacher . . . teacher!
FREDDIE RUNS DOWN THE UPSTAIRS HALL . . .
FREDDIE: Teacher . . . teacher!
. . . And goes into his room.
Freddie runs over to Cade—he holds up the postcard for him to see. He is
very excited.
CADE: Oh. It's from your Daddy.
FREDDIE (*Pointing to the picture on the card*): I saw this one.
CADE: That's right.
FREDDIE (*Pointing to the picture*): Read it.

CADE (*Takes the postcard*): It's the same picture. But different
   words.

FREDDIE: Read it.

CADE: No, no, no. This time you're going to read this one all by
   yourself.

Cade gives Freddie the postcard.

FREDDIE: Too many words——

CADE: Well, there isn't a word there you don't know.

Freddie hands back the postcard.

CADE (*Pointing to the words on the postcard*): Look. What's that?

FREDDIE: London.

CADE: Right. See, what's that?

FREDDIE: London.

CADE: Right. Now come on—you can read it.

FREDDIE: Read it.

CADE: Now come on, Freddie.

FREDDIE: *Read* it.

CADE: You read it.

FREDDIE: *You* read it.

CADE (*Gives up*): All right. (*Reading*) "Dear Freddie. I am back in
   London. I will try to come home on the 15th. Love—Daddy."

Freddie snatches the postcard.

FREDDIE (*Sniffling*): Why? Why is it far? Why?

EXTERIOR—GREENHOUSE   DAY

FREDDIE IS STUDYING HIS FATHER'S POSTCARD, *trying to read it. Carter is
raking leaves—he passes the greenhouse and sees Freddie. He sits next to
Freddie.*

CARTER: What's your Daddy say this time?

Freddie hands over the card.

FREDDIE: Too many words.

CARTER: What's that mean?

FREDDIE: They all go together.

Carter studies him.

CARTER: What you need is a little helper. Like the one I made my
   nephew Joey.

*He has been fishing in his pocket for something, and comes up with a card.
With a knife, he carefully cuts out a rectangular opening in its center——*

CARTER: . . . Now those words won't just run together.

*Freddie comes in close as Carter finishes the cut-out. Carter takes the post-
card and lays the cut-out card over the writing so that only a word or two can
be seen at a time through the "window."*

CARTER: *Now* read it.

FREDDIE: "Dear—Freddie. I am back—in London—I will try—to come home—on the 15th—Love Daddy."

Suddenly Freddie holds the card up to his face and peers through the opening. We go in to EXTREME CLOSE-SHOT *to reveal what Carter has cut up—his business card: "CHARLES CARTER, Home Service, 223 Wicker Street, 345-7602."*

DISSOLVE TO:

INTERIOR—KITCHEN   NIGHT

CADE, CARTER, AND FREDDIE HAVE FINISHED DINNER. *Cade drinks his coffee. Carter reads half of the evening paper. Freddie is occupied with the rest of the paper.*

As Cade watches, Freddie takes his "helper" out of his breast pocket and begins to read words aloud.

FREDDIE: "I am in the—school play—I am a—turkey. But—this—those—are real duck—wings. I am—a turkey. Turkey, turkey, turkey."

CADE: What's that?

FREDDIE: Charley made it. To help me read.

CADE: Hmmm—show me.

Freddie won't give it up. He puts it back in his pocket.

CADE: Freddie——

FREDDIE: No! I want to go to the bathroom.

CADE: All right! Go to the bathroom.

Freddie exits. Cade looks at Carter. Carter puts the paper down flat.

CADE: I'd like to teach him to read *my way.*

CARTER: I think you're doing a fantastic job.

Cade doesn't respond.

CARTER: Is something bugging you, *Mr.* Cade?

CADE: Nothing at all.

CARTER: Ever since I set foot on this place I got funny vibrations from you. . . . If there's something on your mind, I'd like to hear about it. If I bother you, I can just pack up and move out.

CADE: I wouldn't want you to do that.

CARTER: Then why don't you level with me? Is it the boy?

CADE: Yes, I suppose it is. I was hired to be his teacher. I'm a good teacher——

CARTER: I can see that.

CADE: Frankly, I have a difficult time relating to Freddie.

CARTER: All you have to do is be yourself.

CADE: Well, that's easy for you—it's not for me.

CARTER: I still don't see what that's got to do——

CADE: He's attached to you. You're a playmate for him. He'd rather be having fun with you than doing his lessons. All I ask is that you leave the teaching to me——

CARTER: I think I get the message——

CADE: Well, don't misunderstand.

CARTER: Your place is the teacher, my place is the handyman—that's it, *isn't* it?

CADE: Well—yes—if you have to put it that way.

CARTER: I have to put it like it is, Mr. Cade—otherwise things get all mixed up.

He rises.

CADE: Carter——

Carter turns back to face him.

CADE: This has nothing to do with skin.

CARTER: Man, I got past that one a long time ago . . .

INTERIORS—FREDDIE'S ROOM/ KITCHEN   DAY

FREDDIE AND CADE ARE STANDING IN FRONT OF FREDDIE'S BLACKBOARD on which teaching cards are tacked up. Freddie is pointing to each card and giving the meaning.

FREDDIE: Bow-wow! . . . Green! . . . Yellow! . . . Red!

He points to a picture of a stop sign.

FREDDIE: Stop!

He playfully pushes Cade on the bed.

FREDDIE: Stop!

He claps and laughs—quite amused with his action . . .

NOW CADE AND FREDDIE ARE SEATED ON THE RUG. There are educational toys all around them. Freddie is attempting to fit different shaped blocks into the properly shaped boxes.

He attempts to jam a square block into a round opening . . .

FREDDIE: Doesn't fit.

Cade helps him.

FREDDIE AND CADE ARE SEATED AT THE KITCHEN TABLE. Cade is holding up objects for Freddie to identify . . .

CADE: . . . and this one is a cup . . .

FREDDIE: Cup.

CADE: And just under the cup is a saucer.

FREDDIE (*He can't quite make it*): Sau—sau . . .

CADE (*Pronouncing it slowly*): Sau—cer.

FREDDIE: Sau . . .

CADE: *Sau—cer.*

FREDDIE: Sau . . .

Billy Shulman and David McCallum in *Teacher, Teacher.*

CADE: It's a saucer.

FREDDIE: Sau . . .

CADE AND FREDDIE ARE WORKING OVER A LARGE WHITE PAD. He is teaching Freddie to write the alphabet.

Freddie traces Cade's letter "A" with his finger.

CADE: Okay—you do one . . . careful.

Freddie draws a rather crude "A."

ANOTHER SCENE WITH FREDDIE AND CADE—this time they are practicing the alphabet on a lined pad.

Freddie draws a neat "A" in the lined space. He turns to Cade for approval.

FREDDIE AND CADE ARE SITTING TOGETHER IN ANOTHER LESSON . . .

CADE: . . . and what does a cook do?

FREDDIE: Cooks.

CADE: Cooks, right! And what does he cook?

FREDDIE: Food.

CADE: Food! So—you eat what the cook cooks. Now what does the cook cook?

FREDDIE: Food.

CADE (*Slowly*): Food—say, *food.*

FREDDIE (*Carefully*): Food.

CADE: Now where does the food go?

FREDDIE: In the stove.

CADE: No—where does the food go when you eat it?

Cade points to his mouth.

CADE: It goes in there, doesn't it?

FREDDIE: Mouth.

CADE: Show me where it goes.

Freddie opens his mouth.

CADE: It goes in your mouth. *Mouth.*

FREDDIE: Mouth.

CADE (*Drawing the word out*): Mouth.

FREDDIE: Mouth.

CADE: You look very silly doing that.

Freddie giggles.

CADE: Now—c'mon, be serious. Now then, if you have a cook, what do you have to have for him to cook?

FREDDIE: Food.

CADE: Give me the name of a food.

FREDDIE (*A pause as he thinks*): Beans!

CADE: Beans—where do you get beans?

FREDDIE: From an animal.

CADE: From an animal? They don't grow on animals—a bean animal?
Freddie laughs.
CADE: No. What's the name of an animal with beans—? He's a bean?
Freddie laughs at this nonsense.
DISSOLVE TO:

CLOSEUP   A CALENDAR
WE SEE *the date . . . the fifteenth of the month.*
DISSOLVE TO:

EXTERIOR—DRIVEWAY   MORNING
FREDDIE IS FULLY DRESSED AND IN THE DRIVEWAY WAITING FOR HIS
FATHER.
Cade comes out in robe and pajamas.
CADE (*Calling*): Freddie . . .
He goes to Freddie.
CADE: Freddie, there's plenty of time. Your Daddy hasn't left London yet—probably hasn't even got on the plane. You see, there's a different time there—
FREDDIE: Why?
CADE: Why—well, you see as the earth goes around the sun—
Cade uses his hands to demonstrate.
FREDDIE: No! (*Then, pointing*) When I get up, the sun is there . . . When I go to sleep, the sun is . . . *there.*
He makes a big arc with his hand.
FREDDIE: Nothing goes around *any*thing. It just goes *up*—and down.
CADE: Well, wait a minute—you see—
FREDDIE (*Interrupting*): I *see* it!
CADE: C'mon—let me explain something to you . . .
They start toward the house . . .

INTERIOR—FREDDIE'S ROOM   NIGHT
FREDDIE IS CROUCHED ON THE FLOOR *near his bed. Cade and Carter are standing over him.*
FREDDIE: I hate you!
CARTER: Freddie—c'mon, Freddie. Freddie, your Daddy's just been delayed.
FREDDIE: Go away!
CARTER: Your Daddy's just been delayed.
He can't get through to Freddie.

FREDDIE: Go away—go away!

CADE: Your Daddy's just been delayed. He's coming home, Freddie.

FREDDIE: I hate you!

CARTER: He's coming home.

FREDDIE: Go away!

CADE: Your Daddy *is* coming home.

Carter picks Freddie up and puts him in bed.

CARTER: Come on, now, simmer down.

FREDDIE: Go 'way!

Cade has put Putnam's cable in Freddie's hand.

CADE: Let me read it to you.

Freddie grabs the telegram and tears it to shreds with his teeth.

CARTER: Come on, Freddie——

CADE: He's been delayed but he *is* coming home.

FREDDIE: No. You tell lies! You tell lies!

CADE: No. No. It's not a lie. He is coming home late Friday.

Freddie pulls the covers over him. Cade turns to Carter.

CADE: You have any ideas?

CARTER: Will you leave me alone with him a minute?

Cade nods and exits.

Carter goes to Freddie who is under the blankets. He puts his hand on Freddie's neck.

CARTER: I think I know what you need, son.

THE CAMERA PANS DOWN to Carter's hand resting on Freddie's back.

SLOW DISSOLVE TO:

INTERIOR/EXTERIOR—THE WORKSHOP   DAY

CARTER IS PLANING A PIECE OF WOOD.

We hear the soft sounds of two children playing in the background.

Cade enters the garage workshop from the rear door.

CADE: I'm looking for Freddie—it's time for his lesson.

CARTER: Right out there.

He points with his thumb. . . . Carter and Cade walk to the wide front door of the workshop.

Outside, Freddie and JOEY, Carter's nephew, are playing kickball.

FREDDIE: Joey, Joey, catch.

JOEY: Okay—here.

CARTER: How about that?

CADE: Who's the child?

CARTER: My sister's kid.

CADE: I wish you'd consulted me.

CARTER: I didn't think you'd mind. I bet that's the first time Freddie has had anybody to play with.

CADE: That's not the point. I'm responsible for that boy. I promised myself I'd teach him something useful, at least how to write his own name.

CARTER: Is that so important?

CADE: You're damn right it's important. Niles Putnam isn't going to live forever, you know. Someday that boy will have to leave this prison and face the world. Why, just to cross the street, he'll have to read a "Don't Walk" sign, and know the difference between the Ladies' Room and the Men's. Why, I can't teach him anything if you have him out there playing games all the time.

CARTER: I was trying to help.

CADE: I'm a trained teacher, Mr. Carter. If I need your help, I'll ask for it.

CARTER: I was thinking more about what the *boy* needs . . .

He resumes planing the piece of wood. Cade watches the boys for a moment . . .

THE TWO BOYS ARE KICKING A SOCCER BALL. *Freddie kicks it over the fence.*

FREDDIE: Get the ball, please.

JOEY: You get it. You kicked it outside.

FREDDIE: You get it!

He looks at the fence.

FREDDIE: I can't go out.

JOEY: You get it. You kicked it over.

FREDDIE: No. You.

He tries to push Joey toward the fence.

FREDDIE: You get it, please. Please. Please.

JOEY: Stop pushin'!

FREDDIE: Please!

Joey pushes Freddie back. Freddie gives him a bear hug.

JOEY: Quit huggin'!

Freddie continues to hug, pushing Joey toward the fence. Joey becomes frightened.

JOEY: Let go! Let go! Uncle Charley, Uncle Charley!

He shoves Freddie away from him just as Cade runs to them. Cade thrusts Joey away from Freddie.

JOEY: Freddie, I'm sorry, I'm sorry.

Carter runs over to them. Joey rushes to him.

JOEY: Uncle Charley, he pushed me.

CADE *(To Freddie)*: Freddie, are you all right?

FREDDIE: He hurt me.

CADE: Where?

FREDDIE: My hand.

He shows Cade a scraped hand with some blood on it. Carter steps toward them.

CARTER: Let's see that.

CADE (*To Carter*): I'll handle it.

He gives Freddie a handkerchief.

CADE: All right, Freddie, you go on up to the house and wash your hands. Go on.

Freddie hides alongside the workshop. Cade turns to Carter.

CADE: You better take your nephew home.

CARTER: They were just playing. Don't make a big deal out of this.

Cade stares at him angrily and turns and walks back to the workshop.

JOEY: I'm sorry.

CARTER: That's all right, Joey. You'd better go down to the station wagon and wait there.

JOEY: But——

CARTER (*His eyes on Cade*): Do as I say. I just want to go and get some tools. Go on.

Joey goes. Carter turns his back on Cade and walks into the workshop.

FADE OUT.

ACT THREE

INTERIOR—THE WORKSHOP   DAY

CADE IS LOOKING OUT the workshop window. Carter is gathering his tools together and placing them in his tool chest. It is obvious that he intends to quit.

CADE: Carter, I didn't mean——

Carter turns on him, blazing.

CARTER: What the hell did you mean? Don't you think my nephew has feelings?

CADE: I didn't mean to hurt his feelings, but Freddie is a handicapped child.

CARTER: They're both handicapped——

CADE: I have to decide what's best for him!

CARTER: For him? Or for you? Mr. Cade, I'm gonna get out of here but before I go, I got a word for you. Every time you look at Freddie, it's to get him to do something for you. Every time you come near the pressure is on. (*Sarcastically*) You're like those folks who give their kids piano lessons. Because they love music? No. (*Imitating*) It's "play a piece for the people." "Say a big word for Uncle John." Do your trick. "Say something in algebra for Aunt." Come on, Freddie, come on, look at the picture—say the word—for Mr. Cade. (*Then grimly*) You're always trying to get Freddie to do something to make you feel better! (*With pure scorn*) Why can't you for God's sake just let him be what he is——

He throws the last of the tools into the tool chest, and with a loud bang slams the cover down and exits from the workshop.
Cade stands where he is.

EXTERIOR—DRIVEWAY DAY
CARTER'S STATION WAGON WHIPS *around and down the drive.*
We see the trampoline . . . Freddie has retreated to it.
DISSOLVE TO:
INTERIOR—PUTNAM'S STUDY DAY
THE PHONE IS RINGING. *Cade comes down the stairs, enters the study, and answers it.*

CADE: Putnam residence. Hamilton Cade speaking.
PUTNAM'S VOICE: Cade? This is Mr. Putnam.
CADE: Hello.
PUTNAM'S VOICE: I'm at the airport. Just got in. Finished the job sooner than we thought. How's Freddie?
CADE: Fine, just fine.
PUTNAM'S VOICE: Good. Any problems?
CADE: No, no—nothing special. I—ah—I had to fire the handyman.
PUTNAM'S VOICE: Oh? Well, that's no tragedy. As long as the boy's all right.
CADE: Would you like to speak with him?
PUTNAM'S VOICE: No, he'll just get anxious. I'll get a taxi right away and surprise him.
CADE: Right.
PUTNAM'S VOICE: You okay? You sound a little strange.
CADE: No—I'm fine, fine . . . just fine. (*Pause*) Ah—Mr. Putnam?
PUTNAM'S VOICE: Yes?
CADE: I got your son off the trampoline.

He hangs up.

EXTERIOR—TRAMPOLINE DAY
CADE IS WALKING DOWN THE DRIVEWAY toward the trampoline. Freddie is bouncing up and down on it, monotonously.

 CADE: Freddie?
Freddie ignores him.
 CADE: Freddie!
Freddie ignores him.
 CADE: Stop jumping, Freddie. Freddie, come off that trampoline!
Freddie continues bouncing.
 CADE: Listen, Freddie—I'm sorry I made your friend go away, but you and I have a lot of work to do together. Freddie, stop that! When your Daddy gets here, we're going to show him all the things we've learned. We're going to read to him and we're going to copy out all the words from the cards. We'll really show him all the things we can do.
Freddie continues to jump.
 CADE: Come off the trampoline—! Stop doing that!
He grabs at Freddie and Freddie falls.
 FREDDIE: You hurt my arm.
 CADE: I didn't mean to. Look at me. Do you hear me? Look at me. Look at me. I'm your teacher, aren't I? And I've taught you a great deal, haven't I? *Look* at me, *look* at me. I taught you how to read and write from your cards. Didn't I? *Didn't* I?
Freddie makes no response.
 CADE: I did, didn't I? I've taught you a lot of things.
Cade realizes his own total defeat.
 CADE: I did, didn't I?
 FREDDIE: I make nice pictures. I make nice pictures.
Cade turns and walks back to the house.
Freddie stares after him.

INTERIOR—PUTNAM'S STUDY DAY
CADE IS TAKING DOWN THE SIGNS he has placed around the room for Freddie. He is waiting for Putnam to arrive home.

EXTERIOR—TRAMPOLINE DAY (*Slow motion*)
FREDDIE BOUNCES up and down, up and down, up and down . . .
We hear the voices that Freddie hears in his head . . .

 CARTER'S VOICE: How old are you?
 PUTNAM'S VOICE: You be a good boy now.
 CADE'S VOICE: Fire engines . . . merry-go-round.

David McCallum and Billy Shulman in *Teacher, Teacher*.

DISSOLVE TO:
INTERIOR—PUTNAM'S STUDY   DAY
CADE CROSSES THE ROOM AND POURS himself a drink.
There is the sound of the door as Putnam enters the front hall.
    PUTNAM'S VOICE: Freddie! Freddie, it's Daddy! I'm home!
Putnam comes into the study and sees Cade.
    PUTNAM: Hey! Hello, Mr. Cade. Where is he?
    CADE: He's back on his trampoline.
    PUTNAM: No. He's not there.
Cade stands, alarmed.
    PUTNAM: Where is he?
Cade runs out the front door; Putnam runs up the stairs.
    PUTNAM: Freddie?
PUTNAM IS RUNNING through the house shouting.
    PUTNAM: Freddie! Freddie!
He runs into Freddie's room.
PUTNAM FINDS FREDDIE'S NOTE on the bed.
PUTNAM COMES HALFWAY DOWN THE STAIRCASE as Cade enters the house.
He shows Cade the note.
    PUTNAM: Look at this!
    CADE (*Reads it*): Where was it?
    PUTNAM: It was on his bed.
    CADE (*Reading the note aloud*): "I—gone—see—my—fren."
Cade shakes his head in disbelief.
    PUTNAM: He couldn't have written that. Where is he, Cade?
    CADE: He wrote this . . .
    PUTNAM: Cade, where is my son?
    CADE: He wrote it. He *wrote* it.
    PUTNAM: If my son wrote that note, I'll build you a prep school of
       your own. But if anything has happened to him, I swear I'll
       kill you!

EXTERIOR—A SUBURBAN STREET   DAY
FREDDIE IS WALKING . . . He stops in front of a lawn to study a set of lawn-ornaments: A mama duck and four ducklings following her. The last duckling is lying on its side.
Freddie goes right up to the ornaments, and fixes the fallen duckling so that it, too, is upright. . . .
A STURDY BOY OF FREDDIE'S AGE comes wildly down a hill on a skateboard, shouting——
    BOY: Look out, look out! Get out of the way!
THE CAMERA FOLLOWS HIM and reveals Freddie at the foot of the hill just standing there, watching in amazement.

The boy manages to swerve and miss Freddie, but falls. Picking himself up, he rushes toward Freddie full of fight.

    BOY: What's the matter with you, anyway?

But Freddie goes and picks up the skateboard, and hands it to the boy.

    FREDDIE: I have to find my friend.

Freddie walks out of FRAME, *leaving the boy puzzled, and somewhat comprehending, turning the wheels of the skateboard with his hand . . .*

FREDDIE IS WALKING DOWN ANOTHER STREET . . .

He stares at a stop sign. For a moment he frowns. Then his lips move, forming the letters—S—T—O—P. Then aloud——

    FREDDIE: Stop.

FREDDIE IS AT AN INTERSECTION . . .

The sudden sound of a blow-out is heard, and then the chunketa-chunketa-chunketa of a car rolling on the rim.

Freddie looks in the direction of the sound—fascinated.

The car drives into FRAME *and onto the shoulder of the road with a flat.*

As Freddie runs over to it—a WOMAN gets out of the car. She opens the trunk of the car.

    FREDDIE: That's a jack.

    WOMAN: Yes, it is and I don't know how to use it.

Freddie comes right up to her—and puts his hands on his hips—like Carter. The Woman turns to him.

    WOMAN: Is there a garage around here?

    FREDDIE: My Daddy's got one. But I can fix it.

    WOMAN: Are you sure?

Freddie nods his little nod.

    WOMAN: Well, if your father's got a garage . . .

She looks at Freddie with some concern as he lifts out the jack.

    WOMAN: You can't handle that heavy tire——

    FREDDIE: No such word as can't.

Just the same, the Woman helps Freddie lift the spare tire out of the trunk.

                  FADE OUT.

FADE IN:

EXTERIOR—ROADSIDE   LATE DAY

FREDDIE HAS FINISHED CHANGING THE TIRE, *and he steps back, hands on hips, to look over the work.*

    FREDDIE: *That's got it.*

He smiles up at the Woman.

    FREDDIE: There's no such word as can't.

And he starts away. But the Woman catches his arm.

    WOMAN (*Gently*): What's your name?

FREDDIE: Freddie.

WOMAN: How old are you?

FREDDIE: Thirteen years old.

WOMAN (*Very softly*): Thirteen.

The Woman opens her purse and takes out a dollar. She hands it to Freddie.

FREDDIE: What's that for?

WOMAN: It's for you.

Freddie studies the bill curiously.

FREDDIE: Thank you.

WOMAN: You're welcome. Freddie—where do you live?

FREDDIE (*Pointing*): With my teacher. I can read!

He reaches into his pocket and takes out the cut-out "reading helper" Carter made for him. As the Woman studies it——

FREDDIE: You look through the little window to see the words.

He takes it and holds it up to his eyes.

FREDDIE: See?

WOMAN (*So gently*): I see.

She takes the card and reads aloud——

WOMAN: "Charles Carter . . . Home Service . . . 223 Wicker Street . . ."

Then she takes Freddie by the hand and leads him to the car door, opens it— and Freddie climbs in.

INTERIOR—THE CAR   LATE DAY

WHILE THE CAR IS IN MOTION *Freddie is holding his precious card up to his eyes and peering through it.*

We see what Freddie sees, framed in the card: a street in what is obviously a poorer part of a small city like Stamford or Norwalk—no ghetto, but a row of self-respecting frame houses with little front yards.

Now into the frame of the card comes Carter's station wagon with the ladders on top, parked in the driveway.

The car stops and Freddie jumps out. The Woman waits until he enters the house.

INTERIOR—CARTER'S HOUSE   LATE DAY

FREDDIE RUNS THROUGH THE HOUSE *looking for Joey. Carter follows him.*

FREDDIE (*All excited*): Where's Joey? Where's Joey?

CARTER: Freddie, now you simmer down. Joey went to the grocery store with his mother. And the first thing you're going to do, young man—you're going to call Mr. Cade on that phone.

FREDDIE: No!

CARTER: No? Since when do you sass me back? You're asking for a spanking!

FREDDIE: What's a spanking?

CARTER: You might just find out!

Carter sits down at a telephone table.

CARTER: You come here while I make this phone call. . . . You stand right here.

After he dials, he reaches out and pulls Freddie toward him and onto his lap.

CARTER: Come over here. . . . (*Into phone*) Cade? Oh, Mr. Putnam. This is Charles Carter—the Carter Home Service. The handyman? . . .

WE ARE IN PUTNAM'S STUDY . . .

Putnam is on the phone—Cade is standing near him.

CARTER'S VOICE: Yes. Yes, sir, I understand, Mr. Putnam . . . Your son's right here.

THEN, AT CARTER'S HOUSE . . .

CARTER (*To Freddie*): Freddie—say hello to your Daddy.

Freddie puts his mouth right close to the phone.

FREDDIE: Hello . . . (*Pause*) Hello? Hello? Hello? (*To Carter*) Why doesn't he answer?

CARTER (*Into the phone*): It's all right, Mr. Putnam. Yes, he's just fine and I'll bring him right over . . .

EXTERIOR—PUTNAM'S DRIVEWAY   EVENING

CARTER'S STATION WAGON PULLS UP the drive.

INTERIOR—PUTNAM'S STUDY   EVENING

FREDDIE BURSTS INTO THE ROOM, followed by Carter and Joey. Freddie runs to his father.

FREDDIE: Daddy! Daddy, you came back!

PUTNAM: Where have you been?

FREDDIE: I found my friend!

He hugs Joey.

JOEY: Quit huggin'!

CARTER (*To Putnam*): I'm Charles Carter, Mr. Putnam. I don't know how he found my house, but he did.

Freddie takes the dollar out of his pocket.

PUTNAM: Well—where did you get that?

FREDDIE: I fixed a tire.

CARTER: He earned it.

PUTNAM: You earned it?

FREDDIE: Hmm-mm.

Putnam examines the dollar in disbelief. Then he hands it back to Freddie.
JOEY: Can he come home with us?
FREDDIE: Can I?
PUTNAM: Well—we'll have to ask your teacher.

INTERIOR—CADE'S ROOM   EVENING
CADE IS PACKING HIS SUITCASE. *He puts the note that Freddie wrote in the suitcase atop his clothes, but leaves the suitcase open.*
Putnam knocks and enters.
PUTNAM: What's going on?
CADE: Just packing.
PUTNAM: What for?
CADE: I fired myself.
PUTNAM: Why?
CADE: For using Freddie.
Putnam takes Freddie's note from the open suitcase . . .
PUTNAM: You're a fool.
CADE: Yes. I know that.
PUTNAM: You're also a damn good teacher.
CADE: Yes. I know that, too.
PUTNAM: Why don't you stick around a couple of weeks till I can get some recommendations off to my buddies at Hillsgrove?
Cade shoots him a quick look.
PUTNAM: Just a suggestion.
He holds up the note.
PUTNAM: You mind if I keep this?
Cade's look softens . . .
CADE: No.

INTERIOR—HALLWAY AT FOOT OF THE STAIRS   EVENING
CARTER COMES DOWN THE STAIRS *carrying Freddie's small overnight bag. He passes Cade, who is in the living room reading the paper.*
CARTER: Where are the kids?
CADE (*Nodding toward the study*): In there. . . . Carter, I'm sorry about this morning.
CARTER: Forget it, man . . . you're a fine teacher.
CADE: You're not so bad yourself.
Carter goes toward the door of the study—then——
CARTER: Of course—I wouldn't want you flying a plane.
ON THE FLOOR OF THE STUDY, *Putnam is playing with Freddie and Joey. Putnam is demonstrating a toy that has steel balls attached to strings.*

PUTNAM (*He extends one ball*): Now—watch this. . . . What happens when I let two balls go?

JOEY: I don't know.

Putnam demonstrates . . .

PUTNAM: Now how about what happens when I let three balls go? *For a moment, he holds the three balls out on the ends of their strings—then lets go. The gadget behaves according to Newton's first law of dynamics and the children are delighted.*

THE CAMERA TILTS UP *to reveal Carter in the doorway, entering, followed by Cade.*

CARTER: Mr. Putnam, can I have them now?

PUTNAM: Sure.

CARTER: Okay! Freddie, Joey! Let's go!

They tear themselves away from the toy.

CARTER: Say goodbye to your Daddy. . . . I'll wait for you fellas in the car.

Freddie hugs his father. He is about to leave without saying goodbye to Cade when he notices Cade standing slightly off, watching.

Freddie runs to Cade, who bends to embrace him.

FREDDIE: Goodbye, Teacher.

CADE: Goodbye, Freddie.

PUTNAM: You better hurry up, it'll be dark soon.

FREDDIE: I know why it gets dark.

PUTNAM: Why?

FREDDIE: Because the sun goes to sleep.

JOEY: No. That's wrong! Because the earth revolves around the sun.

FREDDIE: What's *revolves?*

CADE: Well—revolves—revolves is to turn——

He takes Freddie by the shoulders and slowly turns him.

CADE: You see, the world turns—you see, if you're the world, you turn—like that—see——

He is turning Freddie.

CADE: You're going around. And—and—I——

Cade stops. He looks at—then gestures to—Putnam.

CADE: Your Daddy—look at your Daddy—your Daddy's the sun. Now you're the world and your Daddy's the sun. . . . Now you can see the sun . . .

He turns Freddie to face his father.

CADE: It's day.

He turns Freddie to face away from his father.

CADE: Night.

He continues to turn Freddie. When Freddie's face is turned away from his father, he keeps his eyes shut.
    FREDDIE (*Eyes shut*): Night!
He turns to face his father and opens his eyes . . .
    FREDDIE: Day!
He stops, facing his father.
    FREDDIE: Daddy? I'm the world! . . .
He looks at his father expectantly . . . Then——
    PUTNAM (*Softly*): And I'm the sun.
Cade sets Freddie turning again.
    CADE: Faster—Day—Night—Day——
    FREDDIE: I'm dizzy.
Putnam crosses over to Freddie and sweeps him into his arms, proudly, joyfully.
THE CAMERA LINGERS *on Freddie's face.*

FADE OUT.

MY SWEET CHARLIE

By *RICHARD LEVINSON and WILLIAM LINK*
From the Novel and Stage Play by DAVID WESTHEIMER

World Premiere
National Broadcasting Company Television Network
January 20, 1970

DIRECTOR: *Lamont Johnson*

PRODUCERS: *Richard Levinson and William Link*

EXECUTIVE PRODUCER: *Bob Banner*

*A Bob Banner Associates Production in Association with Universal City
Studios, Inc.*
Sid Sheinberg, In Charge of Production

THE CAST

MARLENE CHAMBERS: *Patty Duke*

CHARLES ROBERTS: *Al Freeman, Jr.*

TREADWELL: *Ford Rainey*

MR. LARABEE: *William Hardy*

MRS. LARABEE: *Chris Wilson*

GRADY (DRIVER): *Noble Willingham*

SHERIFF: *Dave Ward*

289

FADE IN:

EXTERIOR—A FERRY   DAY

THE CAMERA IS VERY CLOSE on *something as yet unidentified; it is soft and there are glints of sunlight on it. Gradually it resolves itself into the hair of a young girl.* AS THE CAMERA PULLS BACK WE SEE *more of her . . . and to be charitable, she isn't much to look at—seventeen, scruffy, totally forlorn. She wears a faded blouse and a plaid schoolgirl skirt.*

Her name is MARLENE CHAMBERS *and we get the impression that she'd rather be anywhere on earth but here.*

ANOTHER CAMERA ANGLE

Marlene is leaning on the ferry railing, a cardboard box tied with a string at her feet. Somberly she turns toward:

THE WATER   HER POINT-OF-VIEW

The Gulf of Mexico—torpid, catfish gray, its dull surface unrippled by the wind.

BACK TO MARLENE

The ferry is nearing shore but she doesn't seem to notice. She is isolated from the others on board, as if she has staked out her own small island of loneliness.

ANOTHER CAMERA ANGLE

FEATURING *a vintage Ford V-8 parked nearby in a line of other cars.*

The DRIVER *is a beefy man in his forties. His sleeves are rolled up on his thick arms and an old felt hat is pushed back on his head. He wears an incongruous pair of jet-age sunglasses which he lifts to watch Marlene with ill-concealed curiosity.*

EXTERIOR—THE PIER   DAY

AS THE FERRY BUMPS AGAINST THE LOG PILINGS *and the bustle of unloading begins. The cars all ignite their motors and* REV UP, *waiting to drive off.*

ON MARLENE

She sighs and turns from the railing, picking up her make-shift suitcase.

ANOTHER ANGLE

As she moves toward the front of the boat. The Driver noses his car up behind her and taps the horn. She turns, startled, and they exchange a few words—a pantomimed "Want a lift?" and her hesitant acceptance—their voices lost in the noise of disembarkation. A moment later she is in the car and it rumbles off the ferry onto dry land.

EXTERIOR—THE LANDSCAPE   DAY
A HIGH ANGLE, PANORAMIC SHOT *of the Gulf Coast, with the car looking like a centipede in the far distance. The landscape is depressing . . . flat, marshy, and sparse, with no hills or mountains to break the monotony. There are clumps of salt grass and an occasional stand of pines edged by palmettos. The towering theatricality of the Texas sky reduces everything to miniature.*
CLOSER ANGLE   THE CAR
As it cruises along a flat strip of road that begins nowhere and arrows off to the horizon. WE HEAR *country* MUSIC *and the raucous fiddle* SOUNDS *hang in the still air.*

INTERIOR—THE CAR   DAY
THEY HAVE BEEN TALKING—*or rather, the Driver has. Marlene watches the scenery without really seeing it. The* MUSIC *pours out of the radio.*

> DRIVER: . . . Y'know, I got me a little girl a' my own about your age. Sixteen.
>
> MARLENE: I'm seventeen.
>
> DRIVER: Is that a fact? (*Turns down the radio, studies her*) You ain't cold, are you? I can turn on the heater. I got me a fine heater in this old car.
>
> MARLENE: No sir, I ain't cold. Not at all.

He puts his arm up on the seat behind her, smiles . . .

> DRIVER: Just want you to be comfortable.

She's pressed against the door as far as she can get, but she huddles into herself even more.

> DRIVER: Her name's Bobby Lee. My little girl.
>
> MARLENE: Yes, sir.
>
> DRIVER: Don't have to sir me. Name's Grady.

He gives her an affectionate pat on the arm, his hand lingering just a moment too long. Marlene tenses, stares through the windshield.
THROUGH THE WINDSHIELD   MARLENE'S POINT-OF-VIEW
Up ahead, on the right side of the highway, is a combination gas station and general store. It dozes in the sun; a lone, old-fashioned gasoline pump is standing in the dusty front yard. Beyond, to the left, a small peninsula curves out into the Gulf. The tops of houses are barely visible through a screen of trees.
BACK TO SCENE

> MARLENE (*Pointing*): Up there, mister.
>
> DRIVER (*Disappointed*): Where'd you say you was goin'?
>
> MARLENE: My aunt's. Like I told you, mister?
>
> DRIVER: Your aunt don't live there, I can tell you that for sure.

Ain't nobody live's in those houses, 'least not this time 'a year.
Summer folks all packed up an' gone.

MARLENE: Oh. (*Quickly*) Well, my Aunt Donna, she don't exactly
live right there. She—she's supposed to, you know, pick me
up? At the store. The one right up there.

DRIVER (*Peering through the window*): Looks to me like she ain't
there yet.

MARLENE: She said—she told me to wait for her. So if you'll just
let me out . . .

*He's annoyed that their ride together is ending so abruptly, but he removes
his arm from behind her and slows down, pulling off the road.*

EXTERIOR—THE STORE   DAY
THE CAR COMES TO A STOP. *With relief, Marlene opens the door and starts to
get out.*

INTERIOR—THE CAR   DAY
DRIVER: Hey—how come you ain't in school?
MARLENE: . . . Graduated.

EXTERIOR—THE STORE   DAY
AS MARLENE TAKES HER CARDBOARD BOX *from the back seat and closes the
door.*

MARLENE: Thanks a lot, mister.

The Driver watches her for a beat. Then he takes off his glasses.

DRIVER: Who you runnin' away from?

MARLENE (*Defensive*): Nobody!

DRIVER: Well . . . you take care of yourself, hear?

*He puts the glasses back on, shifts, and pulls onto the highway in a boil of
dust. Marlene watches him go. She looks around, lost and lonely, then she
goes up the two front steps of the store, opens the screen door, and goes in.*

INTERIOR—THE STORE   DAY
IT IS COOL AND DIM, *with shelves well-larded with produce and packaged
goods. There is an ancient soda-cooler in one corner and five-gallon milk
cans stand about. The owner of the store is a flinty, no-nonsense man in his
mid-fifties. There are lines of bitterness around his mouth, but his manner,
though blunt, is not hostile or unkind.*

*His name is TREADWELL, and as Marlene comes tentatively into the
room he is busy transferring the dregs of three or four ketchup bottles into
one bottle. He does this with great care and precision, not looking up at her,*

as if a full ketchup bottle is a thing of manifest importance. Marlene clears her throat but he doesn't seem to notice.

MARLENE: Mister . . . ? Excuse me——

He finishes his task, caps the bottle with a sense of satisfaction, and for the first time regards her.

MARLENE: Ah—is there a bus go by here?

TREADWELL (*Nods*): Right on by. Takes the folks in town where they can get gypped.

MARLENE: It don't stop here?

TREADWELL: Oh, it stops, all right, if they's somebody waitin'. Where you off to?

MARLENE: Uh, New Orleans. I'm goin' to New Orleans.

TREADWELL: There's one by here goes in that direction. (*Beginning to take an interest in her*) Your people in New Orleans?

MARLENE: Yes, sir. When's it come by? The bus.

TREADWELL: Eleven tonight—if it's on time.

MARLENE: Not till eleven?

TREADWELL: Don't let it bother you none. You won't have no trouble hitching a ride before then.

MARLENE: I don't expect I'd want to do that, mister. Hitch a ride.

TREADWELL: Then what was that car Ah just heard? Didn't you get out of that?

MARLENE (*Flustered*): Well, I——

TREADWELL: Never mind. You hungry?

MARLENE: Sir?

TREADWELL: You look sunk-eyed. How about if Ah fix you a sandwich and get you some pop?

MARLENE: I guess that would be nice.

Treadwell begins making her a thick sandwich of baloney, mayonnaise, and sweet pickles. As he does:

TREADWELL: Ah'm Mr. Treadwell. Ah own this valuable hunk of real estate . . . what's yours?

MARLENE: Sir?

TREADWELL: Your name?

MARLENE: Marlene. Marlene Smith.

He gives her the sandwich and opens a bottle of soda with a church key. Her hunger is evident as she takes a big bite from the sandwich. Treadwell watches her, amused.

TREADWELL: How come you're runnin' away from home?

MARLENE (*Protesting through a mouthful*): I'm not. No, sir. My momma and my daddy moved to New Orleans and left me with my Aunt Donna till they found a place.

Ford Rainey and Patty Duke in *My Sweet Charlie*. Courtesy
of Universal Pictures.

TREADWELL: If you say so, Miss Marlene Smith.

MARLENE: It's true.

TREADWELL: Well, it ain't none of my business. Nobody can tell about kids nowadays anyway. Flying the coop all over the country. Glad Ah don't have none. You want another sandwich?

MARLENE: No, sir, this one's fine. How much do I owe you?

TREADWELL: Seein' it's you, about five dollars.

MARLENE (*Stunned*): Five dollars!

TREADWELL (*A slight smile*): Let me tell you something, Marlene. In this world, before you take anything from anybody, you find out how much they 'spect you to pay for it. Ah mean anything. From anybody.

MARLENE: Yes, sir.

TREADWELL: Ah ain't goin' to charge you nothing. Ah invited you. When somebody invites you, you don't never ask how much.

MARLENE: Well . . . thank you. I expect I better be going.

TREADWELL: Changed your mind about hitchin' a ride?

MARLENE: Guess so.

TREADWELL: Just be careful who you ride with. No wild boys. And when you get to New Orleans, you look around for a nice place for a little store and you let me know, hear?

MARLENE: Yes, sir, I sure will. Thanks again for the sandwich an' all.

She picks up her cardboard box and starts for the door, turns back as if to say something, changes her mind and exits.

Treadwell is obviously puzzled by her. He returns her pop bottle to the rack and goes to the door.

EXTERIOR—THE STORE   DAY

AS TREADWELL COMES OUT. A jetty stretches off into infinity and Marlene is standing looking down at the water.

ON TREADWELL

He is concerned—it crosses his mind that she just might be about to jump.

ON MARLENE

As she turns away from the jetty and walks back to the highway.

ON TREADWELL

Watching her go.

DISSOLVE TO:

EXTERIOR—SKY   DAY

GULLS, wheeling and swooping. The vast sky is turning darker; the sun is sinking in the West.

EXTERIOR—HIGHWAY   DAY

MARLENE IS STILL WALKING, her pace much slower now, the box a burden. The Gulf is to her left, and just ahead are the beachfront houses she saw from the car. She hears an automobile approaching, turns to signal she wants a lift but it races by and once more the road is empty. She takes off one of her shoes, shakes out a pebble, and puts it on again. Then, from overhead, there is the RUMBLE *of thunder.*

CLOSE SHOT   MARLENE

As she looks up into the sky, distressed. She hadn't bargained on a shower, or even worse, a storm, and she realizes for the first time that it's growing dark. She looks toward:

THE BEACHFRONT HOUSES   HER POINT-OF-VIEW

A variety of structures, some larger and more expensive than the others, making up a small beach compound. The area is apparently deserted. An abandoned lighthouse thrusts into the sky.

BACK TO MARLENE

She is still worried about the impending storm, and she starts up an oyster-shell path toward the first of the houses—it's painted white with green shutters on the windows and has an inviting front porch. Suddenly the squall breaks, sending down a splattering of raindrops. She holds the cardboard box over her head and runs through the rain, finally reaching the house and taking shelter under the porch roof.

ANOTHER CAMERA ANGLE

As she watches the rain somberly, realizing that it may be an all-night affair. A rusty swing dangles nearby and she sits in it, creaking slowly back and forth, hugging herself against the damp chill.

CLOSE SHOT   MARLENE

Sad, bedraggled, a drop of water running down her nose.

ANOTHER ANGLE

As she gets up and tries the front door. It's locked. There is one large window and she scrapes against the sill, but it is firmly secured. Frowning, indecisive, she peers beyond the edge of the porch and notes that there is a lull in the storm. She holds the cardboard box over her head again and runs down the front steps.

NEW ANGLE

As she dashes around the side of the house, trying one window after another. Most are screened, but on one the screen is loose. She pries it open, and to her relief it slides upward. She tosses her box inside and crawls in after it.

INTERIOR—LIVING ROOM   DUSK

MARLENE GETS TO HER FEET and looks around.

   MARLENE (*Calling*): Anybody home . . . ? (*Louder*) Hello?

No answer. Some of the furniture is sheeted and there are no signs of current occupancy. The room is furnished in a rustic fashion, with knotty-pine tables, pine-panneled walls, and a fireplace. A spinet piano stands in one corner next to a portable phonograph on an end table. To one side is an archway that connects with the kitchen-dining area at the back of the house.

ON MARLENE

As she explores the house THE CAMERA *browses with her. She tries the light switches but the electricity has been shut off. There are candles and matches on a sideboard and she lights a few, setting them up in holders. As she passes the piano she hits a few of the keys aimlessly. The* SOUND *is unnaturally loud. She looks into the sleeping area, spots a transistor radio, and takes it with her.*

Finally, she goes to the kitchen. There is a table in the middle of the room, cabinets, an icebox which turns out to be empty, and an old-fashioned stove. To her delight when she tries to light the range with a match it springs into flame. She rubs her hands over the fire for warmth, then opens one of the cabinets.

ANOTHER ANGLE

It is filled with supplies—cans of pork and beans, Spam, okra, Vienna sausages, hominy, packages of cereal, jars of instant coffee, etc. There is also a small can, somewhat different from the others. Curious, she takes it down.

THE CAN   HER POINT-OF-VIEW

The bright-colored label reads: "Chocolate-covered Ants."

BACK TO MARLENE

As she makes a face and returns the can quickly to the cupboard. Then she takes down a can of pork and beans and a box of crackers, and begins a search for a can opener.

 MARLENE (*To herself*): C'mon, can opener, where are you?
She roots around in the back of several drawers and finally finds one. Its discovery is a victory for her.

 MARLENE (*Holding it up, triumphant*): Marlene Chambers, you're
  startin' to get lucky.
She goes to work on the can.

 DISSOLVE TO:

INTERIOR—LIVING ROOM   NIGHT

THE RAIN POUNDS ON THE ROOF . . . *Marlene is huddled in a big chair, wrapped in a blanket from the upstairs bedroom. Candles burn and the transistor radio is* PLAYING *dance* MUSIC. *She is spooning out the last of the pork and beans from the can. Content, she sets down the can, stretches like a cat, and dips into a magazine rack beside the chair. She comes up with a few that hold no interest for her, then spots a movie magazine among them. She draws a candle closer and opens the magazine, begins paging through it.*

CLOSE SHOT   MARLENE
The magazine doesn't hold her attention. She lets it close and stares for a
long moment into space. Then, almost as much to her surprise as to ours, she
begins to cry. . . . The magazine drops to the rug.
                                              DISSOLVE TO:
EXTERIOR—THE BEACH HOUSE   DAY
A BRIGHT, SUNNY MORNING, *no sign of rain.*

INTERIOR—KITCHEN   DAY
SUNLIGHT STREAMS IN *through the windows. Marlene is standing at the stove*
drinking coffee. She finishes, savoring each swallow, then carefully washes
out the cup. She replaces it, along with the dishes she has used for breakfast,
in the cupboard. She picks a crumb off the table with her finger and takes a
final look around.
She likes it here; she doesn't really want to leave but she feels she should be
on her way. She picks up her cardboard suitcase and goes to the door.
          MARLENE: Well . . . g'bye, house.
She goes out. THE CAMERA HOLDS ON *the kitchen door for a long beat—then*
it opens and she comes back in. She unsnaps her purse and removes a small
roll of dollar bills. She peels off one of them, takes a sugar bowl from the
cupboard, and sets it on top of the bill in a prominent place where it can eas-
ily be seen. Satisfied, she retraces her steps to the door and leaves the house.

EXTERIOR—HIGHWAY   DAY
THE CAMERA IS ON MARLENE *walking by the road, her thumb up to hitch a*
ride. Cars and trucks tear by in fast blurs. She has been at it for at least half
an hour with no success. A bit forlorn, she looks back over her shoulder.
THE HOUSE   HER POINT-OF-VIEW
Like a refuge beyond the trees.
BACK TO MARLENE
She drops her hand and trudges along the highway, her bright spirits of the
morning already dissipated. There is a SQUEAL OF BRAKES *from off-camera*
and she turns, startled.
NEW ANGLE
As a souped-up sports model angles off the road and pulls abreast of her. It is
packed with some of the local high-school bucks, out looking for an aimless
good time. They are all in their late teens. The car is a mass of psychedelic
art work and there is a bumper-sticker reading: "DON'T LAUGH, MIS-
TER, YOUR DAUGHTER MAY BE INSIDE."
          FIRST BOY: Hey, there, want a lift?
          SECOND BOY: Where you goin'?
Marlene just stares at them, not sure what to do.

FIRST BOY (*Laughing*): She don't know where she's goin'.

THIRD BOY: C'mon, climb in. Got car stereo in here.

MARLENE: I'm not hitchhikin'.

SECOND BOY: No? Then what you got in that box—your lunch?

More merriment from the car. Marlene grows angry.

MARLENE: I *live* around here!

SECOND BOY: Sure you do.

MARLENE (*Pointing toward the house*): I live right back there. Just goin' for a walk.

FIRST BOY: Well don't walk too far. Might not find your way home.

They laugh again, but it's obvious there's no more sport to be had.

THIRD BOY: C'mon. Let's go.

With a chorus of "by-bye's" they pull back on the road and rocket off. Marlene watches them go. Another car or two shoots past but she is no longer interested. With a new sense of purpose she turns around and starts back in the direction from which she came.

EXTERIOR—THE BEACH HOUSE   DAY

HIGH ANGLE, SHOOTING DOWN, *as Marlene marches around to the kitchen door. It's almost as if she now has title to the place. She pauses, surveying the house with a sense of satisfaction, then goes in.*

INTERIOR—KITCHEN   DAY

AS SHE CLOSES THE DOOR *and drops her suitcase with an air of finality. She puts water on to boil, then spots the can opener. With a small smile she picks it up and talks to it as if they are old friends . . .*

MARLENE: Can opener—you an' me are gonna get to know each other.

MONTAGE SEQUENCE:

SHOWING *Marlene's possession of the house as well as the passage of time.*

WE SEE:

Marlene cleaning and dusting in the various rooms.

Marlene making the bed.

Two more dollar bills accumulate under the sugar bowl.

Marlene at night, reading more movie magazines.

Marlene removing a pie she's baked from the oven.

Marlene taking a bath while the transistor radio blares with rock-and-roll.

Another dollar bill goes under the sugar bowl.

Marlene on the beach, wearing a man's coat she has taken from a closet, kneeling at the water's edge constructing a sand castle.

Marlene, sitting on the porch swing at night drinking coffee.
More cans coming down from the shelf.
Marlene taking the last dollar bill from her purse and putting it under the
sugar bowl. There is a stack of fourteen dollars now.
A CLOSEUP of the sand castle, eroded now, as water swirls around it.
HOLD for a long beat, then:

SLOW DISSOLVE TO:

EXTERIOR—THE BEACH HOUSE   NIGHT
DARKNESS except for a flickering light in the bedroom window.

INTERIOR—BEDROOM   NIGHT
MARLENE HAS FOUND A KEROSENE LAMP *and it sits on the bedside table, giv-*
ing off a faint illumination. She crawls under the covers and turns down the
wick until the light goes out.
CLOSE ON MARLENE
As she closes her eyes, luxuriating in the clean sheets, serene. In a moment
or two she will be asleep. But—abruptly—there is a SOUND from downstairs.
She is instantly alert, sitting up in bed.
Silence. She shrugs—probably just her imagination—and settles down
again. But the sound repeats itself—there is the unmistakable RASP of a
screen being pulled off.

INTERIOR—LIVING ROOM   NIGHT
WE SEE A SHADOWY FIGURE, *ill-defined in the moonlight, lift the window and*
climb inside. The figure knocks against a table, mutters under its breath.

INTERIOR—BEDROOM   NIGHT
MARLENE IS BOLD UPRIGHT *in bed again, almost paralyzed by fear. The*
NOISES *continue. Silently, she brushes back the covers and forces herself to*
get out of the bed. She slips on a robe, which is just a bit too large for her.

INTERIOR—LIVING ROOM   NIGHT
THE CAMERA IS ANGLED ON *a man's feet.* THE CAMERA FOLLOWS THEM
across the living room and into the kitchen.
ANOTHER ANGLE
As Marlene creeps from the bedroom.
THE ARCHWAY LEADING TO THE KITCHEN   HER POINT-OF-VIEW
There is dim moonlight—the intruder's shadow shifts across the floor.
BACK TO MARLENE
Almost against her will she moves furtively toward the kitchen. There is the
sudden loud SOUND of tap-water being turned on. She freezes, looks long-

ingly toward the front door—it is her nearest escape route—but curiosity gets the better of her fears and she edges closer to the kitchen.

THE KITCHEN   HER POINT-OF-VIEW

SUBJECTIVE CAMERA, PANNING *under the arch and finally coming to rest on a man's broad back. He is bent over the sink, lapping up water from the spigot like an animal. At length he turns the water off and wipes his mouth with the back of his hand. Then he straightens up and his face comes sharply* INTO FOCUS—*a black face.*

BACK TO MARLENE

Absolutely stunned. She can't help herself—she cries out involuntarily——

MARLENE: It's a nigger!

ANOTHER CAMERA ANGLE

The man hears her, whirls. Their frantic eyes meet, then she runs and dashes for the front door. He goes after her, inadvertently knocking a glass to the floor. The two of them struggle in the moonlight. Marlene tries to get the front door open but he pulls her away, slamming her against the wall.

MARLENE: Ow!

He grabs her by the wrists. By this time, because he is Negro, she is almost as outraged as she is frightened.

MARLENE: You let go of me!

His face is very close to hers and she can see him clearly. . . . He's about thirty—compact build, a strong, intelligent face. He wears a torn, stained white shirt and the trousers to what was once an expensive suit. There are bruises on his forehead and his broad nose is flared with his labored breathing. His name is CHARLES ROBERTS.

ROBERTS (*Intense*): Keep your voice down!

Marlene stares at him, open-mouthed. Not only has he attacked her, not only is he giving her orders—but worst of all, he sounds like an educated Northern white man.

MARLENE (*Defiant*): You just let go of me.

He glares at her and she almost unconsciously lowers her voice . . .

MARLENE: You're hurtin' my wrists, y'hear?

Roberts releases her.

ROBERTS: You're lucky I didn't break your neck. (*Looks around*) Where are they?

MARLENE: Who?

ROBERTS: Your parents.

MARLENE (*Blankly*): My parents? (*Then, quickly*) They—they went to town. To the picture show.

He studies her, wondering if she's telling the truth.

ROBERTS: Then you're alone?

MARLENE: Uh-uh. Not a bit. I mean, they're coming back any minute.

ROBERTS (*Musing*): The other house was locked. This is a summer bungalow, isn't it?

MARLENE: . . . An' you better not be here when they do. My daddy don't take no sass off nobody. So you just be on your way, boy.

He turns a look of quick hatred on her. With cold anger:

ROBERTS (*Slow, measured*): I am thirty-one years old and it's been a long time since I was a boy.

Marlene is speechless. He reaches past her to chain the door from the inside, then moves around the room restlessly. Finally he spots the radio, looks back at her.

ROBERTS: You listen to the news today?

MARLENE (*Sullen*): No.

ROBERTS: Where's the phone?

MARLENE: You don't see one, do you?

ROBERTS: No phone?

He shakes his head and continues to prowl. Marlene has half-conquered her fear and watches him with the moral superiority of the lady of the house.

MARLENE: Suppose you just tell me what you're doin' here?

ROBERTS: What do you think I'm doing?

MARLENE: Huh? Oh. Stealin', that's what you're doin'. You got no business in this house and you know it.

ROBERTS (*Turns and looks at her*): I guess that makes two of us.

MARLENE (*Startled*): What are you talkin' about?

He flicks a light switch on and off.

ROBERTS: No electricity . . . everything closed up. The owners won't be back for months. You broke in just like I did.

MARLENE: That's a lie!

ROBERTS: Is it?

MARLENE: I *live* here. My daddy——

ROBERTS (*Imitating her*): Your "daddy"—if you ever had one—is a long way from these parts.

MARLENE (*Indignant*): Now lookie here——

ROBERTS: Lookie here? All of a sudden she's talking Chinese. You must be very educated to speak another language.

MARLENE (*Heated*): Don't you talk smart with me!

ROBERTS: All right, I'll talk dumb, so you can understand. I have a hunch you're very good at dumb talk. So I'll make it simple. Is there any food in this place?

His tone has infuriated her. She turns away, refusing to answer. Annoyed, he takes a quick stride over to her and swings her around.

ROBERTS: I said—is there any food!

MARLENE (*Standing up to him*): Find out for yourself.

ROBERTS: Okay——

He grabs her by the wrist and yanks her roughly toward the kitchen.

MARLENE (*Howling*): Hey! *Hey!* Now you *stop* that—you let go of me!

INTERIOR—KITCHEN   NIGHT

ROBERTS RELEASES HER ABRUPTLY *and starts to light candles. She presses back against the sink, glaring at him. He crosses to the cupboard and opens it.*

ROBERTS (*Whistling under his breath*): What'd you do, rob a supermarket?

MARLENE: It was here when I—I bought it at Mr. Treadwell's and it's mine and you can't have none.

ROBERTS: Who's Treadwell?

MARLENE: He owns that store on the highway, that's who.

ROBERTS: What store?

MARLENE: Onliest one there is around here. He's a friend of mine an' he comes by all the time to check on me.

ROBERTS (*Skeptical*): Why's he do that if your "daddy's" around?

MARLENE (*Groping*): Well, because . . . because—(*Then, firmly*) I don't have to answer none of your questions! Don't you get uppity with me!

ROBERTS (*To himself*): Uppity! (*For the first time he laughs, though his laughter is touched with bitterness*) Lord, they really say it, don't they?

Marlene continues to glare at him as he begins wolfing down a package of oatmeal cookies. Then his eye falls on the money under the sugar bowl.

ROBERTS: Funny place to leave money.

MARLENE: I reckon folks are entitled to leave money wherever they want to.

He ignores her and is lifting a cookie to his lips when an owl HOOTS *outside. He stiffens.*

ROBERTS: What was that?

MARLENE (*Derisively*): Ain't you never heard a owl before?

It puts her one up on him and they both know it. He continues eating in silence for a moment while she watches him.

MARLENE: Somebody beat you up, didn't they?

ROBERTS (*Grim*): Somebody tried.

MARLENE: Sassed somebody, didn't you? Well, serves you right. You Northern . . . people come down here and think you can——

ROBERTS (*Interrupting*): Who, said I was from the North?

MARLENE: Sticks out all over you. An' just 'cause somebody beat you up's no reason to bust in here an' act ugly to me. Wasn't me that did it.

ROBERTS: You'd like to, though, wouldn't you?

MARLENE: Now lookie here——

ROBERTS: Chinese again.

MARLENE: I'm tellin' you that picture show is just about over. They'll be home soon. So you'd better git while there's still time.

Her tone, her air of superiority, is beginning to rub him the wrong way. He has a desire to hurt her, but since he is not a physical man he uses words as a weapon.

ROBERTS: Nobody will be home soon because the people who own this place are long gone.

MARLENE: They're not!

ROBERTS: They are. And stop trying to convince me you live here. By no stretch of the imagination do you belong in a decent house. Because you know what you smell like to me—a tar-paper shack in the middle of a swamp somewhere.

Having put her down he turns away—but she is suddenly on him, clawing, raining furious blows with both tightly clenched fists. Surprised, he wards her off, until she finally moves away, her anger spent. There is a long pause; it's obvious she's ashamed of what she's done.

MARLENE (*Grudgingly*): I shouldn't of done that. But you got no right to talk to me that way.

ROBERTS: If I had any brains I wouldn't talk to you at all. But don't take it personally. I figure you're about the norm for this neck of the woods.

MARLENE: Now lookie . . . look here, I had just about enough of this. When you gonna get out of here and leave me alone?

ROBERTS: I'll worry about it in the morning.

MARLENE (*Dismayed*): Morning!? You mean you—you're gonna *sleep* here?

ROBERTS: That's the general idea.

MARLENE: But—you can't! You just can't! I was here first! I found this house and it's mine!

ROBERTS (*Flat*): In point of legal fact, you have no more right to be here than I do.

MARLENE: I do so!

ROBERTS: Why?

MARLENE: Because I'm——

She stops, but he knows what she was going to say.

ROBERTS: Because you're white? Sorry.

He turns and walks out of the kitchen. She's not sure what he's just said but she goes after him.

INTERIOR—LIVING ROOM   NIGHT

ROBERTS DROPS DOWN EXHAUSTED *onto the couch.*

MARLENE: If they catch you here——

ROBERTS: If they catch me anywhere.

MARLENE: It'll be lots worse if they catch you here. With a—with me.

ROBERTS (*Regarding her thoughtfully*): If they catch me here, they'd catch you here. And I have an odd notion you don't want to be found.

MARLENE: Why'd you have to bust in an' spoil everything?

ROBERTS: Look, you're beginning to bore me. I haven't slept in two days. So go to bed and leave me alone.

She stands her ground. Irritated, he gets to his feet and starts toward her. Something in his manner, something fierce and just barely under control, makes her start backing up.

MARLENE: You'd better not try anything.

ROBERTS (*Caught short*): What?

MARLENE: You know what I mean. You know exactly what I mean.

He gets it and starts laughing harshly.

ROBERTS: You are something else. You are really something else. No, Snow White, I wouldn't worry about that if I were you. Because have you ever looked in a mirror? You are *ugly.* U–g–l–y.

MARLENE (*Stung*): That's what *you* say. If my daddy was here——

ROBERTS (*Correcting her*): Were here.

MARLENE: If my daddy were here——

ROBERTS: I know, he'd sic the hounds on me. But he's not. (*Pause, then evenly*) It's just you and me. (*Takes a step*) Now go to bed.

She backs away quickly.

MARLENE: I'm goin' but not 'cause you said to. I'm goin' 'cause I'm good and ready!

She goes into the bedroom and SLAMS THE DOOR.

INTERIOR—BEDROOM   NIGHT
THE CAMERA IS CLOSE ON HER FACE as she presses her back against the door,
her eyes wide and frightened.
        MARLENE: Oh, Mama, what am I gonna do?

INTERIOR—LIVING ROOM   NIGHT
AS ROBERTS CROSSES TO THE TRANSISTOR RADIO and turns it ON, switching
the knob until he finds a news broadcast. Then he settles back, his eyes star-
ing into the darkness, his tension evident on his face.

INTERIOR—BEDROOM   NIGHT
MARLENE HAS FLUNG OFF THE ROBE and is hurriedly pulling on her clothes.
She slips into her shoes, picks up her purse, and creeps to the door. She opens
it silently and listens. The only SOUND from the living room is the low mur-
mur of the newscaster's VOICE.
NEW ANGLE
As she closes the door with excruciating care, allowing the lock to settle in
the latch without a telltale click. She moves to the window and slides it up,
puts a leg over the sill. She looks back toward——
THE CARDBOARD BOX   HER POINT-OF-VIEW
It sits empty on the dresser. Her few possessions have been put away.
BACK TO MARLENE
She decides against taking the time to pack it. At the moment all she wants
is to be out of there as quickly as possible. She swings up her other leg until
she is sitting on the sill.

EXTERIOR—THE BEACH HOUSE   NIGHT
THE GROUND IS NOT FAR BELOW, though it's still a risky drop.
She screws her eyes shut, takes a deep breath, and pushes off. She lands on
her feet and pitches forward, but she quickly recovers and stands absolutely
still, listening. The house is quiet. She peers into the darkness, orienting her-
self, then takes a few tentative steps that gradually turn into a run.
ON MARLENE
Running over the dark terrain, trees sweeping by, zigzagging in and out of
islands of moonlight.
CLOSE ON MARLENE'S FEET
They pound the rough earth.
ON MARLENE
Her mouth is open, breathing hard. She is not only running from the black
man in the house, but from herself and her problems. At last, completely out
of breath, she slows down and finally comes to a stop, leaning against a tree.
ANOTHER ANGLE

She feels safe now—for the moment she has out-distanced her fears. She dusts herself off and runs her fingers through her hair. Then, feeling better, she starts to walk. She has only taken a few steps, when——

CLOSE SHOT   ROBERTS

He suddenly lurches up in front of her, almost FILLING THE FRAME.

ON MARLENE

Stunned. Her mouth opens in panic.

ANOTHER ANGLE

As he grabs her, his big hand sealing her scream inside her throat. For a terrible instant she thinks he's trying to smother her. Struggling fiercely, she sinks her teeth into his palm. He cries out, then hauls off and slaps her savagely across the face. She goes reeling to the ground, but she scrambles to her hands and knees, looking up at him in mute dread.

> ROBERTS (*Shaking with anger*): Get back to the house!
> MARLENE: You hit me. . . . (*Almost uncomprehending*) A nigger hit me.

He yanks her to her feet.

> ROBERTS: Move!

Now the tears begin. For the first time that night she begins to sob, her whole body trembling. Burying her face in her hands, she runs past him, plunging blindly in the direction of the house.

INTERIOR—KITCHEN   NIGHT

MARLENE STUMBLES IN, *still crying, heading for the living room. Roberts enters after her.*

INTERIOR—LIVING ROOM   NIGHT

SHE RACES ACROSS THE ROOM, *tearing open the door to the bedroom and* SLAMMING *it behind her.*

INTERIOR—BEDROOM   NIGHT

SHE THROWS HERSELF FACE DOWN *on the bed, sobbing.* THE CAMERA HOLDS ON HER *for a long beat, then——*

NEW CAMERA ANGLE

As the door opens and Roberts comes in. She swings around on the bed.

> MARLENE (*Screaming*): You get out of here!
> ROBERTS: You're not hurt. I didn't hit you that hard.

She turns back to the pillow, face down, blotting him out. Roberts stands in the doorway for a moment, then moves into the room.

> ROBERTS: Don't try anything like that again. Understand? (*No response*) All right, sulk. But listen. I'm not here because I want to be. But I am here. And I've got to stay a few days.

She is absolutely motionless.
Roberts looks down at her, worried. He taps her shoulder lightly to see if she's all right. Marlene whirls a tear-stained face on him.

> MARLENE: Don't you touch me!
>
> ROBERTS (*Pulling back*): I was only——
>
> MARLENE: Just stay away! If you try to take advantage——
>
> ROBERTS (*With a derisive snort*): Take advantage? Lift that burden from your mind, Snow White. I told you—you don't exactly turn me on.
>
> MARLENE: Get out of here and leave me alone!
>
> ROBERTS: Gladly.

He strides to the door, yanks it open. Behind him, she has buried her face in the pillow and has started to cry.
Roberts pauses.

> ROBERTS: Look . . . I'm not in the habit of hitting women. But you shouldn't have run out of here. . . .

She doesn't answer him. He gives it up as a lost cause and goes out, closing the door behind him.
ON MARLENE
Twisting her head, calling after him:

> MARLENE: I ain't half as ugly as you.

She sinks back on the bed.

EXTERIOR—SKY   DAY
GULLS ARE CIRCLING *far out over the water.*

EXTERIOR—PORCH   DAY
ROBERTS IS GETTING THE LAY OF THE LAND. *His eyes move restlessly. Though the sun is up, it's obvious that he's cold. The fresh day means nothing to him.*
SHOT OF THE HIGHWAY
A car approaches.
BACK TO ROBERTS
As he draws back into the shadows.
THE HIGHWAY
The car comes closer, tears by.
BACK TO ROBERTS
The SOUND *of the automobile dwindles. He thrusts his hands in his pockets and heads for the kitchen door.*

INTERIOR—KITCHEN   DAY
MARLENE SITS AT THE TABLE, *nursing a cup of coffee. She is fully dressed*

and maintains an air of wounded silence. She doesn't look up as the screen door BANGS *open and Roberts comes in.*

ROBERTS: This is the most God-forsaken place I've ever seen. Nothing but water and that one road.

She greets his attempt at conversation with icy indifference. He crosses past the table on his way to the stove.

ROBERTS (*Wry*): Thanks for making me coffee.

The water in the pan is still hot. He spoons instant coffee into a cup, adds sugar, and water.

ROBERTS: Everything's instant these days. (*A glance at her*) But they tell us to be patient.

No response. He brings the cup and saucer over to the table and sits down. Immediately, Marlene gets to her feet, picking up her own cup, and crosses to the sink. Roberts watches her, shrugs. At the moment he couldn't care less. They both drink their coffee in absolute silence.

DISSOLVE TO:

INTERIOR—BEDROOM   DAY

CLOSE ON THE COVER *of a movie magazine.* PULL BACK TO SHOW *that Marlene is lying flat on her back, holding the magazine straight up in the air and reading it from this impossible position. The door opens and Roberts enters. He looks around the room, opens the closet door.*

MARLENE (*Curious in spite of herself*): What you lookin' for?

ROBERTS: Blankets. It's cold in this house at night.

MARLENE: Only blankets are the ones on this bed. An' you can't have them.

He sees the robe she was wearing.

ROBERTS: What about this?

MARLENE: You get away from that. It's mine.

ROBERTS (*Picking it up*): It's big enough to fit me.

MARLENE: I said it's mine.

He ignores her and puts it on. The sight is so ludicrous that Marlene can't help but giggle.

ROBERTS (*Embarrassed*): What's so funny?

MARLENE: You. If you could just see yourself.

Despite his pretense of indifference, he casts a furtive glance in the dresser mirror. A slow grin spreads over his face.

ROBERTS: Why, hello, Charlie. You could be the first black Miss America.

MARLENE: Who's Charlie?

ROBERTS (*Suddenly somber*): Nobody. Nobody at all.

MARLENE: That's your name, isn't it?

ROBERTS (*Evading her question by Uncle Tomming it*): Tell you the truth, Miz Scarlett, we don't have no names. We ain't bright enough to remember 'em.

MARLENE: He can't even talk like a nigger when he tries. He is a mess.

Roberts takes off the robe and puts it back in the closet. Marlene returns to her magazine, pretending to ignore him. He turns, and studies her for a long moment.

ROBERTS: The more I think about it the stranger it gets . . . your hiding out here.

MARLENE: I ain't hiding.

ROBERTS: Yes, you are. Like a stray cat.

MARLENE: I ain't. Anyway, it's none of your business. (*Irritated*) Besides, what are you botherin' me for? This here's my bedroom an' I want some privacy. It's better you keep out. You won't get no ideas.

ROBERTS (*To the room at large*): Beautiful. She still thinks I have designs on her. (*To Marlene*) It's about time you disabused yourself of that notion. You're a lot safer with me than some white man. (*Cruelly*) Matter of fact, you'd be safe with anybody, the way you look.

MARLENE (*Stung*): *Would* I? Well, some people *like* the way I look.

The way she says it makes Roberts glance at her searchingly.

ROBERTS: Oh?

ON MARLENE

Defiant. She knows all this talk about her ugliness simply isn't true. Roberts observes the expression on her face.

ROBERTS: You're looking pretty smug. You mean you had yourself a boy?

MARLENE: Don't you dare talk ugly to me!

ROBERTS (*Amused*): She's blushing.

She lowers her eyes and he continues to study her.

ROBERTS: You're red as an Indian. I must've touched a nerve.

MARLENE (*Hysterical*): Get out! *Get out!*

ROBERTS (*Retreating*): I *did* touch a nerve.

MARLENE (*Pushing at him*): You get out of here!

He backs out the door and she BANGS it shut. She glares at it, riding the wave of emotion. She starts across the room—then she suddenly stops, a look of pain on her face. She grips her stomach. A low moan escapes her lips and she sits down on the bed, doubled over. She doesn't move.

DISSOLVE TO:

EXTERIOR—THE BEACH HOUSE   NIGHT

WE SEE FLICKERING LIGHTS from several of the downstairs windows.

INTERIOR—KITCHEN NIGHT

MARLENE IS HAVING A SULLEN DINNER at the table in the light of a kerosene lamp. Roberts bangs around clumsily at the stove, cooking a meal for himself. He pours it from pan to plate and sits down across from her. As before, she rises instantly—no black man is going to sit with her—and leaves the room.

INTERIOR—LIVING ROOM NIGHT

MARLENE SETTLES ON THE COUCH and puts her plate on the coffee table. A moment later Roberts comes in carrying the kerosene lamp.

MARLENE: Stop following me.

ROBERTS: I think we should have a talk.

MARLENE: What about?

ROBERTS: A subject of mutual interest.

MARLENE: There ain't no such thing.

ROBERTS: I want to leave.

She looks up at him eagerly.

ROBERTS: But I can't if you're going to run right out and report I was here.

MARLENE: I won't. I swear I won't. Cross my heart and hope to die.

ROBERTS: Are you a Christian?

MARLENE: 'Course I'm a Christian. Everybody's a Christian.

ROBERTS (*Annoyed*): How would you know? Ever see a black face in your church?

MARLENE: You've got your own churches.

ROBERTS: And you burn them down.

MARLENE: I don't know nothin' about that.

ROBERTS: I'll bet you don't.

MARLENE: Well, I don't. How come you're always blamin' me for everything? And what's my bein' a Christian got to do with anything?

ROBERTS: Because I want you to swear on the Bible. Are you willing?

MARLENE: Sure I'm willing.

He takes a Bible from a shelf and sets it in front of her.

ROBERTS: Put your left hand on the Bible and raise your right hand in the air.

She raises her right hand as high as it will go.

ROBERTS: Half that high will do nicely.

She lowers it to normal swearing position.

ROBERTS: Now repeat after me . . . "I swear on the Holy Bible . . ."

MARLENE: 'I swear on the Holy Bible . . .'

ROBERTS: "I will not tell anyone at any time . . ."

MARLENE: 'I will not tell anyone at any time . . .'

ROBERTS: "That Charles Roberts——"

MARLENE (*Interrupting*): That's your name, ain't it?

ROBERTS: Isn't it. And you'd better forget it. Put your hand back on the Bible.

She obeys.

ROBERTS: "That Charles Roberts was here . . ."

MARLENE: 'That Charles Roberts was here . . .'

ROBERTS: "Nor will I try to communicate . . ."

MARLENE: 'Nor will I try to communicate—' You know somethin'? It sounds just like you're readin' all that right out of a book.

ROBERTS: Don't interrupt. "With anyone concerning him."

MARLENE: 'With anyone concerning him.'

ROBERTS: "So help me God."

MARLENE (*Does "cross-my-heart"*): 'So help me God.'

She takes her hand off the Bible. Roberts regards her carefully.

ROBERTS: Do you believe your word is sacred? Even when it's given to a black man?

MARLENE (*Insulted*): What do you think I am? I wouldn't give my word to a Nigra or anybody 'less I expect to keep it.

ROBERTS: Nigra. I'm getting up in the world.

MARLENE: When are you leavin'?

ROBERTS: Now's as good a time as any. I don't suppose you'd know if the highway patrol is very active?

MARLENE (*Blankly*): Uh-uh.

ROBERTS: That store you mentioned—Treadwell's. Where is it?

MARLENE: Mile. Mile an' a half down the road.

He nods to himself, picks up her coffee cup and drains it. She's so eager to have him gone that she doesn't object. He sets down the cup, takes a last look around, and starts for the door.

MARLENE: Hey!

He turns, half expecting a word of farewell.

MARLENE: Lookie—if you get caught—you won't tell nobody about me bein' here?

ROBERTS (*Wry*): I'm really going to miss you.

He goes out. She hurries after him and chains the door. Then she pirouettes around the room, delighted to be rid of him. It's her house again.

MARLENE (*Sing-song*): Ding-dong—he's gone!

EXTERIOR—HIGHWAY   NIGHT
NO CARS, NOT A SOUL. *Roberts' shadowy figure moves along the gravel shoulder.*

INTERIOR—TREADWELL'S STORE   NIGHT
THE CAMERA SLOWLY PANS *the darkened interior: Pyramids of food-stuffs, shelves, a pot-bellied stove.*

INTERIOR—TREADWELL'S BEDROOM   NIGHT
AN ASCETIC CHAMBER *with a few furnishings. Treadwell is asleep.*
CLOSER ANGLE
ON *Treadwell's sleeping face. From off-camera there is a small* SOUND. *Treadwell senses it rather than hears it, shifts position in the bed, still asleep.*

INTERIOR—STORE   NIGHT
WE SEE ROBERTS' SHADOW *outside the window. He is straining, trying to raise the window.*

EXTERIOR—STORE   NIGHT
ON ROBERTS, *his muscles tightening. The old latch gives way with a rusty* SNAP. *He hesitates, standing absolutely still. Then he carefully lifts the window and climbs inside.*

INTERIOR—STORE   NIGHT
ROBERTS MOVES FURTIVELY *around the room, looking for something specific.*

INTERIOR—TREADWELL'S BEDROOM   NIGHT
CLOSE SHOT
As *Treadwell's eyes open.*

INTERIOR—STORE   NIGHT
ROBERTS PASSES BY A HEAP OF DUSTY CAMPING EQUIPMENT *and then sees a clothing rack in a corner of the room. It is a length of pipe braced by two uprights and its hangers support a variety of hunting jackets, out-of-style spring coats, Army fatigue shirts, and rainwear. Roberts earnestly runs his hand over the material, seeking the warmest fabric.*

INTERIOR—TREADWELL'S BEDROOM   NIGHT
CLOSE SHOT

On an automatic-action double-barrel shotgun within reaching distance of the bed. Treadwell's hand enters FRAME, *grabs the gun.*

INTERIOR—STORE   NIGHT
ROBERTS HAS DONNED A WINDBREAKER. *He doesn't like it, takes it off.*

INTERIOR—TREADWELL'S BEDROOM   NIGHT
TREADWELL'S BARE FEET SOUNDLESSLY TOUCH THE FLOOR.

INTERIOR—STORE   NIGHT
ROBERTS RETURNS THE WINDBREAKER *to its hanger and removes a sheepskin coat. This seems more like it. He slips it on, luxuriating in its warmth, buttons it up the front. Then he crosses quickly to the open window. He is about to climb out when he thinks of something, goes back to one of the shelves, and digs into a box of chocolate bars. He stuffs some into the pockets of his new coat and returns to the window.*
CLOSE SHOT   ROBERTS
Putting a leg over the edge. There is a sudden, shattering ROAR. *The top of the window frame explodes, the wood splintering, and the glass tinkling down. Roberts casts a panicked glance over his shoulder.*
TREADWELL   ROBERTS' POINT-OF-VIEW
Treadwell stands in an open doorway, an ill-defined bulk with features barely discernible. THE CAMERA ZOOMS IN ON *the blued metal of the shotgun.*
        TREADWELL'S VOICE (*Harsh*): Stay where y' are!
BACK TO ROBERTS
Hurling himself through the window.

EXTERIOR—STORE   NIGHT
ROBERTS HITS THE GROUND, *rolls, and is up on his feet running.*

INTERIOR—STORE   NIGHT
TREADWELL STRIDES ACROSS THE ROOM, *sweeping a stack of cartons out of his way. He reaches the window, shotgun raised, looks out.*
A FIGURE   TREADWELL'S POINT-OF-VIEW
It is racing along the fields that border the highway—an impossible target, already out of range for accurate firing.
BACK TO SCENE
Treadwell slams down his weapon, furious. He turns on a light and crosses to an old-fashioned wall phone. He is cranking the bell.

INTERIOR—BATHROOM OF THE BEACH HOUSE   DAY
A BIG CLOSEUP OF MARLENE *brushing her teeth. She goes at it with a great*

zest and energy, humming to herself. Finished, she rinses, examines her face critically in the mirror, and leaves the room.

INTERIOR—LIVING ROOM   DAY
MARLENE, DRESSED IN THE ROBE AND STILL HUMMING, *comes bounding down the stairs.*
CLOSER CAMERA ANGLE
As she stops dead.
ROBERTS   MARLENE'S POINT-OF-VIEW
He is huddled on the couch in deep slumber, the sheepskin coat thrown over him for a blanket.
BACK TO MARLENE
Her face falls.
  MARLENE: Hey!
She marches down the steps and shakes him roughly by the shoulder.
  MARLENE: Hey!
NEW CAMERA ANGLE
As Roberts jolts awake, ready for anything.
  ROBERTS: Wha——
  MARLENE: What are you doin' here? You said I could have my
   house back!
Roberts sees who it is and rubs a hand across his eyes.
  MARLENE: After I swore on the Bible an' everything.
  ROBERTS: I need some coffee.
He pushes himself to his feet and heads for the kitchen. Marlene goes angrily after him.
  MARLENE: Why'd you come back?

INTERIOR—KITCHEN   DAY
AS ROBERTS COMES IN *and sets water to boil. During this:*
  ROBERTS: Because I got within speaking distance of a shotgun.
  MARLENE: Shotgun?
  ROBERTS (*Bitterly*): Your friend Treadwell is a light sleeper. I was
   shopping for a coat after hours, and he came charging in with
   both barrels blazing. (*To himself*) I think I got out of there be-
   fore he got a look at me.
  MARLENE: Why'd you have to come back here? Why can't you go
   someplace else?
  ROBERTS: There isn't any place else.
  MARLENE: You tryin' to say this is the only place in the whole
   wide world?
  ROBERTS: I don't have the whole wide world to choose from.

MARLENE: All right, so you came back. Don't mean you got to stay. Wait'll it's dark an' you try again.

ROBERTS: Too risky. For all I know they might be combing the area right now.

MARLENE: Just 'cause somebody busted into Mr. Treadwell's? They wouldn't take the trouble.

ROBERTS: They would if that somebody were me. So get it through your ignorant head—I'm staying.

MARLENE: An' after I swore on the Bible.

He ignores her, makes coffee, and takes a long, grateful draught.

MARLENE (*Muttering*): Burnin' my butane. Drinkin' my coffee.

She stamps out of the room.

INTERIOR—LIVING ROOM DAY

AS MARLENE ENTERS AND THROWS HERSELF sulkily into a chair. Roberts comes in, drinking from the cup.

ROBERTS (*Frustrated*): Why don't they have a phone in here?

MARLENE: S'posin' they did? You ain't got nobody to call.

ROBERTS: No? (*Studies her*) Isn't somebody, somewhere worrying about *you?*

MARLENE (*There is poignancy in her belligerence*): What do you care?

ROBERTS: I don't. I was just trying to make it simple enough for you to understand. There are people wondering and worrying about me. Can you understand that, Snow White?

MARLENE: I don't like it when you call me that. So stop it.

ROBERTS (*Condescending*): Propriety insists I call you *something.* What's your name?

MARLENE: None of your business.

ROBERTS: No? After we've been living together in the same house——

MARLENE: We have not either lived together!

ROBERTS: Sorry. (*Mockingly*) I mean inhabiting the same house.

MARLENE (*Exasperated*): It's Marlene . . . Marlene Chambers.

ROBERTS: How'd they happen to stumble on that? I thought they went in for Emmy Lou and Sally Jo around here.

MARLENE (*With pride*): For your information, I was named after my great-grandmother. She had a big place in Atlanta.

ROBERTS (*With irony*): Must be nice to have ancestors. I don't know the names of mine because they were changed when they got off the boat.

Marlene shakes her head, gets up, crosses to the door.

MARLENE: That's all you ever think about, ain't it?

ROBERTS: What?

MARLENE: Bein' a nigger.

She goes out.

ON ROBERTS

This hits him hard. In her casual way she has offended him. He strides to the door and enters the porch.

EXTERIOR—PORCH   DAY

MARLENE SITS IN THE SWING, aimlessly propelling herself back and forth.

ROBERTS (*Cold*): I think about a great many things, but normally being a Negro is not one of them. Except when some ignorant cracker rubs my face in it.

MARLENE: Don't blame me. It ain't my fault you're black.

ROBERTS: Do you think I'd rather be white?

MARLENE: Wouldn't you?

ROBERTS: It's amazing the way your mind works. It's classic. If I were white you think I'd be a better man?

MARLENE: You wouldn't be no worse.

Roberts throws up his hands.

ROBERTS: You can't argue with a white.

MARLENE: You sure been doin' it.

He turns away, dismissing her, and leans on the rail, his eyes on the water of the Gulf. Marlene continues to rock, back and forth, back and forth . . .

DISSOLVE TO:

INTERIOR—KITCHEN   NIGHT

CLOSE ON THE LIT KEROSENE LAMP. THE CAMERA PULLS BACK TO SHOW Roberts, eating at the table. Marlene is taking inventory of the cupboard, removing the remaining cans and counting them.

MARLENE (*Muttering to herself*): Looks to me somebody's been gobblin' like a hog.

ROBERTS (*As he eats*): Just what I've been thinking. Where do you put it all?

MARLENE (*Whirling to face him*): Least I paid for what I ate.

ROBERTS: You paid?

She indicates the bills under the sugar bowl.

MARLENE: You're so smart, where'd you think *this* came from?

ROBERTS: I thought . . . you mean that's your money?

MARLENE: It sure ain't nobody else's. Least it *was* mine. Every day I put in a dollar till I didn't have none left. An' that's a whole lot more than you did.

ROBERTS (*Amused*): Well, I'll be . . .

He leaves the table and makes his own inventory of the cupboard.

ROBERTS (*Musing*): Even if I wasn't here it couldn't have lasted long. The way you pack it in. Where does it go?

He looks at her. She is uncomfortable under his scrutiny. Her hand steals to her stomach.

MARLENE: See somethin' green?

ROBERTS: What?

MARLENE: How come you keep lookin' at me like that?

ROBERTS: Because you interest me. You really do. Your being here all alone . . . as if you've got no other place to go. Why?

Her hand steals to her stomach again and the gesture does not escape his notice.

ROBERTS: Your stomach hurt?

MARLENE (*Snatching her hand away*): Yes. 'Cause I got a bellyful of you.

ROBERTS: You certainly got a bellyful of something. (*A sudden insight*) Well, how do you like that? (*Laughs*) And I thought you were such an innocent little girl. Stupid, but innocent. Got ourselves pregnant, didn't we?

ON MARLENE

Shaken, not answering. She shifts nervously under his gaze.

BACK TO SCENE

Roberts is grinning, amused by his discovery.

ROBERTS: And to think it took me all this time to . . . My apologies, little mother.

MARLENE (*Bewildered*): For what?

ROBERTS: For thinking you were too ugly for anyone to look at. Because someone did a lot more than just look.

MARLENE: He was big an' sweet an' smarter than you! An' if he was here he'd teach you to talk to me like that!

ROBERTS: But he's not here, is he? Why?

MARLENE: None of your business.

ROBERTS: He wouldn't have anything more to do with you, would he?

She begins to crumple, but he is relentless——

ROBERTS: They tell me it takes four things around here to make a marriage official. A preacher, two witnesses, and a shotgun. That daddy of yours—didn't he have a shotgun?

CLOSE SHOT   MARLENE

Wincing, deeply hurt.

BACK TO SCENE

ROBERTS (*Pressing*): He threw you out, didn't he? (*Enjoying himself*) Didn't he?

MARLENE (*Screaming*): I hate you!

She is completely shattered. She begins to cry—loud sobbing sounds—slowly she slips down the side of the sink to the floor.

MARLENE (*Hands over her face*): Hate you, hate you, hate you . . .

ON ROBERTS

Looking down at her. He sees how vulnerable she is and he feels a sudden surge of disgust at his behavior. He has used her to vent his own hostility.

NEW ANGLE

As he crouches down beside her. She is almost pitiful, racked with sobs, hands still covering her face.

ROBERTS: I'm sorry . . . I really am . . .

He reaches out to touch her, his hand stopping just short of her shoulder.

ROBERTS: Marlene . . .

THE CAMERA HOLDS ON *this tableau for a long moment, then:*

INTERIOR—ANOTHER KITCHEN   DAY

CLOSE ON A WINDOW AS THE PANE OF GLASS SHATTERS, *exploding inward. It has been hit by a fist wrapped in a moth-eaten olive-drab blanket.*

THE CAMERA PULLS BACK TO SHOW *Roberts standing outside. He reaches through the opening, unlocks the window and raises it, climbing inside. He still carries the blanket.* WE NOW SEE *that we are in the kitchen of one of the other houses. It is ultra-modern, with a double oven and built-in pantries. Roberts opens the pantry doors, frowns as he sees there are only a few cans of food left behind. The refrigerator is unplugged, nothing inside but a lonely wedge of extremely stale cheese. He sniffs it and makes a face. However, he is luckier when he opens a bin under the sink. A smile creases his features.*

EXTERIOR—THE YARD OF "THEIR HOUSE"   DAY

CLOSE ON A BLANKET, *lumpy now, folded like a sack and being dragged along the ground.* THE CAMERA PULLS BACK TO SHOW *Roberts pulling it around the side of the beach house. He stops, hearing country* MUSIC *pouring out of the upstairs bathroom window.*

ROBERTS (*Calling*): Hey, Marlene!

INTERIOR—BATHROOM   DAY

MARLENE HAS JUST FINISHED WASHING HER HAIR. *She sits on the edge of the bathtub, wearing her robe, giving herself a hundred strokes with a brush. The radio blares on the sink. She hears him calling, snaps off the* MUSIC, *but doesn't go to the window.*

EXTERIOR—YARD   DAY

ROBERTS: Are you up there? Hey, I found some food!

No answer.

ROBERTS: Marlene! How long do you think you can go without eating? (*Getting angry*) All right, you're not hurting me. You're only hurting yourself. And your baby.

NEW ANGLE

As her face APPEARS in the window.

MARLENE: I ain't got a baby.

ROBERTS (*Sees her*): You will have.

MARLENE: I don't want no baby and I ain't gonna have one.

ROBERTS (*Shrugs*): Suit yourself.

He drags the sack toward the kitchen door.

INTERIOR—KITCHEN DAY

ROBERTS COMES IN, closes the door, and hefts the improvised shopping bag onto the table.

MARLENE'S VOICE: What'd you find?

NEW CAMERA ANGLE

TO INCLUDE MARLENE standing in the doorway. He smiles slightly—her curiosity was obviously too much for her—and lifts a corner of the blanket to REVEAL a tumble of potatoes.

MARLENE: Potatoes! Sweet or light?

ROBERTS: Sweet or light?

MARLENE: Sweet potatoes or Irish potatoes. Don't you know anything?

ROBERTS: How do you expect me to know what they call Irish potatoes down here?

Marlene crosses to the table and inspects them.

MARLENE: You don't like it when somebody talks to you the way you talk to them, do you?

ROBERTS: How are you going to cook them?

MARLENE: You weren't countin' on *me* cookin' for you, were you?

ROBERTS: If you want some you will.

MARLENE: I don't cook for no——

ROBERTS: No cookie, no eatie. (*Holds up a potato*) Just look at it. Many an Irishman would have killed for this during the potato famine. I'd like to have it baked. With butter and chopped chives and sour cream.

MARLENE: Sour cream. Ugh. When our cream clabbered we threw it to the pigs.

ROBERTS: Well, since we don't have any butter we can't have them baked. And we'd need milk for mashed potatoes. What other way is there?

MARLENE: French fried.

ROBERTS: Are you telling me you can make French-fried potatoes?

MARLENE: We got shortening. But what makes you think I'm gonna be your servant?

ROBERTS: Like I said—no cookie, no eatie.

MARLENE (*Thinks it over; then grudgingly*): Well . . . all right. But if you 'spect me to cook 'em, you have to peel 'em.

ROBERTS: What?

MARLENE: When was the last time you cleaned the wax outta your ears? I said I'd cook 'em if you peel 'em.

ROBERTS: I suppose that's equitable.

MARLENE: Equitable?

ROBERTS: Fair.

MARLENE: Equitable means fair?

He nods.

MARLENE: Why didn't you say fair then?

She is bustling around getting out shortening, a pan, etc. He does nothing.

MARLENE: I thought you were supposed to peel. When you count on doin' it?

ROBERTS: Where's the peeler?

MARLENE: If you ain't the most helpless . . .

She runs water into a dishpan and brings it to the table. Then a bowl, then a paring knife. She picks up a potato. She is very much in charge.

MARLENE: Hold your hands out. . . . Now palms up. Now I suppose you want me to work your hands for you like one of them puppets.

He begins peeling the potato as if sculpting, shearing off big slabs. Marlene, who has gone back to work, glances up from spooning shortening into the pot. She stalks back over to him and stands staring disapprovingly. He looks up at her defensively.

MARLENE: Can't you do nothin' right? I swear, it looks like you never peeled a potato before in your whole life.

She takes the knife from his unresisting hand and peels the potato deftly in a long unbroken spiral. He is impressed.

ROBERTS: Not since I was a kid. My mother always did it. Or the maid.

MARLENE (*Incredulous*): The maid? Where'd y'all get the money to have a maid?

ROBERTS: My father earned it. How does anyone get money?

MARLENE: What is he, an undertaker?

ROBERTS: What gave you that idea?

MARLENE: They make a lot of money, colored undertakers.

ROBERTS (*Imploringly at the ceiling*): I really picked one.

Marlene starts the potatoes cooking.

MARLENE: He a preacher then? Your daddy?

ROBERTS: He's a brand manager for a distilling company.

MARLENE: A what for what?

ROBERTS: You know, I'm continuously impressed by the number of areas in which you're misinformed.

MARLENE: Least I know how to peel a potato.

ROBERTS: He's in charge of promotion and sales for one of the brands of whiskey made by a distillery.

MARLENE: Whiskey? No wonder he makes all that money, the way you people like to drink it.

ROBERTS: Wouldn't it be ironic if it were my old man's brand your old man gets stoned on every Saturday night?

MARLENE: My daddy? He don't allow a drop of sinful whiskey in the house.

ROBERTS: One of those, huh? What does this daddy of yours do for a living?

MARLENE: Farms. He . . . he's got this two hundred acres of bottom land so rich you could eat it with a spoon, an' two tractors an' a cultivator an' I don't know what else.

ROBERTS (*Wry*): It was obvious to me from the first time I saw you that you were a daughter of wealth.

She seeks refuge in contemplating the potatoes. She muses.

MARLENE: What potato famine?

ROBERTS: What?

MARLENE: The one you were carryin' on about.

ROBERTS: Oh, that potato famine. Don't they teach you anything around here?

MARLENE: They teach me plenty.

ROBERTS (*Lecturing*): In the 1880's the Irish potato crop was virtually destroyed by blight. This resulted in wide-spread starvation and a wave of emigration to this country.

MARLENE: You don't have to act so smart about it. I ain't never seen anybody with so many airs.

ROBERTS: If you'd say ain't less often you wouldn't sound so ignorant.

MARLENE: I know there ain't no such word as "ain't." I just can't help sayin' it. But I *do* know what potato blight is. An' rust, an' rot, an' the pip.

ROBERTS: The pip?

MARLENE: Chickens get it.

ROBERTS: Live and learn.

MARLENE: Taters are done.

She dips them out with a big spoon and divides them equally in two plates. Roberts remains sitting at the table. She gets ketchup from the pantry, pours it on lavishly, then goes to her spot at the sink and begins eating standing up.

ROBERTS: Why don't you sit down at the table like a civilized human being?

MARLENE: I'm doin' just fine right here, thank you.

Roberts thinks for a moment, then turns to her.

ROBERTS: Do me a favor.

MARLENE (*Suspicious*): What kinda favor?

ROBERTS: Eat a potato for me.

MARLENE: Eat a . . . why?

ROBERTS: I want to try a scientific experiment. You like scientific experiments, don't you?

MARLENE: Not 'specially.

ROBERTS: Let's try one anyway. It breaks the monotony. Okay? Eat a potato.

She shrugs and dips a piece in ketchup. He watches carefully as she lifts one to her mouth.

MARLENE: Didn't you never see nobody eat fried taters before?

ROBERTS: Not scientifically.

She swallows with difficulty because he is watching. He points to the chair at the table.

ROBERTS: Now, sit down over here.

She hesitates . . .

ROBERTS: Don't you want to help the cause of science?

Mystified and curious, she brings her plate to the table and sits down, her back unnaturally straight.

ROBERTS (*With mock-solemnity*): Now, Doctor Chambers, select a potato of approximately the same proportions and degree of crispness as the specimen previously consumed.

MARLENE: Huh?

He points at her plate. She picks up a potato and starts to take a bite.

ROBERTS: No, no, you forgot the ketchup.

She dips the potato and eats.

ROBERTS: Now for the most important part of the experiment. How did the first potato taste?

MARLENE: Real good.

ROBERTS: How did the second potato taste?

MARLENE: It was good too.

ROBERTS: I see. Then it would be correct to assume there was no difference in taste between them?

MARLENE: 'Course there wasn't. They was cooked exactly alike.

ROBERTS: Q.E.D.

MARLENE: I know what that means—we had it in geometry. It means that proves it. Proves what? I mean what did the 'speriment prove?

ROBERTS: It proved a French-fried potato tastes the same whether eaten standing or sitting.

MARLENE: Anybody knows that.

ROBERTS: Even if the eater happens to be sitting across from a black man.

MARLENE (*She's got the point*): They're gettin' cold.

Both eat avidly.

EXTERIOR—HIGHWAY   DAY

AN OFFICIAL POLICE VEHICLE TURNS OFF THE MAIN ROAD *and heads for the colony of summer houses.*

ANOTHER ANGLE

As it bumps along the ground and finally pulls to a stop a few yards from Marlene and Roberts' sanctuary.

INTERIOR—KITCHEN   DAY

THE SOUND OF THE BRAKE BEING YANKED-ON *cuts through the air like a knife. Roberts stiffens, his fork halfway to his mouth, and Marlene's eyes widen with apprehension. Quickly, he gets to his feet.*

ROBERTS: Pull those shades!

Marlene blinks.

ROBERTS (*Hissing*): What are you waiting for? Move!

His words act like a catapult. She lunges to the windows and begins drawing the shades as he strides swiftly into the living room.

INTERIOR—LIVING ROOM   DAY

ROBERTS CROSSES THE ROOM AND THEN HUGS THE WALL, *inching toward a front window so he can look out. Finally he manages to catch a glimpse of the front yard.*

THROUGH THE GLASS   HIS POINT-OF-VIEW

The parked police car—a SHERIFF *and a* DEPUTY *emerge,* SLAMMING THE DOORS.

ON ROBERTS

Almost panic-stricken.

NEW ANGLE

As Marlene comes in from the kitchen.

MARLENE: Who . . . ?

ROBERTS: The police! Be quiet!

MARLENE (*Stunned*): The police?!

Roberts jams his finger to his lips, points at a corner where he wants her to hide. She scampers to semiconcealment.

EXTERIOR—THE BEACH HOUSE   DAY

THE CAMERA IS ON THE SHERIFF AND DEPUTY. *Whatever their mission, they do not seem particularly galvanized.*

SHERIFF: Check that bungalow over there. I'll take this one.

They separate, the Sheriff heading for the porch and the Deputy crossing to the neighboring bungalow.

INTERIOR—LIVING ROOM   DAY

IN A FRENZY, ROBERTS IS SWEEPING ALL SIGNS OF OCCUPANCY *behind the couch. He races to the door and, his face tightening, he carefully and soundlessly slides the bolt home.*

NEW ANGLE

Marlene clutches at her stomach, her expression bewildered.

MARLENE: Ow!

ROBERTS (*Wheeling on her*): What is it?

MARLENE: It's kicking!

ROBERTS: Marlene, you've got to be quiet!

She nods, ducks out of sight. Roberts flattens himself against the inside of the door.

EXTERIOR—PORCH   DAY

THE SHERIFF SAUNTERS UP ON THE PORCH; *he has seemingly all the time in the world. He tries the door.*

INTERIOR—LIVING ROOM   DAY

THE CAMERA IS CLOSE ON THE KNOB AS IT TURNS . . . *then* ANGLE UP TO SHOW *Roberts, not daring to breathe.*

CLOSE   ROBERTS

Almost sick with fear.

ON MARLENE

Watching him from her hiding place. She, too, is frightened, but she senses that his terror is greater and somehow more desperate.

NEW ANGLE

TO INCLUDE *the front windows. The Sheriff's face* APPEARS *in one of them, his eyes shielded against the sun with his hands, scanning what he can see of the room. The face vanishes and then reappears in another window.*

Patty Duke and Al Freeman, Jr., in *My Sweet Charlie*.
Courtesy of Universal Pictures.

ON ROBERTS
Not moving a muscle.
BACK TO SHERIFF
As he calls out——
SHERIFF: Hey, Walt! Come here.
ON ROBERTS
Agonized by this new development.

EXTERIOR—THE BEACH HOUSE   DAY
AS A PHLEGMATIC WALT TAKES HIS TIME APPROACHING *the porch and then
clumps up the steps.*
DEPUTY: Somethin'?
SHERIFF: Take a look.
He points through the window.

INTERIOR—LIVING ROOM   DAY
THE CAMERA IS ON THEIR TWO FACES PEERING IN.
DEPUTY: What?
SHERIFF: That barometer. Over there on the wall.
ON ROBERTS
His eyes shift.
THE BAROMETER   ROBERTS' POINT-OF-VIEW
AS THE CAMERA ZOOMS IN ON IT
BACK TO SCENE
SHERIFF: Treadwell wanted to sell me one last week. Think I
    should buy it?
DEPUTY: What's he askin'?
SHERIFF: Twelve.
DEPUTY: You can do better in town. I seen 'em for less.

EXTERIOR—THE BEACH HOUSE   DAY
AS THEY TURN FROM THE WINDOW.
SHERIFF: Don't really want the thing. It's my wife. (*Indicates the
    other bungalow*) Anything over thell.
DEPUTY: Nope.
SHERIFF: Same here. That boy's made tracks by now.
DEPUTY: Want to check the others?
SHERIFF: Waste of time. Come on.
They cross the porch and go down the steps.

INTERIOR—LIVING ROOM   DAY
ON ROBERTS, *as he permits himself the luxury of a sigh.*

ON MARLENE

She starts moving out from her concealment, but Roberts holds her with an upraised hand.

NEW CAMERA ANGLE

He looks through the window to make sure they are on their way, then drops into a chair, totally depleted. Marlene approaches him tentatively.

> MARLENE: I guess it's all right now.

He doesn't answer. She looks at him for a moment, then:

> MARLENE: Charlie . . . what'd you do?
>
> ROBERTS (*Meeting her gaze*): Why?
>
> MARLENE: I don't know. I guess I never seen anybody so scared.
>
> ROBERTS (*Defensively*): And you weren't?
>
> MARLENE: Not like you.

She continues to look at him and he shifts uncomfortably. They both realize that what she's said is true.

                                    DISSOLVE TO:

EXTERIOR—PORCH   NIGHT

THE CAMERA IS CLOSE ON A RADIO. A NEWSCASTER *is delivering state and local news in a bored, rural monotone.* THE CAMERA ANGLES TO SHOW *Roberts sitting on the swing. He is holding a safety razor and a glass in his hands, but he does not move as he listens to the broadcast.*

INTERIOR—LIVING ROOM   NIGHT

MARLENE IS CURLED UP IN A CHAIR *with a movie magazine. She also hears the faint sound of the newscast.*

EXTERIOR—PORCH   NIGHT

THE REPORT ENDS *with the local weather forecast, and Roberts relaxes and turns off the radio. He goes back to rubbing the razorblade inside the glass. Then he fits the blade into the razor lying on the swing and cautiously tests the edge on his cheek. Pleased, he goes into the living room.*

INTERIOR—LIVING ROOM   NIGHT

AS HE ENTERS AND CROSSES TO MARLENE.

> ROBERTS: It works. How'd you know you could sharpen a razor-
>   blade with a glass?
>
> MARLENE: My daddy does like that all the time.
>
> ROBERTS: I'd imagine a prosperous farmer could afford new
>   blades.
>
> MARLENE (*Quietly*): You know I was storyin' about that.
>
> ROBERTS (*Beat*): How do you feel?
>
> MARLENE: Okay, I guess. Only it keeps kickin'. (*Angry*) I won't
>   have no baby! I just won't. It ain't fair.

ROBERTS: No, I don't suppose it is.

MARLENE: What am I gonna do?

ROBERTS: Go back home.

MARLENE (*Shakes her head*): My daddy says he never wants to see me again.

ROBERTS: Maybe he's had a change of heart.

MARLENE: That shows how much you know.

ROBERTS: Haven't you got any other relatives?

MARLENE: Just my Aunt Donna. My mama, she told me to go there but I just couldn't.

ROBERTS: But isn't that——

MARLENE (*Getting worked up*): I don't want to talk about it any more!

ROBERTS: Okay, okay . . .

A pause between them. Then:

ROBERTS (*Changing the subject*): What's for dinner?

MARLENE: Nothin' much. We're gettin' low.

ROBERTS: Potatoes all gone?

MARLENE (*Nods*): An' the cereal, an' the pork and beans. And for lunch we finished off the last can of chili.

ROBERTS (*Glum*): We'll be down to the chocolate-covered ants pretty soon.

ON MARLENE

Reacting to this—it's not far from the truth.

DISSOLVE TO:

EXTERIOR—WOODS DAY

CLOSE ON A HATCHET as it bites into the trunk of a small pine tree.

ANGLE TO SHOW Roberts, pulling the hatchet from the tree and taking a few more hard swings. He finally cuts through and the tree topples over.

EXTERIOR—YARD OF THE BEACH HOUSE DAY

AS HE DRAGS HIS BOOTY up to the kitchen door. He is also carrying a lumpy burlap sack.

ANOTHER ANGLE

The door bursts open and Marlene runs out, her face glowing with delight.

MARLENE: Charlie, you got me my tree. Goody!

ROBERTS: We're starving and she wants a Christmas tree.

Marlene helps him cart the tree into the kitchen, looking curiously at the burlap sack.

INTERIOR—KITCHEN DAY

AS THEY COME IN. Roberts hefts the sack onto a counter.

ROBERTS: We're lucky. I found this lying by the side of the highway.

Marlene peers into the sack avidly, then looks at him and shakes her head.

MARLENE: Horsecorn.

ROBERTS: That's bad?

MARLENE: You can't eat it.

ROBERTS (*Disappointed*): Oh. (*Notes a saucepan cooking on the
stove*) What's that? I thought we were out.

MARLENE: Just somethin' I scratched together.

ROBERTS: Marlene, you are a genius.

*She divides the concoction on two plates. He comes eagerly to the table,
holds her chair out for her, then sits himself. He lifts a spoon to his lips as she
watches. It is too dreadful to swallow.*

MARLENE: You're always so picky.

She tries a spoonful but can't get it down either.

ROBERTS: Maybe we should try the tree.

MARLENE: Charlie, what are we gonna do?

ROBERTS (*Pushes the plate away*): You know as well as I do. We've
got to leave here.

MARLENE: Well, sure . . . 'ventually.

ROBERTS: Not eventually, Marlene. Much sooner than that.

MARLENE (*Hesitant*): Like . . . when?

*Roberts looks down at his hands, feeling slightly guilty. He has come to a
conclusion on his own and now he must tell her about it.*

ROBERTS: Well . . . I've been doing some thinking. And I've
pretty much decided to clear out on Christmas day.

MARLENE (*Startled*): Christmas?

ROBERTS (*Nods*): It's the best time to travel. Everybody's home
with their families. The roads are as empty as our shelves.

MARLENE (*Upset*): But that's—that's real soon.

ROBERTS: I know.

MARLENE: But—what about me? What do *I* do?

ROBERTS: You should be under a doctor's care. There must be social agencies. Even down here.

MARLENE: Social agency? I wouldn't go to no place like that.

ROBERTS: Why not? It wouldn't matter to them that you're not
married. They get hundreds of girls in the same predicament.

MARLENE: I ain't hundreds of girls.

She gets up from the table and leaves the room.

INTERIOR—LIVING ROOM   DAY

MARLENE COMES IN, MISERABLE. *Roberts follows her. Suddenly, she bright-
ens and turns to him.*

MARLENE: I know where we can get some food! Mr. Treadwell's.

ROBERTS: Are you out of your mind? Do you think I'm going to break in there after——

MARLENE: I don't mean break in an' I don't mean you. We got money. My nest egg. I'll just go to the store.

ROBERTS: In your condition? It's a couple of miles. You'd have a load of groceries.

MARLENE: I'll hitch a ride.

ROBERTS: What if it's somebody who lives in this area? They'll want to know what you're doing here. So will Treadwell.

MARLENE: I guess he would suspicion something.

ROBERTS: Suspect. Suspicion's the noun. Suspect's the verb.

She mouths what he's just said.

ROBERTS: . . . Anyway, how long would fourteen dollars' worth of groceries last?

MARLENE: At least till Christmas.

ROBERTS (*Thoughtfully*): I wonder if he'd remember *me* . . .

MARLENE: You! He almost caught you once.

ROBERTS: It was dark. I don't think he saw my face. Besides, we're all supposed to look alike around here.

MARLENE: But you don't know how to act.

ROBERTS: What do you mean, I don't know how to act?

MARLENE: You go in there like you are, he'll know you're from up North and he'll suspicion . . . suspect somethin'.

ROBERTS: I'll wear a pair of overalls. I'll manage.

MARLENE: All right, then, show me.

ROBERTS: Show you?

MARLENE: Uh-huh. Act like I was Mr. Treadwell.

ROBERTS: Act like . . . that's ridiculous.

MARLENE: I'm just tryin' to show you. It ain't no use thinkin' you can fool him.

ROBERTS: Of course I can.

MARLENE: You go out and come in like you was comin' to Mr. Treadwell's. I just want to see you make a fool of yourself.

ROBERTS: I go to the store. I go in the store. I tell the man what I want. Simple.

MARLENE: You just don't know nothin'. You do like that, you'll get caught for sure. You don't say anything when you go in.

ROBERTS: I don't say anything?

MARLENE: No, sir! Down here people don't just speak right up like they was from some big city. You go in an' you just wait till he asks you what you want.

ROBERTS: I don't get it.

MARLENE: Lordie, even if you were really goin' to the store we'd starve to death before you got there, the way we're goin'. You just go out and come back in.

ROBERTS: All right, all right.

He goes out the door and comes back in. He looks at her expectantly.

MARLENE: You done wrong already.

ROBERTS: What is it this time?

MARLENE: You ain't supposed to look at me.

ROBERTS: Not supposed to look at you?

MARLENE: I told you, you just stand there an' wait till I ask what you want. Kind of run your eyes over the stuff on the shelves. (*She demonstrates; then, like a man*) You want something, boy?

ROBERTS: Yes, sir.

MARLENE: More Southern-like.

ROBERTS: Yes, suh.

MARLENE: That's better. Now, say what you want.

ROBERTS: Okay. What *do* we want?

MARLENE: Oh, 'vaporated milk, Vienna sausage, margarine. Stuff like that. Now say what you want.

ROBERTS: I'd like some evaporated milk, some Vienna——

MARLENE: No. Not *e*vaporated—'vaporated! You got to talk more Southern-like. An' you looked at me again. Charlie, you can't go to Mr. Treadwell's!

ROBERTS: Oh, can't I!

He stalks out, stalks back in, and sets himself deliberately.

ROBERTS: Ask me!

MARLENE (*Like a man*): You want somethin'?

ROBERTS: Ah wants some 'vaporated milk, some Vienna sausage . . . an' Ah wants to know how the hell I talked myself into going to the store.

MARLENE: Charlie, you sound just like a Nigra!

There is a long beat . . . then:

MARLENE: You'll be careful, won't you?

DISSOLVE TO:

EXTERIOR—TREADWELL'S STORE   DAY

ROBERTS IS STANDING BY THE GAS PUMP. He looks at the bleak facade of the store with more trepidation than he's willing to admit. He steels himself and goes in.

INTERIOR—STORE DAY
AS ROBERTS ENTERS. Treadwell is stacking cans on a shelf. He turns and sees him.
ON ROBERTS
Waiting, expecting to be ignored.
BACK TO SCENE

TREADWELL (*Affably*): He'p you with somethin'?

Roberts swallows his surprise.

ROBERTS: Yes, suh.

TREADWELL: Well, you come to the right place, whatever it is. What you need?

Roberts takes out a list and hands it to him. Treadwell studies it.

TREADWELL: Uh-huh. Ah believe Ah can take care of all this for you.

He begins moving around the store, filling the order. As he does:

TREADWELL: You're not from around here, boy.

ROBERTS (*Bridling at the "boy"*): Yes, suh.

TREADWELL: You mean you are or you mean you ain't?

ROBERTS: Ah mean Ah am.

TREADWELL (*Pausing*): You gettin' smart with me?

Roberts wants to snap back an answer but he holds himself in check.

ROBERTS: Me? No, suh. Ah just means Ah'm from around heah. Ah stays with mah cousin.

Treadwell has gathered the items on the counter and licks a pencil stub.

TREADWELL: Lemme see. Looks like 'bout twelve dollars, seventy cents. You got that kinda money?

ROBERTS: Yes, suh.

He digs out a lump of bills and counts them out on the counter. Treadwell takes them and counts them a second time.

TREADWELL: Thirteen dollars. You 'bout got this money wore out, ain't you? But it spends good as brand-new.

He expects a laugh, but Roberts does not oblige him.

TREADWELL: Tell you what. Seein' it's a right nice order, Ah'm gonna round it off to twelve dollars even.

He waits for a reaction.

ROBERTS (*Forcing himself*): Ah sure do appreciate that.

TREADWELL: You just tell yo'h cousin and all yoah friends Mr. Treadwell treats Nigras right in his stoah, and heah? . . . Anything else?

ROBERTS (*Thinking of Marlene*): Well . . . have—is you got jelly beans? An' lickrish?

TREADWELL (*Grins*): Got a sweet tooth, ain't you? Got one myself.
He digs under the counter for a small sack and fills it with jelly beans and licorice whips.

ROBERTS: How much is that?

TREADWELL: No charge. You bought a nice order.

Roberts is baffled by this small act of charity, but he resists it because it has about it the odor of patronization.

ROBERTS: Well . . . thanks.

He gathers up the groceries and starts to go.

TREADWELL: Hey, boy——

Roberts hesitates . . .

TREADWELL: You tell yoah cousin an' yoah friends. Mr. Treadwell
treats you people right. You heah?

The words "you people" are incendiary to Roberts, but he holds himself back.

ROBERTS: Ah gotta be goin'.

He leaves—and it's all he can do to keep from slamming the door.

INTERIOR—KITCHEN DAY

AS ROBERTS SLAMS DOWN THE CARTON OF GROCERIES. THE CAMERA ANGLE WIDENS TO SHOW Marlene looking at him. She notes his mood, but her attention is drawn to the sack and she opens it to see the licorice and jelly beans.

MARLENE: Goody! You got me candy.

He doesn't answer.

MARLENE: What's wrong?

ROBERTS: Nothing.

MARLENE: What you so mad about, then?

ROBERTS: Treadwell.

MARLENE: What'd he do?

ROBERTS: To be exact, he gave off such a smell of condescension it
turned my stomach. The way he said Nigra——

MARLENE: He said Nigra? Well, there. I told you he was nice.

ROBERTS: Nice? What do you mean, nice?

MARLENE: If he wasn't, he'd of said, you know, the other.

ROBERTS: I wish he had. At least it's honest. There's something degrading about the way he says Nigra instead of Negro.

MARLENE: It's the same thing.

ROBERTS: The hell it is.

MARLENE: It is so. It's just the way we say it.

ROBERTS (*Exasperated*): Marlene, do me a favor. Let me hear you
say Negro.

MARLENE: Sure. Nigra.

ROBERTS: You see! You said Nigra.

MARLENE: I said 'xactly what you told me to say. Nigra.

Roberts feels like he's wandered through the looking glass. It's almost funny —but not quite. Then, patiently:

ROBERTS: Say *knee.*

MARLENE: Knee? Why?

ROBERTS: Just say it.

MARLENE: All right. Knee.

ROBERTS: Now say *grow.*

MARLENE: Grow.

ROBERTS: Now put them together.

MARLENE: What do you mean, put them together?

ROBERTS: I mean say them together. One after the other. First *knee,* then *grow.*

MARLENE (*As if humoring a child*): All right. Knee . . . grow.

ROBERTS: Closer together.

MARLENE: Knee grow.

ROBERTS: You did it! See, you *can* say it. Now try it again. Negro.

MARLENE: Nigra.

ROBERTS (*Groans*): From now on, let's stick with Afro-American.

MARLENE (*Blankly*): What?

ROBERTS: Never mind. (*Offers the sack*) Have some jelly beans.

DISSOLVE TO:

INTERIOR—LIVING ROOM   NIGHT

CLOSE ON THE RADIO, THE ANGLE TO SHOW Roberts listening, as usual, to a news broadcast. He is extremely tense at these times, his body rigid, his breathing hesitant.

INTERIOR—BEDROOM   NIGHT

AS MARLENE PULLS BACK THE COVERS of the bed and then pauses, hearing the drone of the radio from the room below. Curious, she goes to the door.

INTERIOR—LANDING   NIGHT

AS MARLENE COMES OUT OF THE BEDROOM and starts down the stairs in her bare feet, unintentionally silent. Roberts is still hunched over the radio, immobile, concentrating.

NEW ANGLE

As Marlene comes closer.

MARLENE: Charlie——

At the sound of her voice he whips around, startled. His intensity frightens her and she takes a step back.

ROBERTS: What do you want?

MARLENE: Just wonderin' what you was listenin' to.

ROBERTS: What's it sound like?

MARLENE: Well you don't have to jump down my throat.

ROBERTS: Sorry.

He snaps off the radio, rises, stretches, beginning to unwind. Marlene studies him.

MARLENE: Hey, Charlie . . . do you work?

ROBERTS: Of course I work. What brought that up?

MARLENE: Just wonderin'.

ROBERTS: You're doing an awful lot of wondering tonight.

MARLENE: What 'xactly do you do?

ROBERTS (*After a long pause*): I'm a lawyer.

MARLENE: A lawyer? A real lawyer?

ROBERTS: What do you mean, a real lawyer? You think a man has to be white to be a real lawyer?

MARLENE: No, that ain't what I think. I know there's colored lawyers. If it wasn't for them an' the preachers an' some of them others from up North comin' down here to stir up trouble . . .

ROBERTS: You really believe that, don't you?

MARLENE: Ain't that why you came down here? To stir up trouble?

ROBERTS: I don't want to talk about it.

MARLENE: I'm gonna mark that down with a red crayola. First time you ever didn't want to talk about somethin'.

ROBERTS: It's better if you don't know. For your own sake.

MARLENE: What do you mean, for my own sake?

ROBERTS: I don't want to implicate you.

He moves away. But Marlene's curiosity is fully aroused.

MARLENE: Charlie . . . how come you're always listenin' to the news?

ROBERTS: I told you—I don't want to go into it.

MARLENE (*Persisting*): You 'spect them to talk about you, don't you?

He doesn't answer.

MARLENE: Look, I don't mind if you impicate me——

ROBERTS: Implicate.

MARLENE: ——implicate me. Really. I mean, I'm askin' you, so if anything happens it's my own fault. I mean, ain't it?

ROBERTS: Your logic is irrefutable. All right. Just remember, you asked for it . . .

*He thinks for a moment, reaching inside himself and disturbing memories
he'd rather forget. Finally:*

ROBERTS: I told you I was a lawyer. I worked for a large firm—I'm
their token black—and I was getting to feel pretty safe and
snug, pretty important——

MARLENE: Where was it? Your office?

ROBERTS: New York.

MARLENE: I kinda thought so.

ROBERTS: Anyhow, I somehow didn't feel important enough.

During this, THE CAMERA BEGINS MOVING IN ON HIM.

ROBERTS: . . . Too many things were happening. Too many of
my friends were standing up on their hind legs for a change,
demanding things, talking back, shaking the tree. . . . And I
wasn't a part of it.

MARLENE: Why?

ROBERTS: Because I was too secure. . . . Anyway, my father was
born near here. So one day I decided to take a look at my
roots. And when I got here something amazing was happening—a handful of black students on a little upstate campus
were on strike. They wanted power and they wanted a voice—
and they weren't just asking, they were laying down the law.

MARLENE: What'd that have to do with you?

ROBERTS: That's the point—I wasn't sure. But I had to see it for
myself. . . . So I went to the campus—I guess I had some idea
in the back of my mind that they might need legal aid. When
I got there some of the students had decided on a protest
march. And for the first time in my life I went out on a limb. I
joined it.

ON MARLENE

Listening, involved in his story.

BACK TO SCENE

ROBERTS: . . . We left the campus and marched through the main
street of town. All very orderly. Ordinary. . . . And then I noticed that people were waiting for us, lining the street on both
sides, laughing and jeering. And every now and then a rock
would come flying in. . . . We did some laughing ourselves,
right in their faces. And then a white man came running up
and hit me. Why me, I don't know. But he stepped off the curb
and hit me. I hit him back. First time I'd hit anybody since I
was a kid. They swarmed off the curb and grabbed me. Instead of going limp I fought back. I kicked and bit and butted.
Like a madman. And I broke loose. And I ran. Lord, how I

ran. . . . And they chased me. Yelling and screaming and I knew that if they caught me they'd kill me. Then I knew what it felt like to be a nigger. . . . I ran until I couldn't run another step, but I kept running. I came to an alley and I ran in there. I heard one of them screaming "Stop!" and terrified as I was I wondered where he got the breath to scream. . . . And when I reached the end of that dark alley and saw it was a dead end I knew I was cornered.

THE CAMERA IS VERY CLOSE ON Roberts now, a line of sweat across his forehead. He has almost forgotten Marlene in the room.

ROBERTS: I shriveled up in fright and without even knowing how it happened I found myself curled up in a ball, down in the dirt. And then they were kicking me and calling me names and I suddenly realized it wasn't a mob, it was just one man, and I got up out of the dirt. And I looked at him and it was his turn to be frightened. He snatched up a brick and tried to brain me with it but I got it away from him.

NEW CAMERA ANGLE

He stops and it is a moment before she realizes he is not going on.

MARLENE: What happened?

ROBERTS (*After a long pause*): I killed him.

She puts her hand to her mouth in horror and he waits, resigned and bitter, for her denunciation. Slowly her hand comes down. She reaches out and touches his shoulder gently.

MARLENE: Poor Charlie.

SLOW DISSOLVE TO:

EXTERIOR—WATER   DAY

TWO CORKS BOB SIDE BY SIDE on the sunny surface of the Gulf.

NEW ANGLE

TO SHOW Marlene and Roberts sitting at the edge of the pier, their legs dangling. Both are holding fishing poles, but apparently they haven't had much luck. The day is cold and clear.

CLOSER ANGLE

Roberts gets a bite. Elated, he raises his pole, lifting the flip-flopping fish from the water.

MARLENE: Careful!

ROBERTS: Don't worry. I've got him.

But the line, made of rotting string, snaps, and the fish goes tumbling back into the water.

ROBERTS: Did you see how big it was?

MARLENE: Shoot, it was teensy.

Patty Duke and Al Freeman, Jr., in *My Sweet Charlie*.
Courtesy of Universal Pictures.

ROBERTS: You're jealous.

MARLENE: Jealous of that little ol' thing? Anyway, you didn't catch it.

ROBERTS (*Wry*): This is getting bad for my ego. Might as well go back.

They get to their feet and, carrying their poles, move along the pier to the beach.

NEW ANGLE

As they approach the road, Roberts stops abruptly, tensing.

ROBERTS: Listen.

MARLENE: I hear it.

So do we. It is the SOUND of a car drawing nearer.

ROBERTS: Get down!

MARLENE: I hope it ain't——

ROBERTS: Shhh!

He pulls her down out of sight.

NEW ANGLE

A new model sportscar has bumped off the road and is heading toward "their house."

ON MARLENE AND ROBERTS

Watching fearfully: Are the owners returning?

BACK TO SCENE

As the car drives past the house and comes to a stop by the neighboring bungalow. Two people emerge, a man and a woman. They are the LARABEES. The man wears a tailored brown duffel-coat and a corduroy cap. The woman wears slacks and a matching coat, with a bright blue scarf around her head. They are both in their late thirties. They go up on the porch and look at the screen door. They are talking, but from this distance we cannot hear what they are saying.

ON ROBERTS AND MARLENE

MARLENE: What are we gonna do?

ROBERTS: I don't know.

MARLENE: Looks like the screen's latched. Maybe they'll just go away.

BACK TO SCENE

As the man leaves the woman on the porch and walks around the side of the house.

ON ROBERTS AND MARLENE

Waiting, tense.

BACK TO SCENE

WE now HEAR the man's loud VOICE.

LARABEE: Come on back here! Somebody's broken in!

The woman runs around the house in answer to his summons.

ON MARLENE AND ROBERTS

> MARLENE: They're gonna find out! They'll look in our house and find out!
>
> ROBERTS: Don't worry. They won't do anything to you. You'll be all right.
>
> MARLENE: They'll call the police and put me in jail. And everybody will see my . . . see my . . .
>
> ROBERTS: Nobody cares about that. Don't you understand? I wish to God that's all I had to worry about.

BACK TO SCENE

The front door opens and the Larabees come out.

> LARABEE: Let's check the Taylors. Maybe they broke in there, too.

They come down off the porch and move toward "their house."

ON MARLENE AND ROBERTS

> ROBERTS: That does it!
>
> MARLENE: Charlie, what are we gonna do?
>
> ROBERTS: Do? Run. But not you. I keep telling you, you've got nothing to worry about.
>
> MARLENE: They'll look inside and then they'll call the sheriff, won't they?

Roberts half rises.

> ROBERTS: As soon as they get inside, I may have to make a break for it.
>
> MARLENE (*Wrapped up in her thoughts*): Did he say the Taylors? Was that the name he said?
>
> ROBERTS: What?

Suddenly Marlene makes a decision, gets to her feet, and begins running toward "their house," still carrying her fishing pole.

> ROBERTS: Marlene! What are you——?

But she is gone. He sinks back, stunned, into concealment.

NEW ANGLE

As Marlene slows to a deliberate walk, approaching the beach house. The Larabees spot her and come down from the porch. Marlene seems very calm.

ON CHARLIE

Not believing his eyes—she's going to betray him.

ON MARLENE

As she meets the couple in front of the house.

> MARLENE: Hello.
>
> LARABEE (*Suspicious*): Hello. You from around here?
>
> MARLENE: Yes, sir. I live here. In the Taylors' house.
>
> LARABEE: The Taylor house? I didn't know . . . Did you, honey?

MRS. LARABEE: They didn't say anything to me about leaving any-body.

LARABEE (*Challengingly*): The Taylors are in South America.

MARLENE: Yes, sir, I know. That's why they asked us to stay in the house. Me an' my husband. We're lookin' after it for 'em.

ON ROBERTS

He inches closer . . . straining . . . wishing he were a lip reader. Eventually he will get within hearing distance.

BACK TO SCENE

LARABEE: This husband of yours, where is he?

MARLENE: He had to go to town. Somebody tried to bust in last night. He run 'em off but he thought he better report it to the police anyhow. In case they try to, you know, come back.

LARABEE (*Less antagonistic*): They tried to break into the Taylor house too?

MRS. LARABEE: They did break into ours. Didn't you hear them?

MARLENE: No, ma'am, we sure didn't. If we had, my husband, he would have run 'em off. I sure am sorry.

LARABEE: That's all right. It's not your fault.

ON ROBERTS

Closer, listening, almost daring not to breathe. He's marveling at Marlene and hoping she can pull it off.

BACK TO SCENE

MARLENE: I hope they didn't take nothin'.

LARABEE: Wasn't much to take. Just some groceries. But they broke a window getting in.

MRS. LARABEE: You'll have to do something about getting it fixed, Jack.

LARABEE: I sure don't like the idea of coming back down here just for a window.

MARLENE: My husband, he'll fix it for you when he gets back.

ON CHARLIE

His face a study in open admiration.

BACK TO SCENE

MARLENE: Not with real glass, though. He'll, you know, put boards over.

MRS. LARABEE: We surely do appreciate that. Is there some way we can repay you for your trouble?

MARLENE: Oh, no, ma'am. No trouble at all.

MRS. LARABEE (*Indecisive*): Well . . . when are you expecting?

MARLENE: Ma'am?

MRS. LARABEE: Your baby.

MARLENE: Oh. My baby. Pretty soon now.

MRS. LARABEE: Your first?

MARLENE: Ma'am? Oh, yes, ma'am.

MRS. LARABEE (*Smiles*): I thought so . . .

She reaches out and impulsively touches Marlene on the cheek.

MRS. LARABEE: Don't be frightened. There's really nothing to it.
I've had three.

LARABEE: Honey, I hate to break up this girl talk, but if we don't
get moving——

MRS. LARABEE: All right. (*To Marlene*) Well . . . goodbye. I just
know you're going to have a wonderful baby.

LARABEE: Thanks again. If you write the Taylors, tell them Jack
and Laurie Larabee said hello.

MARLENE: Yes, sir, we'll do that.

*The Larabees go back to their car. Marlene stands motionless watching
them.*

ON ROBERTS

Also watching.

BACK TO SCENE

*As the Larabees get into their car. With a wave and a shifting of gears they
are off. As soon as they are out of sight:*

NEW ANGLE

*Roberts bounds out of concealment and runs over to Marlene, almost hugs
her.*

ROBERTS (*Exuberant*): Marlene, you were great!

She collapses onto the porch step.

MARLENE: I'm so scared. How come I'm so scared now an' I
wasn't before?

ROBERTS: Who cares? You got rid of them. I never saw such acting!

MARLENE: Actin'? I wasn't really actin'. Least it didn't seem like it.
I felt like . . . like I really did have a husband. While I was
talkin' to them, I mean . . . (*Pause*) That lady, she sure was
nice. An' the way he called her honey an' opened the car door
for her . . . I wish . . .

ROBERTS (*Softly*): I know. Hey, are you all right?

She nods . . .

ROBERTS: You handled it perfectly. They won't even report it.
Marlene, I'm proud of you.

MARLENE (*After a pause*): We got any boards?

ROBERTS: Boards?

MARLENE: To fix their window with. I told them enough stories without storyin' about that part, too.

ROBERTS: It really bothers you to tell a lie, doesn't it?

MARLENE: 'Course it does. Don't it bother you?

ROBERTS: Depends on the circumstances.

MARLENE (*Without malice*): You would think that. Bein' a lawyer. *He starts to laugh.*

INTERIOR—LIVING ROOM   DUSK

WE SEE THE CHRISTMAS TREE. Marlene has decorated it with paper chains from old newspapers and has even cut out an almost symmetrical star from the bottom of a tin can.

NEW CAMERA ANGLE

She hangs the last chain as Roberts looks at the tree admiringly.

ROBERTS: You're pretty clever with your hands. I had no idea you could do so much with so little.

MARLENE: That's just foolin' around. It don't amount to nothin'. (*Pause*) I mean, anything.

She tries to straighten the star but fails because her stomach makes her awkward. Roberts does it for her.

ROBERTS: I don't agree. It shows talent. Maybe some day you could get yourself a job where you make things.

MARLENE: I thought of that. But first I'm gonna get me my high-school diploma. No matter what.

ROBERTS: Good idea. You could even go to night school.

Marlene steps back and studies the tree. A feeling of nostalgia comes over her.

MARLENE: You know somethin', Charlie? This is gonna be the first Christmas I ever wasn't home.

ROBERTS: My parents never made much out of Christmas.

MARLENE: We did. Mama saved the decorations, you know, an' every year she'd get 'em out again. When I was little I used to wonder what it was made all them lights turn off an' on. (*Reflects*) I still don't know. . . . Do you?

ROBERTS: Know what?

MARLENE: What makes 'em turn on and off that way. What makes 'em do like that?

ROBERTS: It's a circuit breaker . . . something electrical.

MARLENE (*Grins*): So you don't know, neither.

She turns the radio on, fiddles with the dials until she gets a Christmas carol. "Silent Night" is playing.

MARLENE: Listen. . . . When I was in Sunday school and sang that, you know what I sang? 'Stead of "round yon virgin" I sang "brown young Firgin." It was I don't know how long 'fore I quit thinkin' there was this colored girl in the manger with the Holy Family. Named Firgin. Like, you know, their washer-woman or somethin'. Only I never could figure out how they could have a washer-woman if they were supposed to be so poor an' all.

ROBERTS (*Laughing*): When I was little I thought they were all black. I'd get furious when I'd see pictures showing them as white. Except Judas. I always thought of him as white.

MARLENE: You sure must have been a mean little boy.

ROBERTS: And I grew up to be a mean big man.

She grins and turns up the radio . . . "Little Town of Bethlehem" is playing.

MARLENE: C'mon, let's sing.

ROBERTS: I'm not much of a singer.

She hums along with the carol, then begins to sing. Her voice is immature, but pure and sweet.

ON ROBERTS

Lying back on the sofa, his hands laced behind his head, listening. Unexpectedly, he finds himself at peace.

NEW ANGLE

As Marlene finishes the song. A silence expands and a look of sadness comes over her face.

MARLENE: Charlie . . . you're still leavin' tomorrow, aren't you?

He nods.

MARLENE: I wish you wouldn't go.

ROBERTS: I have to . . . and so do you. If worse comes to worse you can always go home.

She shakes her head . . .

MARLENE: Uh-uh. Not in a thousand years.

ROBERTS: Don't you miss anybody?

MARLENE: My mama.

ROBERTS: Your father?

She doesn't answer.

ROBERTS: Marlene, you can't carry a grudge for the rest of your life.

MARLENE: Why not? You do.

ROBERTS: What?

MARLENE: Carry a grudge. Against anybody who's white.

ROBERTS: Why shouldn't I?

MARLENE: I'm white.

ROBERTS: What's that supposed to prove? You're dif——

*He stops abruptly at the realization of what he has been about to say. She
smiles, then stiffens.*

MARLENE: Oh!

ROBERTS: What's the matter?

MARLENE: He kicked, hard.

Roberts goes to her.

ROBERTS: Marlene, if you won't go home it's got to be a social
    agency. You have to make up your mind.

MARLENE: They give your baby away, don't they?

ROBERTS: Yes, but they're very careful about placement.

MARLENE: I wish I could just bring him back here with me to live.

ROBERTS: I wish you could, too. But some day you'll get married
    and have babies you can keep.

MARLENE: Oh, Charlie! Why didn't my daddy talk to me like that?

She begins to cry.

ROBERTS: Hey, easy . . . everything will be all right.

Marlene groans.

ROBERTS (*Concerned*): Did he kick again?

She shakes her head . . .

MARLENE: I had a catch in my side.

ROBERTS: A catch? (*Dubious*) Marlene?

MARLENE: Honest. It don't hurt any more.

ROBERTS (*Studying her*): You'd better get some rest.

She nods, goes toward the bedroom, then pauses and turns.

MARLENE: Charlie. What do you think sounds prettier? Marl*ane*
    Chambers or Marl*ene* Chambers?

ROBERTS: Marlene.

She starts to go out, stops again.

MARLENE: I wonder, would they let me keep my baby?

ROBERTS: If they thought you could take care of him.

MARLENE: I want to. I don't want nobody else raisin' him. I
    want . . .

ROBERTS: What?

MARLENE: I want him . . . to be like you. (*Pause*) Charlie, did you
    hear me?

ROBERTS: I heard you.

MARLENE: Good night, Charlie.

Roberts sits on the sofa, deeply touched.

                    DISSOLVE TO:

EXTERIOR—THE BEACH HOUSE   NIGHT
THERE ARE NO LIGHTS BURNING.

INTERIOR—BEDROOM NIGHT
MARLENE LIES ON THE BED in a tangle of sheets and blankets. Unable to stop herself, she gives a sharp cry. She is holding her stomach and moaning.
NEW CAMERA ANGLE
As the door opens and Roberts comes in carrying the kerosene lamp.

ROBERTS: Marlene . . . Marlene . . . they getting bad?

MARLENE (*Nods*): It really hurts.

ROBERTS: How does it hurt? Does it feel different from the other times?

MARLENE: I don't know. It just feels . . . funny. But it ain't right. It's not supposed to be for a while.

ROBERTS: I don't think so, Marlene. It's time to go.

MARLENE: Now? You mean right now? But we're not sure.

ROBERTS: We're sure enough. We can't afford to take chances. (*Pause, then very quietly*) It's time to go.

MARLENE (*Rising*): All right. I'm ready.

ROBERTS: No, you've got to stay here.

MARLENE: I thought you said——

ROBERTS: I'll go to find a phone somewhere. Treadwell has one.

MARLENE: Charlie, you can't!

ROBERTS: Don't worry about him. We're big buddies now. I get all my groceries there.

MARLENE: But it's the middle of the night. He'll want to know how come——

ROBERTS: I'll say I was just passing by and heard somebody calling for help.

She starts to protest again but has another twinge, effectively ending her opposition.

MARLENE: Tell him you were night huntin'. Possum huntin', with a dog an' all.

ROBERTS: Perfect. I'll tell him that and then I'll be on my way.

MARLENE: But—you weren't gonna leave till tomorrow. You know, when there's nobody around and it'll be safe an' everything.

ROBERTS (*Shrugs*): So the countdown starts a little sooner. It doesn't matter.

MARLENE: Charlie . . . some day, after I've had my baby an' things are all right again . . . will you come see us?

He tries to smile at her, but they both know that he cannot see her again for many reasons.

MARLENE (*A small voice*): I guess I won't see you any more, not ever.

ROBERTS: Whoever comes here will have to take you to a hospital. As soon as you're there tell them to get in touch with your Aunt Donna.

MARLENE: Charlie, don't you dare go wearin' Mr. Treadwell's coat into his store. He'll know you were the one that broke in.

ROBERTS: I'll hide it outside before I go in.

MARLENE: Then what'll you do? Where'll you go?

ROBERTS: Don't worry. I have warm clothes now, and you taught me how to speak the language.

MARLENE: Charlie, I'm scared.

ROBERTS: I am too, Marlene.

He starts to leave, then turns to her. There is a moment of intense silence. Then he disengages himself from her gaze and walks swiftly out of the bedroom. Marlene sinks slowly to the bed.

EXTERIOR—TREADWELL'S STORE   NIGHT
A BLACK FIST POUNDS ON THE DOOR . . . The lights snap on inside.
NEW CAMERA ANGLE
WE SEE ROBERTS waiting, hunched against the cold.

TREADWELL'S VOICE (*From inside*): Don't have to bust the door down. Ah'm comin' . . . who is it?

ROBERTS (*Assuming an accent*): It's me, mistuh.

The door opens a few inches to reveal Treadwell. He has pulled a pair of trousers over his pajamas and carries the shotgun slung under his arm.

TREADWELL: What you want? Don't Ah know you?

ROBERTS: Yes, suh. Ah was in here once. (*Urgently*) Mistuh Treadwell, there's a girl needs help down there . . .

TREADWELL: What girl? Get inside. It's freezin'.

INTERIOR—STORE   NIGHT
AS ROBERTS HURRIES IN AND TREADWELL CLOSES THE DOOR. The storekeeper leans the shotgun against the wall.

TREADWELL: Now, what's this all about? What girl, where at?

ROBERTS: In one of them houses down there. By the watah.

TREADWELL: Shady Cove? There ain't nobody in them Shady Cove houses. Not this time of year.

ROBERTS: Yes, suh, this girl. She's about to have a baby.

TREADWELL: What's she doin' in one of them houses? And how come *you* know so much about it?

ROBERTS: Ah was just passin' by and Ah heard her yellin'. An' she told me to run for the doctuh.

TREADWELL: You gonna have yourself a long run. Nearest doctuh's . . .

ROBERTS: Would you phone him, mistuh? She's bad off.

TREADWELL: Well, seein' it's an emergency . . . guess Ah could give it a try. Sure she's bad off?

ROBERTS: Yes, suh.

TREADWELL (*Grinning*): They'll do it every time. Have their baby in the middle of the night. White, black, don't make no difference. (*He picks up a pot*) Ah'll put on some coffee an' phone. You look half-froze.

ROBERTS: Ah really think you better hurry.

TREADWELL: Oh, you do? (*Studies him*) Look here, boy, you seem awful bothered 'bout this. Sure it ain't your woman in that house?

ROBERTS: No, suh. (*Pause, then*) She's white.

TREADWELL: White? Why didn't you say so?

ROBERTS (*Forgetting his accent*): You didn't give me a chance.

Treadwell eyes Roberts speculatively.

TREADWELL: Where you from?

ROBERTS: Mistuh, can we talk about that later? She's real bad.

TREADWELL: Okay, Ah'll call the doctor. But you just wait right heah. Ah want to talk to you. You heah?

ROBERTS: Yes, suh.

Treadwell goes into the other room, leaving the door partially open so he can keep an eye on Roberts. He begins cranking the wall phone, then speaks softly. His words are inaudible.

ON ROBERTS

He wants to run, to get out, but he knows that if he does Treadwell might come after him. He also wants to make sure that the call to the doctor has been completed. But his nerves are stretched to the breaking point. For lack of something to do he stares fixedly at Treadwell's coffeepot, which sits on a warming hotplate.

CLOSE SHOT ROBERTS

As his tension grows, he casts a glance toward the front door and freedom.

ANOTHER ANGLE

Treadwell hangs up and returns to the main room. He adds instant coffee to two cups and pours in steaming water from the pot.

TREADWELL: Have you'self some hot coffee.

ROBERTS: The doctuh——?

TREADWELL: On his way.

Roberts is flooded with relief. He waves away the proffered cup of coffee.

ROBERTS: No thank you, suh. Ah guess Ah'd better get on home. Mah cousin, he——

TREADWELL: Ah told you Ah wanted to talk to you.

He thrusts the cup at Roberts, who takes it reluctantly.

> TREADWELL: Now how come you told me you was from 'round here? You from up Nawth, boy.
>
> ROBERTS (*Smoothly*): I just didn't want to get in any trouble. I really do live down here. With my cousin. He told me to stay cool and things would be fine.
>
> TREADWELL: Smart boy, yoah cousin. You pay attention to him.
>
> ROBERTS: Thank you, sir. I guess I'll be getting on back.

He starts for the door, setting down the coffee cup.

> TREADWELL: You bettah stay. Show the Sheriff which house.
>
> ROBERTS (*Freezing*): The Sheriff?
>
> TREADWELL: Yeah. Figured the fastest way to get the doctuh was to have the Sheriff pick him up. He'll be comin' here first.

ON ROBERTS

Reacting.

BACK TO SCENE

> TREADWELL: Only take him a few minutes. You might as well sit down and have yoah coffee.

Roberts begins moving toward the door again.

> TREADWELL: Hey! where you goin'?
>
> ROBERTS: I have to go.
>
> TREADWELL: And Ah say you ain't.

Treadwell comes around the counter, his suspicions aroused.

> TREADWELL: What you in such a hurry for, boy? Somethin's real funny. Real funny.

Roberts strides for the door and starts to open it. Treadwell goes after him, grabs him by the upper arm. In a panic, Roberts struggles with him. The storekeeper is astonished that he's meeting resistance.

EXTERIOR—STORE   NIGHT

THE SHERIFF'S CAR COMES BOILING DOWN THE HIGHWAY.

INTERIOR—STORE   NIGHT

ROBERTS HEARS THE APPROACHING VEHICLE *and breaks the older man's grip, pushing him away. Treadwell slams into the wall and Roberts flings open the door.*

> TREADWELL: Stay away from that doah!

But Roberts runs out. Treadwell goes after him.

EXTERIOR—STORE   NIGHT

AS ROBERTS SPRINTS ACROSS THE FRONT YARD *toward the highway. The Sheriff's car is just braking near the gas pump.*

NEW ANGLE
Treadwell bursts from the store.
    TREADWELL: Stop! You hear me?
ON SHERIFF
Piling out of his car. He comprehends the situation in an instant—obviously another robbery—and fumbles at his holster.
ON TREADWELL
    TREADWELL: Stop him!
ON SHERIFF
His gun in his hand.
    SHERIFF: You! Stay where you are! Come back here!
ON ROBERTS
As he keeps running . . . running . . .
VERY CLOSE ON THE SHERIFF
WE ARE IN A FORESHORTENED VIEW of the barrel of the revolver and his eye. The other eye squints.
    SHERIFF: Last chance, boy! I'm warnin' you I'll shoot!
ON ROBERTS
His head raised like a sprinter, sucking in breath, running . . .
CLOSEUP GUN
As the Sheriff's trigger-finger contracts.

INTERIOR—MARLENE'S BEDROOM NIGHT
SHE IS LYING FLAT ON THE BED, her hands resting lightly on her stomach. Suddenly, the SOUND of a distant SHOT. She sits bolt upright as THE CAMERA ZOOMS IN ON her face.
    MARLENE (*Screaming*): CHARLIE!
Utter silence. The echo of the shot reverberates, then dies. Slowly, tears squeeze out from her eyes. She doesn't bother to wipe them away and they roll down her cheeks. She knows. WE HOLD ON her face for a long, painful moment, then:
                EXTREMELY SLOW DISSOLVE TO:
EXTERIOR—THE BEACH HOUSE NIGHT
THE SHERIFF'S CAR WITH A REVOLVING RED LIGHT is parked in the yard. Its headlights illuminate the front porch.
CLOSER CAMERA ANGLE
Treadwell and the Sheriff are standing there smoking cigarettes. They hear footsteps inside, throw down their cigarettes and stamp them out. A moment later, a rumpled-looking DOCTOR and Marlene emerge. Her eyes are dry, almost glazed. A blanket is thrown over her shoulders and she carries the cardboard box with her possessions.
    TREADWELL (*Clearing his throat*): How you feelin', little lady?

No answer.
>   DOCTOR: 'Be fine soon's we get her to a delivery room.
They move off the porch to the waiting police car. Marlene pauses, looks at Treadwell.
>   MARLENE: You'll apologize to the Taylors for me. Tell 'em I'm
>   sorry. An' tell 'em I'll pay for everything when I can.
>   TREADWELL: If it's just them groceries, Ah'll give it to 'em outta
>   the store.
>   MARLENE: I thank you, but *I* want to. They can get hold of me at
>   my Aunt Donna's. I'll write out her address when we get to
>   the hospital.
>   DOCTOR: Let's go. You don't want to have your baby right here.
He helps Marlene into the car, then looks at Treadwell.
>   DOCTOR: Coming?
>   TREADWELL: Ah'll walk back.
The Doctor climbs in and closes the door. The Sheriff turns a haggard face to Treadwell.
>   SHERIFF: What else could I do? I thought he was robbin' your
>   store.
Treadwell shrugs—neutral, placing no blame—but we feel that what has happened has disturbed him. The Sheriff sighs, gets into the car, and slams the door.

INTERIOR—CAR   NIGHT
MARLENE SITS IN THE BACK WITH THE DOCTOR, *who has a reassuring hand on her arm. Her face is expressionless. But as the car starts to move she turns to look through the rear window . . .*

EXTERIOR—CAR   NIGHT
REVERSE CAMERA ANGLE
THE CAMERA IS ON MARLENE *from the outside of the rear window. Her face is very close, childlike, but the eyes are still dry. She forms Charlie's name with her lips.*

INTERIOR—CAR   NIGHT
REVERSE ANGLE
THROUGH THE REAR WINDOW *Treadwell's shadowy form is walking back toward his store.* WE SEE *the beach house recede in the distance. The house diminishes . . . grows farther away . . . until it is as slight and insubstantial as a sand castle. . . .*
>   *FADE OUT.*

BIOGRAPHIES

ELLISON CARROLL is a pseudonym.

A graduate of Harvard University, SIDNEY CARROLL was an editor of various magazines such as *Stage, Coronet,* and *Pageant.* During the Second World War he was a correspondent in the Pacific for *Esquire.* After the war he turned to writing for television, and wrote dramas for such programs as "Philco Playhouse," "Omnibus," and "The Alfred Hitchcock Hour." For motion pictures, he wrote the screenplays for "The Hustler," "Gambit," and "A Big Hand for the Little Lady," which was based on his TV play *Big Deal in Laredo.* Mr. Carroll was awarded an Emmy in 1965 for his writing of the documentary *The Louvre.*

ERNEST KINOY began his professional work in broadcasting in 1948 as an NBC staff writer of such radio drama programs as "University of the Air," "Dimension X," and "The Eternal Light." In addition to *Blacklist,* his television work includes scripts for such series as "Route 66," "Dr. Kildare," and "Naked City," and for such anthologies as "Playhouse 90." For the Broadway theater he wrote the books for the musicals *Bajour* and *Golden Rainbow.* Mr. Kinoy is a past president of the Writers Guild of America, East, and is presently Vice President of the International Writers Guild. He received an Emmy Award in 1964 for *Blacklist*

Collaborators since their student days at the University of Pennsylvania, RICHARD LEVINSON and WILLIAM LINK were film critics for the university newspaper, contributed to the literary magazine, and wrote the books and lyrics for four "Mask and Wig" musicals which toured the East Coast. In addition to writing dramas for various television series, they have written fiction for such publications as *Playboy* and *University Review.* Three of their short stories have been listed in the Honor Roll of the Martha Foley Collection of the Best American Short Stories. For *My Sweet Charlie,* the first drama which Mr. Levinson and Mr. Link both wrote and produced, they received an Emmy Award in 1970.

Before his service in the Korean War, LORING MANDEL attended the University of Wisconsin, from which he graduated with a B.S. degree (with a major in speech and an audited major in music composition). After his military service, he wrote for television in Chicago before going to New York. His TV work includes the plays *Shadow Game, The Raiders,* and *To Confuse the Angel.* Mr. Mandel was nominated for an Emmy Award in 1959 for his *Project Immortality* ("Playhouse 90"); and in 1968 he was awarded an Emmy for *Do Not Go Gentle into That Good Night.* His motion-picture writing includes the screenplay for "Countdown"; and for the Broadway theater he wrote the adaptation of *Advise and Consent.*

Born in Steubenville, Ohio, TAD MOSEL served as a private to sergeant in the U.S.A.A.F. during the Second World War. He earned a B.A. degree at Amherst, and an M.A. at Columbia University. Mr. Mosel has written dramas for many of the major anthology programs, among them "Studio One," "Playhouse 90," and "CBS Playhouse." In addition to *That's Where the Town's Going!* his TV plays include *My Lost Saints* and *Secrets.* For motion pictures, he wrote the screenplay for "Up the Down Staircase." Mr. Mosel was awarded a Pulitzer Prize for his stage adaptation of the James Agee novel *A Death in the Family*—entitled *All the Way Home.*

SAM PECKINPAH was born in Madera County, California, on the side of a mountain which bears the family name and which was homesteaded by his grandfather. After earning an M.A. degree in drama at the University of Southern California (his thesis was in the form of a film), he acted with the Huntington Park Civic Theatre, was a prop-man at a TV station in Los Angeles, and later became a dialogue coach for film director Don Siegel. He was encouraged in his television work by the late Dick Powell; and for the latter's Four Star company he wrote or directed or produced

—or all of these—programs in "The Westerner" series. In addition to *Noon Wine,* Mr. Peckinpah's TV dramas include scripts for "The Rifleman" and "Gunsmoke." Among the films which he has written and/or directed are "Ride the High Country" and "The Wild Bunch."

In addition to writing *Who Do You Kill?* for the "East Side/West Side" series, ARNOLD PERL was also Executive Producer for that series. His other TV writing includes scripts for such programs as "The Big Story," "Naked City," "Chrysler Theatre," and "The Eternal Light." For the Broadway stage he wrote *The World of Sholom Aleichen* as well as adaptations of *Tevya and His Daughters* and Sean O'Casey's autobiography, *I Knock at the Door.* Mr. Perl's work in motion pictures includes the screenplays for "Cotton Comes to Harlem" (in collaboration with Ossie Davis) and "Malcolm X." For *Who Do You Kill?* he was nominated for an Emmy Award in 1964, and received a Best Dramatic Script award in that year from the Writers Guild of America.

After graduating from Barnard College, ELLEN M. VIOLETT was "company playwright" for several years with the Tour Players. Her first television play was *The Lottery,* an adaptation of the Shirley Jackson short story; it was presented on both "Cameo Theatre" and "Fireside Theatre." Miss Violett's other writing for TV includes scripts for several episodes of "Shane," "The Defenders," and "Hawk." For "Omnibus" she wrote the adaptation of *Dear Brutus,* and for "Producers' Showcase," the adaptations of *Rebecca* and *The Skin of Our Teeth.* Her stage plays include *The Color of Darkness—The World of James Purdy* and *Copper and Brass.* She was nominated for an Emmy Award in 1969 for her "CBS Playhouse" drama *The Experiment.*